ALSO BY TIM DEE

The Running Sky: A Birdwatching Life
The Poetry of Birds (co-editor with Simon Armitage)
Four Fields
Ground Work (editor)
Landfill

Greenery

Tim Dee

Greenery

Journeys in Springtime

JONATHAN CAPE
LONDON

1 3 5 7 9 10 8 6 4 2

Jonathan Cape, an imprint of Vintage,
20 Vauxhall Bridge Road,
London SW1V 2SA

Jonathan Cape is part of the Penguin Random House group of companies
whose addresses can be found at global.penguinrandomhouse.com.

Penguin
Random House
UK

First published by Jonathan Cape in 2020

penguin.co.uk/vintage

A CIP catalogue record for this book is available from the British Library

ISBN 9781787330559

Typeset in 12/15.5pt Adobe Jenson
by Integra Software Services Pvt Ltd, Pondicherry

Printed and bound in Great Britain by Clays Ltd, Elcograf S.p.A.

Penguin Random House is committed to a sustainable future for
our business, our readers and our planet. This book is made
from Forest Stewardship Council® certified paper.

MIX
Paper from
responsible sources
FSC
www.fsc.org   FSC® C018179

For my children . . .
Dominic, 13 October 1993
Lucian, 4 August 1995
Adam, 14 August 2019
. . . *offspring*

And now in age I bud again

George Herbert

CONTENTS

17 March 1780

Brought away Mrs Snooke's old tortoise, Timothy, which she valued much, &
had treated kindly for nearly 40 years. When dug out of its hibernaculum, it
resented the insult by hissing.

20 March 1780

We took the tortoise out of its box, & buried it in the garden: but the weather
being warm it heaved up the mould, & walked twice down to the bottom
of the long walk to survey the premises.

Gilbert White

The Way Up

Cape of Good Hope
34°S

21 December. Midsummer. On the kelpy beach at Olifantsbos there was an ostrich with its head in the sand. I thought it was eating flies. The beach is a few kilometres south of my sometime home at Scarborough, on the western edge of the Cape Peninsula in South Africa. It was a male ostrich, with athletic pinkish legs, a long muscular neck and a heavy bustle of black and white plumes. It could have been Queen Victoria getting ready for a swim. Flying above the unlikely *strandloper* were three fast-moving small birds, doing battle with the hot buffet of air salted by the Atlantic and gritted by the beach. Heading south, they followed the shore towards the Cape of Good Hope. They were swallows: the gash of dried-blood at their throats told me that, and the blue, metal-shiny *crick crack* of their sharp wings and deep-cut tails. And they flew, as always, ever so lively.

Cities on the sea, Albert Camus wrote in 'Summer in Algiers', *open out into the sky like a mouth or a wound.* The same evening, sitting on the *stoep* of the house I share with Claire, my South African wife (my only wife – she happens to be South African), we looked out west over the Atlantic from our Cape Town suburb into the sloping midsummer sun. There were more swallows and, in identifying them, I saw not only a bird I knew but also how hard it is to see into the heart of anything for sure. A loose flock was moving south between our house and the ocean – half a dozen barn swallows (the preferred name today for what I have always called simply *swallows*) and the same number of greater striped swallows. I knew the barn swallows had left winter behind them in Europe. I

1

knew the greater striped swallows were intra-African migrants that breed (between September and March) across South Africa and then winter further north in Angola, Congo and Tanzania. I was doing my best as a translocated bird-man, living in a world turned upside down, trying to read it right, but, as I looked, I couldn't help but declare my origins and show my head to be, with the ostrich, somewhere in the sand.

The barn swallows flicked low down at the edge of the land between the weedy surf and the white strand. They looked – they always do – as if they were seeking something. Each knock and slide in their flight appeared an adjustment – a correction made with every wing-beat to the delicate blue-black needle of themselves. There wasn't much land left in the direction they flew – perhaps ten kilometres of beach and rocky peninsula. And I told them there was nothing where they were going but shipwrecks, whale bones, cold sea and, after that, colder ice, with nothing, absolutely nothing, for them to look forward to, and that they'd do better, on this solstitial evening, to turn and head for home.

I said *home*. I had lost my foothold on the map. The winter solstice in South Africa is in June. The swallows were where they should be in December, as at home as they could be. But at that moment I couldn't see them as anything but away. Away from a home (in Britain – as it happens – where some of the swallows that winter in the Cape go to breed) that was mine too, and which, even as I sat next to my wife outside our house, the sight of the birds made me miss.

These Cape swallows in my midwinter (I'd left Britain just two days before), in Claire's midsummer (which has been written into her for ever – hot Christmases), in whatever the time is for the birds there (the non-breeding time, the moulting time, the open-territory time) – they tugged at what I have known for all my life, or thought I have known, of birds and how they work in the world. I heard myself say *home* and laughed aloud to be so found out.

Sometime before 1965, the poet Elizabeth Bishop watched a sandpiper somewhere along the Atlantic seaboard that she knew between Nova Scotia and Brazil. She wrote a poem about the bird.

It is very well seen. I suspect the bird is a sanderling, although it is hard to identify as a particular species of peep (which is what American birdwatchers call small shoreline waders). The poem begins on the sea's edge and at its breaking waves:

> The roaring alongside he takes for granted,
> and that every so often the world is bound to shake.

Bishop said that she saw something of herself in the migrant wader working at the wet seam of the shore. 'All my life,' she wrote, of the poem, 'I have lived and behaved very much like that sandpiper – just running along the edges of different countries "looking for something".'*

I have thought the same of myself, but often what I have been looking for, and trying to steer by, has not been a non-specific 'something', but rather sandpipers themselves, or swallows. For as long as I have been a birdwatcher, birds on the move have given me bearings. If I know how life goes, it is, as much as anything, because of sandpipers and swallows. Thanks to them, I've heard the roaring of the world too, and I find I know a little of its shakes.

Though the birds I saw were heading south, soon enough all the barn swallows in the Cape will fly north and, eventually, out of Africa and into Europe. They journey in their own time, flying all day, a metre or so above the ground, feeding on flies as they go. Their own time turns out to be the right time and they arrive where they need to be on time. Mostly this is the case. Early in the new year the first barn swallows cross the Mediterranean into southern Europe. This might be one definition of the beginning of spring.

Spring moves north through Europe at a speed comparable to the swallows' flights – a speed comparable because it is the right speed for life. In January the mean temperature in Gibraltar is eleven degrees

---

* 'Sandpiper' was first published in Bishop's collection, *Questions of Travel* (1965). All her other book titles might be mentioned here: *North & South* (1946), *A Cold Spring* (1955), and *Geography III* (1976). W. S. Merwin has a sandpiper poem to put alongside Bishop's called 'Shore Birds'. It focuses on their migratory movements and describes them *tracing a memory they did not have/until they set out to remember it.*

Celsius. In July the mean temperature in northern Scandinavia is eleven degrees Celsius. Around about ten degrees, grass and other vegetation begins to green up, and small insects, flies and others, hatch and appear. The season of growth and of birth can begin at this temperature. Swallows can live.

The ten-degree isotherm – a line on a map connecting points where the temperature is the same – moves north across the landmass of Europe from the Mediterranean Sea to the Arctic Ocean at roughly fifty kilometres a day between the winter solstice and the summer solstice. We could call that four kilometres an hour for twelve hours each day. Spring, therefore, moves north at about walking pace. Migratory herbivores following fresh grass are said to *surf the green wave* – we might do the same. In Europe, at any time between midwinter and midsummer, if you started walking at six in the morning in a place where the temperature had reached ten degrees and headed north for twelve hours, you should end your day in the same temperature and in the same seasonal conditions as you began. You would then be travelling with the spring.

Of course, there are mountains in Europe that skew the temperatures – to climb is to go back in seasonal time – and there are the effects of continentality, whereby spring comes earlier to the seashore than to the interior. And who can wake for six o'clock every day and, unhindered, set off north? And north is probably never absolutely north. And each spring arrives on different days year by year in any case. And aren't we now ourselves foolishly tampering with the thermostat and tripping up the time (up to 21.2 per cent of the world's birds are estimated to be threatened with extinction as a result of climate change)? There are these, and there are other corrections to consider, but even if the progress of greenery is a humanly conjured fact, and even if it is in jeopardy – silent springs being more likely each passing year – thanks to our machinations, surely the truth of the season still arrives like an undeniable commandment.

Spring! It is undeniable and irresistible: the arrival and the passage of the growing season demands attention and provokes participation. *Rise; and put on your Foliage*, said Robert Herrick in a May Day (and Mayday) *reverdie* to his lover Corinna ('sweet-Slug-a-bed') who was doubling as a leafing tree.* *Now each holt and hedge in him / Runs green again* says Chaucer of Troilus, the lover (in Lavinia Greenlaw's version). Theodore Roethke knew a birdwatcher's spring in his poem 'The Far Field': *to come upon warblers in early May / was to forget time and death.* *O Earth on holiday* says Rilke of the same days (in Don Paterson's translation).

It takes a certain mannered attitude to find spring *off.* Green is almost always good and is everywhere the sign for go.[†] Spring is here, George Orwell wrote in London in April 1946, *and they can't stop you enjoying it.* Some depressed people get more depressed in springtime, but this is probably because their mood remains wintry and their sap fails to rise with the season to mirror or answer the spring. That is terrible, but the green itself is innocent. There is hay fever too – also misery-making. But few, overall, dislike our salad days and most of us look forward to the spring and want to be out in it, to feel its return as good and to know its multiple lively beginnings – buds, blossoms, songs, nests and eggs.

We could go further. The ancient Greeks had two words for time: *chronos*, meaning chronological time, and *kairos*, which has been translated as *timely* or *the right time.* The author of *Ecclesiastes* knew the same distinction. *Good time encounter her!* says a servant woman of the pregnant Hermione in Shakespeare's *The Winter's Tale.* The right time cannot be measured, but it is good to live in. Who wouldn't, if they could, try a little time-travel in search of more of the right time, trading the notional middle of winter for some early spring in the south, or denying the dog-days of summer, when every engine stalls, by heading further north to keep the spring gears engaged?

---

* In Herrick's time, Londoners went out of their city on May Day and brought home the blossoming May. John Stow in his *Survey of London* (1598) says: 'Every man, except impediment, would, on May day in the morning, walk into the sweet meadows and green woods, there to rejoice their spirits with the beauty and savour of sweet flowers, and with the harmony of birds . . .'

† See, for example, the end of Robert Lowell's 'Brunetto Latini', a marvellous retelling of Dante's *Inferno* Canto XV: 'he seemed one of those/who run for the green cloth through the green field/at Verona . . . and seemed more like the one/who wins the roll of cloth than those who lose'.

Knowing those annually recurring gifts of nature, and registering them alongside our own one-way journey through life, why not try to travel with the season and be in springtime for as long as possible, why not try to start where the season starts, and then to keep up with it, in step, walking a moving green room, travelling under the sun, like swallows out of Africa?

Spring means more to me with every year that passes and takes me deeper into my own autumn. More and more, I want to be stirred by it, shaken, woken. To everything, yes, there is a season, but the more seasoned I have become the more certain I am that spring is the one. Every time calls on us, of course, and we need the spring's opposite as much as it does, since all of life *cycles* and all must go around. But because we ourselves head only in one, terminal, direction, it seems our feeling for the beginning of things, the spring, can only grow.

Some time in my late thirties I realised that my morning was done. It wasn't a profound discovery – we cannot live without getting closer to death – but if it went in particularly deep for me, it was because I have spent every spring I have known keenly, hungrily alive to what D. H. Lawrence called the *world's morning*, waiting for and watching the arrival of migrant birds from the south and feeling renewed, at once well met and made up, by their return.

From around my fortieth birthday I have often felt on the far side of the season, even during March, April and May. From over the hill, I look both back and ahead – mixing memory and desire, as has been said – and yearn all the more. If I want to cry about this I remember the days, twenty years ago or so, when, in their own time, my young children discovered the end of time, learning – I saw it come into their faces – that they too would one day die. When we make life we make a death: it can only be so. The best thing I ever did in the world was being part of the making of my children. The cruellest thing was the same.

Keats can call up the sobbing as well. In his nightingale ode in the soft purple bliss of one springtime dark, he talks about not being able to see 'what flowers are at my feet'. When, later and sicker, he knew he would soon die, he spoke of wanting to stay alive long enough to see, again, 'the simple flowers of our spring'. He did see those once more, but when, in the autumn of the same year, he lay on his deathbed in Rome, and heard his friend Joseph Severn describe his grave plot, Keats said that 'he already seemed to feel the flowers growing over him'. He weakened further as the year drained to midwinter, *spitting out blood for time to breathe*, and he was finished not long after its midnight. The season was starting over but he couldn't go with it, nor could he *simple* its flowers. He died on 23 February 1821, as the days began to lengthen, in the first green bite of the new Roman spring.

Even when I am in midsummer South Africa at the end of every calendar year, I try to get some flowers for my mother in midwinter England. She likes nothing more than a bunch of daffodils at Christmas.

It is my mother who has given me my title. During Christmases past, when staying with my parents, she often asked me to go out and fetch some *greenery*. In the bleak midwinter we craved something of the quickening of the spring. The table needed vegetation. Sometimes I had to buy the stuff, sometimes – better times – I went out with secateurs and cut holly and ivy, and yew and mistletoe if I could, and anything that still had green in it that might stand for the life of the year that had gone and the life of the year that was to come. We weren't Christians, or pagans, or even green-fingered gardeners – we just wanted some green at home for the least green time.

We take flowers to the sick and heap coffins and graves with blooms because they stand for life, for the best of time, for the beginning of things rather than their end. Green is innocent, I said, but we know it to be also unfailingly directed: green leaves eaten by a brown cow make milk as white as egret plumes, the most tender shoot is the most intent thing – it is growing, coming into itself, a fuse lit in the world's morning, bright enough to meet the sun. Greenery is, in this way, another word for the spring.

We anticipate the season more than any other. We are always on the lookout for signs. It is as if, as Henry David Thoreau said (in a March diary entry), 'a man were to warm his hands by stretching them towards the rising sun and rubbing them'. Some of us have had the chance to go in search of the spring, as Keats did too, for something like our health; but most of us mostly stay put, having little choice but to keep to our places. Doing so, the spring comes over us. It is still good. But once or twice, maybe, in our lives we might manage to travel with it for some more of its time. That is better still. To have more spring. I have tried to do that. *I got to my feet* – I like that expression. To journey with the season, hoping to find a pace that feels in keeping and matches its larger rhythms. I also like the suggestive idea behind what musicians call common time, and I have tried to keep spring's account of it for as long as I might carry the tune.

I was born in May and, my mother tells me, I was outside in a pram taking in the sky for much of the rest of the spring as it progressed through the back garden of my first home in suburban Liverpool. For fifty years since then I've been a birdwatcher, and seeing and noting down the new birds arriving in the spring gave me my first understanding of wild time. The second list of birds I started after my life list (all the birds I have ever seen) was a list I kept each spring of the dates when I first saw a spring migrant or summer visitor back in Britain. It was my *First of the Year list*, and I still put 'FOY' next to my first chiffchaff or wheatear or sandwich tern in my notebook. Many bird people do.

'Tell me to what you pay attention', said José Ortega y Gasset, 'and I will tell you who you are.' 'Look deep into nature,' said Albert Einstein, 'and you will understand everything better.' The truth is that these spring migrant birds and the imperative behind their journeys meant more to me than those resident species they joined. The added meaning began with the migrants showing me what I think is something like the kindness of strangers or what Emily Dickinson called in a poem the *transport of cordiality*; it also had to do with these birds having been at home somewhere else, coming most often from Africa, which has been *under* my whole life in many ways, sometime as a mother-ship, sometime as gravy-boat, sometime as ark. There is a line in Nadine

Gordimer's novel *The Conservationist* describing the *bloom* that a man detects on his lover from the times she wasn't with him. There is that for me on those shared birds.

All I did not know went on beginning around me says W. S. Merwin in his poem 'Threshold' about swallows. And barn swallows themselves have a year-round spring, shifting about to exchange spring in the northern hemisphere for spring in the south. They travel *within* the season, as if carrying it with them – one swallow does make a summer in this respect: one swallow is a summer, though I would prefer the saying if it said *spring*.

There are four seasons, I know, in the European year. There are four chambers in the heart, four quarters to the moon, four winds, four apostles, four points of the compass, four string-players in a quartet, there were *Four Quartets* that worried about time, times four. But I see and have always seen the year in two halves. I feel it like that: a coming, spring, and a going, autumn; six months forward before six months back, six months up before six down, six months of lengthening days before six of longer nights, six greening months before six browning, six growing before six dying; in autumn things fall apart, in spring things come together, blood flows into the heart and away from the heart, a clock ticks and tocks, because we breathe in we must breathe out, swallows appear and swallows vanish.

I think of summer as a word for where the end of spring meets the beginning of autumn. I think similarly of winter: there the autumn meets the spring. The crux of Shakespeare's *The Winter's Tale* comes in a line spoken by a shepherd who has found an abandoned baby (Hermione's delivered at full term) at the moment another peasant (his son) witnesses the guardian of the baby being killed by a bear: 'thou met'st with things dying,' says the older man, 'I with things new-born'. These *things* are part of the great rotation of all, where our round Earth spins in such a way that the wheel of life, death and birth, will be everywhere simultaneous, continuous, and somehow rhyming. We can see this in the way that spring begins for some life forms before autumn is out and how likewise autumn eats at spring before it is done.

It is true that spring wouldn't be spring without the autumn. Part of what makes the spring is that its opposite, having preceded it, will also follow it. Spring is about coming around to dying as much as about the birth of the new. And it is also true that there is nothing naturally wrong with winter, unless, perhaps, your lungs are drowning in its damps, or your fingers are as cold as the turnips you must cut. Many flowers need a *winter memory* to germinate. We all, more or less, must be *vernalised* – and go through dark times in order to be born into light.

Those half-dozen barn swallows flying south in December towards one end of the habitable Earth at the Cape of Good Hope, flying low over *fynbos* bushes and flowers, taking kelp-flies around ostriches – even to identify them worked on me as a provocation. Where are they at home? Whose swallows are they? Can anyone, in any case, lay claim to a bird? What do I make of the south knowing that the swallows go there? And now, when I am living as much in the south as I am in the north, how do I see the birds and me bound together by our long-haul commuting, and (to adapt a line by Robert Lowell about Elizabeth Bishop) by our shared *giant memory of one known longitude?*

What does it mean to live so as to avoid winter?

Or to live in sunlight as much as possible?

Or to be always entering wherever you are?

To passage. To be endlessly on the move.

To be coming, always, and to be becoming. To be a rhythmic pulse of wherever you are.

To move north, at the speed of a season. And then south, doing the same.

To be forever temporary. To be permanently now.

To be on time. To be timely.

To be a world clock, a world calendar.

To occupy everywhere but own nothing.

To be at home, without being a home-owner.

To mingle with others that go nowhere but where you meet.

To cross seas under your own steam. To survive a desert.

To go right, until you die.

To take, as a swallow might, the South African Cape to the Nordkapp of Norway and to take back something of the last red Norwegian barn before the Arctic Ocean to the last house (but one ...) before Antarctica. A lifelong *hegira*. In one year, to take flies put up by the feet of an eland, a camel, a brown bear and a reindeer. To see, over the waves at Scarborough, South Africa, an Arctic tern you might have met before, above a fjord near Tromsø or flying past Scarborough, North Yorkshire.

To know, by living it, how this world works.

To have in you something of a perpetual spring, something of what Osip Mandelstam described in a poem as both *the buzz of earth and the buzz of the Earth*.

All of what follows, follows those swallows, and could be said to have come from the traces of those birds. They are among the surest signs that the Earth is alive. Through them I have learned to love the world, and watching them fly, and trying to travel with them, has made the world they know and live in seem lovelier still.

John Buxton used the words *loved* and *lovely* about the wild world and about springtime redstarts, the birds he studied when he was a prisoner of war in Bavaria in the Second World War. He knew the words (he was half-quoting Sir Philip Sidney's *The Defence of Poesy*) were unlikely ones for a book of ornithology made from data got out of a prison. That is why he used them. He watched the birds arrive in the spring from the south and fly through the wire of his prison camp, where he was held captive, to breed. His monograph on the species, published in 1950, is the best bird book I know.* He was a scientist and a poet, and I strive to follow him; but, long before I'd read his book, the redstart had become my favourite bird. The first I saw – I was eleven – secured that title, and the species has held it ever since.

Many of the words here are about swallows – more still are about redstarts. I have tried to make as much of this book about the birds

* I wrote about *The Redstart* at greater length in *The Running Sky* (2009). Towards the end of his book, Buxton says: 'Nor would I change this mystery of the redstart's life by trying to make it seem familiar. That may be the method of science: I do not know. But the method of poetry (and that is my concern) is to make things familiar be as if they were not familiar, to make this too-much-loved world more lovely.'

and other natural manifestations of the spring as I can, but it is, of course, also about me. John Buxton knew that happens when a scientist looks at birds; Elizabeth Bishop knew that happens when a poet does.

It isn't only birds here. In spring, everyone, somehow, likes to set off on pilgrimages. We all spring-clean, one way or another. I am interested in how others have done their spring-seeking – what in the season they were looking for and what they found. Poetry is like a species of spring to literature, and there must be some of that. Music moves with strides through time, and I have tried to listen to some seasonally affected songs. Some people have spent their lives journeying, as migrant birds do, and I have been keen to hear of their travelling. Some have got stuck at borders but others have made it through. Paintings on stones fly through space with the accuracy of the field notes of a naturalist, but also as our dreams navigate the insides of our minds. Some people have collected stones themselves as time-keeping devices; others have found home-scars in rocks that might suit them as coffins. Some have been spring-makers in themselves, and I wanted to meet them or their remains. Bodies in bogs have composed the season. Some have said it with flowers, and I have wanted to botanise with them. I've put on my own weeds. Students of long-gone springtimes have shown me how Europe discovered how to live in the season when it was new for everyone. Scientists have told me how to see inside a reindeer or a brown bear or a swallow. Chronobiologists have wound my clock. I always come back to birds, but there are many good ways to tell the time.

This is a book about the greenery that is spring, mostly made out of birds that are not green themselves, but which I think of as flying green flags through the season. I have written before on birds and on green places. They are what I know. I see through them; they see me through. My bird-thinking depends on recognition or knowing a little of what I am looking at – my cognition comes as *re*-cognition: seeing the same birds, like swallows, year after year, returning into view. My first book, *The Running Sky*, was about birds and about the sky they occupy – their defining habitat (pity the flightless ostrich at Olifantsbos, or the African penguins, on the other side of the Cape Peninsula), which is a zone of life, that we look up towards, and in part live by, but which we cannot fully enter. My second book, *Four Fields*, was about treading earth, and the marks (green interventions and otherwise) that we have made on the Earth's surface, the elemental matter that we stand on; but it was also about the earth underneath, from where everything springs and to where everything, in the end, is inevitably headed. Here, in this book, my words are above all about birds in time and in movement. I share time with birds because they let me depart from myself while making me feel at home in time passing. Migratory birds were doing what they do in a time when I wasn't anything; they'll be doing the same in a time when I won't be anything. The element behind everything here is fire (sunlight, first of all, and its fall on Earth): this book is also about how the subjects of my book one end up in the earth of my book two; and about how lovable the world is, above all, when those living things are moving in the world's morning and are not yet dead.

Time is the fire in which we burn, said Delmore Schwartz. I mostly agree with the gloomy poet: doing our worst as arsonists and clock-breakers ourselves, in a world we have already grievously mutilated, we look set for a planetary holocaust. But nature's great giving (which is more than a gift), that is the fire of spring, the lit green fuse in the world's morning, burns for life and not for extinction. There is also the firetail – the name by which John Clare and others knew my favourite bird, the redstart. That little bird's good fire is the *bonfire* of this book.

The mystery of the swallows at my house at the Cape begins to be explicable. We have some intelligence: spies in the sky have tracked the migrants – rings have been fixed to the birds and the aerial wanderers have been geolocated. We learn more and more of them, but as we do – perhaps even because we know more – the flights of the birds remain beyond our grasp, our minds balk and we struggle to handle the reality. What we gave away in our evolution is what they live by, and this keeps them as marvellous strangers to us. Handling the flyers is not really what it is all about, in any case. In the past we knew they went into the winter dark and they came out of it in the spring. That was miraculous. Now we know more and we do not permit the miraculous, but we still cannot comprehend the birds' flights as anything else, and so they continue to feed our imaginations, educating us sentimentally, and showing us how to feel the world. *Birds return, they flash and mingle in mid-air*, said Horace (via Robert Lowell) in his 'Spring' in 23 BCE; and so they do. *Thick flies the skimming swallow*, said Robert Burns in 1783; and so it does.

I was one hopeless quarter of four friends who went walking in the mountains north of Cape Town, just after the Christmas of the homing swallows. Our aim was to descend the Witels, a river-gorge so narrow in places that you must rock-hop midstream and sometimes swim. This can only be done in the heart and heat of a dry summer. It was idyllic: we could drink the clear cool river-water as we floated along and the dripping banks were lit with crayon-red disas and red-wax gladioli (*Disa uniflora* and *Gladiolus cardinalis*). A Cape rock thrush sang its beautiful simple song: an honorary redstart for me. But after a day, my left knee went berserk and I slowed our party to a near standstill. European bee-eaters urged me on, making a World Service fizz from their short-wave radio calls above us – they might have been resident breeding birds or they might have been winter migrants, ex-Europe, into the South African summer. They hunted the bees that the wet trench had encouraged into this otherwise burned and brittle place. And there were swallows – barn swallows – that overtook me as I skidded with a fibrous crunch from one wet rock into the river. Later, lying on the improvised stretcher or portable coffin I had fashioned for myself from my rucksack, I looked up at the crack of the gorge rising over our heads and could see the swallows flying the course of the wet seam of the river as if they were navigating a coronal suture – the mountain's or, perhaps, mine. I knew I was a goner, but we slept out one more night on a ledge of rock, and twice I woke to see the bright hurry of a shooting star cross the gorge. I wondered whether the brief flare of light had got into my sleep and woken me – it seemed it might. As I lay there, looking up, I remembered that I had been dreaming of swallows. In my sleep, I was depressed by my incompetence as a rock-hopper, but the birds had come to my rescue and, by passing over me, they somehow lifted me out of the crack in the Earth and helped me on.

December & January

Swaffham Prior
52°N

21 December. On the shortest days in midwinter England I want all of the light possible as it sways around the solstice. Having declared winter non-existent and today the beginning of spring, I headed out to try to find the new season in the opening of the year.

I left the house before dawn and walked east towards Suffolk up a farm track between bare winter fields where the sun would come. It came at eighteen minutes past eight. The world never seems to be moving faster than it does at the visible comings and goings of each day, at sunrise and at sunset. Mostly we don't notice it; but at those times we can feel our spinning planet simply by looking towards the light. Here, on one square metre – some hard chalky nubs of soil in a field at the edge of Newmarket Heath – it was possible to feel the Earth in motion. It is ordinary, this movement, ordinary, continuous and vital – everything that lives, lives with its speed – and yet how different life would be if we registered our turning world like this all day every day.

There were snowdrops on the verge. Each looked like the glassy bead of a hailstone frozen on a blade of grass. A wren sang from a frosty ditch – a midget marching band of one. Crows in the bare trees looked like black lamps in the grey air. Hares woke in the brown fields and stretched their ears. The extra minute of light had nothing more to show than what was already present – it showed just a minute more of that. More light but, so, all begins again. Today, there was nothing else to see but there was one more minute to see it in.

Allowing spring to run from midwinter to midsummer, it amounts to 183 days of the year. Almost. The exact time of the solstice shifts a little – the not-quite repeat cycle, or rather its not quite matching our invented time, is one of the good or happy disturbances of our world, the pearl-making grit in our oyster. Our being just *off* a little in how we have configured that world – the mismatch we have made in our timing – is itself a version of the tilted planet that makes the seasons. This uneven errancy gives some buzz and sway to every year. One in four years we must even leap. We feel our ride, consequently, as analogue, as if we drive with a manual gearbox rather than an automatic transmission. That is good too.

On cold days one of my fingers on my left hand gives up on blood and drains itself of colour and feeling. It looks then like a waxy tuber, something revealed that has never seen the sun, a dead man's digit or personal parsnip. On my path this morning a shoelace snagged and I had to take my gloves off and kneel to the cold ground. There was my useless twig, dry of blood. I thought of driving it into the soil, planting its deadness in the dark, pushing beyond the cold chalky rubble-bones at the surface to find warmer, wetter compost ticking over through the downtime. Might I grow there, in the soft machine of spring soil, a living hand for another year?

I turned for home and walked back from sunlit ground into still-frosted shadow. On the top of an ash tree was a singing mistle thrush – a male declaring himself and his plot. Its perch and its singing made the bare tree beneath it look like an exposed lung. Its song was things old and cold made into music. If a colander could sing it would sound like a mistle thrush: cold light, cold air, cold water coming through cold and hammered steel.

It is undoubtedly winter-music, but what you can hear in the mistle thrush's song is the future. It is all intention. From November, long before today's solstice, long before the coldest nights and the shortest days, this singer has been sending itself on, together with everything that has made it, towards what will be, towards tomorrow, towards the spring.

Go and find one: listen to a mistle thrush singing on the year's shortest day and you will know something of what it would be like to take, as a gift for those who arbitrate on matters of dying and re-birth, a golden bough – a token of ever-renewing life – into the winter underworld, and you will also know how it could be that one of those arbitrators was Persephone, who had a split existence, with a happy job as well as a sad one, who was the keeper of the dead but also the grower of spring, the season that is always yet to come but which is always – we hope, praise be to her – sure to.

5 January. Mild. The leftovers of a tar-black Christmas pudding had few takers on the bird table. A blue tit flew to the forsythia bush by the back door and nipped off a new yellow flower and held it in its feet. The little bird leaned in to the cut it had made and drank a bead of nectar. It released its grip and the pale yellow trumpet spun down to our meagre patch of lawn. The severed flower-head landed next to a dis-masted purple crocus that had collapsed with its petals splayed on the short bleached grass like the hands of a broken clock. I hadn't seen it upright and here it was, done already, dead before the best of the year, telling its time.

Midge-like flies appeared at midday above the battlefield. It was ten degrees Celsius.

Bouillon
50°N

6 January. The town of Bouillon in southern Belgium is knuckled in a sharp bend of the Semois River. Today, the water flowed brown and heavy and the old town curved in the river's crook, like a snail drawn up stickily into its shell. In a winterish mist that hung greasily about, I walked the streets with Patrick McGuinness, poet and writer of his childhood there and of its damp ricochet through his life. It being Twelfth Night, or the day after, we fortified ourselves with cakes and ale: Orval beer, made by Trappist monks thirty kilometres away, which arrives silently in brown otter-slink-shaped bottles, with a curling fish on the label, and a *galette des rois*, a huge seasonal almond cake, intended

to be cut and shared at home but which we scoffed in handfuls to keep us going as we went. Traditionally, each *galette* is seeded with a little fairy figurine or good luck token for the year ahead. I bit into ours before I knew what it was.

In Bouillon, we walked, what Patrick called in a Belgian poem, *a symphony in grey major*. Rooks, thinking of bed from mid-morning onwards, muddled above the crooked castle, like smoke off damp coal. Having no leader, they paid court only to themselves until one raven passed high above them on other business and broke the sound barrier with a croak. That set some jays laughing in the bare beech trees on the river bend. Little else, apart from the water, moved. Nothing else sang. Coils of dog shit studded the empty quay like rusty iron capstans. We dodged them and, doing so, I spotted a raft of hairy crud kayaking the river. I had my binoculars (I always do) and could see a tusk of dirty ivory steering the rig. It was a wild boar. The Semois runs through thickly wooded country higher up in the Ardennes and as it goes it must pick up passengers. Here was the busiest and bulkiest item we saw all day: a purposeful giant coconut keen to get on, piss-yellow and turd-brown, albeit quite dead and with a half-rotted head. Perhaps it had mistaken the water that muddily matched its coat and had drowned upstream, though it is hard to think a boar overcome like that, or perhaps it had died on shore and somehow rolled into the flow, but what heave or flood could pick up such a pig? We gasped to see it. And on it went like something flushed in the toilet swirl: shaggy cata-falque, beaver apology, hairy shit, abandoned Kon-Tiki, furry comet. It took the Bouillon bend with a reckless lean like an old motorcycle and sidecar, full pelt, nuzzling at its own froth, spinning in its own maelstrom, sweeping its own shave; all the while keeping mum and cutting free even as stick-nests and carrier bags and other dead flotsam took to it and hitched a ride. Orpheus, done with charming, failed in his wife-rescue, and beyond poetry, singing his head off down river, leaving Europe, as the story goes, looked perhaps like this, a potent mess. Exit: boar.

FEBRUARY

Quantocks
51°N

5 February. I peered into fifteen empty nest boxes in the old tannery oaks at Rectory Wood near Nether Stowey to try to bring to my mind the pied flycatchers I had seen in them last spring which, those very minutes, would be in some green-leaved African trees south of the Equator. Since *now* is almost everything in nature, rarely do we think such thoughts, or reach for such absences. There were old nests in the boxes, curves of dead grass and cupped bowls of moss and feathers, spaces made by the sitting birds. With my hands I felt for them and their ghostly warmth. Some looked like old hats or old slippers on the floor of a wardrobe, others more like the casts of dusty planets or ragged moons. The birds were far away but their home-making shapes were there still in the wood.

I left the trees at dusk and walked on the moor, looking up to the ashy sky in the south. I was thinking of the olden days when heaven was sometimes seen – golden, beaming, angelic – breaking through the clouds. There was nothing tonight but the full moon in the pale sky. On its own, riding high, in the dark wall of the winter night, it appeared more like a frosted porthole than any bird's nest. The sunlit lunar surface looked like the view beyond; the bright prospect seemed warm and alive – maybe that was Africa.

In the six months of spring (or what I am asking to be spring), the moon is full six times (seven some years) and so six (or seven) times is in its every phase. But we sublunaries see each day's moon differently. No two nights of moonlight are alike, nor have they ever been since the moon was born. It comes around but it never quite looks the same. Even a full moon in an open sky, uncaged, appears as a different face every time.

The Giant Impact model of the moon's making suggests that something not quite the size of the Earth, an impactor planet named Theia, collided with our planet and the crash threw off a great cloud of debris that collected as the moon. Some have thought the Pacific Ocean is the impact area, the lunar home-scar, and that the moon was torn from it. The moon's oxygen isotopic ratios are the same as the Earth's, implying a shared origin. Moon dust speaks of where it was made, like the feathers of a migratory bird. The jolt of that crash, it has also been suggested, was what tilted the Earth off its axis. It is the tilt – Earth's angled relation to the sun – that gives us, towards the top and bottom of the globe, the seasons, their variable day lengths and shifting temperatures, and the annual animal migrations that follow the light. Life works consequentially for those of us at the top and bottom of our planet. The truth, as Emily Dickinson said it should be, is told *slant*. Everything follows from that tilt.

The map of spring must be forever re-drawn, said Aimé Césaire. *Notwithstanding unique all over all again* was how Louis MacNeice put it in a poem; talking of the season, Rainer Maria Rilke said the same in 'Cycles' (in Don Paterson's version), one of his fifty-five, spring-loaded *Sonnets to Orpheus* (1922):

> The word is old, but never seems outdated
> And every year arrives like something new;
> though it has come so often. Always anticipated,
> though not once did you catch it. It caught you.

Catching is the thing – or, seen from the reverse angle, our being *taken* by the season.

Zakouma & Ennedi
11°N & 17°N

To get to Chad in mid-February, I took a taxi at three in the morning from my flat in Bristol for an early bus to London; then planes from Heathrow to Atatürk, Istanbul to Kano, and Kano to Ndjamena. My taxi-driver was from Alexandria in Egypt. A smiling, thickset man, coated against the cold of the small hours. I told him that, in travelling to where I was going, I would be flying over his old home. He asked me what I would do in Chad. I told him what I was chasing: birds, migrations, the spring. His dark-brown eyes flashed back at me in his rear-view mirror.

He had studied biology at 'high school', including what he called 'the five stages of evolution theory'.

– Natural selection?

– Yes, *ach*, *ach*, the natural selection!

He had a question for me.

– I have seen these gulls in Bristol with rings on their legs. What is going on? The government watch everything in this country. Are they using the gulls to spy on us?

He had warned his family about this, he said.

– *Ach*, that was a joke!

But still he wanted to know.

– Can the rings tell you, by satellite, where a bird is?

As a boy he'd seen the nets for catching migrant quail on the Egyptian shore of the Mediterranean. And another bird, after rain in the same place, bigger than an 'Egyptian goose' that could barely fly, that 'didn't want to fly'.

It is striking how many people – people who aren't birders – carry with them the memory of one or two vividly recalled but unnamed birds they have seen. Bird people get used to being asked about these. Often a definitive answer isn't really being sought, or if given isn't really welcomed. The bird unnamed is more powerful and has a stronger magic.

What was that heavy Egyptian goose that didn't want to leave home?

– A bustard, perhaps? Or, maybe, a stork?

He didn't know the names. Still his first question nagged.

– Do the rings tell you where the bird is by satellite?

– No, you have to catch them again. Or fix a GPS to them.

He was ready to be worried by the thought of what the gulls of Bristol had seen of him. Perhaps he was moonlighting.

– It isn't a transmitter?

– No, nor satnav.

The drive was only ten minutes, and it is an easy route at three in the morning, but my new friend managed to get lost and took a wrong turn.

– I am too interested in this talk!

Crossing the Sahara, I peered from the plane at the nothing of the desert dark. I wanted to call what I couldn't see a *vastitude* – my doubt about that even being a word suggesting it could be the right one. I tried to conjure a redstart, flying north below our plane as we flew south. I fell asleep soon after, at my window seat, my forehead pressed to the egg-shaped porthole.

In Ndjamena, I met up with Claire and our friends Gus and Margie Mills, who had all come north from South Africa. We were going birdwatching in the Sahara for a week. I wanted to see the desert and I wanted to see some of the birds I expected as spring visitors to Europe on the point of crossing the sand. Before that we would travel south-east of Ndjamena to the national park at Zakouma for a few days. There we hoped to see some of the same migratory birds, with others, in a green place, on the southern fringes of the Sahel, where they had spent their winter.

First, we had one night in the hot and dusty city. From a balcony we watched what we could see over the mud walls around our hostel. There were no women on the streets. Boys played football in a wide public square. Mopeds sputtered, their riders in white or brown thawbs and keffiyehs. Men with sub-machine guns, in sunglasses and soft leather slipper-like shoes, walked among the mopeds and the footballers.

Towards the time for evening prayers, from a line of acacias, three melodious warblers (destined soon for Spain, France or Italy) began singing. It took us some time to work out what we were hearing. We were quite far east for such a westbound bird. And, at first, I wasn't sure how many birds and how many species were present. The song was rich, glutted with notes, and some patches or phrases sounded as if they were being given over the top of others. *Hippolais polyglotta* is the species' scientific name – and what we heard sounded like a speaking in tongues. In the heat and the dust, the honey-gloop of song (three birds, each singing twice at once) and the amplified muezzins from the minarets of three (or was that four?) mosques all warped and phased and fizzed into one hot static soup.

Claire recorded the warblers on her phone. When we re-played the sounds, the birds jumped out of the trees to try to see what it was that sang so like them. I claimed the fresh green of their plumage as a European colour – the salad of the spring of where they were headed – it seemed the opposite of Ndjamena's dust. But the birds had moulted and grown their new feathers in this parched place or somewhere similar (twice in fact: a complete moult after they arrive from Europe in the autumn is followed by a moult of body feathers and some wing feathers in the early spring before they head north). They were hostages to nowhere.

The holy sound system cranked up and the warblers' song began to ebb. The sun sank. From one quarter of the burnt sky, straw-coloured fruit-bats flapped. Some looked like big leathery bees, others like flying machines assembled from wire and waxed brown paper. Their heads hung down as they flew, as if they were looking with amazement at what they were doing. Four or five lost their nerve and crash-landed into the trees, folding their embarrassing wings away and clawing at the leaves.

Birdwatching anywhere in Africa almost always involves a mix of local resident species and visiting birds that are more familiar to a traveller from Europe. The juxtapositions throw the world into relief. In Madagascar I've seen barn swallows from Europe feeding near lemurs and ground rollers. One bird has come from elsewhere in order to be here. One bird that lives here all the time shares these pools or this thorn bush with a bird that comes only for a month or so each year. One is a seasoned migrant; another might live its life within a single tree. A steppe buzzard is on this telephone post in open country in the hinterland of Cape Town and a jackal buzzard is on the next. The jackal buzzard breeds in the gum trees around the farmhouse a kilometre away, the steppe buzzard must fly to the Aral Sea. This bird knows a reindeer and a leopard as its mammal neighbours; that one knows only the leopard.

February in Chad is thick with a mix of birdlife. On our first day out from Ndjamena we saw a Montagu's harrier, three white storks, two northern wheatears and twenty-five lesser kestrels hawking for insects – and a black scimitarbill, a grey hornbill, ten marabou storks, twenty fan-tailed ravens in one wheeling circle, and a scatter of chestnut-backed sparrow larks in the dusty gutters of the dirt road. Every subsequent day blended its birds like this.

In Zakouma, we spent five days travelling around the park watching everything we could. Like the bee-eaters perched outside our cabins – northern carmine and little green – we made loops and sallies, starting out, crossing paths, heading back; we took dawn and dusk drives; we walked when we could; we stood in a storm of millions of red-billed queleas; we flew a sky-circuit in an aeroplane looking for elephants; we shook hands with some park rangers on an anti-poaching patrol; we shook hands with some nomads herding their flock to water; we dodged buffaloes and we followed cheetahs; and all the time a swirl of birds was around us – some in their forever place, others in their home, as I learned, away from home, the *other* life for so many of those due in Europe in a month or so.

A dripping tap across the camp from our cabin was an oasis in the dry season scrub. Almost the first bird I saw there was a male redstart – the bird most needed in every spring of my northern life. The gesture of its flight seemed offered as a gift: the spread of its wings and tail like an open palm – yes, it said, salaam, you are welcome and, yes, here too you might thrive.

There are two seasons only in Zakouma: dry and rainy. It rains between April and October. At that time all the European migrants have gone north. It doesn't rain at all during the dry season. The redstart wintering here will arrive after the rains of one year and leave before the rains of the next; it will never feel rain in all its time in Chad.

We went out. Six lions dozed under a thorn, meat-dreams on their breath; a whitethroat – friend of my springtime runs in the Cambridgeshire fens – ticked and fussed in the leaves above. Watching it, I understood that everything that lived in Zakouma is accommodated. Nothing is *off*. Later we saw a wigeon in a flash of flood-water: it shouldn't have come so far south (they winter in Britain commonly, and breed in Iceland and northern Scandinavia), but still it didn't look out of place. Above the lions, in the next acacia to the whitethroat, was a lesser whitethroat. They rattle from the same hedge on my fenland run as a whitethroat scratches. The bird here was a neighbour now of the whitethroat and might be a neighbour later. Between the thorns of Chad and those of Cambridgeshire, the whitethroat will most likely fly north-west out of Africa; the lesser whitethroat, even if it were heading for the same scrubby fen edge in western Europe, would travel far to the east around the Turkish end of the Mediterranean. The great inhalation of spring into Europe contains these flights up either side of Africa and the shared thorn trees at either end of these little warblers' long journeys. Here they meet and there they might; in between was the desert.

One afternoon, we flew above Zakouma for an hour, hitching a ride in a spotter plane piloted by the park warden, Rian Labuschagne. The protection of elephants there is a major part of his work (it has been successful, but at a considerable cost). Locally, Zakouma's elephants are both wanted and not. The wider world has interests in them too. Elephants are global commodities – bulky containers for various human fantasies and grey projections of various human desires. They are also of a scale out of sorts for the times. They live in herds and they walk with long strides, caring not for borders. They are big, and they appear to be doomed because they now don't fit the terms and conditions with which we have rigged the world.

Following the green that comes with rain, the elephants of Zakouma move like the area's nomadic people – and for the same reasons – wheeling south through Chad. Seeking the same as the nomads seek for their cattle, sheep and goats, makes the elephants rivals. Nomads, Rian said, think they own everything wherever they are; elephants, massively, unconsciously, behave in the same way. Elephants also clash with settled people when the herbivores' seasonal migrations after edible greenery put them in conflict with crop-growing villagers. They can eat people out of their house and home.

Then there are poachers who seek elephant ivory for its high value, in some Asian cultures, as a fantastical revitalising medicine and, in some Arab cultures, as a symbol of prowess, militancy and masculinity. Rian believed that most poaching of elephants, across a huge swathe of Africa, was the work of just a few people, who rode on horseback from Sudan into the rest of the continent. If they need to, these poachers could travel forty or fifty kilometres through the bush every day, avoiding paths and tracking their quarry. An elephant might walk a similar distance. If the elephants move then the poachers follow. When each man has one tusk they travel back to where they came from, each carrying the ivory curving over the back of a horse or a camel.

Our plane ride taught us this sad news when we were done, but first it took us beyond the trappings of the man-made and busted world and out over paradise. It was the best air journey of my life. We flew from half past four in the afternoon for an hour, ninety metres up, with the windows open, crossing acacia woods, spiny thickets, steel-blue rivers, glistening wetlands and a vast grass plain. New, wholesome and distributed truths were to be had at every moment – below us was a *Whole Earth Catalog*. The planet, seen from the air immediately above it, is much more readily lovable than it is down below. In the show-all light the land was brilliantly legible. It works, as well: it has an intelligible lay-out – a *tawny grammar* – that you cannot sense when travelling its thickness. Life seems *just so*. Here

26

was everything, now. Five iridescent green wood-hoopoes planed away from the crown of an acacia; a herd of buffalo walked in and out of their own dust cloud; a dozen crocodiles slinked into a river as our shadow buzzed them; here was a marshy flash dotted with fifty crowned cranes; here, a *pelicanopolis* taking wing; and here, the first ten of 250 elephants between some trees, in a savannah of open woodland, their broad earth-grey backs more like hills than animals, showing them to be absolutely part of the place and, apparently, so close to us that we might have stepped down onto them and ridden their ride.

Everywhere was beautifully occupied. We were making a raw noise and burning the guts of the Earth in order to traverse it, flushing animals and fouling the air, but from the open windows we looked down on a different working of the world that seemed wholly good: a huge *being*, a continent, stretching away in all directions, animal tracks and paths, flight-lines, hoof-casts, elephant-dug dust bowls, a male pallid harrier drinking at a pool, ash-lines of burned tree trunks where lightning had started a fire, fig trees and acacias, the plump domes of their crowns, water lilies, like stars sown below and shining up to those hidden in the blue above, the planetary marks of life, of wear and tear and repair, its joining and its happy blur.

What was the love I felt for the way we moved in the air and passed over this world? Perhaps it was the love I feel at the thought of a whinchat, ninety metres up, alive, as if with all its own windows open, flying into these places for the first time, in the autumn of the year it hatched in a nest of woven grass on a Scottish brae, its flight map uploaded already into its paper-soft skull even as it curled in the dark of its chalky egg; or my equal love at the thought of a returning bird, the same whinchat, coming back the next year, knowing the place differently now having been there already and having entered it, but coming again above these scattered trees and the dry grasses between them, and dropping down to find its place.

Everything below you is helpful – here is *accommodation*. The open woodland spreads apart, until there is more grass than trees, and then just one tree in the middle of some grass, and then just grass. Seeing that reminded me of a passage near the beginning of *Wind, Sand and Stars* where Antoine de Saint-Exupéry, recalling his days as a novice pilot, took advice from a seasoned airman, Guillaumet, about a flight he was to make across Spain.

> But what a strange geography lesson I was given! Guillaumet didn't teach me about Spain, he made Spain my friend. He didn't talk about hydrography, or population figures, or livestock. Instead of talking about Guadix, he spoke of three orange trees at the edge of the field near Guadix: 'Watch out for those, mark them on your map ...' And from then on the three orange trees had more significance than the Sierra Nevada.

He made Spain my friend. Ever since I first read Saint-Exupéry forty years ago when hitch-hiking in Yugoslavia, I have been looking out for those orange trees. Nowadays, thanks to American military and espionage technology we can all see, on any screen, three (and many more than three) orange trees still in the vicinity of Guadix. But they occur in other places too. I thought I might have seen them one May day, when I flew from Foula to the Shetland Mainland in a little plane that rolled off a cliff to get airborne, and which I shared with the island's three schoolchildren who were going for a swimming lesson, already changed into their trunks and costumes and wrapped in their towels. The stony runway we took towards the cliff edge was where, just an hour before, I had found a stone curlew, a rare, overshooting, spring migrant, and as we accelerated to take off, the bird flew from the tussocky edge and briefly kept us company. I thought I saw the essence of those orange trees again when, coming in to land at Maroantsetra airfield in eastern Madagascar, after a local flight from Antananarivo that Claire and I shared with a row of chickens and cockerels in woven baskets who clucked and crowed as we began our descent. They had the first-class seats; we were in economy. Outside, I could see half a dozen teenage children urging cattle off the grassy outfield of the little airport and then standing with their arms outstretched to indicate to our pilot that his way was clear.

As we crossed the great grass plain at Zakouma, I requested out loud that I might return as a nomad. Rian said he wanted the same. Down below us on the grass – I waved at them through the open window – men walked with their herd from a watering place; further on women were striking camp, dismantling a long tent, loading a cart and harnessing brown and white bulls. Of course, I don't like milk, am nervous of cattle, prone to mosquito attacks, am not good away from a shower for long, and so on, but to move like this, after fresh greenness, at walking pace through such a world …

Or could I be a nomad with wings? A whinchat?

With a serious smile, back in his control room at the park headquarters, Rian banished such dreams and, quite properly, fenced all those escapist thoughts. Beneath photographs of butchered elephants (their faces hacked open for their tusks) and photographs of park rangers slain in gun battles with poachers (the living faces of the dead men), he talked about his armoury, the mortars donated by the President of Chad, the Chinese ammunition he issues to his rangers (who once included the pictured six, all murdered in 2012 by Sudanese poachers as they came out of their hidden camp at first light to pray), and he showed us his windowless strong-room with its rocket-launchers and its confiscated ivory, awaiting burning – four curved tusks weighing forty or fifty kilograms each, propped in a dark corner where they looked like abandoned parings of the moon.

We saw a whinchat that same day. There were three feeding on the wet edge of the flood plain we had earlier flown over. Three also-migrant red-throated pipits walked among them, also filling their beaks with insects. The warm sandy streaks on the whinchats and the pink speckle on the pipits' throats flushed as the sun lowered.

I had been in the strong-room but the world came good once more.

An altogether different birdlife then overtook us. We had travelled to the centre of this shallow arena of wet grass to be there when it happened. Twilight is short across central Africa – once the sun drops, night comes fast. Here it was flown in by an extraordinary collection of flapping dirty grey dish-rags that was six million red-billed queleas. These birds took the sun down. As the light slipped, a kind of smoke seemed to breathe up from the trees at the rim of the plain. It could have been rising dew; it could have been emerging midges. There were rolls of it, coils and ropes and drifts, long slung metres, banners, shirts and trousers of it, and now all of it was pouring from all sides and converging towards us, at tree height first, then rippling down in a joined flex to a metre or less above the grass until we were swallowed up as the queleas began to arrive at their roost around us.

My only comparable experience of being overtaken in this way at speed (a speed that is of this world and yet incredible) was standing on Dartmoor in Devon when the solar eclipse of 1999 shut down the sky. In Chad, thousands upon thousands of the little grey-brown sparrow-like birds achieved the same effect. They parted their flocks just enough to avoid us and swirled around the bushes and settled where they could. The noise they made – but *it* seems more precise to describe their singularity – was like a colossal chicken battery. An electric hiss: six million chirrups, twelve million wings, and the rainfall percussion of the shit of every shitter in the flock. It was a muzz, and a brown bleed across the eye; it was a smell, as well; we breathed them, it was the air; the weather had become quelea.

Dynamite and flame-throwers have been used on these birds in other parts of Africa. They are lumped with locusts. Their shared mind moves mountains, eating them to the ground. So many must, of course, eat so much. Seeds they love. Worse, they always want more: they strip one locale and move on, rolling out their avian rapine far and wide. No grain is safe. They plunder. They are excessive. They are themselves excess. There is more than enough of them in the world and yet still more come – invasive immigrants, bad migrants, anti-manna.

To me they looked unfinished. In their hurry to get on, they had hardly bothered coming together. They are like how they live: the condition of their life makes the condition of their life. They are like the moulded flip-flops that are shoeing the world, and that I saw everywhere in Chad, dead soles, broken and pressed into the roadside dirt of every village. They over-produce; they glut; they erupt. There is always too much of them when they come. They are like the rain and the dust. Perhaps they are like us.

Each flock, three thousand birds or more, shoaled and swelled as it crossed the muddy pan and the flooded grass. One flock picked up a waiting male pallid harrier that would have liked to eat a quelea and it rode alongside them trying to enter the herd enough to snatch one bird. The flock decided (how it does this is a mind unread, as yet unreadable) it wanted to drink before sleeping, and it thickened itself lower to the ground and each bird touched down for a moment (enough) before rising again, a thread rippling through the heavy carpet. The descent was weighted from above and it killed the air like a vacuum, pushing the harrier down to make an emergency landing and leaving it stranded on the mud, its grey slump looking like an old flag, over-run and abandoned.

When they reached the bushes where we stood, the queleas streamed in and out of them like dots and dashes. It was very noisy and hectic. The back of some colossal machine had been taken off – a kind of world engine – and all its moving parts were there to be seen working overtime. The birds looked then like lines of code or an epic digital sequence being run at speed, each digit almost always the same as the previous and the next, and all coming into meaning or resolved only en masse.

More and more arrived and each found a place to perch. They carried the last of the light with them, brown motes of it, and as they shelved themselves in the bushes the night fell and they switched themselves off almost instantaneously.

We woke long before light the next morning in order to see the birds leave their roost. At the edge of the site was a buffalo dormitory. A herd of one hundred were waking as we passed, their bed-linen of crushed grass giving off the smell of a cowshed. At six, at the first sun crack, lines of the queleas began unravelling out of the bushes and pouring away in all directions. It was an unspooling with great chatter. In slaps of brown whiplash, whole bushes exited as one. Thick cables headed off. They were still together – they never aren't – but now they were aerial once again, the best joining.

I saw then that the bushes were bare. What, in the half-light, I had thought to be leaves had been birds. A pungent stink came from the late abandoned trees – the smell of the buffalo dorm or of a lion mattress multiplied many times. Beneath each bush were pillows of white-grey shit. On every pillow were one or more corpses – the ordinary, so rarely seen, dying of birds. Yellow-billed kites and European marsh harriers and pied crows came through the roost looking for the sick or the lay-abed. Finally, I saw a take: a marsh harrier in flight extended a leg to its side and grasped a passing quelea. It looked like an automatic gesture. Neither bird seemed to notice what had happened.

After days of such a sustaining feed at Zakouma, we turned north into the Sahel, driving for hours across flat open country through scrubby thorn lands. There was briefly a little tar, then a lot of dirt, then infinite sand. From half a day away from Zakouma, there was nothing green, save for a smattering of dwarfish moisture-hoarding leaves on scattered acacias. Nomads and their herds were moving alongside us; some of the travellers, carrying long sticks, walked with their animals, some rode on horses and carried long spears, some rode on camels and donkeys; the camels looked too big for them, the donkeys too small. At a drinking pond, a little boy in a Barcelona football shirt rode an enormous wide-horned cow out into the water. A Bororo cow – the Bororo people are famous for their cows.

We drove on. Every village had the suggestion of a barricade at its entrance and exit: a piece of string slung loosely across the road between two sticks. Differences between settled and mobile existences define the Sahel: the people, places, and birds. Sometimes a policeman crouched at the roadside; sometimes a scarecrow had been built there. The settled in Chad are in permanent antagonistic negotiation with the moving, but it was possible to drive straight over the string.

These were farmers' villages, with thatched round huts, often decorated at the roof apex with an ostrich egg threaded on a stick, a good luck token for a new couple. In the fields, men and women with mattocks were beating at piles of rust-red sorghum. Sometimes crops are forked up into trees and stored there – they look then like a giant sociable weavers' nest. Other farmers build wooden gantries or use their hut roofs to lay up their unthreshed harvest or hay and keep it out of the browsing range of their goats. The raised stacks provide shade. Families congregated beneath their crop in these outdoor living rooms; others used the shaded space for prayer or as a shop. Milk in old fizzy drink bottles was for sale, cooking oil in the same, petrol in the same.

We stopped for lunch ourselves in the shade of some trees. A dozing parliament of marabous had taken the best acacia. Everything wanted out of the sun. On the dusty ground beneath the dark tangle of a tamarisk, a pair of black scrub-robins mated, their long tails, striped black and white, rising and falling, the male's sooty mantling wings patched with a rufous-red I now knew was the colour of a head of sorghum. There was a lesser honeyguide here and a Vieillot's barbet, and then a couple of Europeans showed themselves: an icterine warbler and a female redstart followed by a male. I was happy, as I always am, to be admitted to their company. A party of nomads on camels had stopped here too and the male redstart, excited by all the traffic, flew close to the animals to take an insect from the stone-baked ground. Heading back towards some cover, it passed between a camel's legs, flying a parable of one sort or another. Before we started off again, the Chadian drivers and cook from our trip took off their shoes, washed their hands, knelt to the earth, and prayed.

It got dustier. Zakouma, now one day behind us to the south – even dried-out dry-season Zakouma, seemed in the memory like a kind of bosom. We were to be weaned as we went north. Everything turned khaki. Trees got rarer and there were fewer birds. I began to count the larks we flushed from the gritty roadside. They were dry-risers, arid country specialists: chestnut-backed sparrow larks, black-crowned sparrow larks, greater short-toed larks, and crested larks. All life in

Zakouma had seemed joined, immersed and interwoven – now the desert began to proclaim an atomised world. The first shock of the Sahara is how little there is of anything apart from the dust. And how particulate all life has become. *Khākī* means dust-coloured in Urdu. *Khāk* means dust in Persian. It is dust – it becomes more obviously sand only some way north – which lies between every observation. Dust – like a migraine – underwrites everything as an aggregate, but because it is itself particulate it scatters everything as well. It holds itself together only temporarily; it is forever wearing down and blowing away. Even the rocks in these places are dust, briefly held upright. All that is trying to live in these conditions appears separated too from the next living thing. Between each observation I made there was much I wanted to call nothing. I know that is not right, but I also know – the desert schooled me so – that *nothing* describes something of the tenuous fragility of the lives that are there, their toe-hold, their panting.

In Abéché, having bought the last green things we could find and a kilo of 'flour of dried meat', we sat in a shaded colonnade outside a shoe-maker's kiosk. His slippers were lark-like. The old man and some apprentice boys crouched on the ground. From goat hides, they cut sandy-coloured shoe-shaped uppers and soles. They softened the leather by hand, rubbing it with amber beeswax. Everything being worked was the colour of one sort of sand or another. In their concentration, the workers had let their own shoes slip from their bare feet, and every now and then one or another of them would unconsciously feel for their footwear with their stretching toes. Watching that was like seeing larks descend in steps of air from the sky to the sand.

Next door was a *Salon de Coiffures* with photographs of rap stars on the walls. The barber slept in his barbering chair as barbers do anywhere. Further along, I noticed that the tailors of Abéché were the only spectacle-wearers in town. Next, there was a *Cabinet Dentaire (Syrien)* and, adjacent to it, a stall selling leather pouffes stencilled with the word *Tchad* and the Playboy bunny logo. The last sign on the colonnade, hanging in front of an empty room, read *Vente de Glace*.

In the town of Kalaït, our next stop northwards, a migrant white wagtail walked the dust-dirt along a street of blacksmiths, its tail-pump passing for bellows. Claire spotted that the blacksmiths had customised old Land Cruiser engine-blocks for their anvils in their desert forges. She loves a Land Cruiser. Iron beaten out from old oil drums was also being recycled as axe-heads, ladles, and hefty tweezers for the removal of thorns. A boy passed us whipping his donkey with an iPhone cable. Camel saddles were for sale. There were house sparrows near the outdoor bread ovens. An old man tried to sell a kid goat by putting it into Claire's arms: we didn't buy it. The bread, flat and singed and a little gritty, tasted like where we thought we were going.

There are various marks on various maps to indicate the southern edge of the Sahara. One of them is the 150mm isohyet for annual precipitation. North of Abéché we crossed the sixteenth latitude – another signifier. I looked around; I was always looking around. My notes from the desert were written in a green notebook. They were mostly done on the move from the back seat of a Land Cruiser. The route was rarely, after Abéché, a road of any kind. Often, whatever there was of a track was harder to travel than the open country stretching away around us. But none of it was smooth, and my notes record the bumps and jolts and lurches like a seismograph. Here is the wadi where we first saw migrant Rüppell's warblers. Now we're leaving an *oued* where there was a dead Arabian bustard. This is sand's soft sift and barn swallows are passing. The substrate wrote itself into whatever I was trying to write. It also encouraged brevity. Sentences are not easy when your writing desk is slewing through sand or juddering over shattered rock. Wherever I am, my notes often amount to nothing more than a list of birds, but here the note-taker was an earwig that walked my pages with ink on its feet. The conditions demanded small-scale scribbles – but the desert also endorsed this. In the face of its *vastitude* – that which was literally blowing into my face, grain by stinging grain – it was impossible to find anything matching or commensurate to say. What use was my little green book to this epic sand world? Who could put into prose the width of the view or the heat of the day: the fizzing emptiness; the blackness your eyes see at the brightest times; the pared-back truth of an unhomed planet; the sense you have of being a bystander on the first day on Earth? My literary tools weren't up to it any more than my body. Nothing in my lexicon could match what I could see. Being light on what Henry David Thoreau called *dusky knowledge*, I have no *tawny grammar* of my own. My mind was sapped and overdrawn. I threw out adjectives and exclamations again and again but they all died in the desiccated air.

The Swedish poet Tomas Tranströmer knew Chad. As a child he was a keen entomologist and planned on becoming (like me, like many) an African explorer. He became a poet and a psychologist instead. In a prose poem called 'Upright' in English, also translated as 'Standing Up', he remembers a day in Chad (this is Robert Bly's translation). Although it is about walking on water and how this is not possible, we might also read it when attempting a sand crossing:

on the banks of the Chari, there were many boats, an atmosphere positively friendly, the men almost blue-black in color with three parallel scars on each cheek (meaning the Sara tribe). I am welcomed on a boat – it's a canoe hollowed from a dark tree. The canoe is incredibly rocky, even when you sit on your heels. A balancing act. If you have the heart on the left side you have to lean a bit to the right, nothing in the pockets, no big arm movements, please, all rhetoric has to be left behind. It's necessary: rhetoric will ruin everything here. The canoe glides out over the water.

For a canoe ride on a desert river, read a car ride across the sand. All *rhetoric* must be left behind.

Piss-stops get mentioned in my notebook because we invariably saw migrant warblers in the thorns nearby, but often that is all I was able to carry away from these places. There wasn't even much piss. My sour dribble made it to the sand – the only moisture to have touched it in ages – but it dried to salty grit as fast as my shadow moved off. Similarly, I am left with a notebook filled with bird names, one-liners and sweat stains, emergency observations snatched in from out of the sun and forever smirched by our dusty progress.

Perhaps the poverty of my data, though, might serve to intimate how it goes for the birds in the Sahara. These migrants (and a handful of residents that survive the desert year around) add up to barely a dot or a dash, a mark or a grain. The weight of one willow warbler moving north across the desert in the spring is somehow to be measured against nine million square kilometres of sand. Each bird is a little green notebook against the Sahara.

Seen from its surface, brought up by its school of hard knocks, the desert is experienced as a world-maker, such that when you are in it everywhere else beyond every horizon becomes *not* the Sahara. You sense the rule of sand even when it is absent. Leaving the Sahara behind means a migrant bird's life might succeed, the white wagtail might make it, but even apparently away from the sand, the birds' lives are still shaped by it – redstarts can only be in an oak wood in an English spring or a birch wood in a Norwegian spring because they have crossed the desert; as they travel, they carry the experience in their bodies, its news like those falls of rain that sometimes dust car rooftops in England with the warm reddish grit of sky-shipped Sahara.

The desert is a world-maker in fact as well as in our imaginations. The subject of the first paper Charles Darwin wrote in the light of his observations and experiences on the *Beagle* was about the dust blown on the Harmattan wind from the Sahara out into the Atlantic; he found it covering the ship's deck one morning in January 1832. In 2016, a paper was published in the journal *Nature* reporting on an analysis of 161 years of dust counts in the desert from 1851 to 2011. It has an excellent title: 'The past, present and future of African dust':

African dust emission and transport exhibits variability on diurnal to decadal timescales and is known to influence processes such as Amazon productivity, Atlantic climate modes, regional atmospheric composition and radiative balance and precipitation in the

Sahel. To elucidate the role of African dust in the climate system, it is necessary to understand the factors governing its emission and transport. However, African dust is correlated with seemingly disparate atmospheric phenomena, including the El Niño/ Southern Oscillation, the North Atlantic Oscillation, the meridional position of the intertropical convergence zone, Sahelian rainfall and surface temperatures over the Sahara Desert, all of which obfuscate the connection between dust and climate ...

The desert is felt far and wide, even on the other side of the Earth. Its dust both conceals and reveals; there are correlations and obfuscations, clearings and cloudings; the Sahara, like the redstarts and swallows and honey buzzards crossing the sand, is blowing in the wind. As to how that hot storm will go, there are now, the paper's authors say, in our era of increased greenhouse gas emissions (which slows down tropical air circulation), lower quantities and reduced transmission of African dust. The future is likely to include increased rainfall in West Africa, a warmer North Atlantic and increased risks of hurricanes. Even as a waning power, the desert looks to remain a hothouse or a forge as its dust blows forward and its dust blows back.

But let us get particular: because there it is possible. Any stop in the desert might feel like a stop in the middle of nowhere, but, because of the migrant birds, every stop we made turned out to be in the middle of somewhere. When we could, we pulled up near trees, for their shade but also because we were drawn inevitably to the feature the tree made in an otherwise empty-looking scene. Then we spotted the birds. There was an olivaceous warbler in that tree. The colour of a drying leaf. And another in that one. And a subalpine warbler in this. Greyish but with blood-rust warming its throat. And the thought came, as we passed more thorns, that every one would hold a European migrant. That every February day and night of my life and many thousands beyond it, this has been the case. That this is where they want to be. That these thorns are warbler banks – they are safe in them, they are saved there. That Europe is in waiting in these grey stunted trees. That the songs of a whole season are keeping quiet in them. And that the thorns are feeding the fat on either side of the warblers' keel-like sternum, to enable them to go out from the shade and the shelter of the tree, to steer headlong into the sky and to deliver to Europe its spring.

We stopped to drink and to pee: in one acacia, one each of Rüppell's warbler, lesser whitethroat, and garden warbler – a Cape Canaveral for Europe; also there, below the tree, a desert wheatear – a migrant from the north but with a name that made it seem at home; and three residents too, a hoopoe lark, three desert larks and three cream-coloured coursers. Resident birds, like these, must be surrendered to the desert to survive. To live here for long you must aspire to the condition of sand and take on its tone. Migrants get away with looking more out of place. The black-and-white face of the Rüppell's warbler seemed flagrant among the thorns.

Despite the strings on the roads in the Sahel, Chad is the least fenced place I have ever been to, but it is perhaps also the hardest country to get across. If your place ends (or begins) in the Sahara desert, it is probably ridiculous to think of erecting any barrier of your own. The in-between lands at the border of eastern Chad, where we were, and Darfur and South Sudan further east, are important pathways for refugee or emigrant peoples coming out of Sudan and South Sudan, Ethiopia, Eritrea and the ruins of Somalia. Local Toubou guides run the human caravan. We wouldn't see them, nor any sign of them as we drove north, our driver and cook Johnny said, waving his arm off to the right. We wouldn't see them, but they would be there.

Claire stopped once in the Libyan desert, on a journey she took before we knew one another, and a migrant yellow wagtail materialised out of the burning sky and dropped to her feet for the shade her shoe had made. She was remembering this as we were surprised by a barbary falcon that appeared as were watching ten pale crag martins feeding in swooping flights along a rock outcrop. There was danger and panic. The falcon tried to drive the martins towards the sandstone cliff whereupon the martins did something I have seen only once or twice before in fifty years of birdwatching. The threatened birds flew closer to us, swinging near, cutting their flight swoops and slowing their wing-beats.

They had it in mind to put us between them and the falcon and sought us out. Little else in our desert days paid us any heed, but I was taken by that.

Five Dorcas gazelles ran for five kilometres in front of us when we were back in our car and heading on north for the mountains at Ennedi. Three were smaller calves; they followed the leading couple. Were we herding them or were they on the move for themselves? Their feet kicked spurts of gritty dust. I thought of their hooves on the stones, and about the word exodus, and then I remembered Saint-Exupéry (whose captive desert gazelles forever pushed at their cage seeking 'the vast open space that will fulfil them') and D. H. Lawrence:

> The gazelle calf, O my children,
> goes behind its mother across the desert,
> goes behind its mother on blithe bare foot
> requires no shoes, O my children!

One swallow, alone, flew north, over the sand towards the sandstone. And then, presumably, beyond it to more sand. I lost it in the dusty heat haze. So long have migrant birds' dashes through the air – a dash on a map, a dash in the mind – been a mystery, we feel their movements as an estrangement. Not being able to configure it ourselves, we think of birds losing what we imagine to be their identity when in transit. They become inconceivable above the desert, or crossing a sea.

People who have had a diagnosis of dissociative fugue lose access to their memory of themselves and their sense of selfhood. Sometimes they adopt a new self; sometimes they might abruptly depart on a journey. It isn't like this for the birds – they are being exactly as they must be; they are being fully themselves – yet we feel it as if it were so when trying to contemplate what they do. Thinking about migration and trying to feel what it is like tips us ourselves into fugue (or fugitive) thoughts that we project onto the migrants.

Unintelligibility might be the truth of those journeys. It is also what we feel looking at the sand. All those flying north every spring have already flown south across the Sahara the previous autumn. To think of that is enough to incapacitate the mind. But for the birds, migration is *common sense*, and their travels are commutes, not tourism. Some birds cross the sand at night because it is cooler and because they have the stars to steer by. Some hide in the slim shade of rocks during the day. Some cross in a single non-stop flight, days and nights long. Some break their journeys and eke out their supplies at oases. Some travel in flocks. Some alone. Millions make it and life goes on. Millions die. Their bodies mummify in the dry heat and they pave parts of the desert. Their soft organs dissolve but their feathers persist and only slowly abrade and granulate after the bird's death, breaking down into a kind of bird-sand that joins all the other sand to build the Sahara.

We camped on the flat floor of a dead-end valley enclosed by smooth sandstone cliffs. Late in the afternoon the sun left and the place became more itself than it had been before. The sun, when up, was in charge of everything below. It felt like high noon all day. Once it quit, at six o'clock, distances that seemed truer appeared, and a quietness, that was the specific quietness of this corner of the desert, could be heard. House buntings and white-crowned black wheatears that had been hiding in crannies in the rock came from these shelters and spread out across the valley floor. The space that lived globally a minute ago became intimate.

In the dark another sort of desert clarity comes. There is no haze or shimmer or sweat. Then, in the bone-show of rocks, the land looks more thoughtful or thinkable. Ample and almost friendly. Near our camp, another night, a golden nightjar started singing. I wanted to see it. Its name is enough of a spur – who wouldn't prospect for that? – but it also made a sound across the sand flats like the last drops of water gulping from a thin-necked bottle. I walked towards it, but it receded deeper into the desert, like a mirage in the dark. As I returned to our sleeping mats, the moon came into the night like compensation for the hidden bird, a golden dew-goblet, damp, massive and full. Jupiter, all silvery refulgence, was visible too with its moons like bees buzzing about its head. The air between us must have been very empty. And yet birds were surely in it, too, moving north, over the singing nightjar, and over us sleepers on the sand.

– In the morning – the cinema!

Leading us into the Sahara, we had an excellent guide, Pier Paolo Rossi, an Italian rock-art obsessive (and, he asked me to say this, member of the Chadian company Société de Voyages Sahariens). We showed him some birds; he took us from one cave shelter and rock painting to another and told us what he thought of what we saw. He was friendly, funny and, in his rock-wisdom, a domesticator of the harshest places. In one place he pointed to a quern-stone on the sand with a worn grinding stone left on the flat-plate of rock: it might have been last used, Pier Paolo said, five thousand years ago or perhaps five days before, by the camel-herding nomads camped nearby. There, as every-where he took us, the desert was made homely.

At Terkey there is an ochre-red rock wall painting of twenty or more horses, all painted galloping right to left, all their riders armed. They have a fabulous stretch to their stride – thirty centimetres between forelimb and hind. In the absence of any painted ground beneath them, they are galloping over infinite space. Nearby there is a leggy white camel with a red rider. And a Toubou-era 'grande vache', like a medieval sideboard.

– And so, arrive the cow!

There followed a magisterial lecture from Pier Paolo on the human history of the desert: on transitions from hunting eras to centuries of nomadism and pastoralism; on the green Sahara; and on scenes in ochre from the heads of Saharans. As he talked, a rogue audience of goats and donkeys appeared and came clattering up to the cave mouth to huddle against the painted animals for the shade of the overhang. A cricket warbler tutted in an adjacent bush, like a museum attendant. Pier Paolo broke off his talk and shooed the living beasts away.

Eight thousand years ago cows arrived in what is now the desert. At this time, wild cows were domesticated in Africa. Hunters became settlers. A restive people stopped. Some wild animals continued to move around the more sedentary people and their cattle. Rock-painting in Ennedi dates from before this time of domestication, from twelve thousand years ago. The climate then was milder, wetter, greener. Painting continued into drier times when the principal subject shifted from wild animals to kept or semi-kept ones. People were painted as they had been before, but where once the human images described people on their way into or out of some psychic adjacency to the animal kingdom, later they became the animals' (more prosaic) riders or herders. Sometimes, in these more recent pictures, they danced still, and sometimes they made music.

We left behind us even the thorns. It was too dry for any tree. Rock and sand only was possible. The sand was once rock. It is all, Pier Paolo said, *alive sand*, all moving at various speeds.

   – A million years it becomes sandstone, and another million years it becomes more sand.

He rubbed his hand on the gritty rock above some beloved images.

   – The destiny is to fall down!

The current desert is relatively young. The same empty plains were once busier, wooded and wetter grass grew, and rivers ran where wadis now flow with sand. Early humans were among the users of these green corridors and reached North Africa through them. Now the desert lays down its conditions of dry life, with migrant birds (among other animals) adapting or evolving to overcome barriers and hazards that the sand throws up. But the Sahara, in the species memory of many of the birds that cross it today, was green. It will be green again (in another 15,000 years) if all hangs on and we lay off (a 41,000-year cycle determines the greenness of the Sahara). Perhaps the subalpine warblers will be around to know it.

I came to hate the sun most days. We all became preoccupied with shade and shelter. Everything we were interested in depended upon it – the birds and the people seeking to move across the desert, and the records of the people who lived there once. The dappled shade of our lunchtime tree-stops was replaced by huddles under the lips of sandstone in shelters we shared with rock paintings, with crag martin nests, with goat-shit middens, and with the graffiti of soldiers from the recent Chadian–Libyan wars. As we climbed to them, sometimes we flushed the tiny pink flakes of trumpeter finches that had had the same idea. They flew off, piping their toy-brass annoyance.

First light struck four heaped stone tombs on the valley floor and raised them up. I noticed them, as I hadn't in the brightness of the day before. House buntings had spotted the early heat and warmed themselves on the black barrows, making domestic the accommodation for the long dead. The tumuli are Neolithic. Bones, not whole corpses, were buried, but recently the tombs were raided by nomads, seeking the crystalline salts produced by a chemical reaction of stone and bone. Now just the stones remain and the corpse-hill left by the looted skeletons. Nearby were three Lichtenstein's sandgrouse, a male and two females. My first. They were exquisite to look at. Most countries with deserts and arid places in Africa and Asia have a sandgrouse. Each species might wear the national sand. Close up – though they are very wary and hard to approach – they all have a look about them of a pigeon in desert fatigues. The trio in front of me, nervous in their short-legged trundles over the wadi's warming shale and sand, were richly marked on their wings, backs and bellies with appropriate colours, like the elaborate marbled endpapers of a Victorian account of desert exploration. They moved like scree, like geology, and every crack of the sandstone, every hot dune, every sand fractal seemed to have been painted into the birds' plumage and then glazed over with a promise of water, giving them a shine that made their dust sparkle.

Around a rock corner, we came upon a hidden trench, somehow worn into the sandstone. It was coffin-shaped like a sand-coloured sink or vitrine and harboured a tuft of colourless dry grass. Two stunted thorns leaned over its two long sides. In each thorn were two subalpine warblers. I was amazed, once more, amazed to conceive of those migrants travelling into the desert, and coming upon this hole in the ground and steering themselves (one by one, or as a loose flock) into the skeletal comfort of those trees. I watched the warblers until they were happy enough for me to lie down in the coffin under them.

Still I think about those warblers there. Often. And the stony comfort of such a resting place that others elsewhere have noticed and used. I find I collect accounts of such beds. To be able to lie down and fall asleep outdoors is one of the greatest gifts of the warming year. In Chad I had my first spring sleep in February.

On 29 April 1802, after a Westmorland spring walk with her brother, Dorothy Wordsworth recorded an entry in what has come to be known as her *Grasmere Journal*:

A beautiful morning – the sun shone and all was pleasant ... William lay, and I lay, in the trench under the fence – he with his eyes shut, and listening to the waterfalls and the birds. There was no one waterfall above another – it was a sound of waters in the air – the voice of the air. William heard me breathing and rustling now and then, but we both lay still, and unseen by one another; he thought that it would be sweet thus to lie so in the grave, to hear the *peaceful* sounds of the earth and just to know that dear friends were near.*

The spring before the Wordsworths had found their resting place/ nest box (both bolt-hole and stamping ground), Coleridge had gone on a walk into similar Lakeland territory; his notebook for 18 June 1801 records another stony bed:

A Hollow place in the Rock like a Coffin – a Sycamore Bush at the head, enough to give a shadow for my Face, & just at the Foot one tall Foxglove – exactly my own Length – there I lay & slept – It was quite soft.

In Book V of *The Odyssey*, Odysseus is shipwrecked on his long journey home from Troy. Cast ashore on an unknown island he crawls

---

* For the (imagined) other end of this story, see Ronald Johnson's shimmeringly lysergic archaeological exhumation of the Romantic poets, and other early nature-writers, among the linked poems of *The Book of the Green Man* (1967): 'this soil, once Wordsworth, lies in silence'.

45

from the beach to a safe haven, beneath the knotted tangle of wild and cultivated olive trees that have grown together (inosculated like the two worthy old peasants who die as entwined trees in Ovid's story of Philemon and Baucis). Their fallen mixed leaves make a bed and a soft pillow and Odysseus sleeps. In Peter Reading's poetry collection C (1984), the story is re-inhabited:

> When I was a boy and read that section ... I was deeply and permanently influenced. Since then the idea of such a comfortable and comforting solitary and impregnable bower has been insep-arable for me from the concept of profound sweet sleep – and more ... Almost every night since that time, except when drunken or erotic diversion has rendered such conceit impracticable, I have snuggled into the warm bed-linen metamorphosing it to dry Sabaean insulating leaves, blanding approaching oblivion.

Reading returned to this touchstone incident several times. It is there in his *Final Demands* (1988 – several collections have titles that had him already dead), and in *Faunal* (2002) we find this:

> Again the Homeric dream,
> Olive and Oleaster,
> under which the fallen leaves are scraped
> and demise commences.

The poet Michael Longley has also re-worked Odysseus' botanical bed-linen. In 'The Bed of Leaves' in *The Ghost Orchid* (1995), the weary, battle-worn wanderer nests himself down, cossetted by a 'mattress of leaves, / An eiderdown of leaves':

> So was his body in the bed of leaves its own kindling
> And sleep settled on him like ashes and closed his eyelids.

At Manda Guili in Ennedi, on the low roof of a rock cleft, cut like an eye in the sand-brown cliff, there were camels painted in white, with long stretching necks, and red reins and red riders on saddles like we'd seen for sale in Abéché. There was a cavalcade of cows, mostly red, some with swollen moon-like white udders. There was a red-ochre cheetah-type feline, its bony shoulders perfectly caught. And among some other humans, there was a kneeling figure facing right, its lower legs tucked beneath it, plucking at the six or seven strings of a harp- or kora-like instrument with a long neck and a bulbing base or sounding resonator.

In an old church in Bristol, I once saw Toumani Diabaté play. He was touring with his younger brother, Sidiki. Both play the kora. They are from Mali and Toumani is acknowledged as a master player. To my ears, the kora, beneath Toumani's fingers, makes the best possible desert music and migration music and movement-across-sand music. I think of it as made in those places and out of them (it literally is, when played on a home-made instrument that uses a halved calabash covered in cow-skin as a resonator and stretched antelope hide for its twenty-one strings). I've never ridden on a camel but I wonder, when things are going well and your caravan is underway, whether a camel ride might sound like a kora tune: those great soft plates of feet moving over soft sand; the looping stride, the stretch and reach; the air that breezes a little cooler at height. Kora plucks can sound also like the scratchy notes of a *Sylvia* warbler, such as a whitethroat, and I associate it with that bird and the sense I have of both bird and tune coming out of or across the desert.

The kora makes string music but it comes like the circular breathing some saxophonists employ to extend their blow – it lasts as long as the journey it signifies. So Toumani Diabaté's kora (a tune like 'Doudou' from 2010, or 'Kadi Kadi' or 'Monsieur Le Maire De Niafunké' from 2004, where he plays with desert guitarist Ali Farka Touré) makes song-lines and flight-lines of exhilarating plasticity. The desert is every-thing and we will never properly get across it, but walk on – fly from thorn to thorn if you can – and we will find a way to live here. So it walks, it flies, it overtakes itself, and it comes home again. It moves us here from there, as a whitethroat flies from its bush in the Sahel to its bush at Wicken or Tubney Fen and we feel it doing so. Both are made in Mali or Chad, both receivable in Cambridgeshire. These tunes have a regular stride to them, a plucked ostinato that plants its feet and sets a beat. A second musical layer comes when this beat sounds its own echo, triggering sympathetic resonances from the whole instrument that gives a ground swell, a deeper pulse, that might be the vibrato (a tune beside a tune) of the purring earth, almost like the feeling of sand when you push through its hot surface. A third musical layer (the playing is extraordinarily dextrous) is then laid over these two: dappled or shaded lines that work in filigree out from the core heartbeat, making sallies and departures, around and back, adventurous, declarative, watery (or holding a memory of water) and thrilling, a kind of lighter, more limpid flow, on top of the traffic below (which is all about getting us there), that will talk about what we might find when we get there, what we might do, what this becoming will deliver us to, and how we might hope to live. It is all – the whole tune, everything the kora says – about how to move: in time, in step, in season, in concert.

As he walked onto the stage at St George's in Bristol I noticed that Toumani limped. He has a bad leg and walks with a broken gait. All the stir and flow of his heartfelt musical path-making is made by a man who struggles to walk. The desert is in that too.

At Manda Guili, in the rock shelter with the ochre harpist, I thought of Toumani and his kora and also of Orpheus and his lyre. In the wadi, below the cave with the paintings, there was a one-tent settlement surrounded by a few trees with a desert crowd of birds: a pair of duet-ting yellow-breasted barbets, black robin-chats and rufous bush-chats, Sudan golden sparrows and northern grey-headed sparrows, and two European migrants – a subalpine warbler (since we reached the desert, the commonest temporary) and a first for our trip, a western Orphean warbler, soon due in Spain. Named for its song, which is thrush-like, declarative and slow, and unusually sweet for a *Sylvia* warbler, it was silent when we saw it. Painstakingly, it worked the crown of an acacia for nourishment, its music superfluous here.

I went back for a last moment with Orpheus on the rock, and looked between his silent cipher in the acacia and the soundless painting over my head. Warmth came, like a hot blanket, off the cliff above me after the sun had left. The shelter was littered. There was a severed goat's foot and a discarded flip-flop pushed into a crack oozing with bat shit. I walked back down towards our vehicles; the guys (Hugo, Issa, Johnny) had had enough: they had prayed and now were playing fruit-crush games on their phones. Everything was quiet across the wadi apart from little pulping fizzes and sweet-sounding explosions.

There were two ways to get to the deep sandstone canyons and the *guelta* at Archei. We hoped to see something of the last crocodiles in the Sahara, so we followed a nomad girl in flip-flops from her camp. Having told us that she was eight and knew the way, she led us swiftly up across a saddle of rocks to a cliff edge that looked down into the canyons and over the water. There were three small West African crocodiles half-submerged in a pool. They might have had parts as the living dead in a dinosaur diorama. They lay, the remnants of a species, in the remnants of the river that made the canyon and had floated their ancestors here before quitting the scene. Except after very rare rain, no water runs in the *guelta* now, and the pools survive thanks only to a seep of water percolating from below.

We watched the crocodiles. Or rather we slid into some stretched minutes of crocodile time, which, for them, is mostly a waiting in the long now of their evolution. The crocodiles are connected to the rock paintings and the rock painters. When the Sahara was green in the *Neolithic Subpluvial* or *African Humid Period*, which ended about five thousand years ago, it was easier to swim into, easier to fly across, and could be home enough for much more animal life than today. The crocodiles looked as though they remembered it.

A white wagtail – *little trotty wagtail* in John Clare's intimate, domestic, English terms – ran after flies on the sand close to the largest of the crocodiles. It might have been the bird we'd seen days before in Kalaït. Wherever it had come from, it was a migrant heading back to Europe to breed – it could be in Denmark in a week. I noticed another. The two birds bounced away in flight over the crocodiles to the other side of the pool. In a similar way they navigate a supermarket car-park in Europe, where they gather flies from the radiator grilles and wheel arches of shoppers' cars. The crocodiles didn't blink.

A minute later the watery end of the canyon was filled with camels. A herd, one hundred strong, was being led there. Their belching conversation, a forever burped speech, echoed loudly off the rocks. It was hard to tell if these moans were of pleasure or of fear. Mostly they sounded, as all camels will, pissed off. One shouting young man on a saddled camel at the head of the herd led them into the water. Some drank, some appeared to swim. The swimmers looked like bizarre theme-park vessels in a Tunnel of Love ride. The water was a kind of bliss for them, but it was only to be had with protestations. One hundred old loveless tramps were taking their annual bath.

– Now the crocodile runs away! Pier Paolo said.

But they couldn't. They withdrew into their pool and waited out the passing blip of time. A study in the winter of 2018 suggested that the three crocodiles we saw are the last of all their kind in Archei. All are thought to be female.

We followed our young guide back down from the cliff to the ground level of the canyon. We said goodbye. There was an olivaceous warbler and a subalpine warbler in one acacia near her tent-house.

– After Archei, Pier Paolo said, I always have the impression to smell like a camel.

There is a deep cave there near the pools. We walked in. Some predator had cached its prey: the bodies of thirty Sudan golden sparrows had been pushed into the sandy floor like dead shoes. We found a hoopoe feather and the skulls of three bee-eaters. These migrants might have been caught elsewhere and brought here, or perhaps they had simply stopped on their journey and made it no further. Slave-traders, Pier Paolo said, at one time used the same cave to imprison their human cargo while they let their camels drink outside.

When I rolled awake from my sleeping mat the next morning, the first bird I saw was a species I have dreamt of seeing ever since I knew it to exist. The blackstart must have been named in the knowledge of a redstart. *Stert* is a Middle-English word for tail. The redstart – long known in the European north of its range – was named early. The blackstart – the *blacktail* – was put into English more recently, and is actually taxonomically closer to wheatears than redstarts. But it does to its tail what a redstart does to its: the red tail of a redstart is lovely of itself, but the real prompt for its name was that this tail shivers, almost continuously, behind its owner.

At dawn, on a scatter of rocks near our camp, two blackstarts were doing the same, signing themselves as soon as they woke, with their quivering wings dropped slightly below their dusty-black bodies, and their darker dusty-black tails trembling. There is not much to these birds. They look like the shadow of another. But the pulse of their tails, like breathing, rising and falling and glancing in the light, put a time signature into the wadi, like a stress mark in a poem or an italicised word. *Whát I do is me: for that I came*, says Gerard Manley Hopkins in his kingfishers-catching-fire poem (with italics and stress marks), and that is one way to think of the starts' tail action. It is the bird's manifest specificity. But I want also to think of it as friendlier than that, like a handshake or a wave, though that sounds an odd thing to say about such an involuntary action, and one made by a bird.

How is it that I feel included in the tail-pump of the blackstarts, as I do of every redstart doing the same – that automatic gesture, that carries on out of sight of the bird, behind it, which I feel to be as close to an embrace as any gesture made in nature? It can surely be nothing of the sort, but there in the Saharan sand, as in the green woods of springtime Europe, was a licence for life – for my life – issued by a bird being itself. 'If I am pressed to say why I loved him', Michel de Montaigne wrote, trying to describe his feelings for his friend, Etienne de La Boétie (he died of the plague in 1563), and the circumstances for the intensity of his relationship, 'I feel it can only be explained by replying:

> *Parce que c'était lui; parce que c'était moi.*
> Because it was he; because it was me.'

North of seventeen degrees we began to hallucinate trees. There are not many friends to be had in such empty quarters. In a week we hadn't seen one cloud. Memories of wetness dried in the dust. The desert seemed deserted – idiot thoughts like that came to me – and it looked impossibly old and like another planet. There was no cover to the Earth at all, only surface, sandstone or sand, wearing away or worn out. The stoniest of silences came and everywhere smelt of cooked juiceless stone. The light tied a tourniquet around my skull. No turban was enough.

– In this way – west from here – it is very empty until Niger, said Pier Paolo.

The emptiness is infectious. As we travelled further into it we were emptied ourselves of things that we knew. As it became harder to find life it became harder to live. It was so flat that every raised grain of sand had its own shadow in the first light of morning – all the world was in these grains. Our shadows, thrown by the sun rising behind us, ran far out across the sands. For one minute only, though – for as the sun hurried up, the community of every shadow was pulled back to beneath our feet and to beneath each flake or grain. After that, the triumph that was overhead cared nothing for shadows and there were to be none to speak of for hours. This was a lonely world more naked than I have ever seen it, less worldly therefore, or more other-worldly, or more dead. Stripped, spartan, remorseless. This is where they die too – swallows, turtle doves, subalpine warblers, white and yellow wagtails. The desert is a mummy-ship, a vast keep or mausoleum.

We accelerated across the hard sand, the widest, most open space I have ever been in, towards a mirage.

– I don't know why, but our direction, *hah* – it is impossible to go straight.

We went beetle-wise, thrown by the flat yet somehow active vastness; the possibility of going anywhere had wrecked our compass and skewed any straight lines we might entertain. Being able to go anywhere we went nowhere. The birds, those that don't die, must navigate better.

Lightning strikes had vitrified the sand where we stopped, making finger-sized glassy bullet cases; they looked like failed tubers that would not grow. I filled my pockets with them and they clinked in their new burrows thirstily like empty flasks.

The trees at Ouei are real. It is an oasis a dozen or more kilometres out west of the massif at Ennedi. An island in the open sea. There are palms and smaller trees, water and gardens. Toubou clans use its water for their herds. The vegetable gardens are fenced. Little Chad flags had been planted along the furrows of turned dirt to try to scare off the attending conference of birds: a black robin-chat and a turtle dove that might have been a local resident, and a migrant white wagtail, three black-headed wagtails, two desert wheatears, a singing eastern olivaceous warbler, a hoopoe and, new for our trip, one chiffchaff and four reed warblers. On Fair Isle in Shetland in June, I've seen reed warblers in another garden at the other end of their spring journey, looking equally out of place. There they had puffed up their feathers against the Shetlandic cold; here they were panting and had drawn their sandy plumage tight around them, making them look long-legged and rangy.

We turned back south at Ouei, against the flow, and began to look for a southern route out ourselves. The panting continued.

Once we passed the tree-line again we stopped for some shade. The birds had already found it. The olivaceous warbler we had seen in the same crown of the same acacia a week before had gone. Reed warblers, which we hadn't seen before the oasis, were now on the move. It was forty-three degrees Celsius. There was no water for the birds, but around the base of the thickest thorn crowded more than twenty small ones, each trying to lie against the trunk. We thought they had found some moisture to drink in a crevice in the bark, but we couldn't feel anything damp. The shade and the relative cool was enough to make them cluster. I have never seen anything avian so abject. It was thirty-nine degrees there at the trunk. All the birds hugged the tree, leaning into it, as I have never seen birds lean. They looked as if they were forgetting who they were. Hosts and parasites were shoulder to shoulder in the heat, two green-winged pytilias and a Sahel paradise whydah, forgoing their usual antagonism. Resident birds mixed with migrants, all makes jumbled in an hour of need. Their beaks were open. They were panting. Four northern wheatears, a reed warbler, and a sedge warbler (the first of our trip) would never be as close in Europe as they were at the tree. Nor would their neighbours: a red-cheeked cordon-bleu, a northern crombec, a little weaver, an African silverbill, a Sudan golden sparrow, and one – not six million – red-billed quelea. Every bird gasped. When we walked close they fluttered, like injured casualties, just a metre out of our way. We emptied our water bottles onto the cracked bark and into the cracked earth.

Back in Ndjamena, one melodious warbler was still singing where it had been when we arrived. The compound guard with a dead arm who slept in the shade on the ground was still asleep. He woke up as we pulled in, and he lifted his inert hand into ours to greet us.

MARCH

Bristol
51°N

2 March. I woke to falling snow and then for two hours walked through it on the route I sometimes run to the Sea Walls on the Downs: plunging into slacks and dunes, sinking to my knees in hidden hollows, sliding down a path where flakes had frozen – my familiar green-grassy city-park place turned Sahara-strange. The cutting wind scattered icy crystal-studs that pinged off my coat and stung my cheeks. Carrion crows, ordinarily cocky, looked sickly and shadowy, sickly and significant.

But here's a white wagtail – a surprise early migrant – flown out of the desert itself, last seen attending to the meat-flies around the crocodiles of Chad, here all *trotty* and pert and finding something to eat under a dripping car that had skidded to a kerb. Its grey back mimed the monochrome scene; its hurry, here, was as there in Chad: it was as busy on the snow as it had been on the sand, divining all possible life with the twitch of its tail. After I had seen the bird, it seemed that my boot-prints in the slush on my doorstep looked like a map of Africa.

Zennor
50°N

6 March. Atlantic Cornwall is good for the intemperate spring-seeker. You can see ahead there. Along the coast path at Zennor, despite the ice in the sky and a heavy-duty ocean kettling itself on the granite

furniture at the shore, I could smell the spring in the marine blow, coming strong and yet softly, sweetly, from offshore. The *Western Approaches* – I always liked that thought: a compass point making headway, and today, a gift from far out was being brought in on the air – things were looking up; so might you.

Not far from Zennor, further along this always novel shore, I saw my only ever mermaids. I was thirteen and on a summer-holiday hike, walking south along the coast path with my aunt and uncle and cousin Tom. It had been a wet and birdless week. All the morning goodness of spring had drizzled away into an enervated July – the month-long slow afternoon. Fledgling gulls in their dirty pyjamas bleated along the cliff tops and stomped on the beaches. Stonechats were moulting out their brightness. All the gorse fire flames were damped. Rain-water and then salt-water had got into my binocular lenses. Wardens at the youth hostels made us wait outside in the soak until opening time. There was just one (teenage, pustular) consolation when, on the sole sunny day, Tom and I were scanning a pebbly bay from a cliff top, and there, as well as a pair of oystercatchers, were two young women lying naked, half out of the sea on the beach, their legs lost in the surf, their wet breasts like the smooth sea-rounded stones that tumbled at the shore. I had never seen real bosoms in the wild before. We were on the point of making an addition to our notebooks when we noticed, on the far side of the same bay, another presumably otherwise equally disconsolate and steaming birdwatcher, peering down with rapt attention on the same scene. That shook the dream from us, and we picked up our heavy bags and trudged on.

There were no mermaids at Zennor in early March, but the wind through the day brought spring inklings ashore in a sky-sized envelope of soft air. Grey became blue. The sea settled, its swell now the swing of the weather from further west, with its greenish tumble on the rocks carrying kinder messages from far out. I could see gannets electing to move onshore with the wind rather than to fly along the coast. And in the same mild bumps of air I watched, on my landward side, a skylark rise from a field edge and sing the opening purling notes of its warm spring song as it climbed above me.

It wasn't spring yet, but the gannet and the skylark could see further from where they were than I could on the cliff path. Edward Thomas, in his poem 'Thaw', looked at rooks high up and busy in their rookery in March, and thought them able to see 'what we below could not see, winter pass'. In Cornwall, the skylark and the gannets were rooking too.

M32, M4, M5, M42, M6, A14
51°N

15 March. A four-hour motorway drive from Bristol to the Fens with, at the roadside, forty active rookeries. Old nests pull the birds back to where they had lived – hatched, perhaps – last year. The birds' past life still acts upon them – the nests retain a sticky power. Only for a month or so after the young fledge do the birds turn away from them. Through the autumn they visit every day, in the mornings on their way from their overnight roosts and on their way back to their dormitories in the evening. From around midwinter they are even more attentive. A good portion of the short day is spent back in their old house. Their nests are significant: to see the birds sitting alongside their former home (we assume it was theirs) suggests the sticks have meaning.

I tried to take in each rookery as I hurried by below. Almost every nest had one rook next to it. Sometimes I saw a visitor to a sickbed. Sometimes the rook seemed to be sitting next to its own head-ache. Sometimes I saw a black bird warming itself at a black bonfire. Sometimes the bare tree looked like a cage with each of its avian occupants tethered to a heavy ball. The nests are needy, that seems sure, and the rooks must attend.

I do this counting on every long solo drive in the early spring. I note the rookeries I pass and estimate the nests in each. They get me by. I count other traffic and other trafficking at other times of the year. By them all I augur. Certain trucks mean well: if I see any labelled *Knights of Old* the day is likely to be good; *Hungarocamions* improve it further (though these are increasingly rare); to pass *The Shore Porters' Association*, 1 Baltic Place, Aberdeen, is still better news; twice in forty years of motoring up and down the M5, I have seen the *Western Combine* pigeon transporter – nothing better intimating home and homing has ever crossed my path.

There are occasions on most motorway drives when you come to and realise that you are alone in a run of the road. Much lies behind you, much ahead, all the cars and trucks of everywhere, but for a while, a thousand metres, you travel on your own, owning the road, having slipped between everyone else and found some space for one minute or so. You are held, in time, and you feel it. Unbidden comes the thought that if you could keep things like this you would, allowing everything to move as it must and travelling yourself with it, as you ought, but able to go with the flow, unencumbered and in a stream of something that feels safe. Never catching up – never being caught. Like birds in a flock. At moments like this you notice time as otherwise dangerous, as otherwise remorseless, the wrecking ball, the everlasting bonfire. And you notice this also because you know – even as you become aware of it – that you will not be able to hold on to the sensation that you are now enjoying of a serene fall, unbruised and elastic. Those gaps ahead of you and behind you are not yours to own or master. Even now you are gaining on the cars in front while others are hurrying on you from behind. But just for a few moments more, the passage of time and your passage through it flood your mind.

When the rooks are hidden by spring leaves, I do hay lorries. I do straw lorries later, as they come out of the granary of the east to bed down the cattle of the west. I do dead animals all through the year. In the autumn, until the rooks begin again, I do the linear orchards of roadside apple trees, carrying and dropping their coralline fruit, the late golden suns that constellate the roadway cuttings and embankments of boring old England.

I first learned about vernalisation and the apple's need for winter from Barrie Juniper. We were working together on Jonathan Davidson's radio drama *Miss Balcombe's Orchard* (a time-travel piece, like many of the radio plays I produced). We recorded the play in an orchard in Oxford that Barrie looked after. He knows his apples. One of his books (written with David Mabberley) is *The Story of the Apple*. He is a botanist and a fruit historian as well as an orchard man. I think of him as an apple-god. We cast him in the play half as himself and half as a fruity species of dryad who spoke apple truths from among blossoming branches.

I had met Barrie in 2007, at a memorial service for the writer Roger Deakin. He stood up at one point at Deakin's Walnut Tree Farm in Suffolk and made an impromptu poetic intervention, reciting William Cory's 1858 adaptation of Callimachus' ancient elegy, 'Heraclitus'. The poem puts a single human death in the company of nightingales and the endless go-around of life. Who, I wondered, would make such a stand? I spoke to Barrie and discovered that he got to know Roger because they had spoken of apples. He talked apples to me too. I asked about golden boughs – could the magic tree have been an apple-loaded branch? I asked about Atalanta, who was stopped in her tracks by three golden apples.* I asked him what he thought of the apple in the Garden of Eden – if the fruit was ripe when Eve picked it, would that season-ally challenge the idea of the garden as a place of constant spring; could another fruit – a pomegranate – be more Edenic? And I asked him about the apple trees of motorway verges, told him of my autumn counts, and enquired what had happened to make these runaway orchards. He said – and he spoke as mischievously as a dryad but as believably too – that motorists and truck-drivers buy apples in service stations, eat them ('The pome, that which is eaten,' Barrie said, 'is essentially a womb') and toss the core (the leftover flower of the apple tree) from their windows, sending it spinning across the hard shoulder towards softer verges where it rots. Seeds can only germinate that have separated from the core ('The placental tissue of the apple core contains germination inhibitors'). Germination also requires cool temperatures. Motorway apple seedlings sprout because the fruit, having been shipped and stored in chilled containers, is then kept refrigerated in service-station cafeterias and food halls, and the combined cooling is sufficient

---

* 'Was it so strange, the way things are flung out at us, like the apples of Atalanta perhaps, once we have begun a certain onrush?' – Eudora Welty, in her story 'Music from Spain'.

to mimic the prolonged chill of winter that apple trees in their wild or cultivated state need to germinate and grow. Their *winter memory* gives the apple the ability to flower; anticipating spring allows it to happen – that is vernalisation.

Tubney Fen
52°N

17 March. At Tubney Fen I flushed a skylark from the straggly grass field. It let out a shivery call as it rose. After a moment it seemed to rewind this or swallow it back, breathing in what it had breathed out; its song began then, spooling on from those first gargled notes. The singing made the lark's body shake as if animated by its own music, its open beak was busy, its wings bowed and trembling. Another skylark rose, prompted by the first, and as it broke into song, I saw a chalky dab of shit fall beneath it back down to the field where I was walking.*

Then a crane called: one brass blast, stretched and bent, as if from an old foghorn on the fen. It could have been the sound of the air itself being hurt, the sky cracking. The bird was flying through the mist half a kilometre away from me. It called again. Cranes are huge in flight, looking improbable and vulnerable. Their long thin neck extends out in front and ripples uneasily, as if being worked like a rope by the oncoming air. Their long legs trail behind them, stick-thin and snap-pable, and always held just below the horizontal, as if at any moment they might need to step down from the sky. And their wings in flight, though massive grey oblongs, look worn out and inadequate, they flap like a dusty carpet being beaten. A cold grey thrum was put into the day as the bird hauled itself past. As it went, it turned its head to take in where I was in the field, the big open pasture, where perhaps it had slept the night before. I could see it seeing me.

---

* There is a poem by Coleridge – 'Aria Spontanea' – that makes an ecstatic, almost excessive organ-recital out of a similar observation on the Quantocks: his lark sings high and travels out of sight, 'tho' twice I beheld its mute shoot downward in the sunshine like a falling star of silver ...' To me, at Tubney, it looked more like a tiny clod of earth.

I went back to Burwell Fen the same evening and bumped into the crane again. It was one of a pair I saw mating on a reedy island in the middle of the sodden fen. One bird climbed on the back of another. It did so with effort and with care, a slow-motion opening and closing of barn-door wings and gentle mountaineering of long legs. The two stayed in congress for only a moment. It happened so fast I didn't even have time to feel a voyeur. There was a rapid, less decorous dismounting and both birds immediately resumed their feeding, jabbing their Stone Age bills at the base of the reed stems after frogs or water beetles. It was hard to believe that they had made an egg.

Tollund
56°N

One spring I went to Denmark twice. On both journeys I was following others – people and birds – trying to live off the land, arriving into it, with spring weather, and making their way, as best they could.

At the end of the season, I went to watch swallows with a man who knows how to read them, and to learn, from another expert in transgenic divination, about the reindeer which had brought human life into the springtime of the place, ushering the very first people into Denmark after the last ice age waned.

In March of the same year, at the beginning of the season, after the (now) brief ice age of a Baltic winter, I went to try to listen to the dark talking and to see some bog bodies – dead people once thought to be the engines for the making of spring.

The most famous of these old bodies, known today as the Tollund Man, is now in the Museum Silkeborg in Jutland. The museum is a very unfussy small-town sort of establishment. I visited with my friend Julia Blackburn, who was at work on a book about human remains, time-travel and Doggerland.* We planned and recorded a radio programme that never got finished and still awaits its waves.

---

* Julia wrote up her version of these days in *Time Song: Searching for Doggerland* (2019).

We met Ole Nielsen, the director of the museum, in the room – lodge–tomb–morgue–chapel – devoted to the Tollund Man. He lies on his side on a tar-black bed in a glass case. His resting place looks part altar, part operating table. He is naked but also somehow not: he is clothed in his persisting skin. He looks like a sleeping whippet as painted by Lucian Freud. The painted dog, like the preserved man, appears tired out but peacefully curled into sleep, and not unhappy, bony with stretched skin pulled tight. Both wear serene frowns.

The room at Silkeborg is dark. There are neither windows nor any natural light. The darkness helps keep the body both dead and alive. A black interior is the best replica of the night – underwater, underground – that the Tollund Man knew for more than 2,000 years. When you enter from one of two doorways your presence is detected and a light flickers on. There are stools you can take to sit near the glass case and the dead man, as at a bedside.

Ole joined us and we sat together. After a few minutes, because we weren't moving about, the lights went out and put us into a dark cave. A shine on the man came off him then, moony glints from his blackened skin. We stayed with him, sitting in the dark, talking.

– He was found in the spring of 1950, said Ole. It was the 6th of May. A Saturday. Three peat-diggers went out to the bog to dig for fuel for their own use. They cut into him. They might have cut more but one of their party was a woman (Grethe, wife of Viggo Højgaard; his brother Emil was there too), and she remembered that an old peat spade had been dug out of the bog nearby and so urged her husband and brother-in-law not to be too savage when they hit a resistant object. And there he was: his face seemed so fresh the diggers wondered if they had come across a crime scene.

It was and it wasn't.

– The police were called at first; then the archaeologists took over. They took him to Copenhagen in a block of peat. An autopsy dismembered him. They sawed off his head and his feet. In those days no one was sure how to keep a body when it was out of the peat. Preservation was hard. If an item that has been waterlogged in a bog is left to dry out it will lose its shape and crumble away. If it is left in ordinary water it will rot and decay. They experimented, learning that alcohol could replace bog-water and fix the body; later, wax was deemed better than alcohol – wax being stable and firm at normal room temperatures.

He's a waxwork?

– Not exactly. For many years just his head was exhibited here. That is how I first encountered him. Only in the late 1980s could he be put back together again. My predecessor, Christian Fischer, assembled all the bits of him that were scattered around various institutions. Now we have him all here. What we see in the case is his real head and a reconstruction of the rest of him. The real parts we keep behind the scenes. They are precious but vulnerable.

– Only recently did we find his toe. When Christian was assembling the body, the only missing part was the big toe of the right foot. It had been clearly sawn off – but no one knew where it was. There were rumours that a man who had worked on the body conservation had asked for it to be buried with him when he died. Then, in October 2016, we had a phone call.

– I have the big toe, would you like it?

– It was the daughter of the conservator. She remembered the Tollund Man's foot in a jar of blue liquid in her childhood home. And one day her father sawed off the toe. He felt, she said, bad about that afterwards. Somewhat guiltily, he took to carrying it around with him in the pocket of his jacket. At mealtimes he would take it out and put it next to his plate on their dining table and think aloud about it and make chat. After her father died, his daughter found the toe in the family home in a willow basket made for Easter eggs. It was nesting there, tucked in with a bit of tissue. She knew it at once; and now we have it and we are happy. We have everything of the Tollund Man today apart from his inner vital organs. If they turn up, we'd be even more delighted.

– P. V. Glob, who wrote *The Bog People* in 1965, guessed the Tollund Man was an Iron Age man. It was a good guess. Today, we know that he is about 2,400 years old. When he was found, hardly anything was known about bog bodies. In those days, as had been the case for a long time, a find like the Tollund Man was mostly regarded as a nuisance.

Bodies were often re-buried, turned back into the peat. No one thought of them as treasure.

The light had gone out. Julia stood up and circled our man. The light came back.

– Raised bogs are where the bog people came from. What is special about them is sphagnum moss. It works like a sponge. The moss can suck up and hold twenty times its own weight in water. It makes a cold, oxygen-poor, sour environment. You could compare it with pickling. That is more or less the process that has kept the bodies. Tollund Man's hands are badly preserved – it is possible they were sticking up above the water for some time and rotted somewhat. To be preserved the body must be covered quickly. The bog juice dyes human skin. The process is like tanning as carried out by nature. The wet bog moss environment also preserves collagen (part of the protein fibres in a body) and keratin (hair). Bog bodies look like soft bags. The skin persists, but the bones are decalcified and become pliant. You can see that Tollund Man's bones look bent – that has happened since he was alive. The calcium has more or less disappeared from his skeleton.

– We think he was between thirty and forty years old.

He looks older.

– He is. He's two thousand, four hundred years old!

The man looked to me like he might have been cast in lava. His skin has the colour and appearance of meconium – the inner soil that a new-born baby expels, a soil which all of us have swallowed at the outset of our lives, which has the darkest green colour and looks like a mortar or impasto made of all the spring leaves of all the past springs.

– There is tranquillity and peace on his face. Someone took care of this man; they closed his eyes and mouth, and laid him down to rest. OK, you think, perhaps death is not so bad after all. But he was hanged. There is a noose still tight around his neck. Not strangled but hanged. Most bog people that we can establish a cause of death for were killed violently. The Grauballe Man had his throat cut from ear to ear – his neck makes a savage grin – and one of his legs was broken so he couldn't escape his wounds. We know these are not normal burials for the time.

Ordinary deaths were cremated. The people never buried a fellow human like these bog people. We assume, then, that a further meaning was attached to these people and to their deaths. Maybe those who killed themselves were put into bogs – this has been considered. Maybe criminals who were punished for offences were put into bogs – this also has been considered. But it seems to us now that these bodies mark not a punishment as such but a sacrifice. We are seeing a religious idea. The people were sacrificed to a god or gods, whoever they might be. The bogs and wetlands were interfaces between the world of humans and the world of the gods. They were places where you reach out for the gods and give them gifts. Tollund Man was put in a pit that had been dug for peat. It was a flooded tomb that had been dug by people. A sacred place was made from a working place.

We don't know how they spoke, these people, or the specifics of what they spoke of, but we begin to be able to grasp some of their thoughts.

– Some bodies were held under the water and were trapped or pinned there with wooden cages or hooks. These were handmade and special. They might have been to prevent the body from floating, but they might also have been more imaginatively being used to keep the body working underwater in the bog, to stop the dead awakening, to keep them down.

– We think that all the well-preserved bodies we know were put in the various bogs at a cold time of year, when the temperature was no more than four degrees Celsius. If it is warm there is a race against time. We assume the bodies were added to the bogs at the end of winter and the beginning of spring – the turning point of the year, when the seasons slide over one another. That was the best time for preserving at least, but it might have been, more significantly, also the time that the bodies were needed. These might be spring sacrifices. Sacrifices for the spring. To make it come.

That his skin survives rather than his bones brings the Tollund Man close. If he were a skeleton our feelings for him would be stonier. Working on behalf of other life to come, his keeping has given the Tollund Man a version of immortality. The murdered man was sent

65

ahead to secure in his dying a future for those he lived among but which he himself would not see. All these years later those survivors – his killers – have long gone and little trace of them remains; but the man who was killed to become a time-traveller in his time, to bring the spring again, has survived, albeit dead, to work on us and on our time.

– We know these people were farming people. They had small fields. They grew various grains: barley, oats, linseed, and wheat varieties. Tollund Man had some crop grains in his stomach. His last meal was porridge (old books call it gruel) – barley, oats, linseed, but also different weed seeds – nineteen in all. These would have been gathered rather than grown. There was no meat in his diet at that point. Nor was there anything green. It might have been a typical meal for late winter or early spring. Just now we are trying to analyse some of his hair to see if this was his normal diet or a special one. It might be an exemplary meal in this way: it might be part of the message the man had to take to the bog. Maybe there was a crisis. Maybe it was understood that a big offering was needed in order to secure growth once more. Maybe that is why he is there. He was to be deposited in the store of the sphagnum moss in the bog. For the spring to come.

The light went off once more. We sat on in the dark.

– I've dreamt about him, Ole said. I spoke to him once and he spoke back. But when I woke up I couldn't remember what he had said.

Julia and I drove to the bog. There is a little brass plaque nailed to a tree at the edge of a path that crosses a corner of the mossy mire. The sign is low-key, like most things hereabouts. This is the exact place, it says. It was breezy when we were there. I recorded some gusts on my machine.

– Tollund Bog: wind in trees.

Green was coming back again in places across the moss, like a pea froth on a boiling pan. In the cool blue sky above, ragged white streamers of common gulls came, four hundred or more, a passage of spring-seeking northbound birds, returning on the wind. But winter still seemed in charge. My feet grew numb and there was sleet in the air.

Perhaps this day was the day the Tollund Man was put in the bog. Maybe a despairing village needed a boost in the green gap when fresh things were scarce, they scraped their barrels for one last bowl, and then they hung up the man they had kept for the purpose. After they had done it, someone closed his eyes and put him under the water, but he might have looked up from his hanging tree and seen, in his last sky, the first white flakes of the new-come common gulls, right there, exactly, as he dropped, deep and darkly into himself.

We went back to the shore at Aarhus to sleep. My room looked over the Baltic. The sea barely stirred. I stood at my window and scanned the night. It was a tired tide that lapped at the shore. Then the moon rose up – one notch from full – and as it climbed the sky, the pearly orb – an old, old romantic moon – unfurled a shimmering sea-road below that flared with magnesium brightness. It stirred and then aroused the eiders that were riding out the night's desultory waves. There must have been five hundred drakes and ducks in one raft: blacks and whites and earth-browns, rising and falling on the soft swell. They had looked, when I first saw them, like casseroles in an oven. But as they bobbed into the highway of moonlight, their colours came back and the males stretched their necks and started to sing. It wasn't a song, though: it was their comedy croon – *ooooOOOOoooo ooooOOOOoooo* – a gossipy commentary on their as yet unrealised ambitions, each exhalation of surprise tempered in a suburban manner. Eiders speak of their ridiculousness before anyone else can call them out. It was a lunatic sound, but it was also very sweet.

I got into bed, under an eiderdown of sorts, listening through the open window. What I could hear was nothing like a sacrifice to the season, but it was nonetheless going to make life happen: two hundred or more nudgers and winkers, gently yodelling their own embarrassment, in the wash of the sea; drawing attention to what they wished to get over, dancing a true dance as only an awkward dancer can, stepping up sweetly, all-in-all, as required.

When I woke the next morning, there was a white wagtail on a boulder on the beach below my room. It was fresh in, for sure. Its tail pumped slowly. The bird looked like a hand-rolled cigarette in a talking mouth. As slight as it was, and even dressed in cautious pied plumage, it was the season incarnate, and I cheered it from my window.

I walked along the beach. A sun of beaten alloy and zero heat came up out of the Baltic. I said hello to a swimming club of hardy Danish pensioners climbing down wooden ladders from a jetty to get into the sea. In the wind, shoals of last year's beech leaves were picked up from the sandy cove where the swimmers were and scootered beyond them over the water. They spun down like gold leaf tipped from a purse and then bobbed back on the tide towards where they had come, in undaunted – undrowned – leaf-armadas. Further along the beach, I disturbed a tree of jackdaws. As I watched their blacks scatter in the lead-cold light, I spotted, high up and travelling north-east, a party of six Bewick's swans. They looked like a washing line of creamy sheets in the northern sky. They were leaving just as the wagtail arrived – it was getting too warm for wild swans in Denmark; they could sense Siberia melting enough for them to begin their return to the tundra.

Later that day, having driven back towards Copenhagen, Julia and I made one more call. The northern suburbs of the capital have now overtaken Søllerød, but it keeps up its small-town local art gallery and museum. I enjoyed their replica great auk, fabricated from the feathers of eleven sacrificed razorbills, but the point of our visit was to see the graves and skeletons of some Ertebølle people who lived on this wet eastern edge of Zealand between six and seven thousand years ago.

In 1975 at Vedbæk, several Ertebølle burials were found in an old peat bog when a car-park was being built and the foundations laid of a new school. The graves contained the bodies of people twice as far away in time from the Tollund Man as he is from us. Several skeletons showed the Ertebølle met violent deaths; but another grave told another story. It is a grave for two bodies, in fact three or more, depending on what species we might count. A woman has been laid out on her back; her baby has been placed close at her right side. If they had bodies they might be sleeping together; if they had flesh, her baby might have just fed from her breast. But they are only bones. All their colour has

68

whitened into their skeletons. Below the fragile gravel of baby bones – it was a boy, and he perhaps died as he was being born – is a fanned scatter of even slighter bird bones. In death, the baby had been positioned on the spread and opened wing of a wild swan. A whooper or a Bewick's, most probably the latter, a local wintering bird.

The mother was young, around eighteen, and might have died in childbirth. It is thought this was her first, therefore only, child. The dress she was buried in, now rotted and gone, was decorated with perforated snail shells. A robe, similarly adorned, was plumped under her dead head as a pillow. There are hundreds of these shells; there are also more than 200 animal-tooth beads, lying between and around her bones and her baby's bones. Thirty-seven red deer and two wild boar had been killed to provide the teeth. The woman's face would have been dusted with red ochre like pollen and her pelvis was also painted red, perhaps to mark the blood that had come there. Her baby had the white swan's wing for his deathbed. A small pale flint knife was placed on his chest. This is interpreted as an indication of the status of the family and a marker that power in this culture passed within families and between generations.

The swan's wing is difficult to see and hard to configure in the gentle scatter and sift of shells and teeth and bones. It is like trying to pick out a constellation in the crowded night sky. But when you know it is there, it is what you want to see – to see love, to see such tenderness preserved from so long ago, to see a human gesture held for thousands of years in that careful placing of an outstretched wing of a bird, the soft touch of a soft touch, a silent swansong, a way out – a winged means of escape – offered alongside a gentle landing.*

Julia and I both wept as we stood there. Then we walked out to the boggy fields at the edge of the school at Vedbæk and sat on the mossy ground. Little dabs of bog cotton grass wobbled in the breeze. In some

---

* The swan's wing is an obol for the afterlife or a ship of death, of sorts. Sibelius' 'The Swan of Tuonela' could be the singing of this scene: Tuonela in the *Kalevala* is the land of the dead; a white swan floats on a river of black water there. A cor anglais sounds the swan. The music was to have been the prelude to a larger work to be called 'The Building of the Boat' that Sibelius abandoned.

old stories, so P. V. Glob said, the downy cotton was used to make clothes for young princes who had been magically turned into swans. There were new-paired greylag geese waddling in the wet as there had been at the Tollund Man's bog. And from an alder tree, just beginning to hang out its pale yellow catkins and wave coolly for the spring, a fresh-arrived chiffchaff – pale yellow as well, a slip of a thing – sang its name. Its name as I know it, at least. In Danish it is a *gransanger*. In their forgotten language we don't know what the Ertebølle called the chiffchaff, although we do know what they thought of swans.

Lake Langano
8°N

It was March; we had time, so I waited for the birds. On the western shore of Lake Langano in Ethiopia in the grounds of a lakeside hotel, I sat on a low wall of sun-warmed rough concrete. Migrant passerines were moving through the trees, and working their way north up the edge of the lake. Langano is in the Rift. In front of me, shading the walled plot of bare earth, was a garden of acacias, jacaranda, bougain-villea and salvadora, and beyond them, a closed-up cocktail bar, a beach of grey gravelly sand and the restless brown water of the lake. Beyond that, misting away into the dusty sky, was the eastern edge of the Rift, and the beginnings of the Bale Mountains.

I came here in a former life. My first time in Africa was a trip to Ethiopia to see my then new girlfriend Stephanie (later the mother of our boys, Dominic and Lucian), who was living there with her parents (her father was a botanist working on the sorghum parasite *Striga*, her mother a teacher). It was January 1988, during the scarred and scarring time of the Derg, the USSR-backed Communist government. To the north there was fighting in Tigray and Eritrea. The whole country was still in the dark shadow of the famine of 1983–85. I was briefly working then for Save the Children in London, and carried medicines from its headquarters to their offices in Addis Ababa. On my first evening, as we drove from the city to Stephanie's home in Holeta, forty kilometres away, the headlights of the car caught the eyes of a hyena making off with a carcass it had pulled from a rack outside a row of butchers' stalls in a village – a village that seemed to be one street-long gruesome shambles. The weight of its bloody cow-rib booty seemed to throw a further lurch into the hyena's already broken gait. In the headlights, its hot-burning eyes strayed and drifted like a falling flare.

The British embassy had a camping ground on the shore at Lake Langano. There was a hut where a Crown-property windsurf board was stored. We put up tents. In a nearby lakeside lodge we ate scrambled eggs for all our meals, served by friendly figures who appeared out of the surrounding bushes like ghosts. I remember using the wing mirror of our car to help me shave. I tried windsurfing and, on one voyage, raced a swimming monitor lizard that came paddling alongside my board like a freestyle dinosaur.

My birdwatching life around that time was at a low ebb. I was living and working in London and my binoculars went unused for much of most years. I shouldn't have been, but I was surprised in Ethiopia by the European birds we saw. At Langano, in the short dusks at the end of the day, a world-scale bird event occurred, as thousands (millions, I thought) of sand martins and *flava* (yellow-type) wagtails materialised out of the sky, flying south above the middle of the lake. The wind often dropped in the late afternoon, and the sun swung low and dust-smudged in the western sky. Everything was dusty at Langano and, from the shore, the flock of birds looked at first like blown dust or like dry-bodied insects hatched from the lake's muddy brackish waters. They moved as one, like exhaled smoke, too far away to see anything of them other than a brownish purposeful flutter repeated over and over. I kept looking and realised that these were European migrant birds heading to roost somewhere in the Rift. The valley was cradling their days and angling their journeys, and I was watching Europe on its way to bed in Africa.

I might have seen some of the sand martins before – above a reservoir outside Bristol in mid-March, the first birds I'd seen out of Africa that year (as is often the case); or crossing the Top Fields at Portland Bill, having cleared the Channel, moments after making landfall; or singing their fizzy mouthfuls over a lake in Breckland with answering

71

nightjars churring from a sandy heath; or, nearby, in and out of burrows (they tunnel eight to ten centimetres a day) in an old sandpit on the Army range near Thetford; or hunting midges in the rain between a field-working short-eared owl and a ditch-diving otter on Mull; or taking flies between salmon fishermen along the Dee, my notional river, in Aberdeenshire ... There were so many there in Langano, coming dusk after dusk, I seriously wondered if all the sand martins of Europe might be passing. In fact, western European birds winter in the central Sahel; only eastern European sand martins fly to East Africa. The birds I saw were not all of Europe's but probably mostly from the then Soviet world of Russia and Ukraine, Bulgaria and Romania. The backers of the Derg, suppliers of MiGs to the Ethiopian revolution's air force, were also sending dust clouds of sand martins on winter missions.

There were these thousands, and then there was one rock thrush. On the cliffs, south of the embassy campsite (just north of where Claire and I were later to stay), I saw a male common rock thrush, perched just one rock or two away from a male little rock thrush, the first a migrant from the north, the second a resident. They were gorgeous, sharing warm and warming brick-red underparts and smoking grey-blue throats and heads – redstart intensities, as now I would describe them. I was slow, though, to work out then what I was seeing, and the birds' variant cuts from the same cloth foxed me until I got back to my bird books in Britain. I had never seen either bird before, and I remember the oddness in discovering that my first common rock thrush was not in Europe but in Ethiopia (and somehow therefore – as I felt – *away*).

I told Claire about the olden days as we watched a pair of little rock thrushes on the same rocks where I had seen the same species in 1988. It turns out she saw her first common rock thrush also in Ethiopia, in 1999. She also saw her first European common redstart on the same trip: she was a young birdwatcher, then, coming up through Africa, from her home in Cape Town, meeting the Palaearctic coming south. That was a good thought. Long before we met one another, we had both made vows of a birdwatching kind, on dusty Ethiopian rocks, to the same migratory species.

* * *

We weren't the only guests at Langano. Ethiopia has changed enormously in thirty years. The hotel where we stayed had become the premier spot in the country for the photography and filming of brides and grooms in various staged outdoor settings. These were being made before the couples got married and would be screened (and given as going-home presents) at their forthcoming ceremonies. I had thought the first pair we saw were actors doing a promotional shoot for the hotel – but they were a little uneasy with one another and with pouring wine. Then on the other side of the terrace another couple settled stiffly into similar behaviour. They were all real brides and real grooms faking ideas of themselves. Night after night there were more, as well as prop-managers and stylists and camera crews. Once, four separate fantasias were underway using the terrace, the gardens, the cocktail bar, the beach and a bandstand-cum-giant-wedding-cake-cum-king-size-bed.

Close up, the theatricals were gripping. We watched from our dinner table, our meal cooling before us. A drone-mounted camera was being trialled. Day-for-night light screens and fireworks were in use. Plants were planted. There were baskets of roses. A bottle of Johnnie Walker Black Label whisky was positioned like a holy icon. One night, an assistant held up a pseudo-moon when the real one sulked behind a cloud.

– Proceed, moon!

We woke up on our first morning at Langano after two weddings, and the first European migrants we saw were a female and then a male common redstart. They fed on the ground, on the little terrace outside our cabin, taking grubs and flies. A white-bellied go-away bird (well named) chased off the female, and a human cleaner sent the male on his way as she swept fallen plumeria flowers from outside a bride's bedroom. But the birds came back, loyal to certain perches and flight angles, and, almost whenever and wherever we looked, there were redstarts around. I was very happy to sit with them.

For days following, we saw the same individuals, learning the little nicks and marks on their feathering. One male had a slightly walled eye; a female had an abraded tail. Then, after three days, these familiars were nowhere to be seen and new birds came. Some stuck around, some were moving through. The same garden was a winter refuge for some and a passage stopover point for others.

On the second morning, the first bird I saw outside our cabin flew off, dodging a wedding dress being pimped into service, and I assumed it was yesterday's male, but it landed side-on to me, and the metal-burn of a white wing-panel shone from it, as bright as its forehead coronet. It was a redstart of the eastern subspecies *samamisicus*, known as Ehrenberg's. They breed from south-east Europe (Serbia, Kosovo, Northern Macedonia, Bulgaria, Greece), through Ukraine, southern Russia, Turkey and in the north-east Caucasus. Thus we learned that both redstart subspecies were in Langano together. The nominate form occurs elsewhere in Europe (including Britain) and across more central and northern swathes of Russia to north-west China. Ehrenburg's is *Phoenicurus phoenicurus samamisicus*, the nominate is *Phoenicurus phoenicurus phoenicurus*. Its name in Latin means *redtail redtail redtail*. It trembles when written on a page as when spoken out loud. The bird's tail does the same, shaking behind it all the time. It is a *focus*, like a fireplace. It makes the bird repeatedly present. And to me it makes the bird the best of all birds.

One day at Langano, we saw redstarts of the *phoenicurus* subspecies, destined perhaps for the ancient woods near Tartu, around the house of the Estonian poet Jaan Kaplinski, where I heard them singing one May morning in the rain and through a muzz of mosquitoes; or headed, perhaps, for the lime trees by a river in Vilnius in Lithuania, where I heard them singing and watched them bathe once when I was searching for the shattered ghosts of Napoleon's retreat from Moscow. At Langano, the same day, we saw redstarts of the *samamisicus* subspecies, bound perhaps for Crimea and the aspen trees behind Chekhov's beach-hut at Gurzuf on the Black Sea coast, where I heard a singing male once; or perhaps they were to fly to the last high ridge of Serbian beeches in the Tara park, overlooking the Drina River towards Srebrenica in Bosnia, where a May breeze once fanned to my sub-standard ears a cracked phrase of a muezzin's call from a mosque across the border and, at the same moment, a snatch of redstart song, which could have come up from either country.

Behind our cabin at Langano, a shaded corner of trees became the best place for redstarts. I walked there again and again. There were often males of both subspecies, and most times there was also a red-capped robin-chat on the ground, turning over the leaf litter like a thrush. That bird was bigger than the redstarts but shyer. In the murky light it appeared mostly red, a ferrous earthy red all over, with just its wings and central tail feathers a darker blue-black. They are widespread in Africa but not much known. They move within the continent: the bird we saw was likely a visitor to Langano, as much as the redstarts and we were. A little rock thrush also came to the leaf litter once when I was watching two male redstarts eating ants off a verandah. There were many reds to see – the patterned quiver and tremble of tails and wings each shifting in the dappled light, all in the shade like the embers of a slow-dying fire, stirred and blown open in their last filmy burn.

It may well be that the redstarts at the hotel had been there before, the previous winter and spring perhaps. Many migrant birds become as loyal to their winter localities as to their summer territories. It sounds like a poem to suggest they swap one tree in Ethiopia for another in Norway, but very likely they do. A redstart may have two homes, in this way, two home-scars.

Many migrants on their first trip out to Africa must find their wintering place without help. They hatch and fledge and depart their breeding places without a destination in mind. Some birds follow their parents, travelling with them, like cranes and storks, and learn where to go from their elders around them; some learn from travelling together as a species and watching one another; but many, especially night-flying passerines that migrate alone, are totally in the dark in their first autumn. Only by being in a place can these young birds establish their non-breeding station. They seem impelled to leave Europe, and know to take a general direction out by a western route or an eastern one, but after that they have no knowledge to guide them.

Eventually they will stop, but it is often a random stopping. Such a place may well be nowhere near sustaining. Many young birds die at this time. If it is a good place then the birds might live. Adults are adults because they have already made a good choice the previous year. That being so, they retrace their steps and repeat their journeys and so become serial residents.*

Much of migratory birds' route-making and stop-over fidelity is only now becoming understood. Europeans knew – or we thought we knew – that barn swallows come back to their particular barn, but, because that involved a concept of home, it was assumed such loyalty would only apply in breeding matters. The other end of the species' year was lost in the vastness of Africa, from where very little was known of what happened to individual birds.

In 1822 a white stork sent an early one-off message when it managed to make it back to its breeding place in Klütz in Germany carrying tangible evidence of where it had been in the winter – a broken spear was lodged in its neck and breast. In the 1960s Reg Moreau assembled as much data as he was able (mostly from ringing) on the fate of individual known birds. There was very little. In his book on *The Palaearctic–African Bird Migration Systems*, which came out after he died in 1970, only once or twice could he write up the biography of a single bird. There was one black-eared wheatear:

> This species has provided a remarkable recurrence in winter quarters at Kano, Nigeria at the southern limit of its range. In January–March 1964 one was observed in the implement park of the local

---

* Sometimes the stochastic errancy of young birds ends up being to the species' advantage. If things go wrong for adult birds on previously proven wintering sites then those youngsters that wintered elsewhere might survive to save the species. It is good for a bird not to have laid all its eggs in one basket. It is good for them all not to winter in the same place. In 1968 drought in the Sahel caused a calamitous crash in the wintering population of common whitethroats. Half the population did not return to western Europe in 1969, but young birds were more prevalent in the population then; presumably they had wintered across more diverse habitats and in less drought-afflicted areas.

agricultural station. One re-appeared in November 1964, was ringed, and stayed till 17 February 1965. During the summer the implements were re-arranged and in the winter of 1965/66 its favourite perching post (on a trailer) was seventy yards from that in the preceding winter.

Barn swallows were the most obvious migrating species we saw at Langano. Every few minutes a loose flock, like quick-done sketches of the same bird, tracked the shore of the lake and flew on to where the cliff edge ran to the water. They followed a line in the air as if it was marked for them – a route sown or sewn into the sky. All were moving north. Sometimes local species, banded martins and rock martins that also used the cliffs, spun up into the moving swallows or pulled down a bird to join their local flights for a hundred metres or so before these passing birds peeled away to re-join their kind. Sometimes we heard European bee-eaters calling, high up and out of view; they were flying north too, along the swallow path. Once, a ringtail Montagu's harrier flustered a swallow flock that it kept pace with; once, three lesser kestrels, also due north, swirled with some swallows for a minute before all moved on in one airy package.

21 March. We sat and waited at the trees on the beach for an hour. There were busy migrants: an eastern olivaceous warbler pumping its tail, two female blackcaps and then a male, a lesser whitethroat, and two male redstarts flying from perch to earth and back again. The warblers liked the salvadora for its berries. The trees' seeds (in the heart of their berries) are dispersed by birds. Over the years, migrants will have assisted in the planting and maintenance of a take-away garden along their route. They have helped themselves in this way into the future.

The olivaceous warbler might be destined for Syria, the willow warbler that appeared next to it might be en route to Greece. They moved on and I saw them take each other in. Another willow warbler came, and a lesser whitethroat. The birds were moving north, tree by tree, gleaning as they went. The Europeans were joined by two green-backed eremomelas, African warblers, the colour of sherbet, two fizzing pixie birds that were going nowhere nor wanting to.

We sat and waited on the rocks at the cliff base for an hour. An amethyst starling visited its nest hole in a dead tree, holding in the centre of its plum-coloured face two emerald-bright grubs. They gave it a green moustache. A little rock thrush sang from the top of an acacia. Two Hemprich's hornbills carved at the air in swoops and turns. A female baboon with baroque buttocks carefully climbed into a fruiting bush and fed. Close to us, a pair of Abyssinian wheatears walked the ground. Claire spotted a migrant Upcher's warbler in a salvadora bush; I scoured my memory for any useful recollection of the one that my friend and expert bird man Mark Cocker had found for me in Cappadocia in Turkey. A sandy-grey bird with a steep forehead was all I could muster. There have now been two Upcher's warblers in my life. That, I imagine, will be my lot.

Cordon-bleus came close. And the wheatears and rock thrushes came closer. We weren't hiding, but we had stopped long enough to become part of the scene. A young girl – perhaps eleven – smiled and said hello as she came past, closer than she would have if we'd been walking. Mocking cliff-chats made sallies from rock to rock. Rüppell's weavers had woven grass nests in a tree where a hollow log had been wedged as a beehive. A male weaver showed off his craft, hanging upside down beneath his new green weave in a sort of ecstatic dance, with flutter of wing and shimmy of tail and a swazzling sound, as if hypnotised by what he had made.

We moved to another spot under the cliffs, disturbing a warthog that ricocheted away, like an overweight cartoon bomb, its tail-fuse still burning down. Above us, there was a migrant booted eagle flying north along the swallow route. A greater honeyguide called and Claire called back, giving the sound with which human Mozambican honey-hunters answer the guiding bird (she is studying both sides of the marvellous arrangement there). A plain-backed pipit went past and then another which, on inspection, turned out to be a tree pipit, a migrant from Europe. It flew up from the ground and landed on the low branch of a tree. The intensity of its presence there gave it today's award for the-one-bird-in-all-Africa moment. You come away from such encounters holding nothing yet feeling anything but empty-handed. The pipit's seconds in front of us implied a whole world running. It made the slightest of turns of its head, and everything streamed away from its quiet, singular, simple presence.

There was a willow warbler in a fig tree. Also there were a dancing black-billed barbet and a noisy mocking cliff-chat. The warbler, one of perhaps 1,000 million in Africa (so Reg Moreau calculated) on the point of heading north, silently picked over the big leaves. Palaearctic birds seem more circumspect than residents, more single-minded in their feeding, less engaged with local issues.

In the last light, we saw a European nightingale, the first I've ever seen in Africa, feeding on the ground like a chat before flying into the dark heart of a bush. Its brown was sufficiently reddish to put it into my magic company. I wondered whether it would sing this year, and where.

We walked back accompanied by the lullabies of tree hyraxes. They make a noise like creaky farts. The moon swung its gondola into the sky. A greenshank called as it flew north over our heads. Its call was cool and pale, a northern music, just at the edges of green: *tew tew tew*.

We drank beer and asked about dinner.

– There is a peanut in this organisation but not just these days.

Therefore we ate *shiro* again and watched the marriage show once more from our dinner table, sitting next to a waiting wedding dress collapsed on a black cane chair, like an ostrich suicide.

On our last evening we walked again below the cliffs. In a tumble of big rocks, we noticed a willow warbler feeding in a small acacia. It flew to a bushy tree next door, directly to a thin branch. We were above it looking down. There it stopped. It plumped itself up, fluffed its feathers, shook and adjusted itself. It kept on turning its head left over its shoulder to rest its beak under its wing. Then it turned back to face ahead. It stopped moving, its eyes closed and it fell asleep. We could see its pulse, its heart beating through its whole body. We could see it breathing, its chest rising and falling.

No sleeping bag, no pillow, no bag of any kind. *Eschew luggage for the expedition is brief*, wrote Peter Reading, who gave me a T-shirt printed with the same text (he was a birdwatcher too and we'd got friendly thanks to his bird poetry). All I need, I carry with me: *Omnia mea mecum porto*, Cicero reported Bias of Priene saying on his flight from his home. *Bahlasa* is an Arabic word from the Abbasid period (750–1517 CE), meaning *he arrived suddenly from another country without any luggage*. Thus, the willow warbler waking after its sleep: supplied, to be delivered, bagless and perfect.

The light at the lake slipped further into the dust. Most things were brown now. The warbler began to disappear before our eyes as a slender-tailed nightjar started churring from a rock just twenty metres away. It sounded like a sprinkler spraying water. As the air cooled, the stone we sat on, like the nightjar's, kept the warmth of the day. We listened. Was the nightjar's nocturne going into the head of the willow warbler? Are there willow warblers in Europe that remember the rocks at Langano and how they purr after the sun goes? What sort of baggage within might be carried by a bird? There was enough light for about a minute more to see the nightjar, and then it too was taken into the dark. We walked back towards our own bed. A hyena laughed.

At the hotel we crossed paths with four weddings in rehearsal. Each appeared more elaborate than the last; there were chandeliers and thrones tonight. The couples avoided one another. The hyena yelped again and the nightjar's song drifted down from the undercliff.

A staging of what is to come before it has happened – that is what I came to Langano hoping to see. The birds of Europe in waiting. I spent my days looking at what was in front of me, but thinking ahead to the spring in Europe. From Ethiopia it was perfect: everything was still going and nothing had gone wrong – an album I could make too, of an ideal time before it has come. Like the wedding clothes put on before the big day, so my redstarts, in their new moulted finery, were working on their moves, their trembles and shakes, thousands of kilometres away from their brides to be.

Brids, birds used to be called, brides and brids.

The next day, I too flew north, back to Britain, now ahead of the birds. The plane that took me there was called *The Sahara Desert*, and the flight attendant who served me my dinner was called Eden.

Nyíregyháza
48°N

In the autumn of 1986, I moved from Britain to Budapest to study Hungarian poetry for a year. Within weeks I was feeling the cold and feeling alone. Never, before or since has my breath been so continuously visible. Never has it dropped to the ground so uncared for by anyone else. A girlfriend I had miraculously found in England after several monkish years came to visit six weeks after I had started in Hungary. I showed her the covered market on the bank of the Danube and the mushroom doctor there who would vet your harvest for toxic species; I showed her a rough-legged buzzard. But we had already lost our touch and gone wrong. Walking together along the Danube and into its hills, through wet meadows in the autumn's dripping mist, we could have spoken to one another as if in a hushed room. We didn't, and she didn't quite have the nerve to finish with me then. We had to do that over a weekend of failed telephone talk once she'd gone back to England; me trying to ration my increasingly desperate steps to the call box at the metro station and then, red-eyed and winded, kneeling to the floor of my landlady's corridor, weighed down by the heavy black handset she'd let me borrow for one final call, and stunned by the cool voice in it coming with the surge of a dead sea, from the far side of the moon.

Three things, that year, got me through to the spring, three things saved me: oranges, music and birds. The winter came in quickly from the east, very cold and very grey. A thick, felted sky blockaded the country for six weeks. The smoke of the chimneystacks along the Danube snagged under the clouds and gritted the city's head. My throat felt as if a chain harrow was being dragged across it day and night. People stayed inside whenever they could and lived on bottled things. I didn't have anything saved, tried the floury apples from the market, and started taking honey as medicine. Then one day the sun, as it might appear through winter cloud, was suddenly for sale on the streets in the form of Cuban oranges. Special stalls were set up outside the city's central supermarkets and train stations. Queues formed for the novelties. I bought my ration, a bag of six. They were cold, almost frozen in my hand, but they had trapped sunlight even more than the honey had, and when I cut through their old skins they bled.

The next day the stalls had gone and the winter resumed. At the weekend a heavy shudder of cloud sank over the river and froze it. All day was dusk, and in the half-light I watched the Danube's water turn thick like vodka. The next morning the river was sealed and it stayed that way for a month.

In my room I listened to the BBC World Service from London with the heat of the African sounds of Andy Kershaw's world music programme drifting in swirls and hisses through the short wave. All things had angled east or west for me, but here was south, a vitamin like the oranges, and I loved it for that: Sona Diabaté from Guinea singing like an oracle; the Kilimambogo Brothers making misery danceable; Diblo, genius Congolese guitarist, turning electric strings into a kind of woodwind; Guinean guitarist Kanté Manfila and his balafon-player Ibrahim Diawara taking watery xylophone music and playing it through the Sahara's sand. I stood to a kind of encouraging attention to one side of my transistor radio trying to fix the bellying signal through my body.

As well as draining the plasma of the World Service, I started making cassette recordings from Hungarian radio when it broadcast entire, uninterrupted records by Western artists. I still have them. One week it was the new album by the Pretenders, the next a concert by McCoy Tyner. I liked these gifts from the People's Republic to its people, the collusion in the snubbing of copyright and hard currency, the hours of rhythm and blues rubbing at the frozen earth, one record playing one song by Chrissie Hynde making the winter bearable for thousands of people. I imagined half the country, like me in the dark, poised for the announcer to finish his cue, holding down Play and Record on their Soviet machines; all of us little Bartóks intent on collecting these precious arrivals from the other side of world.

I bought records as well. Hungarian records were cheap. The shops along the Leninkörút stocked only vinyl and almost exclusively Communist vinyl. Hungaroton, the state record label, was especially cheap and, though living on a grant of £30 a month, most weeks I could still buy an album. I didn't have a record player but filled a box under my bed with disc after disc to ship home.

I bought Bartók and Kodály. I bought a few records by the licensed pop groups the state allowed into its studios. These albums had cautious lyrics written with unwanted listeners in mind. Hearing them again – the singer-songwriter Zsusza Koncz or the faux gruff-rock band Edda – they sound almost unbearably sad: their little stabs for freedom, their aping of corny Western idioms that carried an inflated value in the straitened East, their studied avoidance of saying what they meant. Listening to them today reminds me – Coleridge writes about a similar feeling in 'Christabel' – of watching my children, when young, laughing at appallingly ropey has-been comedians, and my being moved to tears by their innocent joy, and by how all the horrors of life seemed held off by their giggles. The jokes are rubbish, of course, but how could you – why should you? – dissent from the happiness they bring?

Most of all I bought folk records. New accounts of traditional Hungarian music seemed more exciting than anything else, though I may well have been over-reading its meanings just as my Hungarian friends did with Western rock. I was often asked to transcribe songs by the Rolling Stones and the Beatles and spent hours repeatedly writing out the lyrics to 'Imagine'. In return, my new friends tried to explain to me the songs their grandparents knew. We built and dismantled our respective utopias, pastorals and arcadias in this way, working through our flawed understandings, while reaching across the borders no one really wanted.

In the mid-1980s Hungarian traditional music was widely played live in Budapest. I heard it performed most often in dance houses, where my friends tried to teach me some appropriate steps for the loose and sawing strings that had been fetched out of the hay meadows and villages of Transylvania by curious young musicians from the cities of Hungary. They travelled, recorded, transcribed and learned just as Bartók and Kodály had at the beginning of the century. The state sanctioned this revival of folk music, thinking it a sort of peasant pop, neither Western nor market-focused; but listening to traditional songs, especially those lovingly taken from the isolated and vulnerable Hungarian population in Ceaușescu's Romania, didn't keep young people especially compliant in Budapest or Szeged or Miskolc; if anything it nurtured a strange kind of melancholic nationalism in an audience who ought to have been too young to be affected by such things.

I learned about some of the politics behind the music and its various values to its various makers, encouragers and listeners, but mostly I just liked it. I liked it as soon as I heard it and began to tease at the sense of the words, also loving the walking rhythms, the pounding feet of the bass, the way the instruments scraped at the experience of the song over and again: loss re-stated, love coming and going, leavings and dyings, the sour scratch of life and its fleeting joys. It was good to watch, too, and feel yourself overtaken and repaired by the music, wherever or whatever you had been before it started. Never had I felt so mandated to move whether I consented or not. I was lifted from the floor of a dance house in Mohács, first by the stamp of the musicians and the watching crowd and then by the joined throng of dancers the crowd became. I didn't know the words and didn't know the steps but I was never happier in Hungary.

The musicians I watched were playing other people's tunes, singing other people's lives. Sometimes they even did it dressed up in smocked shirts, waistcoats and leather boots, and then they went home after their performances in taxis or on the metro. The smocking wasn't essential, yet very little of this felt fake to me. There was saccharine gypsy fiddle music crying into tourist *gulyás* in one or two Budapest restaurants, but that was only a sad sideshow with its grinning performers like chained bears; dance house music was different. The players were transformed by what they played regardless of what they were wearing. I watched the musicians join a tune, stepping into its river, the equivalent of finding an opening in water, blowing or bowing low and quiet behind it, before rising to meet and fuse with its current. They kept time, the players, and so could join the swim. Birds join flocks in the same way. In that joining you sensed a past, animated and running towards you, across the old Earth through all its weathers. A fiddle tune had been taken from the fields to the city like grass forked aloft as music. My friends and I were students and teachers, not peasants, but we couldn't but move in the way the music made us. At our feet: the antic hay.

From their relatives who still lived and farmed in Transylvania, my friends brought back to Budapest cuts of bacon, jars of berries pressed to jam, and bottles of mind-warping *pálinka*, as thickly viscous as the freezing Danube. The music from Transylvania or *Erdély* in Hungarian (it also means Beyond-the-Forest), imported the same to the city: versions of food and warmth, the life and labours of the fields captured and held, songs cut by people from the big stories of the world. In them there was open-air work: bows cutting like scythes, instruments made like implements, with coincident delicacy and heft, hand-worked and hard-worn. The tunes could be tough as well as sweet. The violin slobbered with tears as often as it forked grass. The songs were bitter at times and cruel. In the winter in the city they released the smell of hay like a bale prised apart, but also the acrid stench of a dug-over dung-heap.

When all else seemed to have left the city the music kept the river flowing beneath the ice. The Budapest winter was almost without birds. Rooks went south in October and fieldfares followed in loose, stepped flocks calling above the Danube as they steered down its length towards warmer hedges. I remember the end of one near-birdless January day in particular. I had walked until dusk on old snow under bare grey limes around Jánoshegy in the Buda hills, seeing nothing, shivering and trying not to think myself ill. I had hurried to cancel my broken love. At a dance house I met a Hungarian girl called Márta and we'd kissed after she had helped me with a *csárdás*. By the end of the evening we were scrabbling at one another in the lift to my flat. There was an understanding, I was learning, that if you had the fleeting privacy of a room to yourselves, you took it. Hold the space, shut the shutters, and slip into the little pool of free time. The city was crowded with children living with their parents and sharing rooms deep into their adult years. There was always a grandmother somewhere. And there were only these rare opportunities. Within hours, I felt guilty about this and then sick.

As I waited at the bus-stop to leave the woods, seventy waxwings flew into a tree just above me, whistling themselves warm. The bus came and, as its doors opened, the birds flew on like a flight of brown arrows. They had never meant to stay. There was a song I had heard sung by Márta Sebestyén with the folk band Muzsikás, whose words I had begun to learn and like: *Repülj madár repülj – fly, bird, fly*. The singer is languishing 'in a love prison', *szerelemtömlöcben*, and urges the bird to carry news of heartbreak out to the wider world. I thought of the song that night back in my room, but ended up taking a different record from my unheard collection, slipping it from its sleeve, to perch it on my finger to peer at its grooves, trying to catch at the trapped sounds. It was called *The Unknown Music of Birds* and had been compiled earlier in the 1980s by a Budapest musicologist, Péter Szőke. Of all the records I hadn't heard it was the one I knew I had to listen to.

The next evening, after making rough duets playing ropey tenor sax to my Hungarian friend József's far more plausible trumpet, I asked if, instead of listening to John Coltrane, our customary jazz sorbet, we could put on the record I'd brought with me. In his flat we sat and listened, drinking the end of last year's wine, the *házibor* grown and made by József's father on the south shore of Balaton, in a season and under a sun impossible then either to recollect or to anticipate. The record began ordinarily with recordings of Hungarian birds. Between them a slow and deliberate announcer's voice gave their scientific names: *Alauda arvensis, Oriolus oriolus, Luscinia megarhynchos, Parus major*, skylark, golden oriole, nightingale, great tit. The birds sang. It was spring where they were. Then, after the great tit as we know it and think it knows itself, came a great tit slowed down, then slower still, then even slower. Deeper and deeper the sounds came, heavier and heavier. And with them, and József's cloudy wine, and the fug from his tiled stove, I was all but taken under. Trills slurred to barks, gulping trawls came from beyond the sound horizon, and a tearing at the night more raw than any folk bassist could make. I heard Albert Ayler in a great tit. And then, the next track, like a sound from a foghorn across the sand wastes of the *puszta*, the saddest bugling ever heard: a heart's journey in winter, *Lullula arborea*. *Teevo cheevo cheevio chee*, as Gerard Manley Hopkins has it. The woodlark: perpetual sprinkler of sweet sad songs on its flights overhead, but here slowed down and down and put into the mouth of a man. I succumbed. Bird song doesn't have to be manipulated to pull us apart, but the baritone soloist from the Hungarian State Opera singing, as Orpheus might, the woodlark, made it so sad it was hard not to cry. I heard the sound of some faraway, gone or buried world, brought up from a time when we all might have sung the same tune.

My sickness disappeared and so did the girl from the dance house, and one day I heard the ice cracking on the Danube beneath me as I walked over the Chain Bridge. The spring hurried in. In the gutters there were still lingering bergs of dirty snow, rusted with thawing dog shit, but I looked from my window and saw a hoopoe flying north over the rooftops of the city. Like a waving hand it raised its crest as it thought about landing. Quickly the rest followed this scout from the south, with swallow song and bridal lilac moving up towards the hills, while in the woods, on the tops, collared flycatchers appeared, the males perfect in their black and white wedding suits, piping their slender metallic songs like smart blacksmiths. Nearby, after a black woodpecker lolloped away through the trees purring its far-carrying call, I picked up a splinter of beech wood that it had just hacked from a hole twenty metres above me, intent on digging itself a future.

In early April I went with Ferenc Márkus, a birdwatching friend, to the far eastern corner of Hungary where, around the narrow knuckle of a pulled punch, the country met the Soviet Union (now Ukraine), Czechoslovakia (now Slovakia) and Romania. I had never then been further away from Britain. We ate slabs of chocolate embedded with whole cherries and we watched, in an abandoned quarry, a pair of huge eagle owls blinking in the slanting afternoon light, looking like old generals in dressing gowns. We walked in the direction of Moscow along a minor road out from Nyíregyháza and I peered towards the borders while Ferenc told me a story about how, as the Prague Spring of 1968 was being done to death, Alexander Dubček was summoned on a train that took him east. The train, driven under instructions that were not the Czech ruler's, straddled the border, not far to the north of where we were, and then stopped, half in Czechoslovakia and half in the USSR. Dubček was told to walk to the front of the train. There, having crossed into Soviet territory, he met Secretary Brezhnev, who gave him an almighty telling off before sending him back down the carriages to what he had once hoped might have been his own country.

It grew dark as we walked and we arrived at our destination: a weather station. Ferenc had a friend who worked there and he ushered us into a room of radar receivers that glowed green with the colour of glacial melt-water. As we watched one screen, the slur of light behind the strobing bar was studded with brighter spots. Antennae were angled towards the Soviet border, and we were seeing clouds of night-migrating birds moving north-east across Hungary and towards the Soviet Union. Angels, they used to be called by early radar operators who saw the same on British screens. They were coming back, regardless of the wire. In the cave dark of the room we sat at the desks and craned into the screens. As I looked down I felt close to fainting. The pools swarmed and swam in front of me, like a sky of stars, as distant but also as touching. The night had rolled out of the east but we could see into it. It sang a night song, like the singers sang at the end of their sets, an *éj dal*. All borders were open. A thaw had set in; the winter was finished, defrosted by smudges of birds made into green light.

Gibraltar
36°N

'So, I have seen Africa!' – Coleridge was on a ship that passed into the Mediterranean in April 1804, and he recorded in a notebook what the sight – his first view of any land beyond Europe – meant to him. How real it was, or how suggestive? Twice, at Gibraltar, in 2005, and again ten years later, I have wondered the same.

First you must get there. I queued to cross the border-causeway from Spain, cleared the customs, passed a naval port, circled roundabouts, slowed up in shopping streets, parked my car, and began to walk a tarmac path, uphill and towards the south. I've made this short journey for more than five days now on two spring visits, but every trip has repeated the experience of the first: the banality of such an arrival, into the generic nowhere of today's anthropogenic everywhere (there being, as Gertrude Stein said, *no there there*), serving only to increase the shock I felt when I reached the top of the rock, which is (suddenly and totally) Europe, and saw from it a matching rock mountain that is (so near and yet) *Africa*! It was as if I had taken a *travelator* (which I didn't want) to the sublime (which I didn't expect). Standing on the rock's southern-most point, where it begins to step down towards the sea, I imagined being able to reach across, touch the rock of Jebel Musa, embrace the *Jeb* from the *Gib*, and thereby rhyme the continents. The sea strait between Africa and Europe is fourteen kilometres wide (at its narrowest), but an epic handshake feels in the offing.

We are related, after all, and all but joined. The rocks are made of the same limestone. And today, as on many days, Africa actually passed over into Europe: the spring was to be seen flying in, arriving dressed as a black kite, through a salting sea haze and harried by gulls, looking shattered and out of sorts. It wouldn't stop, being an airborne thing and not yet fully at home, but I watched it and, hooked by what I had seen, I stayed on to see it happening again and again. Looking south across the sea strait to Morocco, I could see birds coming from Africa into Europe: a dozen swallows flew past and then a shabby line of new black kites. It had been tough to get across, but they had to, they looked (even) as if they had wanted to. I watched them taking in the land of Europe beneath them. They had been there before, but still they looked about. It was their version of a handshake. The swal-lows called as they made landfall, but most of the birds that came over the rock remained silent: black kites flew past like a game of chess in progress; a flight of white storks sailed over without a flap or a note. But still, their passage *speaks*.

On my second visit to Gibraltar – ten years after my first – the sight of Africa was more provocative still, because when I looked south, having climbed to the top of the rock with Claire (whom I didn't know ten years previously), the thought came irresistibly to me that, if we could just get across the strait, we would be able to take the route the swallows fly and walk down the length of the continent to her home, where now I sometimes live too, at the Cape of Good Hope. I have described our house in the southernmost village on the Atlantic at Scarborough as being the last but one residence before Antarctica. Our barn swallow-watching there occurs at the very bottom of Africa. Here, in Gibraltar, just across from the very top of Africa, were swallows now, in March, calling as they flew, having just flown over the first sea they have had to cross, since flying – who knows, perhaps? – from Scarborough beach on the Cape Peninsula, 8,000 kilometres to the south.

To find yourself at Gibraltar in the midst of flocks of birds crossing from Africa – swallows one minute, black kites the next – makes you want to pay close attention, there and then, to the present and moving moment – the birds are arriving into Europe this very minute. But in their progress and their intention, the migrants also proclaim a deeper time and its dynamic permanence – and to look up and out from the rock is also to be shown, or reminded of, lives before and lives to come (innumerable back-stories and countless ways ahead), or to be put within as long a *now* as the world might allow.

Most large migrant raptors and storks cross into Europe from Africa at one of only three or four key points where the continents are almost joined by land bridges or island stepping stones. Human migrants from Africa, seeking to cross to better lives in Europe, also concentrate at these narrows. Dispassionate observers know these places as bottlenecks or choke points.

Think of an egg-timer. Set it up. A spread of sand bulbs to its bottom. Turn it over. The grainy delta drains away, running narrowly through the pinch-thin neck. Something like this is happening in these bottleneck places. The sand equals the birds that must pass north every spring – the great spread of birds that have wintered down the western side of Africa. The same must fly south every autumn. They funnel to the neck in order to step from one life to the next, they mingle and mix as the rope of them thickens in just three or four places. Then they spread out again and occupy the available land.

Cape Bon in Tunisia, Malta, Sicily and southern mainland Italy connect together as the central Mediterranean flyway (but only for stronger flyers and lighter birds – this route has too much sea for white storks). The Bosphorus, and then further passes and crossings around the Middle East into the Red Sea, form the eastern flyway. The western flyway is over the beaches and mountains around the Strait of Gibraltar (the rock plus the surrounding coastline, mostly westwards, of Spain, and Jebel Musa and the mountains of the Rif in Morocco). There are no other short sea crossings in the western Mediterranean, and this flyway serves the whole of western Europe. Since the end of the most recent glaciation in Europe, around ten to eleven thousand years ago, the strait has been central to the movement of birds from western Africa into the whole of the western Palaearctic. The birds that enter Europe in the spring using this route are mostly western African wintering birds, although some have travelled from as far east as Chad, and some might winter as far south as South Africa. Fifty thousand storks and a quarter of a million raptors cross north each spring. Among them are all the black kites that breed in Switzerland; they would have a shorter journey if they came directly from the south, but there is more sea there and they couldn't get across. Some species of birds that cross (most of the white storks, for example) are headed no further than Iberia; others will fly on as far north and as far east as Finland. At the height of the last glaciation, west Africa is thought to have been the main winter refuge for Iberian birds. As the ice began to retreat further north, birds followed behind to spread up into ice-free western and northern Europe. On the other side of Europe, birds that had hidden out in the Balkan refuge moved into eastern Europe and west Asia. Some species existed in both these refuges and re-colonised Europe from two relict populations of the same species. Other populations of some species had been separated long enough to permit their splitting into different species: the nightingale (in the west) and the thrush nightingale (in the east) evolved in this way.

The sand in my egg-timer stands for the birds on the move, but it is also the real sand of the Sahara too. It sometimes comes nestled in the feathers of the birds that have crossed it; sometimes it comes on the wind and falls as dusty rain. Even if it is not visible at all, it still determines how much of life (and even how much life) lives further north. The desert, as I saw in Chad, is hazardous, mostly uninhabitable, and has to be got across. Migration has evolved in its knowledge and as its embattled enemy. Many birds can live in Europe for its warm months but not for its cold months. Then they must go south. Yet south of Europe is first sea and then sand, and few birds are happy there. Those that cannot manage it die; those that can will get to come back across it again. Every redstart, arriving into the European spring, will have already crossed the sand twice. Every one: south across it the previous autumn, north across it in this spring. Every migrant arriving in the spring is already a seasoned voyager, every one is already a survivor.

My second stay on the rock, in another late March, began with clear skies and a fresh but easing south-west wind. These are favoured conditions for passaging raptors, and the first drifts of birds began to appear at about ten-thirty. The shorter the sea crossing, the better for all, the big birds especially: it takes them roughly forty-five minutes to cross the strait; they must mostly make do with the lift-off they start with and hope it sees them over. Jebel Musa, at 841 metres, is almost twice the height of Gibraltar (426m). I watched soaring raptors losing altitude from the beginning of their crossing. Often by the time they reached Gibraltar they were not far above the sea. From the rock, I saw some alter their flight path having been shown better air elsewhere by other migrants. I also saw eagles dipping down to try to find a thermal above the funnels of ships travelling the strait. Prevailing winds in March are westerly, and birds get blown into the wider Mediterranean as they seek to cross it. Many arrived very low to the sea. Those with the biggest wings are often the worst off: griffon vultures, white storks and short-toed eagles sometimes pitch into the water. For those that make it nearer land, warmer rising air around the rock might raise them up again, allowing them to gain height. But even these birds will pass along the rock some way below the summit ridge. You can be very close to them, little more than an arm's length away, almost within touching distance. That means the raptors must also run the gauntlet of the rock's gulls.

Even as we parked, we could see an agitated swirl of big birds high above us, level with the ridge of the rock. It was a mob and a mobbing: white wings and black wings spangled and spun in the sunlight. A drift of black kites from the south had met a welcoming party of resident gulls keen to escort them off the premises. The kites pressed on. They didn't want to stop. Who would? There are 3,000 breeding yellow-legged gulls on the rock. All day long, for weeks in the spring, these birds slip from their nests (or from the side of their partners on their nests) to police the passage through their airspace of anything they regard as *de trop* – all those that are not from there, or wanted, and best shown the door. They are bold. Later the same day, we saw one swinging on the primary feathers of a booted eagle, which was already at its wits' end having struggled to cross the strait.

We were watching the kites and their gull attackers above us from the outside table of a café. The spring was slow so far, Keith Bensusan said. Some western Bonelli's warblers had come through and Iberian chiffchaffs, but not yet any bee-eaters. Keith is the director of the Gibraltar Botanic Gardens. He's been birdwatching since he was a boy. Spotting a migrant nightjar hiding in one of his mother's plastic flower-pots on their balcony got him interested. His first bird book was a guide to British birds – an old colonial leftover. It had red kites in it but not black. That confused him. I asked (I ask anyone I might) about redstarts: he'd often seen flocks of them in the spring, groups of fifteen to twenty birds, in 'a sort of concert' arriving together, touching down, moving along the rock, through the gardens of the town below and so north into Spain and on to the rest of happy Europe.

– But not this year, yet, this spring is slow …

Keith had to raise his voice over the noise of a machine for unsticking chewing gum trodden into the pavement. I looked down for ants (a new parasitic species had been found) – there are more ant species on Gibraltar than in the whole of the United Kingdom. The Barbary macaques, Keith said, were being given contraceptive implants, but not all of them had yet been caught.

We left Keith and walked to the bird observatory and ringing station, and watched for an hour, thanks to Ian, Steve and Yvonne.

– What the hell is that?

It was a juvenile gannet among a tranche of black kites: a disconcerting meeting of a sea giant in baby clothes and a business gaggle of travelling brown overcoats.

I picked out a black stork that was losing height and labouring over the sea. Its red legs and beak seemed flushed with effort. As it came on, it appeared to be being bent by the wind, its neck and its legs forced below its own horizontal, as if it were a tempered steel bar rolling from a furnace to be quenched and cooled.

– Something is hurrying away inland.

It was an Egyptian vulture.

– They welly through.

Three more came in close and flapping hard over the observatory just as a coach party of tourists were taking in the view of Africa. None of the visitors looked up to see the immigrants.

It seems, through your optics, that you can pick out birds not long after they leave Africa, but the birds you can see are actually almost across the strait, perhaps at most three or four kilometres away from Gibraltar. One solitary scribble materialises against the sea. It might be a fly hatching from the blow. Many times I checked my lenses for dust. Sometimes the light slants a little or the haze above the sea thickens for a moment, and whatever was there vanishes. In that case you must start again, scanning for scribbles. But, if you've kept sight of it, three minutes on, the calligraphy can become a raptor. It pulls at the air, as if in an argument with it, to tilt itself towards the rock. A further minute or two and the bird of prey has become specific – a dark-morph booted eagle. It comes closer now and I begin to think of it differently. We are sharing space, as we weren't before. A marathon-runner has entered the arena. We are sitting warmed by the sun-struck

94

rocks. It is struggling. Now it flies closer. I can see its eyes as it passes. It looks around and down at the rocky slopes. By now I had shared ten minutes with the eagle. In its face I saw something of the look of men photographed on the Somme as they made their way back to their trenches. I had seen the same expression on the face of a wildebeest climbing from the crocodile-filled turbid waters of the Mara River in Kenya. It is something like the enigma of survival.

Black kites were the commonest birds moving over Gibraltar that day. After the honey buzzards that come later – beginning around mid-April – the kites are the most numerous migrant raptors seen from the rock. I counted 800. The observatory logged a day-total of 1,203. They came in loose aggregates, almost sociable assemblies, fractions of a vast flock, with the birds always in sight of at least one other of their kind. Stiff-winged but buoyant, they glide when they can and only rarely flap.

The observatory counted 572 booted eagles; we saw 200. These birds mostly travelled alone, or rarely in an accidental grouping of two or three. They flap quite fast, often appearing more buzzard-like than eagle. All these birds will breed, or try to, in Iberia.

We counted seventy short-toed eagles. I've never before seen more than two or three on any day of my birdwatching life. The observatory logged 135. They make surprisingly heavy weather of the crossing, flying a rather laboured flap-flap-glide sequence that must be repeated again and again. Lateral winds deflected them off course, and their round owlish faces and yellow eyes showed their surprise. Some of the birds we saw might have spent their winters as far east as Chad; they are headed for places in Iberia or southern France that are snake-rich.

As the sun angled west in the late afternoon, long sand-pale ridges and ranges opened up to sight on the African side of the strait. It looked as though it had stepped even closer. Still came the continental drift – more eagles and more kites. Among the legions, an osprey made it (flap-flap), and a marsh harrier (one leisurely flap then another flap), and then a raven, the most accomplished of all flyers, not bothered by anything, and able apparently to be *echt* raven wherever it was and whatever it was doing. While the osprey and the marsh harrier would probably be heading for Scandinavia, it might just have been coming home from a day at work.

There were swallows too, an almost continuous slew of them, and swifts (pallid and common), most numerous of all, like gnats everywhere in the sky, a tray of scattered type thrown nonchalantly across the strait. And then, at the end of the afternoon, a flock of fifteen bee-eaters, chattering as they came, a harlequinade. When we turned from the strait at six o'clock and began to walk north, back towards our car, still they came and overtook us, bird after bird, a swallow, ten swallows, sixteen kites, swifts, three booted eagles, swifts, swallows, a short-toed eagle, swallows, swifts, swallows, swifts, swifts, swifts.

Migration has evolved in bird populations where the advantages of a species leaving its breeding grounds outweigh the disadvantages of travel. Swallows' journeys are long and vexed, but more birds survive them than would survive if they were to stay on through the year where they had bred – say, north of the Arctic Circle in Norway. The Palaearctic–African bird migration patterns we see today have evolved in the last ten thousand years, since climatic change at the end of the most recent glaciation. The migrations are relatively young and the migrant species are still likely to be finding their way. 'It is fair to assume', Clive Finlayson says in *Birds of the Strait of Gibraltar*, 'that in such a relatively short evolutionary time, the migratory strategies of the different species are unlikely to have been perfected.' Birds go wrong as individuals, but as species they are also still adapting their patterns of movement. They are still evolving. As all life is. Evolution is relentless.

Like the larger, less easy-going raptors and storks, passerine birds use specific flyways. Almost all birds would prefer to avoid the lengthiest parts of both the Mediterranean and the Sahara. They skirt the sand when travelling in both directions and often cross the sea at the bottlenecks. Clearing the Sahara, even at its narrowest points, depletes the fat deposits of many small birds. South of the sand, before they embark, yellow wagtails and wheatears put on an extra 30–40 per cent of their body weight in fat. That way they can make a 2,000-kilometre journey in one non-stop sixty-hour flight. Having crossed the desert these birds will often then linger around Gibraltar and southern Spain to regain fat.

We can see long-gone years in these present-day flights. Almost all of Europe's pied flycatchers (even eastern breeding birds) enter and exit the continent via the western flyway. Other species drain in the opposite direction: lesser whitethroats, marsh warblers and red-backed shrikes cross Europe to leave via the eastern edge of the Mediterranean – even birds of those species that breed within a few kilometres of the strait at Gibraltar do this. These birds probably evolved in the places to which they remain loyal in the non-breeding season: the ancestors of the lesser whitethroats that breed in the blackthorn hedge at Tubney Fen near my home in Cambridgeshire probably started their post-glacial life in an eastern place. They entered northern and western Europe from the east and they continue to do so every year. The lesser whitethroats I saw in Chad and in Ethiopia do exactly this, entering Europe from the east no matter where they are headed. Their annual migrations re-enact their species' historical journeys. Their evolution is written into their flight plans.

1 April. The lightest of winds came from the east. A thick fog of low cloud smothered the whole strait. A glacier might have filled the Mediterranean overnight. Ships sounded their foghorns from under its ice. We stayed west of Gibraltar in Spain, about five kilometres inland, and climbed up above the cloud into a deep blue sky at El Cabrito. It was silent and still. We set up our watch at the foot of a dormant wind turbine. There was a pair of red-rumped swallows nesting in the old stone building where we sat. Nothing of the coastline or the sea was to be seen below us. We knew the sea was there only because we had been down at the shore the day before. The mountain-tops in North Africa alone matched us. In Morocco the peaks rose from a muffle of cloud. We waited. A bright-eyed man with a long beard and dressed in a camouflage suit appeared. He was a Spanish migration watchman. He had a walkie-talkie that crackled every now and then. We chatted in Latin names for as long as we could and then he opened the book

he was reading. It was a book of photographs of dancing Spanish horses. His name was Jesus.

A new sound has been put into the world, which is the creak of the gantry and of the blades of a wind turbine waking from rest. We heard that at El Cabrito, which is the oldest windfarm in Cádiz province, before we felt the slightest disturbance of air. But some black kites had already found it. Forty-five birds, in a kind of rope, came from below us, out of the cloud into the blue, feeling their way into rising air, finding a thermal stair and climbing it to where we were, and then moving on beyond us, their flock spilling over the lip of the hill and spreading, in the ease of new weather, inland and out across the level country.

Those birds made it past the turbines before the machines started, but we are stealing the wind from other migrants. Soaring birds are known to collide with turbines. A study published in 2019 by Ana T. Marques and colleagues of migratory black kites around Gibraltar in Spain showed that the species is learning to avoid the blades, but also that their evasion strategy often takes them towards less useful air. In this way they are losing aerial habitat. Following our theft of the wind, the birds, that might have shown us the best air, are now being kept from it.

Another party ascended from below us – more black kites, but with an Egyptian vulture leading the assault. It looked like a grizzled old goat as it passed El Cabrito. Along with the kites, lashed into the thermal, were a marsh harrier, two booted eagles and a griffon vulture. Had they crossed from Africa through cloud or were they moving off after a night on Spanish ground? I tried to ask Jesus.

The Mediterranean as we know it is about six million years old. The strait separating the continents has been closed before, with the gates, at what the ancient world called the Pillars of Hercules, shut. There is talk that they will shut again one day, as the African Plate advances northwards relative to the Eurasian Plate. Africa is moving on Europe: the Earth has some migration of its own surface permanently underway. When that happens the kites and their friends could walk instead of flying. Except that they may well have gone on before, like us, altogether elsewhere.

APRIL

Quantocks
51°N

3 April. A new-come *local* swallow always strikes home. I saw my first
of the English spring today, when driving away from visiting my father
and his broken hip in hospital in Taunton (he was on Coleridge ward
– he might have been on Wordsworth). It flashed across the road and
I saw its *roundy* head.

That word, *roundy*, Seamus Heaney heard used by an Irish
primary school pupil in County Cork who had written a short essay
on the swallow. Perfectly captured in its two brief sentences are the
away bird and the *home*, the world traveller and the domestic familiar,
the bird beyond knowing and the bird just an arm's length away:
'The swallow is a migratory bird,' the schoolchild wrote. 'He have
a roundy head.'

On the creaky cassette-player in my old car was Gustav Mahler:
Kathleen Ferrier, the English contralto, singing *Das Lied von der Erde*.
She makes me cry. The most heart-breaking song is the last one,
specifically its last minutes. It is called '*Der Abschied*' – The Farewell. It
is about home and away too: the end of all things, our deaths and our
homes, and the paradox of endlessness of the end of things, the beginnings again, that come, like swallows, from away.

> Die liebe Erde allüberall blüht auf im Lenz und grünt
> Aufs neu! Allüberall und ewig blauen licht die Fernen!
> Ewig … ewig …

The dear earth everywhere blossoms in spring and grows green anew! Everywhere and forever blue is the horizon!
Forever … Forever …

In 1947 Ferrier sang *Das Lied von der Erde* for Bruno Walter. They made a studio recording of it in 1952. It was this I was listening to. Ferrier was ill then with breast cancer and had begun radiation treatment. Her performance of 'The Farewell' is extraordinarily moving and not only because of the timing of its making. The song and the singer disappear before us in sounds that could mark a journey into the earth or (and) a journey out of it. There is a celeste, too, which makes magically ethereal music. I want to call Ferrier's voice *plashed* – it seems to be so woven into the fabric of the music that it might be some utterance of the Earth itself. She makes a sound like a spoken breathing, which could be a voice at its very end but which might also be a voice just beginning, the very first and/or the very last cries of life, out-breaths and in-breaths, *ah* after *ah*.

The effect is what I think of as a *going-music* that, in the ebbing heat of the leaving of life, still feels intensely alive. Both life and death are being sung. The song moves to the horizon and sings beyond it; it sounds in retreat and yet it feels close to our ear. In this it is like a breathing into sleep but also like bird song sung through the music of weather. It looks at last back over the edge of the world and shines there, even as it thins to almost nothing, like the slightest green flash at sundown, like the last song of a blackbird in a darkening wood.

The Kaluli people of Papua New Guinea, who believe all their dead become birds and (more specifically) their songs, describe a forest full of what they call 'lifted-up over-sounding', *dulugu ganalan*, or 'turned-over words'. These concepts were suggested to the Kaluli by birds' abilities to raise their singing above the background of noise, the jungle wildtrack. That birds have such elocution singles them out and makes them humanly important to the Kaluli. They are the voices of their dead living in birds. 'To you they are birds,' said Jubi, a Kaluli man, to the anthropologist Steven Feld; 'to us they are voices in the forest.' In the last moments of 'The Farewell', as sung by Kathleen Ferrier, we can hear those forest voices too.

Orpheus, who sang – spellbindingly – both to and through nature, would have been familiar with such sounds. Kathleen Ferrier sang him too, in another much-loved performance. In Christoph Gluck's seventeenth-century opera *Orfeo ed Euridice* (all three roles, Orfeo, Euridice and Amore, were sung by women), Ferrier's devastated (ruined and emotionally crushed) interpretation of Orpheus' aria to the dead Eurydice became a show-stopper and was often requested. 'What is life to me without you?' she sang. In many versions of the myth Eurydice is not returned from the underworld where Persephone is the sometime queen (see the agonisingly moving poem by Rilke, for example, 'Orpheus. Eurydice. Hermes'), but in the opera, Eurydice is spared forever-death and is delivered back to life and re-united in a happy ending that is a new beginning with Orpheus.

Ferrier's performances of these songs on the brink of death are especially moving when we know the singer herself wasn't allowed much more of her own life, let alone a second go at it. For her there was no return to the sunlit world of blossom and greenery. She was headed to another sort of forest. She was forty-one when she died in October 1953. Her final public appearance had been in February that year when she sang *Orfeo*.

In the Fens, at the other end of my journey from Somerset, as I arrived at our house, I could see a male swallow on the phone wires overhead. They had got back to Cambridgeshire at the same time as they had reached Somerset. A pair has bred on a roof beam in the open-fronted garage of the house opposite ours for at least six years. Not the same birds – they die long before a sixth spring – but successive pairs have made their residence there, and have raised chicks each year. The sweet gabbling fizz of the bird's song sounded like some sort of domestic dial-up tone. After wiring up its place by singing outside for a minute, it dropped through the dark gap of the garage entrance. I could hear it calling inside. Its quick sharp notes came back off the stone walls and the wooden roof as though it was measuring its space. The bird seemed happy, then, flying and singing, to be settling there.

Bellaghy
55°N

I have been twice to Bellaghy, in County Londonderry, where Seamus Heaney lived as a boy. My first visit was near the beginning of one spring and the second at the end of another. Both times I travelled with poets and novelists: Paul Farley, then John Burnside and Tessa Hadley (Tess is also my cousin). We went to talk about writing about places, Heaney's especially. On each occasion, he both was and wasn't there.

Heaney died in August 2013. The following April, when I went to Bellaghy, his grave was still young, bare and earthy, a slab of turned peat. A body was obviously buried there. On the mound someone had placed a bunch of cut daffodils. It was his birthday – 13 April – the first birthday that he would not know in the first spring since he died. The dark earth was also dotted with a confetti shower of wet blossom sent down from the blackthorns beyond the graveyard wall.

A blackbird sang from the same thorns, and summoned the poems I knew Heaney had written featuring the bird. In these, he had both resisted and succumbed to the birds' dusky magic: the soot-fall of their looks and the elegiac cadences of their song.* 'It's you, blackbird, I love,' Heaney wrote in 'The Blackbird of Glanmore' (his adult home, near Dublin), where he is put in mind of the dead and the dying by a bird he knows well on his lawn, even as the same bird asserts its blackbird particularity and refuses to be loaded with any human baggage.

I had come to Bellaghy from a Heaney commemorative conference, fifty kilometres away in Belfast. Its logo was a blackbird. After a day of talking, I walked the rainy city through a rush-hour of traffic slush and watery light. From early March onwards there are several weeks when the birds' evening

---

* Across Europe, many different poets have heard the same. I talked once about blackbirds with Adam Zagajewski, remembering his birthplace in Lvov from far away in Houston, Texas, where he wrote of the birds' 'sad, sweet cantilenas'. And, the last but one poem in a three-volume English translation of Bertolt Brecht's poetry is a blackbird/death reckoner: Brecht wakes in a hospital bed and hears a blackbird and is calmed, as if shriven or absolved, by its singing, such that he feels closer to being 'nothing' and able 'to enjoy / The song of every blackbird after me too'.

song, and the evening itself, and much human homing happens at once, and for those hours the blackbirds are often louder than anything. In Belfast, on my phone I recorded two males singing from facing rooftops on a terraced street where their territories met near the Botanical Gardens. Their songs were strikingly loud, as if they had been turned up and pushed through the wet dusk. Some dark soil was singing, and yet – since it was song – it was awake and alive above everything; I heard the birds, as the poets have, declaring for life then, even as they endorsed the night.

After Heaney's grave, Bellaghy in April was a sad place to see. Hard times had fallen on the small town. A flesher's survived – 'J. Overend & Sons – Home-Reared Beef and Lamb' – and I shivered at the business, its name and the family's tasks. Many of the other shops were gone, their fronts boarded, or rather blinded, with window-sized stickers of garish vegetable scenes, a digitised cornucopia, with greens too neon and too lurid.

I walked to see Heaney's old home at Moss Bawn (the wooden sign on the house now gives it as two words; Heaney always made it one). It was still alive. A young boy kicked a football on the grass in the front; there were chicken sheds and some old buses laid up in the yards behind. It looked like a Heaney poem, although, from the road, I couldn't see the well that gave him so much to write about. Perhaps it has gone. The sound of its hand pump being worked up and down made a noise that he heard – thinking back as a writerly adult – as the Greek word *omphalos*. Repeated with each effortful stroke, it (so he described in a radio talk in 1978) announced the place – *omphalos omphalos omphalos* – as 'the navel and hence the stone that marked the centre of the world'.

You can step from these heartbeat-headquarters at Moss Bawn and walk along the Lagans Road back towards Bellaghy, just as the boy Seamus did to his primary school. Arriving at the country lane, I found I knew it already, thanks to his poems. Now paved, where once it grew weeds down its spine, it still bucked and bumped as it crossed the boggy ground. In 2014, someone had dumped a dead TV in an oil-skinned flash of water that was poisoning an old orchard. But the spring was, otherwise, underway. New green curves of soft grass fringed the flood. The bare shins of the nearby birch trees looked cold, but their twiggy ends were opening into small punches of leaves. A swallow

– *roundy head* and all – appeared in front of me from nowhere and surfed the undulating road just as a glance of the sun raised steam from the wet tarmac. The road dried, as the swallow's wings and back did, lifting a sparkle from the black and brightening the blue bird. It was new in – I could feel that – but it looked at home already.

There is a poem in Heaney's last collection, *Human Chain* (2010), which is set in, and between, a graveyard and a childhood. 'A Herbal' is really a sequence of small poems that might have been made from nature notebook entries. The lines are short and the vocabulary simple. It begins: 'Everywhere plants / Flourish among graves', and the poem grows out from this thought of living wreaths. It describes various vegetable moments and plant memories, spots of time shared with green leaves and other flowering things. The grass blows in it, as if through a life, going 'with the flow', growing *everywhere*. With other simple and ordinary plants (bracken, broom, blackberries, vetch, docks and rush) it makes a wildtrack for existence, a daisy chain or garland of wild plants that might speak – and somehow medicate – a life. Near the end of the poem, still mapping a local flora, the lines lengthen and the nature observations become incantatory. A habitat or an ecosystem is being described or sung, similar to that which Charles Darwin, on the final page of his *Origin*, evoked as the 'tangled bank' of life.

Heaney, channelling the poem's Breton originator, Guillevic, is *seen through* (as I have said I am by birds) twice over by the (mostly growing) place around him: it sees him through, giving him enough to live on, and it sees through him, showing what he is made of.

> Between heather and marigold,
> Between sphagnum and buttercup,
> Between dandelion and broom,
> Between forget-me-not and honeysuckle,
>
> As between clear blue and cloud,
> Between haystack and sunset sky,
> Between oak tree and slated roof,

I had my existence. I was there.
Me in place and the place in me.

People are made up by places. So are birds. In May, at the Hortobágy fish-ponds in eastern Hungary, nearly every stand of reeds has a male great reed warbler shouting about itself and its living space. I heard them there one spring in the mid-1980s Communist era when their noise was hourly drowned by sky-splitting Soviet warplanes; and I heard them another spring, thirty years later, in the same place, more than a decade after the sign of a metre-long silvery carp leaping towards a silvery red star had been removed from above the entrance gates to the one-time state fish farm. The song sounded the same in the European Union as it had in the Warsaw Pact. But although the bird was making it there, and was also intent on making its own offspring there, the singing was mostly made of somewhere else.

To look at, great reed warblers are like enlarged and galumphing versions of other reed warblers. Their song is equivalently magnified and coarsened. They *ack-ack* at their surroundings, making an angry noise, rough-grained and gravelly, like the splutter of an old generator or pump. Even when long up and running they sound like they are forever just starting over. I haven't heard one sing since I have worn a hearing aid – but the distorting crackle of the wind that strains my machine's dynamic capabilities delivers a memory of the singing bird to me most days that I spend in the open air.

The last one I heard was on its wintering grounds in southern Zambia. A male gunned from a scrubby mound of trees in a neglected grassy field near a guava orchard. Great reed warblers have long been known to sing in their non-breeding quarters and were assumed to defend territory there. They return, with fidelity, to the same spots, commonly in wooded savannah, after their summer breeding in wetlands across Europe (though they are absent from the British Isles). Claire, who has bird business of her own on this farm near Choma in Zambia, remembers hearing a vocal bird behind a snack bar on the road to town. It sang year after year, until one season the tree was silent because, presumably, its returning singer had died.

Marjorie Sorensen studied the great reed warblers at Choma and asked why, when singing is costly, they continued their chunter in these trees, in their supposedly quiescent off-season or downtime. She tested three seasonally related hypotheses, asking if winter song was prompted by rising testosterone (in preparation for their breeding season in Europe), and whether such singing allowed the birds to defend Zambian non-breeding territories (as earlier bird-workers had thought), or gave them practice for their next breeding time in Europe. Working with Claire and Susanne Jenni-Eiermann, Marj's data supported the last hypothesis. The warblers' fricatives and gutturals are them practising for their next spring's scat and attack.

There was further news. Great reed warblers are peculiar in the progression of their moult. On their autumn journeys from Europe into Africa, they pause for two to three months to shed and regrow their flight feathers before continuing on to their final winter sites, further south, where they finish their remaining feather exchanges. Such staging sites for migrant songbirds are more and more nowadays being discovered. Other migrants including sedge, marsh and olivaceous warblers also part-moult on interrupted southward flights.

Where the birds' new feathers grow is recorded in the feathers themselves. Earth asserts its place and signs itself differently in its every square metre, in its every plot. Now we are beginning to know how to read – via the analysis of mineral profiles and stable isotopes – these identifying or determining traces. No soil that grows no shrub that feeds no caterpillar that is swallowed by no warbler is quite the same. Birds absorb isotopes from their food and deposit them in their feathers. They are legible there. The feathers last about a year, so the birds travel with these marks. Knowing where the outside of a bird was put together can indicate effects that have been carried over from conditions earlier in its life. Meagre rainfall in the Ethiopian Rift will tell in the reedbeds of the fishponds of eastern Europe. Great reed warblers that moult flight feathers in Ethiopia and grow new ones there, bring something to Zambia later in their winter that was written into their bodies in Ethiopia. In the trees of the guava orchard they finish their moult. They then take something of Zambia, as well as something of Ethiopia, with them to the Hortobágy in Hungary. Their young, from there, will be dressed in Hungarian feathers until they too grow more African over the months and the years of their life.

The places are in them.

Isotope analysis can help us see back in time as well as to other terrain. Around 62°N in Sweden, the ice in the last ice age was particularly thick. It persisted there after it had thawed both to the south and to the north. Willow warblers – they sing in Choma too during their winters – colonised the new available breeding lands around the ice: one population, coming from the south-west, went south of the lasting glacial conditions, and the other, from the east, went north. The ice separated these two subspecies. When it melted, the birds met, but ever since have retained morphological differences (they can be distinguished by their DNA) and different migration routes and wintering grounds (told by isotope analysis of their feathers which identifies the widely separate areas where they moult): birds from southern Sweden move south-west through Iberia to winter in western Africa; birds from north Sweden move through south-east Europe to winter in eastern and southern Africa. The ice now gone is still somehow marking the lives of these birds for one half of the year, and for the other half, they continue to head home to the widely separate parts of Africa they started out from as a species many thousands of years ago.*

I took Seamus Heaney's book with his herbal poem to Bellaghy and read it there. And, there, I realised that his lines in the poem about wanting to have a sound recording of his footsteps through the wet grass of a field came from a nearby place.

---

* Great reed warblers also have two wintering areas. Western European populations winter in Africa, eastern birds go to south-east Asia; suggesting that in the last glaciation the species may have had two refugia, like the Swedish willow warblers, from which birds spread separately north across Eurasia when the ice disappeared.

Many animal migrations have evolved in response to climate changes. Salmon started out as freshwater fish before being driven out to sea by ice age freezing of land masses. At sea they survived, but retained their ancestral tie to fresh water, so when the ice melted they re-colonised rivers, now as migratory fish.

At Bellaghy, the fortified manor house or bawn, which was built during the Plantation era of the 1620s to dominate the scene and to assert English rule, is now a local history museum. They show a film of Heaney walking in gumboots through the sodden marshy fields of the Strand, in front of Castle Island, at Lough Beg outside Bellaghy. I watched it on my second ghost hunt. As he walks, Heaney describes the three selves and the three times he senses in Bellaghy: a dreamtime and a dreaming self; a historical-time and a historied self; and an auto-biographical time – his own self in his own lifetime.

A taxi took us out to the lough where Heaney was filmed, white-haired among the cotton grass. It was mid-June when we were there. We had to slow for a tractor pulling a trailer, loaded, thick and heavy, with new-cut silage. As it took a corner, a fridge-sized green berg calved from the top of the heaped mass and slid down its side. The shredded grass was juiced and darkening, as if it bled. Just minutes after its harvest it looked very old, like coal with a green lustre. In the cut fields, slurry was being spread on the aftermath to foster new growth. A second and often a third take are possible here. Where the grass had been cut, the peat showed black beneath the green stubble, and now a spatter of black slurry – residue grass that has passed through a cow – was lumpily scattered on top of it. Every field that hadn't been cut and dunged was planted with living cows, head-down and heavily working the green.

– It'll be *aromic* round about, said Noel, our taxi-man.

Nowhere else as here, in my corner of Europe, have I seen swallows so at home and so emphatically in residence. Around the dairy farms no patch of sky was without them. I saw them fly into old barns and out of new ones, disappearing into assorted darks – doorways, window spaces – and loosing themselves back into the air. I watched them for a second time on the Lagans Road. They were plentiful in Bellaghy. In the windowless library at the new Seamus Heaney HomePlace building, we talked about places and place-making and the benison bestowed on our places when swallows nest. The building there was too new for them to have yet found a purchase, but some birds were sizing it up – their flights often seem like this, suggesting measurements and tailoring and sewing and the unrolling of fabric. They were the last birds I saw outside the centre before we started our talk and the first I saw when we finished. Later, I watched them at dusk in Magherafelt, hawking over the Church Street Lounge, and the Mid-Ulster Back Care Centre. And I saw them the next morning, as we left, dipping and cutting, casting and flitting, above the 'one-stop shop' in Castle-dawson that offers 'Quality Blinds Shoes Fishing Tackle'. As always, their own *everything everywhere* zest was good to be with.

On this second visit, Heaney's grave in St Mary's churchyard was no longer raw. Since I had seen its beginnings a headstone had been raised. It names him, alone; and he lies tucked into a corner next to the graveyard wall, shadowed in part by an ash and a sycamore and a thorn hedge that lean over the stones from the edge of a rough field beyond. No one could be buried here further from the church.

– He was an atheist, said the man at the bawn who showed us the film.

It drizzled when we were there. Sycamore keys – still green – spun onto the grave. Swallows came low over the tombs and clipped the trees, seeking insects knocked down by the wet. The unpolished slate headstone freckled with rain, and the low grey stone kerb edging the grave – the bed frame for the body beneath – spotted black.

The bed itself is gravelled. That is a common funerary practice, but the only writing on the stone, apart from Heaney's name and dates, points us to it. Just above the gravel, at ankle height at the base of the headstone, we read: 'Walk on air against your better judgement.' This sounds, perhaps especially for an atheist buried at the limits of a cemetery, like a version of Pascal's wager. Maybe heaven *is* available? But, as in many lines in many of Heaney's poems, the words on his headstone return upon themselves and caution against any single reading. There is dissent and acceptance at once: believe, then, although you are in doubt, take risks though you are cautious, leave where you are and head off – although you know this already to be your place.

It took him a long time, Heaney said in another poem, to credit marvels, and he was never really certain that he should. His poetry was always busy, as Coleridge said we all ought to be, keeping alive the heart in the head. That seems a journey enough from reason and fact. But the headstone words – walking from stoniness to air if they are to do their work – want to have it both ways: a sceptical faith is granted space while a project (the afterlife) gets a heavenly lift-off from what, on a grave, sounds perilously close to an angelic cliché.

The gravel, though, brings us down to earth. The aggregate below the text is more stonily direct – it is the sort of stuff we walk on more commonly than air – and the line makes bigger play in its source poem than as an epitaph: the stones in 'The Gravel Walks' (published in *The Spirit Level*, 1996) are as stony as they need to be. The Bellaghy area is rich in fine sands and gravel and much has been lifted from local beds: 'Pebbles of caramel, hailstones, mackerel blue … Gems for the un-deluded. Milt of earth.' The poem praises the motility of these stones – rocks that move, gravel walking – and the shuck and crunch of ballast, its quality as basic material, like the wayside flowers of 'A Herbal'. But as with the flowers (and as Heaney does in many poems), there is a further gathering, or an aggregation, of a locale and its nature and its people, a gathering that holds tight to the particular but sends it out far and wide (here it is sealed in rhyme and given as an appropriate, if contrary, idea – mobile mortar):

> So walk on air against your better judgement
> Establishing yourself somewhere in between
> Those solid batches mixed with grey cement
> And a tune called 'The Gravel Walks' that conjures green.

'The Gravel Walks' is an Irish reel. It walks and talks. It flows. Its end meets its beginning. It is lively. It grows. It goes around and it need never stop.*

A 'good poem', Heaney said in *Stepping Stones*, 'leaves you walking on air.' I recorded him for the radio once down a line from a Dublin studio. On

---

* *My passport's green*, Heaney wrote in 1983 in 'An Open Letter'. He meant Irish, but perhaps not only that.

air, his voice – his voice alone, nothing more, though nothing more was called for – arrived soft but strong, from under the Irish Sea to where I sat in a windowless cubicle in Bristol. Before we started, I'd asked him to move a little further back from his microphone to stop his plosives popping. Otherwise there was not much talk. He read and I recorded, listening to the poems filling my ears. I knew them in his voice already. Once heard, his poems speak only as he spoke, even when lying quietly on his pages. Still today, after his death, his books remain talking books.

He read some of his bog-body poems, 'The Tollund Man' and others. They sounded properly dark; his reading was flawless, and we were done in fifteen minutes. Another encounter marked the only time I caught his eye. He was beginning to speak a poem at an event in the British Library when my mobile phone started up into life. He looked up, towards where I stood in the audience as I fumbled and blushed. The poem, I think, was 'The Underground', one of two that he read when he was awarded the David Cohen Prize for Literature in the early spring of 2009. It is an underworld poem and orphic: Heaney recalls his honeymoon to London and being late for a Prom and running with his new bride up from the Underground towards the music at the Albert Hall. As they run, the buttons on Marie's 'going-away coat' spring off from it. Then, later, 'now', he goes back underground, alone, more darkly, re-tracing their steps and, like Orpheus, hoping that his wife is still with him, wanting to keep her, but not daring to look back.

For a time there was a Seamus Heaney exhibit at the Bellaghy Bawn. The film we watched there remains a treasured document, but other material has been moved across town to the new HomePlace. There, among the relics, are a desk and Heaney's schoolteacher's bag from his early working years. The HomePlace also has his sandy-brown duffel coat. It hangs empty and apparently floating in the boxed-in air of a clear-walled case. I've seen Emily Dickinson's ghostly white dress doing something similar in her upstairs room at the Homestead museum in Amherst, Massachusetts. Heaney's toggled duffel, outdoors garb now suspended indoors, struck me as sadder still, buried mid-air out of the light, a dead man's going-away coat brought only halfway home.

* * *

As I fished about at the graveyard in Bellaghy, trying to find where the line of poetry on Heaney's headstone came from, a loose paper fell out from one of my books. It was a cutting from the *New York Review of Books* from 2004 that I had kept folded in *Human Chain*. Heaney had published a poem there in memory of the poet Czesław Miłosz (who died that year) made out of the end of Sophocles' *Oedipus at Colonus*. 'What Passed at Colonus' is about a required departure underground: a last rite at a time of ripeness. At the end of his life, with his family crimes behind him, blind Oedipus must leave the lit world for a still-more-blind dark. He is called and he must go, stepping down to plough himself back into the earth where, like a spring in reverse, a stream goes under, as water will swim down a drain in a gutter or as a river in limestone sinks into a swallet or swallowhole. Oedipus takes leave of the living and steps downhill walking into his own grave. A strikingly active or operative geography is enacted as Heaney describes the beginning of this journey.*

> He walked to where the stream goes underground
> And a steep bank paved with flagstones
> Leads down to a lintel in the earthwork.
> And there he stood, studying what next,
> Between a stone cairn and a marble plaque
> To the dead of our late wars.
> Other wars and words were in my mind,
> Another last look taken upon earth –

---

* A similar – equally stirring – effect happened the first time I saw mourners and other visitors at the Vietnam Veterans memorial in Washington DC, disappearing as if into the earth, down the incline dug to house the name slabs, and able, there, to travel so far – half under – with the dead, whose names are listed on the stones that build the retaining wall of the cutting. It makes for an equality of the living and the dead: the extant must be temporarily buried alive in order to spend time with the extinct. Something there is also to be said here (amid talk of swallowholes) about the way that swallows and other hirundines fly so low over water sometimes that we can imagine them slipping beneath the surface where, as was long thought (including by Gilbert White, who never quite gave up the idea), they might sleep out the little death of each winter.

Roads shining after rain
Like uphill rivers – so that I all but
Wept for his loneliness.

The remembered (italicised) lines that Heaney adds to Sophocles are among the last words the poet Edward Thomas wrote in a notebook before he was killed at the Battle of Arras in April 1917.

How what is beneath marks and determines what lives above is a recurring theme for Heaney. Ways down and ways back up were for him a permanent circling-cycling subject, from the soil-fed 'Digging', the first poem in his first book (published 19 May 1966), to the final words he wrote. The last poem in his *New Selected Poems* is dated 18 August 2013 (he died twelve days later), and is for a young grand-daughter. 'In Time' imagines her future as a grown woman after Heaney has gone, while, 'for now', an old man and a toddler move to music across a floor, 'in step' and in touch with the earth: 'we foot it lightly / In time, and silently.'

Heaney's last ever writing, his son Michael said at his funeral, was a text message he sent to his wife minutes before he died while being taken down for surgery in hospital. Don't be afraid, he wrote in Latin: *Noli timere.* The words are in Matthew's gospel (14:27) in the Vulgate. Jesus' disciples, on board a boat in a storm, see him walking on the water towards them. They think he is a ghost, but he tells them it is just the man they know and they shouldn't be afraid.

If he could walk on water, they might walk on air.

It was just before the middle of the year when we visited Lough Beg in the footsteps of Heaney's *wildtrack*, and there were six summer-plumaged migrant black-tailed godwits in the shallows. They were wading up to their waists in the water and fed in the hidden mud by dipping their heads below the lough. Were these brick-red birds still on their way north and intent on breeding, or had they already turned south having failed in their mission? Either way, seeing them there, all bright and fresh yet half-submerged, they looked as if they were on hold, or remaindered, or out of time. It is hard to tell the status of such creatures as the year tips over from spring to autumn, from the becoming season to the ending one. Time is in everything living, but some life seems out of it. The godwits half-buried in the water looked like that. But, as we walked to and from the lough, skylarks kept up, above us, *persisting*, carolling through acres of damp sky over acres of dewed grass. And between the two, the wet air and the wet earth, a snipe, one little tossed sedge-brown rocket, went up and came down.

Highnam
52°N

24 April. Gloucestershire: a male song thrush hatched and fledged and grew in the wood here. In its first weeks it listened to all the music that came to it. In the winter it survived quietly among bare trees – its only talk a *seep* every now and then. The next spring, before the leaves appeared, daylight drilled into its head, such that in March it opened its beak as it never had before and for the first time in its life it sang. Its song was the same song its father had sung – the child had heard its parent sing and took up the same notes – but it was its own too and accented by other sounds that it lived amongst. Reaching into itself, it pulled out a music that was mostly song thrush but which gulped, at moments, just like the nightingale, which the thrush had heard the previous May. In April, the wood thickened with other songs and insects and leaves. One night, a male nightingale that knew the wood's shadows below it, for it had hatched there too, came down from the sky and began its own singing to mark its place and to coax any female that was following in the dark. In the time the thrush had kept to these trees, the nightingale had been beyond the middle of the world at the Equator. In the first creep of daylight as the nightingale sang on, it heard itself being sung by the song thrush. This voice-throwing, this mimicry, probably meant nothing to it – the nightingale stayed where it was and sang without changing its tune – but I heard both singers and both songs too and felt, as I worked out what was going on, how time opened all around me in the wood and how the

past ran back, from the path through the trees, and was made visible, as vivid and as sharp as the cuts that the singing birds were making at the morning air.

Roadwater
51°N

28 April. I walked with my cousin Tess for an hour from her house up a green valley at the edge of Exmoor. We hadn't gone out on a nature trail – we were talking, mostly about our sets of elderly parents, hanging on to their lives nearby – but as we went along field paths and high-banked lanes, we were florally instructed. Tess knows flowers better than me, and pointed out what we were passing: bluebells, green alkanet, yellow archangel, greater stitchwort (Star-of-Bethlehem), some early purple orchids next to some red campion, hart's tongue, some vetches, a small round-leafed fleshy plant on a dripping bank that Tessa knew to be a pennywort, and woodsorrel that we tasted for its apple flavour. I did the birds: three swallows, four chiffchaffs and the continuous sound of perhaps twenty-five singing blackcaps.

Nothing was special, but everything was timely, and as we walked alongside it as it sang or grew we were made happy in the day.

For the same reason I love the company of the naturalist's calendar that Leonard Jenyns kept through the middle of the nineteenth century in the neighbouring village to my sometime home in Cambridgeshire. I often carry it with me and read it like an almanac. I've dreamed of wrapping myself in it – a bivouac for the year. Species by species, and day by day, Jenyns recorded what was singing or flowering, laying eggs or fruiting, etc., etc. Year by year he calculated mean dates, earliest days and latest days. His printed list is a time-map: in the parish of Swaffham Bulbeck *this* happened *then* – all is told for hundreds of animals and plants. It is the true catalogue of a true green man.

Jenyns (who also had another name – appropriately – Blomefield) was offered the job as ship's naturalist on the *Beagle*, but suggested Charles Darwin should go in his place, preferring nature study closer to home. He also seems to have been wary of simultaneity and abundance in nature (the sort of experience that might be likely on a voyage to the tropics and beyond); his calendar shows him to prefer one thing after another rather than everything now. At school, the ardent young naturalist had come across Gilbert White's *Natural History of Selborne*, and was so impressed by the attentive acuity of the old parish observer that he copied out White's book in longhand, fearing he would never see it again. He wanted not to miss anything of it. And not missing anything – seeing how the world goes by being with it as it goes – is the heartfelt message of his sober list. To everything there is a season: Jenyns was a clergyman as well as a naturalist. He liked that thought, wanted to live with it, and he looked for evidence of it happening and he wrote it down.

At Roadwater, there is a home-made produce stall on the dead-end lane where everything sold benefits a cats' home. I bought something of last year's spring: a jar of raspberry jam. A handwritten label on the damson jam said it was *with stones*. Feeling good about seeds as well as fruit, I bought that too.

Caterham & Dulwich & Bristol
51°N

I loved to skip as a child. To skip along a path, not with a rope: to skip home ahead of my parents or around a school playground like a horse. To skip and find a spontaneity that felt more animal-like than any other motion: an upright fling, a series of crestings, a rhythmic quasi-musical crossing of the ground. It was a way to dance when running, and it was fast and warming and not tiring. It made you feel elated but it also made you laugh – I remember it somehow always tickling me. Whenever I have seen antelopes or gazelles displaying, by stotting or pronking, I am reminded of it still and can summon the sensation of that exuberant forward-travelling airborne stride, and the memory of being a child and of being in time. You can see the same in Vaslav Nijinsky (film survives of him dancing *Scheherazade* in 1910).

He skipped and stayed up there longer than anyone – *I merely leap and pause*, he said.

Occasionally, school classes of 'Music, Movement and Mime' allowed skipping, but it was never enough, and you weren't supposed to tear away out of the hall and across the whole world. And it was awkward too – I knew even at the beginning of my primary years that it wasn't boyish (in the same way, I soon learned the grown-up name for hop-skip-and-jump was triple jump because no one wanted to say skip). Girls did it arm-in-arm in duos or trios around the playground. But boys didn't. They had to lock shoulders in a phalanx, as if for a rugby scrum, and chant to collect followers: *Who wants to play – WAR?* The word was stretched and growled, for martial effect, to WHOR-ORR-ORRR!

But there was the maypole. We had one in my first school in Caterham in Surrey. Skipping was part of that. It was a sanctioned seasonal expression – you were to skip around the maypole full of the joys of spring. It was still girlish but it was good. In and out with a partner, you went, weaving or braiding the ribbon you held that was tied to the crown of the tree, until the net it made tightened and became like a cage or a nest, and drew you and all the dancers in towards the trunk, where the skipping had to stop. And then you began again, meeting the tune, and unwound, and someone else was ready to take the ribbon from you and everything started over again.

There wasn't much skipping in secondary school. The closest I got was in 1972 when, aged eleven, I danced in an all-boy ballet interpretation of *The Rite of Spring*. After my maypole school, I was sent for two years to Dulwich College, where only two good things happened: the Van de Graaff generator in the science building made my hair rebel and stand up on end (it was otherwise cut horribly – punitively – short, obeying school rules); and dancing to *The Rite*, when a group of twenty or so of us eleven-year-olds got all chthonic. The music was Stravinsky's. To me, at that age, it sounded more rocky than sexual. It had a stamping beat. But the steps we made were the choreography of a young teacher who knew more than his dancers. We were to dance Persephone's story. The resulting spectacle – two performances only – must have been the equivalent of watching a boys' choir singing the breaking of their voices without knowing what had possessed them.

On instruction, I borrowed a dark purplish bedspread from my mother as a sort of poncho or shroud that I was required on occasion to burst or sprout from. At one point, we spirits of new growth, emerging from the earth, had to reveal burning candles from under our shrouds; they were to flicker in our outstretched hands with the small but intense flame of a snowdrop or crocus or violet. My candle wobbled as I produced it and I spilled hot wax onto the back of my hand that burned and then crusted there, and, worse still, the flame flickered and went out. I was a dud. But before I could get too upset, the music took over and the scene changed and we had to stamp. This was before Pina Bausch and the Tanztheater Wuppertal had patented stamping and made their brilliant and definitive body-slapping, mud-slinging, nightie-wearing *Rite*. I liked our Dulwich stamping – it was the closest I'd been to skipping for a while; and even my singed eleven-year-old self recognised the power of a song of the earth, especially as I stomped it out.

Bohemia
49°N, but not ...

My final stop in theatre – this is all true* – was as the First Gentleman in Shakespeare's *The Winter's Tale* – his most spring-obsessed play – in a production in 1977 at my second secondary school. I was sixteen then. It was a small part, but I got a mention in a review in the school magazine, written by my English teacher whom, up until then, I had doted upon. Such, she wrote, was the woodenness of my performance that, when I appeared, the whole play was infected with a kind of theatrical dry rot.

---

* It is also true that the first dance I had with a girl at the first proper disco I went to as a teenager was to Blue Oyster Cult's 'Don't Fear the Reaper': *seasons don't fear the reaper*, they sing.

My character was one-third of the trio of on-stage reporters who appear in the fifth act to relate the finding of Perdita in Bohemia with some consequences of the discovery of her true identity as the daughter of King Leontes of Sicilia. We three functioned like those newspaper headlines spinning into focus that Hollywood movies used to employ. Time is moving on and the story must hurry towards its end. Passing business has to be described so that the next dramatic revelation can happen on stage. Time itself had already had a walk-on choric part in *The Winter's Tale*, collapsing – as time never does – sixteen years (the springtime of a life) in 'a swift passage' between Act III and Act IV. We gentlemen spoke in order to speed through some further minutes on the play's clock.

During the short run, both the Third Gent (it was Vince Lawlor) and I shared a cold and we stood on stage having spoken our lines while little globes of watery mucus gathered and then wobbled and then fell from the ends of our noses. Girls, from another school in Bristol, came to play the female roles and excited the dressing room and flustered our leading boys (we sniffling gentlemen knew our place). Otherwise, our production was a traditional one. We wore tights. We had slippers specially made with snail-curl toes. A bear-suit was ordered and severe directorial work was done to make its entrance as unfunny as possible.

My lines described part of the aftermath of what Antigonus was doing at the moment of his famous *Exit pursued*. The well-meaning Sicilian lord had laid the banished Sicilian royal baby, as yet un-named Perdita, on Bohemian soil rather than carry out King Leontes' orders to kill her. Alongside, he had left a 'fardel' of her papers (the documentation many refugees lose on their journeys), that would testify who the baby was – the legitimate daughter of Leontes and Hermione and not the bastard child, as the jealously deranged Leontes had believed, of his queen and Polixenes, the king of Bohemia. The baby survives but Antigonus doesn't. The Third Gentleman's report includes a gruesome and arresting line conjured by a novel preposition: 'He was torn to pieces with a bear.'

The talk of all of us more or less wooden gents was around the hinge or crux of the play that delineates stations in a human life, but which also describes the movements of circannual change. An elderly shepherd found the baby Perdita, while his son, called a clown (an old word for a peasant), witnessed the fatal bear attack and the simultaneous sinking of Antigonus' ship with the loss of all 'poor souls' on the (famous) sea coast of Bohemia. 'Thou met'st with things dying,' the father says to his son: 'I with things new-born.' And, from this moment, almost exactly halfway through the action (my Penguin edition has fifty pages before this line and fifty pages after it), *The Winter's Tale* becomes a play about the spring and the possibility of life growing from death. It does this by asking its world, and ours, to awaken its faith in cycles of natural change, including understanding ecological succession – how flowers follow others through the season – and to believe that if old branches can sprout green leaves, then stone statues might breathe with love.

'Blossom, speed thee well!' says Antigonus to the bundle that is the infant Perdita as he lays her on the earth. And much of the remainder of the play is about what happens in the spring or, to put it more humanly, about how spring works on people and on their *becoming* through time. Sixteen years from the fardel, Perdita is a young woman and embodies the season. At first, she is apparently as gauche as its first pale blooms. But she warms up (as her mother will do much later when her statuesque body comes alive). Women in Shakespeare regularly explain flowers to men, and Perdita is his most subtle of botanists. She speaks particularly affectingly of the flowers that token the beginning of spring at a time when they are no longer to be had.

The Bohemian sheep-shearing festival, in the play's fourth act, where Perdita appears as a kind of green woman or mobile bower, takes place in the middle of the year, right at the end of six months of spring. Dressed in flowers and *put-on foliage*, Perdita says she feels 'goddess-like pranked up'. Although she looks the part, she is unsure about playing the season, feeling not spring enough herself, lacking its truest flowers, and also unentitled, a 'lowly maid' to 'gracious' and

120

'high' Florizel, her boyfriend and Polixenes' son, who is here, under-cover himself.

Perdita is not la Bohème; neither does she yet know that, by birth, she is as aristocratic as Florizel. Her *becoming*-story makes for dénoue-ments and some unknotting of the drama. Across the long scene of cozening, dancing, rumpus and myth-mining, as well as the unfolding stories of high-born gardeners and the daughters and sons of the soil, much play is made around nature and nurture, flowering and deflower-ing, sex and death. There is also darkly plumbed talk about what we make of the meaning of spring – how it eats time far beyond the flower-arranging of pastoral, how rarely we feel the season ourselves, how often we are to one side of it, knowing it has gone before or is only to be had by others and elsewhere, and how we intuit that it can never be fully ours to hold on to or to live by. A blossom on the ground is already a (failed) fallen fruit: few signs so early in the season intimate its end. *Et in Arcadia ego.*

Perdita knows she is in floral drag, but also that she is physically in the springtime of her life. These two conditions – an embodiment and a body – do not quite rhyme, and a tender jarring sweetly clouds the day. Spring seems to bring forth elegies for a world that is still in the process of being born. A beginning is always the beginning of an end; we are dying from the moment we hatch. With such knowledge written into its life, the season struggles to be the simple author of itself: perhaps, the play suggests, it was invented by the autumn. At the end, which we will all get to, my tears certainly suggest something of this, coming as they do nowadays every time I see or read how various old-timers can get just a whisper of new life.

For a time, in Act IV, flower-power emboldens Perdita and armours her with a green florescence, like a floral clock or a kind of May Day hi-vis jacket: 'Sure this robe of mine', she says, '[d]oes change my dispo-sition.' She argues with the disguised King Polixenes about the mutu-ality or symbiosis of art and nature, and about dressing up. They are both, in fact, dressing down. He's hiding his kingliness and she has lived as a foundling, cared for by the shepherd and his family. Her suit for the day is bedecked in flowers, but she won't wear 'streaked gillyvors' because they are forced, unnatural hybrids, and tarted or 'painted' into beauty by human gardeners.*

Polixenes says all art derives from nature, but improves it, but Perdita – closer in years to nature than to art – is not impressed. He sounds to her like a grown-up defending the supposed wisdom of age while actually justifying its complacency. Dressed in her weeds, she sets to limning her flora, like a benign version of those terrifying Irish women who still sometimes attempt to buttonhole you on the street with lucky lavender. She hands Polixenes a bouquet of high-summer herbs, old men's flowers, 'rosemary and rue'. For middle-aged Camillo, she has mid-season blooms: '[h]ot lavender, mints, savory, marjoram ... marigold'. Then, although the spring has finished and its signature flowers are dead, she comes into herself, and speaks beautifully of those ground-breaking shows, no longer to hand, that she would, if she could, bestow on Florizel.

> I would I had some flowers o' th' spring, that might
> Become your time of day ...

As she continues with her hypothetical flower-gathering or *simpling*, everything is delicate and pale, yet all is underwritten by the darker subterranean surge of ancient stories. Shakespeare knew Arthur Golding's 1567 translation of Ovid's *Metamorphoses*. And Perdita transmits its sex–death power:

> O Proserpina,
> For the flowers now that, frighted, thou let'st fall
> From Dis's wagon! Daffodils,
> That come before the swallow dares, and take
> The winds of March, with beauty; violets, dim
> But sweeter than the lids of Juno's eyes

---

* The gillyvor, most likely, is the clove pink; it is described in Richard Mabey's modern herbal, *Flora Britannica*, as 'chief ancestor' of carnations, and was introduced to Britain, probably from southern Europe, by the Normans: 'Some traditional stations include the walls of the gents' toilet at Rochester Castle, Kent, and the remains of Beaulieu Abbey in Hampshire.'

Or Cytherea's breath; pale primroses,
That die unmarried ere they can behold
Bright Phoebus in his strength – a malady
Most incident in maids; bold oxlips and
The crown imperial; lilies of all kinds,
The flower-de-luce being one: O, these I lack …

Look again at the word 'take' in this speech. It is small and casual-seeming, but it holds a whole world: the wind that blows the daffodil, the daffodil that shows the wind, the time of both seen in a dozen words. It is close to a cliché, perhaps – flower-talk often is – but one that is true, like all good snapshots from nature, and one that feels seen for real. It is a field note made *with beauty*.

It is also sad, I think, or at least seasonally affected. Of all her flower talk, Perdita's report on early spring – on the flowers she lacks – moves us most. Hers is an after-the-event description of a desired now, a summoning of a time we hope will come again but which is already, and somehow always, in the past. And since we were all in the Arcadia of a first spring once, we all feel the loss and the *lack*.

Perhaps because it marked both the beginning and the end of my acting life, I've remembered most of my First Gentleman's lines. Every time I've seen or read the play since, and involuntarily often at other moments, the words gain on me like an auditory hallucination. I hear them in my head, moments before they must be said.

– *I was by at the opening of the fardel.*

It is like hearing the pre-echo or ghostly first bars of a song, before the actual sound, that could be caught sometimes when listening closely to vinyl records. You heard the cast of a sound waiting for its own body – an echo heard before its source. Something of this I hear in the way a woodlark sings, and in the way Perdita talks, so tactfully, of the spring flowers – she raises them before us, only to say that she cannot actually do that, as she lacks them, and they are dead already. This is like hearing a prompt from off stage for the season, something *sotto voce* or subterranean, the dead speaking of the life that they once lived. It is also itself prompt – an intimation of the right time coming at the right time, promptly. The spring lives like this for all of us grown-ups, I think. It is as much gone as it is here; it is as much going as it is coming.

This sadness is in the play. It's an old man's play. It's late. Despite its title it is actually an autumnal play about the spring. Hermione, revealed at the end – the statue that moves and is warm (neither petrified nor wooden) – is reborn to life with Leontes, but she hasn't begun again: she cannot; she hasn't been preserved – like all the other characters we've kept up with, Hermione, when hidden away, has got old. Crucially, wonderfully, warmly, humanly, she has got old and she has got wrinkled. In that is life.

Etna
38°N

'Comes over one an absolute necessity to move' – so goes D. H. Lawrence's opening sentence in *Sea and Sardinia*. His book describes a trip he took with Frieda, his wife, known to him then as the 'queen bee', in January 1921. They had been living in Sicily for almost a year, and left it for a week to visit Sardinia 'to see', as he wrote in a letter, 'if I should like to live there'. There was always movement in Lawrence's life – a constant need and desire for it – but it was always also awkward and challenging. The strange, involuntary but emphatic tension – a prevailing continuous present tense – of that first sentence captures and enacts something of Lawrence's travel bug. We feel him being impelled or swept up and we arrive with him mid-scene into the moment. He never called time on his affliction – his restlessness – nor did he ever succeed in turning his endless questioning into a fully viable answer, nor, therefore, did he ever come to a halt. He knew all this for himself, although not necessarily at the time he packed his bags or determined to: 'I suppose,' he wrote in a letter from Sicily at midsummer 1920, 'one carries one's own self wherever one goes. But one undergoes a metamorphosis also.'

26 April. Coming over us, the absolute necessity to move: airborne raptors – honey buzzards – were passing above our heads, dark and

angled forms, like scattered tiles pressed into the blue. They had assembled in the distance, materialising from the hulking grey shadows of Mount Etna and slow-beating their way over the intervening hills. We stood beneath their path, on a last ridge before the Strait of Messina. They all followed a road in the air, a route made in part by the wind that strung them together and steered them onwards, and in part by the needle of their own internal compass that gave them a sense of direction.

– *Falco!*

We had learned what to shout within moments of arriving at the spring migration camp on the hilltop. There were a dozen watchers from half a dozen countries looking keenly overhead. Claire and I had joined them for a couple of days to watch the life of the skies and to make a small contribution to some air-traffic control by shouting out some numbers.

Sicily is on the mid-Mediterranean flypath. Honey buzzards that have wintered in Africa and want to get to eastern Europe and western Russia to breed must fly across Sicily. Birds only step this way that can manage a considerable sea crossing. Leaving the African shore at Tunisia or Libya, they must fly over sea, some pass over Malta, then more sea, then fly the length of Sicily, then jump the last sea at the Strait of Messina, and then make European continental landfall in Calabria.

The camp intends to see the birds on their way and take note of their details. A dog-Latin had grown up between the watchers. Birds' scientific names were used to call them out as they appeared, and their position was then described in pidgin-Italian.

Anna Giordano started these waiting-and-watching sessions thirty-five years ago. I talked to her as we scanned. The camp began as a way of 'repressing' some of the illegal, though then commonplace, shooting of birds of prey in Sicily. When Anna was fifteen, in April 1981, she was offered two dead kestrels by a party of huntsmen, as an intimidating first-blood present.

– It was terrible to know – to learn about birds in that way. In Calabria they even eat the honey buzzard. And here they were shooting everything.

Since the 1980s Anna has worked 'to control the mountains'. She began by putting people between the guns and the birds.

– We had to hide our binoculars. They followed us with guns. So we had to carry guns as well, to camouflage ourselves.

Other migrants follow this route as well as raptors. As we spoke, Alpine swifts, common swifts and a yellow telegram of four golden orioles zipped along the ridge, heading for mainland Italy.

– The hunters dig bunkers or hide in old ones from the war. We had walkie-talkies, but the hunters were coming into our radio channel. We had German volunteers, but we couldn't use German because the hunters had been to Germany as guest workers, so we had to use Arabic.

Ten bee-eaters came, and another five golden orioles (three males together), and then an Eleonora's falcon, double quick. The deliberateness of all the movement was exciting to see; you sensed the commitment. The falcon seemed to open up the morning air, and after it, the raptors started flowing.

– *Falco!*

We were one thousand metres up at Dinnammare on the eastern side of the wooded spine of hills that run above Messina. A booted eagle went north, and then the honey buzzards began, six, then five, then two, then six, then twenty, then six, then thirty. Small heads, long tails, a reptilian marquetry about the barring of their breasts – 400 passed over in the first two hours we were there. Singles came sometimes and then flocks. Once a flock of fifty-one. The visible effort they put into their flying was such that it made you want to get out of their way.

I lay on my back for an hour. Part of me was a child again – lying like this, and looking up at the sky, always takes me back: perhaps I remembered my pram; perhaps it was a view I had more often in boyhood; perhaps when you are shorter you are more aware of life happening above you. I watched the sky and thought of all the springs and all the honey buzzards that had gone this way. Some puffy clouds toppled over me, and that strange falling feeling came of an upward vertigo, though I knew myself cradled by the earth beneath me. Honey buzzards appeared; they beat their wings but they seemed to be shifted by the sky itself, as if rather than travelling through it they were travelling with it, flowing with it and drawn by it at once. The passage ran like a tide and I thought I could feel the tow.

The moon, half of it, showed in the sky as thirty honey buzzards went over.

– A honeymoon!

We exchanged words in all our languages for the same, keeping our binoculars to our eyes. Three marsh and two Montagu's harriers passed, and four common buzzards.

Etna was away to the south of us but still huge. Its bulk had a scale and a constancy all to itself, as if its world was measured differently. The mountain speaks 'a true *Language*' – Coleridge wrote in a note of 1804 when he sailed the Mediterranean and thought of Etna. Today, its snowfields and lava runs appeared to smoke as the sun worked over them. At moments the whole mountain was magnified and hugely present just beyond the next ridge; then it slipped off into the African distance; never was it anything other than total.

If you are tectonically minded, Etna lies not in Sicily but at the top of Africa. The volcano sits above where the African Plate meets the European Plate. This is where the continents run into one another. There is a volcano there for that reason. In these terms, this ground truth, the honey buzzards we saw coming from Etna towards us were at that moment passing from Africa to Europe.

The winds, Anna said, were shifting.

– They will be taking a lot of different roads from now.

Two female Montagu's harriers were followed by a female pallid harrier. All appeared to be being steered from behind. I tried to cement my wobbly knowledge regarding the separation of these species. The pallid was slightly bulkier with more two-tone underwings – dark secondary coverts and paler wing-tips. It worked when I was there; beneath them, then I was sure.

We kept on looking. Anna's eyes were bloodshot. Administering the camp takes its toll. She has hunter-enemies too. She has kept the shoe of a man she had fought with on catching him uninvited in her room. He'd been sent, she said, as a frightener. Every month or so, some threatening message is left for her; once a fire was set in four places around her house. She was only saved by 'my father', she said, pointing to the sky. I wasn't sure if she meant a divinity, or the brilliant blue, or the buzzards.

I asked her about the human migrants from sub-Saharan Africa forced to camp in ghettos and shanties around Catania not far below where we were.

– All Sicily is a mess, she said, looking up again.

She preferred New Zealand.

– Auckland is so clean – you can walk barefoot there.

Honey buzzards are easier to think about, perhaps. Very few passing migrant raptors actually land on Sicily. And they make no mess.

Two young women arrived with trays of local strawberries – small, dark and sweet – as a reward for our counting. We dabbed them in the *zabaglione* of cloud that Etna was pushing our way. Bee-eaters came above us. Twenty-five, then twenty, then another twenty-five. One flock cut a rope of honey buzzards. Bee-time is the thing: when there might be bees or their grubs to be eaten, then the birds of spring can come.

27 April. A south-east wind forced a change of scene, and we headed to the grey pumice beach and the old lighthouses on the north-east tip of Sicily at the Strait of Messina. It is only three kilometres from here to the mainland of Italy, but the crossing is hard going. Storks were struggling above the whipped-up sea: four whites and then four blacks, and then another five blacks. They looked like sailors' sheets slapping in the wind. The same wind had stolen a balloon shaped like a mermaid from a child's hand and was hurtling the little shrimp across the strait. An inadvertent awkward squad of six little egrets – too close to one another at one moment, blasted apart at the next – had to take evasive action to avoid colliding with it, they didn't really have any spare energy for emergency procedures. A booted eagle made a start on the sea crossing but was blown back. Yelkouan shearwaters were doing better on their home territory, but even they were beaten about by the shifting wind. As they sheared to steer into the channel, their pale undersides took the sunlight and made them look like the splash of a wave. A female pallid harrier worked the same run of water. The browns and

whites of the landbird and of the seabirds slipped and passed between them. The harrier and the shearwater: named for their efforts on the wing, here up against it.

We were on the beach at four in the afternoon, watching another female pallid harrier commit itself to the crossing and pulling a lesser kestrel with it, when news came through on people's mobiles that the hunting season in Malta had been suspended earlier than expected. There were some Maltese birdmen visiting Anna. They had been campaigning in a referendum on the island. It had failed to secure a real end to the entrenched persecution of all birds there, but a compromise had been offered, with hunting permitted only if no protected species were shot.

– They shot cuckoos and nothing happened, but today a kestrel was hit and the body fell into a schoolyard, and so perhaps now the killing season will close.

There were cheers and applause on the beach. Anna kept her eyes high. Two Eleonora's falcons and a hobby hurried out to sea. A sand martin hurtled past as well. There were probably guns waiting on the other side, but at least the migrants were alive when they left her watch.

1 May. The next day we went to Etna, but it appeared to be shut.

First, we drove, tumbling upwards, in Sicilian *autostrada* chaos: the local speciality, where a multi-lane highway turns a bend or passes through a tunnel and becomes a single-track country road. Near the end of the civic tar, Vulcan's replaced it, with a trench cut for access through the black-snow of the lava that had smothered an old route. Then there was a car-park and the white stuff itself, snow patches on the anthracite black, and, in a snapped-off pine at the snow-line, a cuckoo calling. The climb had taken us from a Mediterranean landscape to a Nordic or Icelandic one. We were under the same sky but had come to a dark place.

It was hard to imagine anything making a living thereabouts. The cuckoo sounded insane. Standing in the raw, stony spread of a lava field there is no earth to be seen. There is nothing green or any crumb of soil. You are on Earth but, you realise, you are without it.

We followed an old ox-cart route once used to take tourists towards the top. The peak was shrouded, clouded or smoking or both: it could have been a cooling tower, a steam bath, a fog factory, a hell vent; I didn't see it unobscured all day. In a scraggle of totem-pole trees that hadn't been swept away or turned into matches by the last lava run, there were coal tits and firecrests. Tiny birds with brave little names, denoting the elementary life that must be lived on a volcano. Each made of bonfire colours. Each with whisper calls like little fuses.

Black prevails otherwise on the volcano. Everything has been burnt: Etna (it encourages these catastrophic anti-lists) is its own shroud, wrecking yard, swarf bin, and slag-heap. It has one story only – its own – like a black hole, like an ocean, like the Sahara. In August 1804, Coleridge saw some powdered lava and thought it a marvel: 'for it exactly resembles the Dross-dust before a Forge Door'. The world has been worked over and is here done in. No matter how high we climbed, it seemed we were still in the outskirts of some perpetual *Zona Industriale* that had begun at the rusty seaside in Catania and surrounded us all the way up to the top. It is all outskirts, Etna, a daggle-arsed mountain, dragged in its own dirt, its own acid reflux, its own landfill.

Yet the strangest of all reconnoitrings to be made is that Etna is not the end of the world but its beginning. Once, I walked the length of the island of Surtsey off Iceland, which was born from the sea in 1964, but the lava on Etna where we were was younger still; I have never stood on anything younger on the planet. But what a baby-face! I got on my knees to try to love the new world close up, to conceive of its future, as it were, as alive, as soil, as a green tomorrow. Down towards the sea, fields of old lava grow vines and apricots and other favoured fruits. But on these higher slopes that is unimaginable. The lava is the new-born insides of the earth, yet it appears not as a child, or as a future, but as afterbirth, as leftovers, as slag. Even the tinkle or rattling metallic clatter the stuff makes, when you kick a lump of it, suggests an item exhausted and done with. It is cooked. It is the end of a Marmite jar. It is the old, old crumbs that have been toasted a thousand times at the bottom of my toaster, and which, flushed every six months from the machine, are spurned by my garden birds on their feeding table.

130

We walked on, crossing lava that had flowed in 1614. It was bare. Moon-clinker. Shakespeare had written *The Winter's Tale* and *The Tempest* in 1610–11. He died in 1616. Etna had flowed and the lava had run between those years. It was warm down there: the rock is still cooling, and its ashy black takes the sun and adds it to the heat of the Earth's core. On a few lava spreads, there were occasional lichen stains of grey-green rust: 'like mould on blackberry jam' said Mary Taylor Simeti in her Sicily book, *On Persephone's Island*. Otherwise, there was nothing else growing. Lava scratched at my hands and knees and tore at my soles. It hurt. Even in hiking boots it was like walking barefoot.

A bar in the top car-park was throwing a country-and-western party with a band of fiddle-players and a pedal steel guitarist: May Day on Etna. Some confused Sicilians, wearing cowboy hats and cowboy boots, were dancing. No one looked fully comfortable or appeared at home. I wondered if Empedocles might have stood for a while and watched the same. Empedocles on Etna: the miserable Sicilian-Greek thinker who could no longer feel any joy in life and who is famous for having pitched himself headlong into the volcano's crater in 434 BCE. He would have passed the car-park on the way to his launch pad.

Matthew Arnold, troubled and self-tormenting Victorian poet, was drawn to Empedocles and wrote a long dramatic-poem about him. He saw in the ancient suicide a reflection of his own thwarted happiness, his ambitions that had come (he thought) to nought, and his sense of failure. In middle age, wrote Arnold of his alter-ego, Empedocles finds his 'spring and elasticity of mind are gone: he is clouded, oppressed, dispirited, without hope and energy'.

It is spring itself that Arnold's Empedocles overlooked: he lived it but it passed him by; at a time when he should have been alive to the present, he was dreaming of an unattainable future. Worse still, he half-knew how wrong he was:

> Is it so small a thing
> To have enjoy'd the sun,
> To have lived light in the spring,
> To have thought, to have done …

By the time he realises the answers to these queries, it is too late. Arnold's poem focuses on the philosopher's pitch-black depression, and tracks him up the volcano and, to a last resort, into the black hole of its crater: 'Receive me, save me!' is Empedocles' cry as he jumps into the 'sea of fire'.

Etna was a perfectly awful landscape for Empedocles. The mountain is like a cast of his damaged mind, a sort of Mount Rushmore for his interior bleed. It makes a backdrop, a black-drop, to his mood, this springless place, 'this charr'd, blacken'd, melancholy waste', as Arnold puts it. But Etna also lives at its smelting heart, and the furnace in the crater might, Empedocles thinks, be a place to begin again, to burn up into something new; that is why Empedocles jumps. 'Oh that I could glow like this mountain!' he says.

Maybe mountains get the philosophers they deserve. Or philosophers, the mountains. No other mountain moves as much as an active volcano. Etna went to Empedocles as well as he to it. Both tramped about. Having written his poem, Matthew Arnold, frozen rather than cooked as a poet, suppressed it – 'jettisoned' is Ian Hamilton's choice term – believing it too 'morbid'. And – like a body moving through a glacier – Empedocles as a poem was hidden for years and only surfaced decades later.

One of the ancient tellings of the Empedocles legend records that, although he finished himself off by diving into Etna's crater, intending to vanish without trace, the volcano had other ideas, and coughed back up one of his flip-flops.

The Valle del Bove below the crater on the eastern side of Etna is perhaps the worst place. It is a vast dead tongue of lava, seven kilometres long and four kilometres wide. It lolls in the ashen mouth of the mountain, a deadly black glacier reaching its dry lick down towards the sea. It is scored with deep grey-brown-black gouges that claw at its black flesh. Nothing grows there. It seems a vast NO. We sat on a sharp ridge to the south of the Valle and looked on in horror.

Then we saw a black redstart on a lava tuft: it looked like a midget astronaut stranded on Mars, but was, it turned out, a perfect volcanic bird, ashy all over apart from the hot throb of its glowing tail which pulsed like molten lava breathes. And then a robin sang, red breast stirring, from a beech sapling behind us that had just come into leaf, a brave green thing that had made it up the slopes and found enough to root into. And swifts came silently, combing the air above the lava tongue, and then, above them all, five honey buzzards pulled themselves north, over everything. A lava-black raven flew up towards the raptors, moving as if it was the owner of the sky; the honey buzzards shifted a little but carried on.

West of Etna, 150 kilometres into the interior of Sicily, we walked for a day on light karst limestone (another rocky cemetery, for sure, but far easier going), hiking up and down, and into and away from, the season, at Pizzo Carbonara, the highest mountain in the Madonie range (its peak is at 1,979 metres)

The sky was bright and galloped hard all day. We started off in spring. On the green floor of a wood of cork oaks there were man orchids and flowering ghost-white asphodels; in the scrub at the wood edge, turtle doves purred and a cirl bunting threw back its yellow head to address the yellow sun, full on.

As we climbed, we travelled against the season and back in time: to baby leaves unfolding, to blossom, to buds, to bare winter branches. We were walking up through the southernmost beeches in Europe. The trees grow in swallowholes or *dolina* depressions on the hillsides. Soil accumulates there that is otherwise rare: between these stands were slopes of shattered rock. Much old snow still lay on the hill. Around the base of some of the beech trunks it was deeper than my boots, but the trees' growing tips had new unfolding leaves that had been wooed from out the bud. Many had only just shucked off their chrysalis casings and their leaves were still soft and droopy. The spent casings lay thick beneath the trees; you could see the subtle pinkish-yellow interior of these, like a soft leather glove. A party of rock buntings had found some knocked-down buds on the snow and pecked at them, part unfurling the tight-wrapped green flag of the leaf within to eat it. Below every leafing tree were also some new leaves that had already been dashed down. On the white snow they looked as green as green could be. It was sad to see them dead in life. I took more photographs than I needed.

Above the snow flew a raven, some hooded crows and a coal-black dive-past of choughs. Then, in a sun-warmed thawed-out clearing, we came upon a hummingbird hawkmoth moving from one dwarf purple flower to another. Sand crocuses, I think they were, *Romulea columnae*. Wearing its padded overcoat, looking as if it had been cut from a tiny carpet, the moth unwound its tongue and drank deep from each purple trumpet. There was a wren, a chaffinch and a blackbird too: bird familiars of lowland England are upland species here.

Close to the summit the beeches shrank back to bushes, not trees. Above 1,765 metres – Claire checked her watch – all the leaves were still locked in their cases. But a blackbird sang from a corrie of snow. And a small tortoiseshell appeared at our side and twenty-five bee-eaters – migrants all surely – fizzed their fizz over a cairn at the peak. The chough flock were excited by the multi-coloured parade. The bee-eaters' purr from 300 metres was like the hawkmoth's at three centimetres. There were two female northern wheatears – migrants also, but perhaps destined to stay and breed high up here – finding flies in the ice. Insects had been frozen into it on a colder day and then thawed by today's sun. The wheatears were the same dirty piss colour as the snow.

From the top, we could see Etna to the east, preposterously large despite the kilometres, and, down below us, we could see the lush green interior, where the spring was flat out, the one vast joined *campo* that is Ceres' plain. From the summit, we walked back down towards it, travelling three months in an hour, through the song of three woodlarks, a firecrest, and two chiffchaffs. After the snow had ended there were orange-tip butterflies everywhere. At the foot of the mountain, two elderly men, out botanising from Palermo, were kneeling to a bank of orchids. They shared their finds: a dwarf yellow flower no one could name, and a not much bigger sombre bee orchid, *Ophrys fusca*, with a pale green-yellow flower that was apparently being visited by a nosy bee – fabulous mimicry done in deep velvety purple with a mesmerising three-dimensionality in the soft fret of the flower-lip.

When we got to the plain, honey buzzards came over the green fields. They flew lower than they had over the lava, as if they sensed the ground beneath them was friendlier. At a quarter past seven in the evening came five, then six, then fourteen birds, all knowing where they were going, all flying north-east in a ragged train. There were nightingales installed in the scrub beneath the buzzards. I thought they sang louder as the shadows of the raptors passed over them.

I wanted to see Enna. The town is near the middle of the green plain. Enna has long been known as 'the navel' of Sicily. And I wanted to see Lake Pergusa nearby, where Persephone was abducted into the underworld. Pergusa is a place where we could say that the spring was born. We have the seasons because of a deal struck nearby. Ovid located his version of the spring-story here; Milton in *Paradise Lost* followed suit:

> that faire field
> Of Enna, where Proserpin gathring flours
> Her self a fairer Floure by gloomie Dis
> Was gatherd, which cost Ceres all that pain
> To seek her through the world.

Persephone's story explains spring's coming and going. She was Demeter's daughter. Zeus was her father. Every agricultural culture around the ancient Mediterranean imagined a narrative – a vegetation myth – to explain the natural phenomena of the seasons; every farmer had need of a Persephone. There are multiple stories about her, many associated with vegetation and spring growth and her life as a chthonic deity, and many associated with – the opposite of that – her queenly rule in the wintry death-lands of the underworld. She was also known as Kore. The Romans called her Proserpina.

Demeter was the goddess of corn. Enna was one of the ancient homes of the cult of Demeter. As Demeter's child, Persephone was the daughter of fertility herself. Demeter is Ceres in Roman myth. In Roman times, the surrounding plain was known as the greenest place in the most fertile island in the Mediterranean. It was a breadbasket. A loaf, bright yellow with maize flour, is still baked in Enna today.

Persephone became the hostage bride of Hades when he, the over-lord of the underworld, abducted and raped her and then made her his queen. Hades was her uncle, her father's brother. He was also known as Pluto and as Dis. He snatched her from near Enna at the lake at Pergusa when she was in a meadow picking flowers (*simpling* like Perdita in *The Winter's Tale*). Seeing a narcissus covered in a hundred fragrant blooms, she had wandered away from her companions. As she reached for the flower, the earth around her tore apart, as if ploughed up from beneath, and there was Hades in a tractor from hell, a golden chariot pulled by four black horses. She screamed, abandoned her posy, and was taken below to be herself deflowered.

This is a story of the fall. The end of spring was born at that moment when Persephone and her flowers were dashed down; seasonal change was effected there and then. The agricultural year was also set going. At Enna, prior to Persephone's kidnap, it was like Eden before the apple: 'continuall spring is all the yeare there founde,' said Ovid (in Arthur Golding's translation). Afterwards, spring would come as just one part of the annual seasonal round.

One bright day in early spring, on a wet flash of green *fynbos* studded with new flowers in a valley floor in the Kogelberg mountains, east of Cape Town, I watched a troop of baboons picking blooms and digging bulbs. They walked on all fours, using both their hands to tear at the greenery before them, passing tiny yellow-petalled flower-heads from their fists to their mouths and scrabbling in the sandy soil to unearth a root or a bulb. They foraged alone (even the babies were picking at the vege-tation), but in a scatter and with an intention that suggested a family outing – a shaggy array of them spread attentively across the green, each occupied with their own feed, but each aware of the joined troop. There are leopards here too and the baboons were on their guard. For an hour I watched them picking flowers and moving together and apart. As the afternoon lengthened, the sun came strong and low into the valley and it lit the dusty fur of the animals' heads and backs, giving them all golden manes. I saw then a whisper of our earliest days, and I wondered how Persephone might have looked as she bent to the fair field at Enna and picked her plants; we all once must have gathered in this way at the green.

Looking for her daughter and failing to find her, Demeter abandoned her normal role as goddess controller of all crops and vegetation. She searched for Persephone, day and night, dipping two pine trees into the flames of Etna and carrying them as torches. The growing season failed – continual spring was to be replaced by continual winter – and famine would have prevailed had not Zeus taken steps. He sent Hermes to persuade Hades to release Persephone. Hades agreed, he would share custody of Persephone with Demeter, but he tricked Persephone and made her eat some pomegranate seeds, with the consequence that she could not permanently leave the underworld for the world of light and had to divide her time and 'parteth equally the yeare between them both' (Ovid, via Arthur Golding). So it is that our year is split in two, and that seeds must do the same, must lie dormant in the dark and cold winter soil; so it is that warmth and light come back in the spring; so it is that the underground breaks out and grows green.

Such legends have shaken and stirred all interpretations for the seasons of the year, but they have also sponsored explanations for the tides and times of human life. As well as being about the getting of greenery, the story of Persephone is about her own growth and emergence. Demeter as a mother is forced to contemplate the passing of her own spring and to consider her daughter growing up and replacing (or even becoming) her. In losing Persephone, her mother is discovered as out of step, and unable to share the daughter's (forced) rite of passage. 'Flowers are fucked into being, between sun and earth,' said Lady Chatterley's lover in D. H. Lawrence's novel. Paradoxically Persephone comes into her own springtime as the victim of Hades: she is fucked into being between the earth and the underworld further beneath it.

Downstairs for half the year, living like a hostage who comes to identify with her captor, Persephone darkened and toughened. As queen of the underworld – often depicted crowned with a wreath of asphodels, totemic flowers of the death zone – she had great power as arbiter over the fates of the dead who had been sent down to the halls of Hades.

Most had to be, and remain, dead, but some she could *undead*. She was not always hard-core; every mortal was destined to come under her jurisdiction, but she and Hades permitted some returns to the upper world. It was Persephone who held sway when Orpheus sought to spring his dead wife, Eurydice.

The *gloomie* message is that it has to be like this. Persephone's story is like a *Lehrstück*, a learning-play: it tells us how things are. We learn it as we live it: perpetual spring couldn't work; a little death, a winter shutdown, an after-dinner sleep, is part and parcel of life; 'the best way out is always through', as Robert Frost had it in a poem. So, be prepared. *Ere your spring be gone, injoy it.* Know what you've got before it goes. But know that there is no true getting to be had. No real purchase on those pretty flowers. And, don't spend too much (time or effort) either. Winter needs to be kept alive in order for spring to follow. Above all, know that *you grow old while I tell you this*: that there is only one spring for all of us on Earth, *the brief span of life forbids our opening any long account with hope*, and *those who cannot use the present are not wise*.

Three of the great traveller-writers to Sicily made extra preparations – telling ones – for their spring pilgrimages to and from the island.

Before he left Messina with Frieda to go to Sardinia for a week in January 1921, D. H. Lawrence packed in a little bag what he called his *kitchenino*. It helped them eat in a pinch, and Lawrence preferred to cook rather than dine out; it and its contents are mentioned several times in *Sea and Sardinia*:

> Methylated spirit, a small aluminium saucepan, a spirit lamp, two spoons, two forks, a knife, two aluminium plates, salt, sugar, tea – what else? The thermos flask, various sandwiches, four apples and a little tin of butter.

Before he left England in early 1804, Coleridge made a list of what he needed for his travels to Gibraltar, Sicily and Malta.

138

A Jacket & Hood to fit on to my green Bag/to sleep in.
Umbrella –
Pencils for presents –
Portable Soup. Mustard

He also took a pair of green-tinted spectacles to be able to look better at the Mediterranean sun and not be dazzled by its light.

Goethe travelled in Italy between 1786 and 1788. His bag was important to him too. He was in Sicily for the spring of 1787, from March to the middle of May. He was especially interested in the botany and geology of the island. Have a look at Etna only from a distance, he was told: 'If you are wise, you will let others tell you about the rest.' He did as he was advised and didn't climb the lava (he had already gone up Vesuvius – a 'shapeless heap'). But even at lower altitudes, tourism was not easy. In Sicily, Goethe made do with a sort of sleeping-bag-cum-portable-mattress. He had been loaned a 'large leather bag' and in Caltanissetta on 28 April he was forced to fill it with chaff to make his own bed. It proved a 'godsend'. In Catania on 2 May, he had another bad night: 'Our sleeping quarters was so uncomfortable that we seriously thought of having recourse again to Hackert's leather bag.'

Goethe was unimpressed by Enna. He had admired the surrounding plain – the Granary of Italy, so called – and the lowland green: '24 April. I swear that I have never in my whole life enjoyed such a vision of spring as I did at sunrise this morning.' By the time he got to Enna, however, it was raining; and the wet (no matter that it was good for the greenery) underlined the mismatch between the place as imagined and the place as experienced:

The ancient Enna gave us a most unfriendly welcome – a room with a plastered stone floor and shutters but no windows, so that either we had to sit in the dark or put up with the drizzling rain, from which we had just escaped. We consumed some of our remaining provisions, spent the night in misery and took a solemn vow never to let ourselves be tempted again on our travels by a mythological name.

Ten kilometres south of Enna, Pergusa still looks as Ovid described it. It is not obviously a dramatic place. The lake sits in a shallow volcanic basin rimmed with woods:

> Trees encircling it
> Knit their boughs to protect it
> From the sun's flame.
> Their leaves nurse a glade of cool shade
> Where it is always spring, with spring's flowers

(Ted Hughes' lines in his re-telling of 'The Rape of Proserpina' in his *Tales from Ovid*). When we were at the lake it had just rained – a curtailed roll of thunder and a swift cloud dump – and the trees looked heavy-leafed and dark. At the wood's edge there were asphodels – timeless death veg: tall, ghost-grey flowers with sickly milk-green leaves. Nearby, towards the shore, an old man was gathering wild asparagus, pulling bunches from the ground – green tops, blanched root stems – and stowing them in a plastic carrier bag. Out on the open water, beyond the green spears of new reeds, was a pair of black-necked grebes, birds made of soot and of gold. Looking like uniformed doormen of an upmarket nightclub, they swam head-on towards one another, with a perky posture, jet-black heads, blood-red eyes, and a sheaf of dazzling golden corn tufting their cheeks, like extravagant makeup.

Pergusa is today a race-track *autodromo*. The lake is roundish and surrounded by a multi-lane paved circuit. Cars – low-slung, finned, souped-up – were tearing along. The five-kilometre loop took them about three minutes. We watched an assortment of machines going nowhere fast. It all seemed germane: here was life being clocked, here was a race to run, here was a flower-picker, here were bouncers or gatekeepers, and here were tractors from hell, burning fuel, eating the sun, exhausting everything.

You couldn't cross the tracks. A high fence kept everyone, apart from the drivers and their mechanics, from the circuit and the lake beyond. The water at Pergusa is brackish apparently. It appears to neither arrive into the lake nor leave it. It sits like an unblinking dark eye. The men at the trackside, and some others standing at the fence, including the man with his bag of asparagus, looked at the racing cars with glances similar to how they might once have looked at a woman.

Taormina
38°N

On a bus ride he took, with Frieda and their *kitchenino*, into the Sardinian interior in January 1921, D. H. Lawrence made an observation about the nature of Italian landscapes:

> the wildest country is half humanised, half brought under. It is all conscious … Wherever one is, the place has its conscious genius. Man has lived there and brought forth his consciousness there and in some way brought that place to consciousness, given it its expression, and, really, finished it. The expression may be Proserpine, or Pan, or even the strange 'shrouded gods' of the Etruscans or the Sikels, none the less it is an expression. The land has been humanised, through and through: and we in our own tissued consciousness bear the results of this humanisation. So that for us to go to Italy and to *penetrate* into Italy is like a most fascinating act of self-discovery – back, back down the old ways of time.

A letter to Compton Mackenzie, now lost, from December 1919 from Lawrence said that he had been driven from England by the 'melancholy of elms'. That wasn't the whole story, but in March 1920, Lawrence and Frieda rented a house for a year (initially) at Taormina between Catania and Messina in Sicily. While finding it he stayed at the nearby Hotel Bristol, which he liked. In one of his first letters from their new home, he reported 'a great V of wild fowl wavering north up the straits – *Heimweh*, or nostalgia then, for the north: yet I am wavering South.'

Lawrence liked the feeling of living at the edge, of getting away, away certainly from the centre: 'one hop, and you're out of Europe: nice that'. But, though he became a resident, he was really a long-staying tourist, and one of many. For the rest of his life his idea of home was vexed. In eastern Sicily, there were numerous wintering foreigners along the strait, snow-birds like him, from the north, including 'a parterre of English weeds'. He wrote satirically about them, but he also felt the same towards local people: 'frail streaming contact is what I like best: not to know people closely'.

Their house, the Villa Fontana Vecchia, had its back to Etna, and Lawrence never climbed the mountain, but he felt its presence throughout his stay in Sicily. He drank Etna wine, characterised the mountain as a person ('He puffs flame at night, and smoke by day'), and reported its snow cover to his correspondents. Spring came early that year and Lawrence was amazed: 'It is beautiful, and green, green, and full of flowers.' As almond blossom gave way to peach blossom, he detailed in letters the succession of plant-life – its press up through the earth – like various postcards from paradise. He wanted to believe that he had been delivered from, or stepped out of, the supposed 'world', which he contained in inverted commas, and had joined the real one, without borders, where we (and the snakes and the fruit trees) might live better lives. For a time, at least, spring in Sicily facilitated that dream:

Beautiful flowers are out. There is a tiny blue iris as high as your finger which blooms in the grass and lasts a day. It is one of the most morgan-schön [sic] flowers I have ever seen. The world's morning – that and the cyclamen thrill me with this sense. Then there are the pink gladioli and pink snapdragons and orchids – old man and bee and bird's nest. Sicily seems so fascinating in the interior. If I can only get some money and finish this novel I shall walk into the middle of it.

He never finished anything such that he managed the interior – neither Enna nor Pergusa, nor anywhere else. He was writing all the time in Sicily. *The Lost Girl* and *Mr Noon* were written in 1920 as well as his *Psychoanalysis and the Unconscious*. *Women in Love* was published, and much of his correspondence is taken up with rights and agents and editions and editors. Instead of travelling he worked on books, painted his bookshelves 'bright green', ate *nespoli* from the garden, and noted the Sicilians grew wheat, semi-shaded, under olive trees.

It got hot quickly. By early May the earth was 'terribly dry', spring was spent and time seemed awry:

It is strange how it is September among the earth's little plants, the last poppy falling, the last chicory flower withered, stubble and yellow grass and pale autumn-dry earth: while the vines are green and powerful with spring sap, and the almond trees, with ripe almonds, are summer, and the olives are timeless. Where are we then?

As the heat increased, he spent all day in his pyjamas, barefoot. He looked at Etna from afar and wrote a poem featuring cold lava that was solid and hot lava that he compared to a snake. He also wrote his magnificent 'Snake' poem, with a real animal in it, which drank from a water-trough ('my water-trough') and then disappeared into a 'black hole'. Lawrence's pyjamas feature as well. His flower poems from this time on Sicily denote miraculous appearances too and make a botanical–phenological diary of his year: 'Bare Fig-Trees', 'Bare Almond-Trees', 'Almond Blossom', 'Purple Anemones' (the flowers Persephone brought up from hell, little 'caves of darkness' on 'the meadows of Enna' – imagined, not seen, by DHL), 'Sicilian Cyclamens' and 'Hibiscus and Salvia Flowers'.

He took nourishment from all these rooted things. As a perpetual migrant, he might have paid more attention to birds in flight, those Vs he'd seen searching for a home, but he looked down more than up and took, as he always had, the pulse of life by flowers. Spring would come from the earth for him, not from the air. It grew up rather than flew over. Flowers were what moved him – their arrival or their coming.

Their need for roots was a harder lesson for Lawrence, and he mostly wouldn't allow it. He was not content to stop, himself. Indeed, he couldn't stop himself.

Throughout his time in Sicily, he always had his eyes on somewhere else. Within weeks of arriving in Taormina, he declared it not a long-term answer: 'Sicily is not far enough.' The grass was greener everywhere else, as it always had been and always would be. 'I might drift off anywhere,' he wrote. There was a plan, which 'thrills me to my marrow', for the South Seas with Compton Mackenzie by boat (with a romantic gypsy name – the *Lavengro*). Lawrence was an expert traveller (pleased with his well-designed *kitchenino*), and he dispensed detailed practical advice to visiting friends on porters and tipping and the best trains from London and how to smuggle tea and sugar from England. He was much less experienced as a sailor, and rather idealised the idea. He's very funny – and self-revealing – about Robert Louis Stevenson, whom he recognised as a fellow habitual runaway:

> Idiot to go to Samoa just to dream and get thrilled about Scotch bogs and mosses. No wonder he died. If I go to Samoa it will be to forget, not to remember.

Yet he never was a forgetter himself, nor could he ever quite forgo his roots.

As each destination was closed to him or shut down, another beckoned from beyond the horizon. Norway would be good ('to see the birch trees moving and hear the water among the stones'). There was a farm he knew of in Connecticut ('America seems to you looney? Well I don't care …'). Herm in the Channel Islands with Compton Mackenzie was an option when the South Seas escape route hadn't opened up. His trip to Sardinia was a scout-out for a new base ('it isn't a place to live in'). He might go to Germany with Frieda. Northern Italy was possible. The Mediterranean by sea could work. Spain was unknown and therefore interesting: 'the one European country that still attracts me'. Malta he did get to from Sicily, and loved it for a minute before hating it ever after: 'it sounds so thrilling ... Perhaps it'll be a fiasco.' It was: too British with 'marmalade and legs of mutton and Bass'. Venice was the same: 'Love Venice to look at, but not to smell, and not to live in.'

When he was hot he wanted to be cool, when it rained in Sicily he wanted away, when it was parched, the same. 'I can't', he wrote, knowing himself well even as he reiterated the same madnesses, 'I can't quite find my direction: can't quite make up my mind in which direction to turn my nose, to try a flight.' The only thing he seems certain about at this time was that returning to England was a no-go. That was never on the cards, although the Mediterranean heat did make him miss its flowers and its sustained temperate greenery (the equivalent of Stevenson's bogs and mosses): 'Alas I can't bear to think of cowslips – There are no flowers like English flowers, say what you will. Here it never rains.'

Lawrence's permanent itch shows him to have discovered that movement – physical movement but also intellectual and imaginative journeying – was where his life was lived most intensely. He was in a kind of lifelong flight (from his place and from himself), but he did his best to make that vital, to make being on the run good for self-growth and good for a big life. If you had a sense of how the world's time goes – and believed in what you knew – there was nothing better than to find a way to keep in step with it. Who wouldn't want to be 'morgenschön'? You don't necessarily have to sail to the South Seas to do that. Nor do you need capacious lungs that can help you walk up a volcano. You must be open, that is all, open to the opening of life – and that is best done in what is surely the best time of day on Earth, the world's morning. Find that, cut back to the old rhythms, linger while being ready to be on your way, keep your *kitchenino* primed and, if you can, be happy.

He was arrogant and contradictory, of course, grumpy and a mess; and, in some ways, the least open of anyone. He was born D. H. Lawrence and lived as him for the rest of his life. And he knew this of himself. The novels and stories are thick with this knowing and the constant, necessarily questioning, struggle to both know and to become or try to become someone else. And he lived like that too. On the penultimate page of *Sea and Sardinia*, at the end of a chapter called 'Back', describing his return to Sicily, he had written:

Andiamo! Andiamo! Let us go on. Andiamo! – let us go hell knows where, but let us go on. The splendid recklessness and passion that knows no precept and no schoolteacher, whose very molten spontaneity is its own guide.

By the end of his time on Sicily (he left in April 1921 for Germany – for a while), his best answer seemed to be to sail away from everything: 'I think it will be the ship' – 'I am serious about this so don't laugh. It has always been my heart's desire to have a boat.' In time, he did build one himself: in the autumn of 1929 he wrote his poem 'The Ship of Death', and on 2 March 1930 he set sail.

Heligoland
54°N

If anywhere *invented* bird migration it is Heligoland, the German island at the bottom-right corner of the North Sea. As a young birdwatcher, as soon as I heard of the place I wanted to go. Birds on the move have been studied there for more than 150 years and, in that time, the island has become a synonym for avian traffic. It also has lent its name to a means of catching it: the *Heligoland trap*, an island invention, remains, at many bird observatories, the preferred method for funnelling small migrant birds towards a collecting box.

Heligoland is famous for its falls of migrants. No bird word excites me (still) more than that one: *fall*. Landbirds on migration often have to cross the sea, but bad weather or wrong weather can bring them up short. A fall happens when concentrations of exhausted or disoriented migrants are forced to stop. A great rush can follow a hold-up. This happens once or twice, in places like Heligoland, most springs and autumns. Birds fall out of the sky.

For landbirds to be at sea is not good. Countless numbers must pitch into salt-water. That has been witnessed – drowning woodcocks picked up by trawlers, a blackbird seen trying to swim the North Sea off the Norfolk coast, and, off Heligoland, a song thrush, a snow bunting and a brambling. Think of Icarus' unnoticed splash, as painted by Pieter Brueghel, and the same, noticed as unnoticed by Auden, in his poem, 'Musée des Beaux Arts'. It is goodbye for those birds, surely. But if the dashed-down birds have somewhere to land then a fall can be in the offing. A landfall. Coastal areas – first ports of call – are fall zones. Ships can be too: leaf warblers might leaf the rigging; migrant raptors, merlins and short-eared owls, following the flocks, might come on board and feed on stray water rails and whacked-out redwings hiding on deck. But falls are island events above all: emergency landings on crash pads surrounded by the sea, oases of solid ground mid shifting wet, front-line and respite care, with food banks and temporary accommodation.

The opposite happens to seabirds. Bad weather drives pelagic species onto land – the last place they want to be. Little auks are *wrecked*. Gannets have been found grounded and incompetent in beet fields in the Fens. A friend saw a Manx shearwater hiding behind a dustbin in Bedford. Skuas are driven deep into the maw of the Wash and even up the rivers that drain into it. Odysseus will know his journeys are over – he is told this by Tiresias – when, having carried an oar from his ship and walked far inland, he will meet people who know nothing of sea-going and will mistake his oar for a farm implement, a winnowing fan. Seabirds inland are bewildered in reverse – their salted sea-going adaptations: great oars of wings, smell-maps of the ocean, deep-diving skills, piratical manners, etc., are all out of place in the muddy fields of any interior state.

My landlocked, sometime home county of Cambridgeshire records ocean-going great skuas harried up the River Nene, past the village of Foul Anchor (named for its haven – offered in the teeth of the same storms that dictate these birds' dislocated flights). The burger bar at Severn Beach, near my sometime second base camp in Bristol, is a good place to take shelter to watch storm-driven Leach's petrels as they try to avoid coming ashore. You know how bad the winds are in the Southern Ocean when, in False Bay at Cape Town, my some-time third lodging, a giant petrel, eater of penguins, also known as the glutton and the stinker, and looking, truly, like a wolf in sheep's clothing, flies between the surfers at Muizenberg and over the sand that is blowing furiously inland from the beach towards the sewage works.

We took a tourist catamaran from Hamburg. It was a soaking day in mid-April. The ride out of the Elbe felt weirdly like a journey down-hill, with all the rain of Europe running away to sea. We voyaged through beige and dun and underfelt, a swatch-book offered by the dullest of decorators: the clouds (brown) walled any view and dribbled into the broad muddy river (brown), the banks of which (brown) got further apart and sank lower until they were gone (drowned). Our boat seemed to be moving no faster than the tide. The wet sheepy muffle to everything called for beer just after breakfast. The sheep themselves, on the riverside bunds, lent their dripping fleeces as mops to the saturated sky. Two white-tailed eagles sat, a grumpy kilometre apart, hunched on the shore, head down with massive nicotine-stained bills, and droplets of rain gathering on the ends of their sniffling eagle noses.

We stopped at Cuxhaven. Bright-coloured rainwear trooped into our steamy lounge. We motored on, past a low fumous stir of knot above the mud flats, into the yawning mouth of the Elbe. The sea now gave a little slap to the hull and put a little green in the drink. A first gannet came alongside. The tannoy crackled into life as the captain explained our course through the ships at anchor: *They are waiting for their orders*, he said. Some were destined to come inland towards Hamburg up the river we'd just left, some would take the Kiel ship canal to the Baltic, some were going further across the North Sea, the German Ocean, to Scandinavia or up the east coast of Britain, some were going west, down the Channel, *la Manche*, and out towards the shipping lanes of the Atlantic, and the joined seawaters of the world. We went on, north-west through the Wadden Sea, until about an hour out, Heligoland loomed, novel in its verticality, slight at first but red and substantial, and, at last, something to head for.

Heligoland is currently two islands. Dune Island, just a narrow channel away from the main island, is flat and pale, like a sandy bank left by a falling sea. Nobody lives there. It appears as a drying seal hauled out on a low-tide beach. The main island comes in three parts: a textbook flat-topped rock shelf with sea cliffs and a lighthouse; a raised beach area at the foot of one side of the red cliffs; and a southern flattish apron, where the sea business of ships and a harbour is carried out behind the straight lines of engineered breakwaters and seawalls. Some parts look more man-made than others, but human handiwork lies behind all of Heligoland.

As you come in from the south-east by boat it is disconcerting to see that the whole of the main island is walled, even in its wildest, rockiest quarter. The sixty metres of sandstone cliffs once met their maker, day in and day out, but are now kept from the sea by a heavy-duty concrete mole. This prompted in me – before we'd even stepped ashore – a sinking feeling: the island looked like it was held captive, the whole of Heligoland a maintained idea.

We were staying in the youth hostel. We watched birds as we walked there. Electric vehicles overtook us, half golf buggy, half milk-float, purring in their anodyne way, as they shifted boxes of new landed goods and fresh disembarked tourists who preferred floating to walking. As we went, we worked on separating migrants from residents – birds and people. We passed hotels and shops on the harbour walls, skirted a town of tight-huddled houses pressed against the main island cliff, and then took a paved path, away from the same cliff, on what looked like a former beach, overgrown with grasses and elders, brambles and thorns.

This land was once sea. The Germans, fortifying their strategic edges in the 1930s, had moved rocks from elsewhere and pulled sand from the waves, and built out over it all to make more *Lebensraum*. The raised beach is just one instance from at least two centuries of confusion about what Heligoland might be: a *terrain vague* to be defended sometimes and at others attacked, a rock to breach or to wall, a beach to detonate or to extend, an island to enlarge or to disperse – an archetypal sand-castle never quite as its masons would have it or as physics would allow.

On that man-made flat north-north-west side of the island there is a children's playground, a trampoline park, a mini golf course, a sea-water power station, a football pitch of plastic grass and then, at a rocky beach, the hostel. Of migrants we saw four wheatears, a willow warbler, a chiffchaff, a male blackcap, four tree pipits, two white wagtails, and three goldcrests. Not an obvious fall, not an impressive haul, but not quite nothing either. Because we'd just landed we couldn't tell whether these birds marked the beginning of a concerted arrival, or were left-overs from previous arrivals yet to move on. Or were they simply part of the drift of ordinarily passing birds that turn up along many land edges through Europe as part of the twice-yearly exchange of millions of migrants?

It is always exciting to see even a common migrant, like a willow warbler, *being* a migrant, and demonstrating that by feeding on the ground, between the thorny stumps of a rose garden in front of a block of holiday apartments. Birds out of place get birders going. There was a wren, a few house sparrows, starlings, jackdaws and a carrion crow too. We decided these were residents and looked at them accordingly. They were less exciting. But then there were others that made you feel they might have been stranded on the island and have a different history. The blue tits and great tits on Heligoland looked like that – I couldn't see them as residents without thinking of the unlikeliness of a blue tit flying over the sea for one hundred kilometres. What would possess a bird, which I know best as an English garden resident, to do such a thing? And then I saw a hooded crow that made me look back for the carrion crow, which perhaps I had passed by too casually. One or other species probably shouldn't be there.

That *shouldn't* is what excites – the hunt for differences, for novelties, for vagrants. To best feel the smooth running of the spring, search out the snags and burrs in it; know the flow by feeling it stopped; see up into last night's sky by flushing those who have fallen from it at a mini golf course at dawn. Students of ornithology were helped on Heligoland to see how migration goes right for many birds by learning how it goes

150

wrong for a few. A bird that doesn't need to land on Heligoland is a success. It is on its way to where it must go. A fallen bird is often a failure. Though many patch up or repair themselves and continue their journeys, others have undoubtedly arrived at a premature or truncated end and, with little prospect of a way on or out, can only slump into whatever kind of funeral parlour the island provides.

At the youth hostel, as outside many of the island's cafes and hotels, there were outdoor seats: chairs wrapped in wicker baskets that allow visitors to be in the sun but out of the wind. To sit in them is like settling into a giant nest or putting on a heavy and creaking greatcoat made of sticks. We had arrived as migrant visitors ourselves, too early to check in, so we took two of these chairs and sat for an hour looking back at the sea we had just crossed. Almost instantly we fell asleep.

I grew up believing Heligoland almost English. Almost English it was once, yet in fact it hadn't been that for nearly a century. But books anchor places they describe, settle them in their time, and detain them there in the reader's mind. And I got to know of Heligoland because of old books: most of all Heinrich Gätke's *The Birds of Heligoland* (1895, written in German by Gätke, translated by Rudolph Rosenstock); then William Eagle Clarke's (such a name!) *Studies in Bird Migration* (1912), where I learned also what the Kentish Knock is; and then a chapter in Ronald Lockley's *I Know an Island* (1938), recording an autumn visit in 1936 when Heligoland was preparing for war (he noted newsreel films of goose-stepping in the island's cinema as well as a record fall of woodcocks).*

---

* In *The Running Sky*, I wrote about Lockley on Heligoland and redstart studies – their migratory restlessness observed on the island when they were caged and spring or autumn could be simulated by daylight-mimicking lamps. I hadn't been there then.

Gerard Manley Hopkins wrote another migration tragedy, and of the Kentish Knock beyond Heligoland, in 'The Wreck of the Deutschland', his long poem about the drowning – martyrdom, to him – of five Franciscan nuns in December 1875 who were fleeing anti-Catholic persecution in Prussia.

Gätke, by birth a Prussian, was shipwrecked on Heligoland when fleeing (as a defeated liberal) the aftermath of the 1848 uprisings in Berlin. He'd known the island before his landing there, when he'd visited it as a hunter. Because the British then controlled it, he was able to take refuge. He stayed on, like a blue tit perhaps, married a native, and didn't leave Heligoland for twenty-eight years. As well as making one of the first systematic studies of bird migration, he also worked as the government secretary, a colonial civil servant, and as a painter of landscapes and sea scenes. He died on Heligoland in 1897. By then, the student of migration had become its sage.

In the course of his life, Gätke collected thousands of the birds that had been trying to use the island 'as a resting place'. His book – 'Nature herself put the pen into my hand,' he said – came from decades of observations. Bird study in the nineteenth century almost always meant bird murder. The island was a sanctuary to passage birds, but it was understood as such only by being simultaneously turned into a slaughter-house. Gätke was one of many men with guns on Heligoland. Most hunters had their eyes on the meat value of their quarry; he was interested in rarity and diversity.

On the last of his book's 600 pages there is a photograph of Gätke, captioned 'The Author In His Shooting Dress, 1893'. He's holding a large, dead, immature gull (perhaps a great black-backed) in one mittened hand, with his rifle in the other. He looks like bad weather and is wearing a severe woolly hat and a thick bearskin smock that he might have grown himself. His long bifurcating grey beard lies like a frozen waterfall over the fur. His eyes have the faraway stare of a polar explorer.

The first entry on Gätke's Heligoland bird list is a 'Greenland Falcon' (a race of the gyr falcon). He killed it – the first known to him on Heligoland – in October 1843, and he says it started him off on his studies. Many more died. Some birds got away. Some were not sufficiently interesting to be taken for study. Migrant redstarts were commonplace on Heligoland, and there is no mention in Gätke of his shooting or collecting any, though he must have done. The species, Gätke says, occurs in 'immense swarms' on both spring and autumn passage when 'all the gardens and especially the potato-fields teem with countless thousands of these birds'. He has little else to say; the brevity of his account and his passing description of the bird's abundance is telling: redstarts were once so common they were barely noticed. They made for the aggregate of bird migration, part of its raw bulk and its backdrop. Numbers like this are no more. I have seen fewer, far fewer, than 1,000 redstarts in fifty years of looking for them.

Rare redstart species did get shot on the island. One Moussier's redstart, normally a resident North African species, arrived somehow on the island in the summer of 1842.

It was shot by Oelrich Aeuckens, and sold by him to a young law student named Jochmus, from Lüneburg, who used to come here annually for sea-bathing. I had at that time scarcely laid the first foundations of my collection, and had no idea what value this example was to Heligoland. Afterwards I made repeated and urgent efforts to obtain it back, but unfortunately without result. At last I gave it up as a bad job, as I was told that the bird had gone to ruin. It was a pretty male in rather worn plumage …

I've only ever seen Moussier's redstarts on their home grounds in Morocco. They are exquisite. My first was a male, on 7 January 2007, in a valley of juniper trees south-east of Touama. I wrote in my notebook:

Magnificent and confiding; with a brighter breast than the red earth beneath it; its underparts more orange than a common redstart, with striking black and white head patterning (a white 'tiara' the book says), and a brilliant white wing-patch. Plus tail quiver!

One page of Gätke's book is about a black-throated green warbler. A single bird. The first European record of this American species was one killed on Heligoland in November 1858 'by a boy with a blow pipe'. The next entry in Gätke is on the goldcrest, the smallest European bird and one of its commonest migrants. As with the common redstart, there are no deaths to report. Instead, Gätke turns poet–theologian:

Imagine a mild and clear evening in spring: the sun has set long since, and the voices of all the feathered wanderers are hushed in sleep … Suddenly through the silence, like half in a dream, the fine clear note of our little wren [goldcrest, he means] is heard, and soon afterwards the bird is seen rising from the neighbouring bushes, through the still luminous evening sky; at measured intervals its call note – 'hiit-hiit-hiit' – is heard as it flies off, in slightly ascending spirals, over the neighbouring gardens; then from every bush – here, there, near and far – the cry is answered, 'hiit-hiit, hiit-hiit, hiit-hiit', in loud clear tones, and from all sides its travelling companions, wakened for the journey, rise upwards, following in the wake of the earliest starter – the latter, however, when the answering voices have announced that all the sleepers are aroused, ceases circling about, and rises, with breast erect and brief and rapid strokes of the wings, almost vertically upwards; soon all assemble in a somewhat loose swarm, the call-notes are silenced when the last straggler has joined the departing flock, and the tiny wanderers vanish from sight. While we are still listening to their call-notes growing fainter and fainter in the distance, and straining our eyes for one last look at the little songsters, the first faintly gleaming stars appear in their stead in the deep transparent ether above. Later still, as we gaze upwards to the night sky sown with innumerable points of light, we imagine that those myriads of shining worlds are all that move between us and the Infinite, while all the time in the heights above us are travelling thousands, nay, millions of living creatures towards one fixed goal – small and weak like this little wren of ours, but all guided as safely and surely as the farthest gleaming stars.

After all the counting and the killing, and the exceptional vagrants, and then the goldcrest night-flight poetry, Gätke still had no solid answers about what migration was or how it could be undertaken. He must have known from seeing goldcrests on Heligoland that they weren't all *safely and surely* guided, but no one, nowhere, knew much more than the deaths of those which went wrong and the departures of those which, apparently, went right.

Shortly after Gätke published his book, the Hungarian ornithologist Otto Herman drew up a list of some of the contrary opinions of various researchers as to the basis of migration. Gätke's theories (a version of his sky-rising goldcrests and his dream-ornithology) feature among many others:

> Naumann: There are definite routes of migration.
> Homeyer: There are no definite routes of migration.
> Weismann: Birds learn how to migrate.
> Gätke: Birds migrate by instinct.
> Palmén: Orientation is traditional.
> Weismann: Orientation is congenital.
> Gätke: There is no leadership.
> Weismann: There is leadership.
> Wallace: The weather has no essential influence.
> Homeyer: The weather has an essential influence.
> Naumann: Temperature plays an important part.
> Angot: Temperature is not an incentive.
> Lucanus: Flight occurs at 3,000 feet.
> Gätke: Flight occurs at 35,000 feet.
> Braun: The original home of birds is the tropics.
> Deichler: The original home is not the tropics.

Birds don't carry bags. Or passports. That is often the first thing I say when people ask me why I like them so much. It helps explain why I want to follow them. They travel with messages, not suitcases; they themselves are the messages and they bring news from elsewhere and from other times. (The metaphorical potency of birds in our imaginative lives has much to do with their flights and their passages, their being elsewhere – they are literal

155

metaphors.*) Never are they so obviously making their way in the world, without needing bags, as when you see them dropping down from the sky, having flown over oceans of water to land on an island in a patch of cover near your feet. An island that you have got to by car, then train, then Tube, then plane, then metro, then boat, then golf buggy. An island you have arrived at, trailing behind you an anchor or tail that you cannot shake off – the crenellated death-rattle of little suitcase wheels on concrete and tarmac that stops your ears and all of your ease.

So it is that when the hostel opens, you put your bag down, button your coat, because it is colder outside the wicker basket than you'd thought, and now spitting with rain, and you head out to walk every path you can. Hours later you come back, but within minutes you feel you should be out again. It must be happening or about to; there must be new birds dropping in; there are gardens you didn't check properly and a patch of scrub that you feel should harbour something.

So get out again.

It goes on like this for days.

There wasn't much to see. It was a good time of year but this wasn't a good time this year. We met with no falls. Still, I went out and did the rounds. Claire worked on emails and kept warm indoors and I walked alone, getting up early, clocking the wind and working a magic strip along a breakwater where I'd allowed myself to get excited by some wheatears and whinchats. I was out all day – I felt I must be. After dark, in our spartan room under a dismal energy-saving bulb, I read about the good old days – a carpeting, abundance, the gold rush.

Britain gave Heligoland to Germany in 1890. It got Zanzibar in exchange. It's a kind of pub-quiz fact. Alongside the history of colonial geopolitics, the insanity of such a trafficking speaks to the extraordinary truths of bird migration that Heligoland has shown (and still shows)

---

* I have seen removal vans in Greece with the word 'Metaphore' written on their sides. It means *Removals*. In Ancient Greece 'metaphero' meant *I carry from one place to another*. Migrant birds are their own metaphors.

and the odd ersatz or untruthful feel of the present-day human island. It is an escape place for birds, and for people, but it also teaches that to truly get on you really need to get out.

As I waited at a fence overlooking an allotment for a warbler I hadn't properly seen, it occurred to me that it was possible, likely even, that since the islands were swapped, there had been one or two individual birds – barn swallows, perhaps a common tern – that had been on both Zanzibar and Heligoland. That was some consolation to me. Some, but not much.

For eighty-three years in the nineteenth century the British administered Heligoland. The island (one, sometimes two) has long been inhabited. The dead have been stored there since prehistoric times and the living have kept them company. Danish kings claimed ownership by 1231. The last Frisian king, Radbod, had retreated there after his defeat by the Franks in 697. Most agree the island's name means Holy Land, though some etymologies suggest it comes from *Hallaglun* or *Halligland* meaning *a land of sand banks, which cover and uncover*. The people lived by fishing for herring, cod and haddock, by wrecking and, its opposite, piloting ships into the sandy Hanseatic coastal regions, and by hunting seals and birds (breeding seabirds and migrants). The Danes lost Heligoland to the British in 1807 during the Napoleonic Wars.

So far, so Fodor's, so Baedeker, so Wikipedia, except for all this sandy coming and going. To this day, some of Heligoland's residents are still, long after Radbod, Frisians. In Heligolandic Frisian, they call their home *deät Lun*, meaning *the Land*. The land as opposed to the sea – the sea being everything otherwise that is the case. It's a name rather like those people have given themselves through history that translate as *the Humans* or *the People*, which means, in other words, we are it, and everything else is not. When you are on Heligoland, *the Land* seems a reasonable name – it is the only place you can see that you can stand on. And it is the land – the island's *landedness* amongst so much malevolent wetness – that has made the place significant for migrant birds.

This land has, however, not been reliable as solid ground. Heligoland has undergone remarkable changes in its recent history. Depressed in the hostel, I watched from my utility bed a Pathé newsreel film called *Heligoland Goes Up*. On 18 April 1947, the British destroyed as much of their former enemy's island as they could, using 6,400 tonnes of explosives, causing, so says the clipped and brisk voice on the newsreel, 'the biggest man-made explosion since the atom bomb went off at Bikini'. Hitler's base for the Battle of the Atlantic was no more: submarine pens, gun emplacements and underground tunnels were 'blown sky high' into a '12,000-foot column of smoke'. On a ship fourteen kilometres off Heligoland, Lieutenant Commander Frank Graves of London pressed the button 'at the fourth pip of the BBC time signal'.

The Big Bang, it was called at the time. The island was ruined, but also re-configured at once. Almost every building was demolished. The detonation created *Mittelland*, an in-between cratered terrain, dividing the *Oberland* (the cliff-edged old island) from the *Unterland* (the apron of lower ground around the harbour). After the explosion no one lived on the island for several years. It was formally returned to Germany in the spring of 1952. Thereafter, a kind of holiday-camp incarnation of the Nazi-era military base/labour camp was built. Different, though not unrelated, offshore resources were to be cached – the island as defensive bulwark, with submarines primed in their pens, was recycled as an off-limits warehouse of treats, a tax-free haven. Cheap booze, fags and smells were shipped to Heligoland to be bought discounted there, and then re-exported back to the mainland.

The island had been dismantled and re-built before. Few places have been so manhandled. At the end of the First World War, the losing power's military kit and infrastructure was removed but, within a few years, re-arming Germany re-built and fortified once more. Heligoland, in fact, turns out to be all *Mittelland*: neither quite here nor there, neither coming nor going, but rather pausing temporarily somewhere in the middle. How oddly appropriate, then, that one of the island's peacetime claims to fame was its sponsoring of another take on the Big Bang. In the late spring of 1925, driven half-mad by hay fever on the mainland, the physicist Werner Heisenberg sought refuge as a temporary migrant, on near treeless and (hence) pollen-light Heligoland. (To this day, the island retains the feel of a spa or sanatorium alongside all its cheap intoxicants.) There, able to breathe in fresh salted air, Heisenberg exhaled the beginnings of quantum theory.

Maybe the migrant birds at the tail end of spring helped him. Maybe he read Gätke. Goldcrests and willow warblers are to migration what atoms and subatomic particles are to quantum mechanics – descriptions of the smallest scales of energy. As Gätke looked up at the ascending flocks of spring-departing goldcrests without being able to see, let alone understand, how they were doing what they were doing, while knowing that they were doing it, and had done it the previous year and would do it the following, so quantum mechanics, part conceived by Heisenberg under the same North Sea skies, asserted that the exact location of a particle in space cannot be predicted, only the possibility of finding it at different locations.

The two mysteries are surprisingly close: to feel the rub of the ordinary magic of migration – the persisting strangeness or the invisible but sensed presence of its gritted flow – we might try exchanging *goldcrest* with Carlo Rovelli's *electron* in his explanation of Heisenberg's equations:

Heisenberg imagined that electrons do not *always* exist. They only exist when someone or something watches them, or better, when they are interacting with something else. They materialise in a place, with a calculable probability, when colliding with something else. The 'quantum leaps' from one orbit to another are the only means they have of being 'real': an electron is a set of jumps from one reaction to another. When nothing disturbs it, it is not in any precise place. It is not in a 'place' at all.

Walking the circular path around the island takes you to these fantastical thoughts – I allowed myself all this because I wasn't seeing any goldcrests. Waiting on news from elsewhere, I was going out each new morning *into* the uncertainty principle. I checked the sky and I looked at the flag outside the hostel to deduce the wind direction but I didn't know what I would find. I stared at the sea, knowing there must have been birds – small, hurrying landbirds – moving over it. I saw nothing. I dreamed one night of waking to find Saharan sand lying on the canvas roofs of the plugged-in re-charging golf buggies, and that sometime Saharan birds were stepping through the granular deposits. I persuaded my lungs that they were being tickled with the lime-flower pollen of all of Germany to the south of us, and that surely there would be an icterine warbler, a lime flower made into a bird, in the brambles at the edge of the observatory garden. But there was actually next to nothing.

23 April. Out from six in the morning. Two complete turns. It was very cold, with a hateful wind from the north. I spent an hour loitering at the hedged allotments on the *Oberland*. Between the neat furrows of bare soil were shuttered summerhouses, arthritic fig trees, fallen gnomes and concrete seals balancing half-rotten concrete balls on their half-rotten concrete noses. My tally was poor, dribs and drabs, ones and twos: one male, one female wheatear, a fieldfare, one willow warbler, and two chiffchaffs. The warblers were puffed up fat against the cold. There were daffodils and some blossom on the thorns, but everything growing seemed pinched and *behind*. The most luxuriant cover was in the cemetery around the church. But a sign said birdwatchers were not permitted. What about those in mourning for *birdland*? Gätke is buried there too. I dithered, then walked on south: one siskin, one redpoll, one goldfinch, six linnets, a maudlin whimbrel on the grass caldera of the *Mittelland* hole, a blue-headed wagtail, ten more chiffchaffs, two willow warblers, two redwings, a white wagtail, then a pied, which I knew to be more – a little – interesting, since pieds are the British race and mostly resident, and so, somehow, I could build this bird a known past, out of my own known past, back home across the shitty seas …

I met another birdwatcher. We compared notes. He said as we parted: 'Carry on seeing nothing!' I add the exclamation mark; in fact he said it without one. The day continued like that – flat. There was one small fillip: a male ring ouzel on the *pit-pat* mini golf course perching on a rotting-concrete Rhineland castle.

On the seawall–breakwater at the *Unterland* was the second-best bird of the day, a male whinchat, flycatching above the hissing kelp on the beach. I had last seen a whinchat in Chad, feeding in the middle of a vast grassy plain. I proposed to myself that this was the very same one and, drawing a map in my mind with a line from Zakouma to Heligoland, I felt lifted for a moment.

24 April. The next day my circuits featured snow, sleet, hail and sun. A wet and grounded woodlark on the football pitch got me started, but not much followed: two male blackcaps, four chiffchaffs, a sparrowhawk and a male ring ouzel on the lawns by the swimming pool (the same as the mini-golf bird of yesterday, I think). The seawall seemed a better place, perhaps because of the flies coming from the kelp: thirty white wagtails, two fly-catching willow warblers, one tree pipit, two male blackcaps, another male ring ouzel, the whinchat again and two male and one female black redstarts. It still wasn't a fall, but at least some birds had come down overnight.

I hung about the children's playground, trying to look innocuous, counting birds with rings – blackbirds, an oystercatcher, a herring gull, a white wagtail – there were lots, almost every bird that was a Heligoland resident seemed to have been caught and tagged. For the first time in my life I disliked the idea of ringing. I tried not to think of a ball and chain.

Heligoland means less than it once did. Its meaning drains from it: migration has been interpreted from many places now, people smoke less and have less need for the island's discounts, a German who wants to go on holiday when the swallows arrive could head for Spain just after Christmas, the spring rush is not what it was, the falls are thinner, numbers of spring migrants are down. On Heligoland they still have the chutes that took rubbish and rainwater and sometimes disoriented birds from the *Oberland* to the sea (Lockley was bemused by this and wrote about them; the island's water tasted gamey, he said, because so many lost birds had accidentally taken the chutes to rainwater tanks and drowned); but since the sea isn't really there any longer at the base of the *Oberland* they are not really used any more – I watched a gardener kicking his garden trimmings over the cliff edge at the bottom of his plot to land on the Nazis' new ground at the *Nordostland*. There are 180 steps from the *Oberland* to the *Unterland*, but there is also now an electric lift down the outside of the cliff.

25 April. Two fieldfares by the trampoline. The male ring ouzel again at the mini golf. I wished it gone. Its value had diminished with each sighting. I didn't like the me who felt that way, but it was true. It was warm and windless in the lee of the seawall and there were twenty white wagtails hurrying to jump for flies, a male ring ouzel (again) checking out the fuss, two acrobatic willow warblers, the whinchat, and the three black redstarts. There were nods here, as at our hostel, across the breakfast room.

An elderly woman had fallen over in the *Mittelland* crater. She had blood on her face. The island ambulance is garaged next door in the *Klinik*. It appeared, flashed its lights for ten metres, and pulled up, never needing second gear. The paramedics trotted to the woman. I watched from the rim of the crater. It was a scene my children might have staged during their Playmobil years. The woman was crying. I could hear her sobs. Her glasses had twisted and bent as she fell. Her dog was distraught and barked at the ambulance crew.

Once more around the island, in the evening. There is a small (700 pairs in 2016), newish colony of gannets on Heligoland (the only breeding gannets in Germany), and in recent years a black-browed albatross, mislaid in the northern hemisphere, has spent time on the cliff top making the best of its relations – a vagrant trying to blend in, hoping perhaps for identity papers, the right to stay, for a mate. Albert the albatross at Hermaness in Shetland tried the same with the gannets there for many years in the 1980s and 1990s, without luck. I'd hoped to see the Heligoland bird and went looking every day, also without luck. The day we left, it appeared back on the cliff, having been cruising the North Sea.

Some of the gannets were grazing the grass on the cliff top. I'd never seen that before. Passing birds, some with seaweed streamers in their beaks, flew into the wind above their cliff and, as they neared the lawn on the top, they paddled with their feet and stepped down. Immediately they looked awkward and too heavy for their legs. Their wings slumped below their bodies. But they were excited by the grass and pecked keenly at it, sometimes dropping their seaweed haul in the process, sometimes managing to juggle it to the back of their beaks. I tried to

162

see what the grass was for: none of the nests seemed to have it visible in them; nor did any bird I saw eat any.

Herodotus described the nomadic Scythians as the supreme riders of the Asiatic steppe, but somewhat chaotic in their funeral behaviours. In their *kurgan* graves (the place they would be stopped longest of anywhere), they tumbled together the bodies of kings, their sacrificed servants and their butchered horses. Gannets seem like that. On the move they are untrammelled. At home – though that isn't really the word – they collapse, and make shit-heaps to live on that sometimes kill them. The colony is a slovenly mess. They might carry no bags but gannets are hooked on clutter. Everything that a gannet does on land happens in the small space it has secured for its nest. One day it has a mound of filth to lay an egg on – the next day the whole of the North Sea to feed in. A 2016 tracking study of the Heligoland gannets found the species mostly fishing north and north-west of the island, with the birds flying around wind-turbine farms en route. But every ocean-going supremo is shambolic at home. Their domestic hygiene isn't helped by the way they gather, for nest material, stray and drifting plastic ropes and netting (90 per cent of nests in 2016 incorporated visible plastic). Plus they often live among the ruins of their own. In 1991, the very first gannet chick that hatched on Heligoland died after it became entangled in plastic rubbish in its own nest. Several nests I could see had dead gannets woven into them. A dead guillemot – like a bijou memento mori – adorned another. Two gannets were mummified into swirls of crap. One nest had a skeleton gannet at its heart, the spread bones of a wing made the cup for a second, a third hung from a stretch of blue rope between one ledge of nests and another.

On 18 September 1798 Coleridge arrived by boat in Cuxhaven. He'd sailed from Yarmouth and crossed the North Sea in two days. He'd written 'The Ancient Mariner' by then but this was his first time on the sea out of sight of land. He had a good passage. He seems to have barely slept and mostly walked the deck wrapped in his everything-proof suit, 'my great coat', which had a collar so big it could be used as a hood. The sea was rough. He liked it. William Wordsworth and his sister Dorothy, who were travelling with him to Germany, suffered badly, taking on a 'frog-coloured appearance' like most of the other passengers, with Dorothy 'vomiting & groaning & crying the whole time!' Coleridge sailed on untroubled; the sea crossing seemed made for him. He watched the waves and befriended a Danish passenger; they drank together and then danced 'appropriately intitled reels'. At four o'clock in the morning, far out at sea on the second day, he saw a bird in the dark: 'a single solitary wild duck'. 'It is not easy to conceive,' he wrote, 'how interesting a thing it looked in that round objectless desert of waters.'

He slept a little then, but not long after,

I was awakened by the cry of land! land! It was an ugly island rock at a distance on our left, called Heiliegland, well known to many passengers from Yarmouth to Hamburg, who have been obliged by stormy weather to pass weeks and weeks in weary captivity on it . . .

Coleridge and his party weren't forced to take shelter, and they made it to the mainland and on into Germany (where, among many discoveries and adventures, he would be disappointed that the poets he met – in his mind, men who were parts of nature – wore wigs). The duck near Heligoland was perhaps an image of Coleridge himself. Interesting to observe in the middle of the sea. But it was also, surely, actually a duck. Also interesting to observe in the middle of the sea.

Walking around Heligoland, I was often put in mind of Gibraltar. Thinking of Coleridge passing Heligoland reminded me that he had seen Gibraltar from the strait in 1804 and had landed on the rock; he didn't much care for it. The narrator on the Pathé newsreel calls the island 'the Gibraltar of the North Sea', and the connection is obvious: another rock, at the edge of a continent, looking out to sea; another trapped place, sterile as a human destination (*there is no there there, encore une fois*); and another avian focus, magnetically marvellous to birds and looped into the lives of many thousands of them over thousands of years. A causeway ties Gibraltar uncertainly to Spain, but from the top of the rock your eyes invariably travel to Africa across the narrow strait and the shadowing mountains from where, in spring, the migrants head out towards you. A concrete wall has caged Heligoland, though the bund is not for its birds and it hasn't made an aviary. Being on it, your eye is always lifting to the sea on all sides, to the reality of that, and to the determining sky running over everything; you can see no other land, and the birds come from above, touching down without possessions or possessiveness of any kind, coming to earth – if all goes well – to re-fuel, but not to linger and with no intention to stay. Lying on my back on the top of the rock at Gibraltar and watching as flock after flock of black kites crossed the strait and passed over my head on their way into the European spring, was a way to feel the world turning. Sitting on a bench on the cliff top at Heligoland was a way to feel it stuck. I saw, far from the island though heading towards it, a little flock of six lapwings. Coming closer, they all stepped down in the sky, rounding their wings and dropping hundreds of metres through the air. I thought they were arriving and would land, but after their first airy tumble they re-grouped and climbed again; they had seen the place but didn't need it and they picked up speed, beating their wings more emphatically, and flew on, over the island and beyond it, over the sea.

Very small the island became in our leaving of it too: the red cliffs bled behind us, the fudged mess of the barricaded and re-claimed land looked like a pummelled flotation device, deflating as it slipped beneath the horizon. Then came the pitch of the sea, with the wind in charge; and just one last marvel at the thought of a goldcrest in such a world, when a fellow tourist at my side on the deck unwrapped a toffee and let the golden-green sweet paper slip from their fingers to be carried overboard and hurried away, up at first, and then down towards the dark water.

MAY

Ham Wall
51°N

1 May. May Day dawn chorus eavesdrop. I was producing a radio outside broadcast that added Somerset birds to a relay of world-waking music, a wave of sung air circling the globe, as the sun of the new day fell upon it, from east to west across Europe, from Russia to Ireland.

We sat at the edge of a reedbed and waited for the dawn to come to us. We didn't sleep – or dream – but listened to the stirring and throat-opening and then full song of perhaps one thousand birds from eleven at night until half past six the next morning. Every minute was different: the air, the light in the night clouds, the dark at the earth, and then the sky opening and all the rest.

It is always dawn somewhere; somewhere the first splash of light is falling onto the Earth. That light, in the spring, wakens birds into song. Dawn is the spring of the day – it is the most audible and the happiest performance of the noise of time. In early May, the dawn chorus moves around the northern hemisphere at about 1,300 kilometres per hour. If there is such a thing as *godspeed* that is it. Every minute, about twenty-one more kilometres of the Earth's surface are lit up and come alive with bird song.*

---

* I came to this calculation via William Empson's essay on the speed of fairy flight in Shakespeare's *A Midsummer Night's Dream*. In the play, Puck says he can get around the world, avoiding daylight, in forty minutes. Empson says that journey time is close to what Yuri Gagarin took on his one mission to orbit the world on 12 April 1961. I checked some figures: NASA says it took Gagarin 108 minutes. Empson's forty seems out, unless he was correcting Gagarin's figures by allowing for the fact that the

166

In the last ninety minutes the noise was so good, and so full, that we shushed all our supporting human talk about the science and poetry of bird song and simply listened to it. It was a marvellous dumbfounding, and far better (for me) for the fact that I had nothing to do with its making. We just opened the faders on our portable mixing desk and edged up the world.

The order of service: marsh frog – heavy water; reed warbler – the Rotavator; moorhen – a practice nightmare; coot – the handyman; gadwall – burp one; tufted duck – burp two; water rail – the gaoler rattling the cage; bittern – afflatus; grey heron – a sleeping sulk; tawny owl – if I must; Cetti's warbler – big sneeze; sedge warbler – the Singer sewer; blackbird – all-day gravy; song thrush – serious dictation; wren – look at me; great tit – no, look at me; reed bunting – old money in your pocket; blue tit – toy drummer; dunnock – unwanted lacework; carrion crow – prang; blackcap – extreme unction; chiffchaff – coaxing a flame; willow warbler – a running tap; whitethroat – a night-time itch; great white egret – harrumph; little egret – get your hands off me; cuckoo – like it says; garden warbler – a cryptic crossword.

We finished, having passed on the world's morning and the new day, and handed over to *Today* (so-called) and the news (likewise) on BBC Radio 4. The human team climbed into a van and we were driven back to Bristol. For a few minutes, we chattered in our elation and in the welcome warmth of the electric heater, but quickly everyone fell asleep in exhausted abandonment, everyone except for me. It was a sweet

---

cosmonaut orbited the Earth not just above its surface – say, at Puck's height, held up by three strong men in the Globe theatre (as he was said to be) – but rather where Gagarin actually was, ninety-one nautical miles (not thirty as Empson says) up and away from all of our shows, our mathematics and our dreams. These figures will also vary according to the latitude of the Earth above which the orbit occurs. It doesn't really matter. In John Clare's poem on a nightjar, 'The Fern Owl's Nest', he describes the bird's flight as being 'as quick as thought'. The image startles me as much as the flight of the bird it describes does. It makes you feel your thinking. Empson's attention and his calculations have a similar effect. They vivify the play beyond its life on the stage or page and animate its interests, and they pique ours: how fast are we going; how does the speed of the turning Earth compare to the speed of our minds, and what is the speed of a dream compared to that; how is time sometimes arrested and sometimes hurried; when Lysander in the play tells the actor impersonating the moon to proceed, does he mean to start talking or to journey on?

sight – like a coach party of big babies. The last hour and a half of our transmission was the best radio I had ever done: the truest *broadcast*, a perfect account – unedited, unmediated, and unannounced. A true time-song – articulate, genuine and complete. It was of itself – no more than what it was, but it really *was* what it was. And that I was less the author of it than any other programme I had ever made left me with the sensation of being free in the world at large. It also kept me awake. It was near enough the last programme I made before I left the BBC after thirty years as a producer.

We've already heard from Seamus Heaney's poem 'A Herbal'. In addition to its benign flower-pressing, it mentions the word I learned in my radio life that I liked the most. It was – for me – also radio's most lovable concept. So loved, indeed, that I ended up making a television film about it just before I stopped working in its realm.

> Remember how you wanted
> The sound recordist
> To make a loop,
>
> Wildtrack of your feet
> Through the wet
> At the foot of the field?

'Wildtrack' is radio-speak for the sound behind the sounds you seek, a gathering of background or what we also called *atmos*, the audible substrate, identifying where you are and betokening it, giving sonic context, but also helping in editing or unifying – tidying – the voice or voices to be heard in the foreground. All edits are less obvious set against a wildtrack; it helps whatever is being said to flow; it is time-coded sonic glue.

Wildtrack is the acoustic of everywhere; it is bird song, it is wind, it is seawash, it is rainfall, but it is also traffic, aeroplanes overhead, footsteps, train shunts and church bells, a marketplace, school playgrounds at dinnertime, voices of trees in a forest. It underwrites the main business but it itself says a lot.

You felt safe if you came away from a recording with plenty of wildtrack. Without it, there could be trouble. It is very hard to fake. Old radio hands on seaside missions used to keep a slice or two of bread near their recording kit to clinch the crucial sonic signifier by making the gulls yawp. I learned early to collect two minutes, at least, of everywhere.

Birds were my bag throughout my years at the BBC, but almost all of my productions were about people, and I never worked for the Natural History Unit. But birds came, in any case, through the air into my programmes. The longer I worked on the foreground – on the so-called *story* – the more I found myself wanting to pay attention to the wildtrack, to bring the background to the front, to regard the substrate as substantial and to make what was passing into the present.

As I neared the end of my three decades of radio-life, wildtrack grew ever more important. Partly this is because, being headed in only one direction, I am drawn to life that might loop, which goes around and comes around; partly because I love all bird utterance and its world-speak, even as (perhaps, because) my hearing thins and fails; partly because, more misanthropically I suppose, I increasingly feel I have heard enough, sometimes more than enough, of our blabber. I've imagined ditching all the talked-out guff I had gathered, and just sitting, deep into the dark, day after day, listening to my tapes, wildtracks and clips of *atmos*, all those incidental sounds, all those songs of the earth.

The first radio programme of my own imagining and configuring I made at the BBC was about the spring song of the nightingale and the value, if any, of considering the bird a natural artist. Thirty years on, one of the last programmes I was involved in was the spring dawn broadcast. As the light came back, that morning, the wildtrack opened up all around, the world was sounding. And sounding full. Enough.

Bristol
51°N

2 May. Bike ride with greenfly mascara. Roadside graffiti: *Nothing Lasts Forever*.

Totleigh Barton
51°N

3 May. No moon; instead a tawny owl wood-shanty from the copses and hedges by the River Torridge in Devon. They *woo*-ed it. There were three males, each a field apart. All tawny owl hoots sound brown, and I think of the birds themselves like that, as soft brown *woo*-planets making their way through the dark. The singers at Totleigh preferred to solo, maintaining their hoot rhythm and the gap between sounds, as foghorns of neighbouring lighthouses must. At dusk, they began with good intentions. One bird left fifteen seconds between its calls and another more like twenty. But they are also compelled to answer any rival. So each prompted each and both soon got stuck in a log-jam. Then a third pitched in. The honourable hoots sounded less hurried than the fuck-off hoots, but both soon crowded in concert. The retaliatory hoots then began to sound strained and creaky. Eventually, after an hour, one bird shut up and the other two calmed down.

I was listening to the owls while watching the last of the light. I had seen an otter earlier, treading water at speed down river, and a dipper, fast and bulbous, flying the same meander, and I was feeling, accordingly, very mellow. In a wet pasture by the river there were cows as bulky as wardrobes. They would normally scare me somewhat, but not tonight. The milky white flanks on some of them appeared like doors opened onto moonlit prospects. Somehow the creamy pink cuckoo-flowers in the same field had sequestered portions of the same daylight-saving light. A cow and a flower shouldn't look similar, but the night allowed it. As I walked back through the herd one of the cows mooed. Another answered from the dark side of a hedge. And that started the owls off again.

Bristol
51°N

4 May. A knife-throw of swifts over my flat; my first of the year. They climb the sky – never otherwise is the air made so substantial, never shown so conquerable.

Wicken Fen
52°N

Every year I can I go to see woodcocks roding. For the last thirty years, in the Cambridgeshire fens, along a line of willows at the edge of a reedbed, I have seen the birds' dusk flights once or twice most springs. They are a favourite bird but I hardly know them.

Springe is a woodcock word (they were trapped with them); and my total woodcock bag is thirty sightings in my birdwatching life: one got up from my feet outside my front door, one flushed beneath a goshawk, one in off an autumn sea, two hurrying above two winter motorways, one migrant over my head on a city street at dusk, one migrant out of an island garden, and twenty-plus separate craft on their lonely spring orbits.

Lonely, it seems to me, is the woodcock's road. Its *rode*: a circuit required and undertaken in the sky after a life lived with all meaning on the ground. A rode: a figure followed in the air. A rode, up there, measured in falling light across a plum-dark sky: love-flights or territorial anger-management – males mandated on spring dusks to perform slow-flapped crossings of the night's hearth in order to declare themselves to the earth. The rode – a word kept only for the bird: a word kept lonely, a dance otherwise no longer danced, some wonky ballet, and the dancer, dirty old man as reluctant after-hours debutante, and most probably a stranger to deodorant, like a badger forced to fly.

Such crepuscules witnessed twenty-plus times. Or dreamt. They go round and come around again. They are all old-timers, and their rode is a ritual carried out with unthinking purpose. Every spring the wood-cock takes the same path through the night air as it did last year or as its father did or as its father's father did. I have grown old under these flights.

Roding is more surprising for being so unlike a woodcock. The birds are the soil's thing and hide in it until they are steered – unearthed – skywards by some seasonal worm in their heads towards the coming dark. Beating the bounds, flying his via dolorosa, the male repeats his course waiting for the shadows to endorse his downward return. Meanwhile he moves stiff with phantom gestures, ghosting a display, slowly and deliberately, low across the fuzzy evening sky.

As he goes he speaks a kind of Linear A. 'To the present writer the sound seems to defy description' – said Alfred Newton in his 1896 *Dictionary of Birds* – 'though some hearers have tried to syllable it.' *Psst. Psst.* And a piggy grunt. Tonight, above the fen, I felt I understood him. He was a businessman stepping awkwardly into a dance, not drunk enough to lose his inhibitions at the disco, except for the accidental farts he let off as he went. My father in 1975. But the usher of dusk, I thought a woodcock once, or a shambling clerk with a heavy ledger making his way through pea soup. You can look and have your visions, but everything summoned by the bird and its rode draws backwards and downwards, and it is always old, gone or going, and of dust or mud. Dreams and other night things shuffle the same tarot between them: bats, owls, nightjars that are also known as goatsuckers, crakes mooncalfing, swifts lifting from the planet to sleep on the wing. But among them, darkly, the woodcock is dirtiest and oldest of all.

They feed feelingly, seeking the movement of a worm through soil. They bend their beaks underground. And they live in this fashion, as night workers, like a geophage or a *turd-bird*: long beak, lizard feet, streaked brown plumage, and all their antiquity scored with brief squeals, snores, grunts, and methane blows. Old, far-off, unlovely things. And *only* old, it seems. The woodcock hides twice over from now in a double cloak of dark: the night's fleece and the soil's suit. I have never seen one on the ground, yet there is no bird more grounded. It would prefer to do all of what it must do, to run its gamut, when close to the earth and at night. Only for minutes of its year will it show itself voluntarily upwards. And even then, stiffness hobbles its dressage. Otherwise, it is a night-soil bird and it carries with it something of the dirt inside us all. It is old like shit is old. Or like a worm-cast is old, being made from double-buried earth that has already moved through a body, from earth that has itself been buried within the earth.

At its home in the dirt the woodcock has long kept a wooden shield half-hidden in leaf mould, its prize for the bird least resolved on modernity. At the tournament the jousting also-rans included corn-crakes and stock doves and willow tits. But since the woodcock has for so long made his rounds and always looked the part, a macroceph-alic boy crowned Queen of the May every year, the half-masted bard permanently installed at the Eisteddfod, everyone else has given up imagining they could ever win, and it has been charitably decided that the woodcock best keep the trophy for all time.

'Almost present, not quite absent: *I am not here, I am something else* . . .' – Elizabeth Bletsoe has a poem on the woodcock in her sequence 'Birds of the Sherborne Missal'. Is it any wonder that we struggle to configure the bird for today? What workshop could new-fangle a wood-cock? How would it look? A Kelmscott smock? A Leach pot splashed with telluric glaze? An artisan pie? Is there someone that will scan its barcode of browns and digitise a bird whose feet and beak are still stuck in the mud? Might you steampunk one from worms and wood waste, a whittled stick for its hard bits, mud and leaf rot for all else apart from a pair of ripe blackcurrants for eyes?

'Its plumage . . . could not be briefly described' – Alfred Newton again. Take, if you will, instruction from the soil. Put out the light. Roll the bundle you have gathered beneath your blind fingers in the earth. Assemble the black back-story. Feel how you have made a snowman-bird in night-shades. And know, even as it shrugs into life, how ancient it is already, how the woodcock gathered words to it in the olden days and remains *cock-shutt*, trapped by them, like a dinosaur tarred and feathered in Latin. Learn how birds do not carry bags but nonetheless come with baggage.

I asked the British Trust for Ornithology, who promised to survey the bird for a year, to put me in touch with their woodcock workers. Could I run a wire? Meanwhile, I was forced back to the old books. I stared at Thomas Bewick's *woodcut*: a *wodwo* with a beak. I word-processed a feathered variorum. The brainless bird with the bending nose that lives by suction and winters on the moon. The 400 served at an archbishop's banquet in the autumn of 1465; the 470 drowned that were picked up by a single fishing boat off Lowestoft in the autumn of 1928; the one accidentally brought down by a 'sixpenny rocket' on

Guy Fawkes' Night in central London. Other stories of woodcocks ferrying or piloting tiny, enfeebled goldcrests across the North Sea. Wordsworth, who, as a boy, stole trapped woodcocks from other hunters' *springes*. Tolstoy giving lines to Levin's dog, Laska, in *Anna Karenina*, when the dog, Levin and Oblonsky go hunting snipe, and Levin blurts a question and receives news of Kitty, whom he thought he had lost, at the very moment a woodcock flies towards them – 'What a time they have chosen to talk . . . And there it comes flying . . . Just so, here it is. They'll miss it . . .' And Gilbert White's notes on being sent a milk-white woodcock, plump and in good condition, and his worrying otherwise about worms – 'Many times have I had the curiosity to open the stomachs of woodcocks . . . but nothing ever occurred that helped to explain to me what their subsistence might be: all that I could ever find was a soft mucus, among which lay many pellucid small gravels.' Then I saw one flying over the M42, *towards* Birmingham in a way that made it inevitable that I would italicise its direction of travel. And I tried to remember how T. S. Eliot (was it?) said of *eldritch* that the word itself was what it meant – ghostly, weird, and out of date – and I thought the same of my *wode cucs*. I went on and ate one on toast in Lexington Street in Soho. Half of one: split in two, my friend Robin taking the right half, me the left. The sticks of the beak and the legs were like a scaffold lifting the flesh to our mouths. The toast was brown, the bird browner. It tasted so. There was bracken in it, and something of the soil around the leg of a mushroom.

I set my heart on learning the sequence of the weave of dead browns that stripe a living woodcock's head – paler, darker, paler, darker – and I sought a paintbox of words for that earthenware bird that would do more than indicate one tone as a variant of another, but every time I started looking at the pictures (all I had to go on), the dome of the bird's head (a schoolteacher's head, or Philip Larkin's, or Moby Dick's) and its beaded eyes (those blackcurrants with a bit of stoat) fixed me in such a way that nothing new could go in beyond what was imme-diately yet bafflingly there. Thus I learned how camouflage messes with the mind as well as with the retina.

* * *

My sometime home county of Cambridgeshire has fewer woodcocks than almost anywhere else in Britain. In the Fens a flight or two come from further east in the winter on what Gilbert White called *moonshiny* nights to crouch in ditches and drains. If the fields flood or freeze and if you are lucky, you might see a woodcock trundle the wheeled wooden siege engine of itself out into the open. I never have. The bird really wants woods, and the county hardly holds more than a handful. Three or four winters ago, my neighbour saw a pair hanging from the belt of a huntsman just outside our village. Thirty years ago on a misty November morning, I put one up from a window-box garden in the centre of Cambridge by opening my then front door. I remember the shock more than the bird, the fluster rather than the feathers, the rifled air.

At Wicken Fen, somewhere near the middle of the southern peat fens, there are trees growing out of the drying swamp, and since the 1950s woodcocks have found them bosky enough to hide beneath. The fen is one of only two or three sites in the county where the birds now breed. Through the spring they rode above the trees and out over the reeds and sedge, their transects and commentaries cutting through the firework flights and the tribal drumming of snipe, the woodcocks' wetter cousins, equally seasonally surprised into the upper air but showing more spirit and buoyancy there.

Walking the flatness of the fen, your thoughts travel further than your destination, just as the bird's rode turns upon itself in its journeys and knots the end of its flight to its beginning. Unravel that rope, then, feel fingered by the *Scolopax*. The fens were forest once; the bog oaks that still occasionally rise like whale-backs through the wasting peat declare it. Read the woodcock as bog oak or golden bough: a wet tree kept underground until it surfaces, old and intact, still leafed though made of rot; or an endlessly leafing branch that might allow passage across the dark lands.

The great energy gift of nature is that it arrives and is experienced in a permanent present. Its *nowness* and its *thisness*, its specifics, cap any sense we might have of the world ageing. It is the same for all the seasons and all their life. We die but the Earth renews. But we experience renewal as a permanently breaking wave. This follows this, now follows now. The flight of birds is an especially potent account of this: it is time hung in the air and made visible. But with a roding woodcock, we encounter a flight that carries more of the mulched life it is made from than the animated life it is flying now. This tells us how much has happened before the moment of our meeting. And the brown woodcock, rotting or golden-rusting for ever, an old apple from an old Eden, is a bird flying out of the past.

In the 1930s the British Trust for Ornithology ran their first wood-cock survey. A modernising zeal was abroad in British ornithology. The woodcock-surveyor-in-chief was W. B. Alexander. For £5, from a second-hand bookseller in Cambridge, I bought a bound reprint from the pages of the *Ibis* of Mr W. B.'s findings. A questionnaire had been devised and distributed seeking information on the birds' breeding, migration, and wintering status, on the 'chief enemies' of the woodcock and on noteworthy roding behaviour. It also queried the best of the woodcock myths – 'Have you ever seen parents carrying their young?'

Some birds are too known for their own good, too surrendered to the bird people. On this list today we might put avocets, marsh harriers, and even bitterns. Such special birds in Britain, birds you might go looking for purposely, can seem owned, managed and all but tethered in their reserves and guarded places. The woodcock is not. It is still more anomalous because it was once known better than it is now. Woodcocks are birds in retreat. With the red grouse, they are the last wild birds in Britain that are more familiar to those who want to kill them than to those who would love them if they could. All the records of American woodcock in Europe come from hunters' bags. No one who might love the living bird (and close relative of the European species) has seen them alive on our side of the Atlantic.

It is spring. Imagine a sleeping woodcock lit by the sun on the floor of a wood. It is disappearing somewhere between the living light and the dead leaves in a drowsy doze. So cryptic is the incubating bird on the ground that its nest is hardly ever found. David Lack, the author of the first Cambridgeshire county avifauna published in 1934, knew of only one modern record. He describes its finding at Chippenham Fen with the social politesse of a man marking a dance card: 'The keeper, Mr Mercer, who knows the bird well, showed the nest to Mr Allen, the estate agent.' The finder, like a canine pointer, shows his master the bird, who authenticates the rustic's record.

Via their lairds and lords, it was the keepers of Britain who supplied sightings of woodcocks carrying their young. Alarmed adult birds are supposed to help their flightless downy chicks to safety by picking them up. As well as roding the skies in its limping sex dance, the woodcock will carry its own children aloft to escape the trappings of the down-there world it otherwise loves. In this way the bird might show itself to us at the very moment it is fleeing from us. In this way the past and the present meet. People on the ground have witnessed these flights; book-writers are not so sure. Gilbert White, who was both, wondered if the injury-feigning distraction flight, where the bird depresses its tail between its legs, might make a woodcock look as if it were carrying the little bag of a baby. But W. B. Alexander reports on his reports: 'Keepers in Hampshire, Worcestershire, Glamorgan, Cheshire and Lancashire have sent particulars . . .' Some woodcocks dropped their young mid-air, and these were watched falling or were found, lonely, on the ground, other chicks were seen being lifted further by their parents: ninety-seven were held between the legs, or between the legs and breast; thirty-eight were carried in the adults' feet or claws; nineteen were partly supported by the adults' tail and thirteen partly supported by their bill; seven were seen riding on their parents' backs.

One recent autumn, I met an artist in Bristol called Luci Gorell Barnes. She works with refugee and migrant women on some allotments in the city, where they meet to grow vegetables and talk. On one wintry morning, at Speedwell, as Luci was arriving to meet the women, she found a freshly dead woodcock in the gutter of the road. They are extraordinary to see close up, fabulously intricate in their markings, and Luci picked up the casualty and showed her group. They were sad to see the dead bird, but impressed by its plumage. The mood of the women was transformed, however, when Luci told them how, when in danger, the adult birds are believed to carry their young to safety. Many of the women – they had come from Sudan, Somalia and

Yemen – had done the same with their babies and children on their dangerous journeys to Britain.

Maramureş
48°N

For a rainy May week in northern Romania, Claire and I walked up and down the season. The new spring birds had arrived in a cloud. Many migrants might not have been wet since their time here last year. There was a male redstart in an apple tree in Săpânţa. I watched as raindrops rolled from its quivering tail, rinsing the colours and making the matt momentarily sparkle. In the same village and the same downpour, a black redstart sang from the brick-tiled chimney of a house. Beads of rain ran from its shaking tail too.

In the murk of a soaked beech wood we found a red-breasted flycatcher. The rain fell as if indoors. The beech trunks blackened with it and the mulching leaf mould of last year's leaves sweated. Everywhere was in shade; everything was sopping. I saw a flying mosquito hit by a raindrop. Andrei Tarkovsky – obsessive and heroic cinematographer of interior precipitation – would have enjoyed it. The flycatcher was hard to locate. Its tiny voice wandered through the aisles of tall trees. We found it low down on a beech branch after twenty minutes of searching. It was sandy-brown in the dinge – I could see very little red – and its metallic chivvy of a song was thin in the dripping nave of the forest, but it sang phrase after phrase with quiet persistence. We watched and listened. I had only seen the bird on passage before and had never heard one sing. After one round of its fragile music, it jumped up into the air and turned over itself and re-landed – a perfect back-flip. It flew off then at speed and we didn't see it again. We marked where we had been with the bird, like Hansel and Gretel on their walk, bending twigs and scuffing the dead leaves, so that we might find our way back to see it again. But overnight the rain worsened, with the cloud coming lower on the hills and swamping the beeches, and we had to abandon our search.

Down in the valleys we could see further, but it was still wet. Cut hay was lying in sodden swathes in the fields like mouldy carpet. It was sad to see. There was dashed-down cherry blossom too and new green leaves rent and fallen. I had one of my it's-already-over-before-it's-properly-begun moments and I moped for a while. I know these maudlin moods. They often come to me around my birthday on 20 May. As a child they used to trouble me – when exactly was the spring; what day was its best day; was there a day when everything was alive; how could we enjoy the new green if there was already something eating it or breaking it off the trees; if a snowdrop has died what possibly could be happy about a cuckoo? A bird's egg has to be broken for its contents to live, but eggshells always look abandoned and sad. I found the shed casings of leaves distressing too – the brown scurf dead on the ground. I still do.

In Romania, in a layby outside a village shop selling mostly pig fat, trucks carrying beehives towards the meadows of the Carpathians were waiting out the wet. I bought one jar of pine honey and one jar of meadow honey – last year's captured sun. The makers of this year's honey were locked in their wooden towers on the flat-beds of the trucks. As I was making my purchases, a dog ran past – a medium-sized, medium-coloured, basic dog. In its mouth it carried a small white dog, dead. It was going at quite a lick. Behind it, panting in pursuit, came two smaller versions of the paramedic–undertaker–cannibal. We followed by car but couldn't keep up.

A road crew were wearing plastic bags on their heads. Some had fashioned carrier bags into jerkins, and one man had a bin bag as a cape. There were men in the wet fields wearing suit jackets and steaming like the horses they were standing next to. Another walked in his soggy tracksuit carrying a chain-saw at his side as someone else might hold the hand of a child.

Despite the weather, tree pipits sang along the field edges, and nightingales and thrush nightingales (both are here) sounded loud as we drove past in the wet, making a buzz-hum like an electricity sub-station. We saw a hepatic cuckoo, a liver-red variant of the bird. A black stork flew across a valley, as if paddling the raft of itself through the watery air. By a spating river, choppy with mud, in the now driving rain, we heard an eastern olivaceous warbler singing – a double dousing for a bird just days out of the drouthy Sahara.

We tried to motor out of the rain, but it was everywhere. In a high meadow sounded the wet cloche of sheep bells, dripping wool and bleating animals. Their shepherds were at work, making cheese in a makeshift dairy, a plastic sheet strung over a gantry of fresh-cut hurdles. From the temporary roof, they hung bags of the curd. In the blotted air they looked like various swimming moons.

22 May. It shone bright – jay-blue bright – at six in the morning, but the rain came again. By the time we had got to the Bicaz Canyon everything was cold and slippery. The limestone cliffs ran wet with the cloud they had fleeced. The river, full in its flow, was loud. We couldn't see the top of the gorge; the canyon was packed with the grey kapok of cloud. A raven came low and made its *okk-okk* call; another, out of view, made a weird whistle through the cloud, as if each knew the other was there and one (though which?) was steering the other. Two pairs of grey wagtails had made mossy green nests just above the river. They looked as if they could be squeezed like a sponge. We walked up the narrow twisting road at the bottom of the canyon where the walls on either side leant together and came close to touching. My neck grew sore from peering upwards. An hour into our patrol, Claire spotted our target, the most marvellous fluttering mouse – a wallcreeper, descending the cliff face, walking down out of the clouds towards our drowning company.

It was a bird come from above, and it made the damp world tremble and fizz in its enlargement. Who could have dreamt up such a creature? It has no legs to speak of, but tough little feet. With these it happily crawls up and down sheer and severe rock. It has a curved beak that can get into crannies and find hidden insects. It has a mouse-bright eye in a surprised-mouse face. Between its beak and its feet, it wears a sensible grey coat. When I first saw it in Bicaz, I wasn't sure if I was looking at a bird or at rainwater sluicing over a bump of rock. But then, as it moved, it did the galvanic thing that wallcreepers do – it flicked open its wings and switched on the whole drab and dripping limestone wall: putting colour into the grey, electricity into the cloud, softness into the hard place, movement into the stone, and warmth into the cold. Its wings were broad and rounded, like the palm of a hand, and decorated like a silk handkerchief, black to the rear and red to the leading edge, with brilliant white spots on the outermost red feathers and on the first four primaries. And it showed this magic readily to us. Like a conjuror opening their empty fist to reveal a precious cloth, so the wallcreeper unfurls its wings and throws across the cliff, for a moment, a deep red cape, old rose-madder red, more lovely for being old and for moving, with the colour drag making it hang or float about the mouse-creeping bird. It does this not in order to fly. The bird we saw never flew: it preferred to walk down and then back up the vertical rock face, out of the cloud and back up into it; but, every few seconds as it came and went it flicked open its wings. In this respect it is a redstart that can walk down a cliff. The wallcreeper's flicking is its signature, or what the books call a habitual expression of excitement or alertness. And it is comparable to a dipper's dipping or bob and a redstart's tail-shiver. They do it more when they are nervous or extra-excited. They use it as a distraction. They use it as a threat. They use it in courtship. But they do it mostly just because they do, and they wouldn't be themselves if they didn't.

We waited, but the bird didn't descend again; maybe it kept on climbing and cleared the cloud, walking higher into the blue, its wings flicking like tinder to the day.

Wallcreepers live vertically: in the winter they descend to lower altitudes and in the spring they climb. Their seasons take them up and down, not south to north. They are altitudinal migrants. It still amazes me to know that in the winter of 1976 I saw a wallcreeper in a quarry near the Cheddar Gorge, south of Bristol. I learned of its vagrancy on the grapevine of bird news and begged my father to take me to see it, without fully knowing what a wallcreeper was or why I felt impelled to try to see one. We stood below the quarry face with a gang of other birdwatchers and saw the wallcreeper's creep. It was an alien life form to me – utterly bewitching but too exotic to understand or love. I hardly knew rare birds then and had no way to think myself into its life.

Stranger still, the next winter the bird returned. Its first errant migration had become a habit. Imagine a wallcreeper flying away from its natal cliff (the nearest breeders to Somerset are in the French Alps or the Cantabrian Mountains in northern Spain), winging over flat fields and then across the swell of the sea. The old red cape flickers and pulses. The gypsy mouse-bird finds vertical stone once more and decides it is at home. And imagine it, voluntarily, doing that again.

23 May. The rain stopped properly in Romania for just one day. We walked as much of it as we could. The Székely Hungarian village of Torockó (known as Rimetea in Romanian) lies south of Cluj in what I think is the greenest valley I have ever seen. The village hugs the valley floor between, to the east, an isolated, almost naked limestone whale-back of a mountain, Székelykő, and, to the west, the more wooded Trascău range.

Wanting some sun, we began to walk up the limestone as soon as we arrived. We crossed a terraced hillside, bony with stones, where shepherds moved their sheep, and climbed beneath a soft shower of woodlark song coming from several singers stowed in the sky. We flushed another from the ground and it flew to the one tree on the hillside, a cherry, where it sat quietly until we passed.

Looking down into the valley below, beyond the grazing terraces, to a patchwork of farmed rectangular strips, it was all green, astoundingly so. Seen from above, every strip (they alternated, between grass being grown for hay and arable hectares growing crops) was a different tone. Every shade was there. Every hue. Green galore. But how hopeless seemed my vocabulary for that view: to get such colour down is as hard as to paint the Sahara. All the available words for the various greens seemed defeated by the growing Hungarian *zöld* before us: lime, emerald, menthol, avocado, eau de nil, pea, sage, malachite, beryl, eucalyptus, olive, jade, sea, Lincoln, Chartreuse . . . Green: vegetable, breeding, deciduous and evergreen, salad and meltwater, bottle and arsenic, gasoline, gaberdine, frog, asphodel — *that greeny flower*, a copper kettle, a lightning rod, the mirror's old silver, a rotting bone, duckweed and apple, greengage and laurel, turned turtle and sap . . . None of them, not one of them adequately let in the light, and none of them seemed appropriately alive. Any qualifying terms I tried to add showed only the dead hand of capture. In the same way, picked bluebells die as true bluebells from the moment they are picked. The green below us was living growth, was raw and wild electric fluid, was surge and rustle and flow. *How many colors are there in a field of grass to a crawling baby unware of 'Green'* – wrote the film-maker Stan Brakhage. *A green acre* – said Gertrude Stein on celery – *is so selfish and so pure and so enlivened*. It is like light – it *is* light – and it is as hard to speak of.

Then we saw something that wasn't green but was everything green means. We walked the limestone ridge to where it fell away towards the fields, and at that point we saw a bird fly up into the chalky blue from the chalky rocks. It was a male common rock thrush making a display flight. The first I had seen since the winter migrant I saw in Ethiopia in 1988. It flew deliberately, describing a circuit in the air, with climbs and flounces and falls, and it sang fluting notes as it went, sounding somewhat gargled, like a blackbird in a hurry.

It flew out and up from the ridge and then performed a kind of emphatic slump above the green valley. As it did, it showed a pearly white square on its lower back and rump. The red on it – its tail, the warm tile red of its breast and belly – was wonderful to see, and the equally warm slate of its back was welcoming too. It was thrown up into the air, singing all the while. Its flight was made with a kind of knowing brokenness. A little fluttering smudge moving out over the broad sweep of the valley. It seemed like a sideshow, an event on an edge, yet because of this it was affecting. It was done perfectly and, because the doer was totally occupied in its doing, everything was believable, and everything that lay behind the doing became lovable. 'Don't show me your soul,' George Balanchine used to say to his dancers: 'I want to see your foot.' A truth came through the bird's act: it was a flounce that wasn't, a tossed handkerchief that wasn't, a throwing down of a gauntlet that wasn't. It made those necessary moves, but it was alive differently behind all of them, and it showed this secret living thing – plainer than its performance but bigger and better than it too.

On the way down the mountain we saw a human version of the same. Dancing is not where any of us live full-time, but (like skipping) it can be a way to show that we are alive, to kick up our heels, to show our feet. A boy, perhaps ten years old, had been sent out to help get his family's sheep folded for the night. He'd gone up the hill, whistled instructions to a dog and, having sent the flock down the terraces, turned to follow them back himself. He was out of sight of all of them now, and of his father who was at the fold at the edge of the village. He joined a dusty track, and as he did he skipped two or three strides, and then hopped two or three steps. A little dust-cast of his fun came up from the path.

We followed him down through sheep bells and dog barks. Below a spring, there were wild strawberries growing. And butterflies I didn't know – a fritillary and another with chocolate brown wings marked with orange spots. A quail called, hidden in the grass, and a scops owl started up. In the village we stopped at an open window on the street, where an old lady in a pinafore and a headscarf was selling home-made *pálinka* (52 per cent alcohol), the clear spirit drenched in fruit (plums, I think). We passed our money and she smiled a golden grin and passed back an old cola bottle filled with her medicine. We enjoyed a nip, sitting in the square, as the village cows came wending home. They did so like children from school. Ten cream-coloured giants appeared in the square with no one driving them. There were soft moos and softer bells. Cow by cow they peeled off and turned down the lanes to their homes. Two stepped this way, one another. They knew their routes. Every house in the village is a farmhouse and most have broad wooden gates opening onto barnyards. Where two cows were expected, the big gates had been opened. Where just a single cow was due, it was only the small pedestrian gate. These are little more than human width but the cows squeezed through, their moony udders, full of the day's greens, slapping side to side and hitting the wooden uprights as they walked.

Székelyudvarhely & Tara
46°N & 44°N

'Most happenings are beyond expression,' wrote Rilke in the first of his *Letters to a Young Poet* (17 February 1903). 'They exist in a world where a word has never intruded.' Quite a lot of being a birdwatcher revolves around not seeing birds. I have learned much that way. I'm also lucky to have been at some *happenings* like those that Rilke describes.

Twice in European springs, I have managed to see more, or to see further, by seeing nothing or not much. Once I waited for hours in a wood for an animal that didn't come. A second time, in a similar place in a different country, what I was waiting for did eventually appear. And then I felt I had seen an animal as it might appear to itself rather than to me.

These times, each in half-light or less (a dawn, a dusk), I sat and waited and watched for hours on the edge of a clearing. Once I was the captive of nothing, and once I was swapped, like a hostage, from being nothing's prisoner to being something's audience. On both of these occasions (with and without a target in view) I had the sensation of being able to see beyond my own seeing, to feel time *out of mind*, as it were, and to witness the world going on, as it does when we are not there.

Lauren Hartke, the subject of Don DeLillo's novel *The Body Artist*, spends hours, when grieving for her husband, watching a webcam relay of a deserted road in the small Finnish town of Kotka. 'The dead times', she thinks, 'were best.'

I have known that good dead time in a clearing near Ivó, north-east of Székelyudvarhely, in Romania, where I waited in hope of a brown bear.

We had gone out with Gyula, a bearded forester in a green suit. He thought there were twenty bears in the Hargita Mountains. To have a chance to see one we had to hide.

It was dusk when we arrived. It had rained earlier but the sky had half cleared. The forest was thick with beech and fir trees. As we walked up, shushed to silence by Gyula, we saw a firecrest busy in the needles of a pine, and both a black woodpecker and a grey-headed woodpecker flying over the muddy track. We climbed into Gyula's hide. He locked the door by wedging his rifle against it, and from beneath his bench took a bottle of *pálinka* (a capercaillie on the label) and filled glasses

185

and passed them to us, all without a word. We looked out on a clearing that he had felled: a tangle of branches and tree stumps with, at its centre, one beech still standing. A wire was stretched from the tree to another at the clearing edge, and slung on it was a blue plastic barrel. Every evening at seven, a shower of maize kernels was released from it as bear bait. We got to the hide just after a drop.

Nothing then proceeded to happen. A chaffinch landed and a jay came down three times to the maize. Two planes passed high overhead. The light began to pack itself away. The leaves on the beeches appeared to be just sitting where they had grown. On the far side of the clearing, the air became soupy, and eventually I couldn't tell what was trunk and what was night. The singing of song thrushes in the surrounding woods got more vehement – a sort of towelling at the passing time – and then dimmed. The distances opened up by their evening song closed as the last light went from the sky. When the moon rose – somewhere out of sight – the night actually got brighter, but the light felt hoary by then, like light reflected from a tarnished mirror. It shone obliquely on a stage where there had been action – you could sense that – but where there was none now.

I stared. No bears came.

Being a ghost might be like this, or being dead. Perhaps I was thinking about that, or about the word *clearing*, or perhaps I was not thinking of much at all. Time slipped, and it passed the point where I was expecting to partake in whatever moment might arise, and we – the clearing and Gyula and Claire and I – arrived into some other realm. Moonlight broke in around this point, and then I could see more of the night forest's nothing-that-is-everything. And I could also see the nothing-that-is-everything that was there the previous night, when we weren't there, and the same careless but intimate immensity that would be there the next night when we wouldn't be there. 'Let it come down,' one of Banquo's murderers says in *Macbeth*, of the rain and the night and death, collapsing each into each with his knife strike. In the clearing I felt I knew what that meant, and what that felt like.

A cloud blurred the light of the moon, and the spaces between the tree trunks on the far side of where I sat lost their various blacks. Yet in this blank my seeing grew. I was next to nothing and was looking at a place that was regardless of me. I saw the forest without knowing it as explicit, as close to plainly as might be possible, as if the optic nerve behind my eye were transmitting while my brain was asleep. I registered the sensation of being there as I perceived it and not as I knew it. I saw but I did not know and, because I was not doing any of the knowing, the place became more itself.

I did not come to this thought. It came to me.

The day had ended hours before, but now I could see its end – the going of the light and so the going of all that the light makes known in the daytime; the emptying of everything without the removal of anything, which is how nature goes when we are not there. I knew it was ordinary but I felt it as a vision. The night's bearlessness made this happen. The absence of a bear helped me see in the dark. If I had seen a bear, I would have seen nothing else; without the bear I could see everything.*

It was once thought that bears were born formless and were licked into shape by their mothers. The bears at Ivó were there somewhere like this but were still shadowy and latent, not available to me, and not yet available to sight.

We walked back three hours later in the dark. There was a clatter of feet off the track ahead of us.

– A deer, said Gyula.

Another year, another bear-watching site. This time in the Tara National Park in western Serbia – a clearing, another eye open to the sky, in a montane beech and spruce forest, similar to Romania but with taller

---

* Writing about Wordsworth's 'There Was a Boy', Thomas De Quincey describes a comparable *relaxation* into seeing: 'after waiting to no purpose [for an owl to call], his attention began to relax – that is, in other words, under the giving way of one exclusive direction of his senses, began suddenly to allow an admission to other objects – then, in that instant, the scene actually before him, the visible scene, would enter unawares . . .'

trees. There was a maize-dispenser like a vending machine. And there was more bait: two spotty young men in tracksuit trousers and vests had hauled a dead cow to the clearing. Perhaps it could tempt a brown bear. As soon as the cow was toppled from the trailer to the muddy ground, flies found all its soft parts and entry points. Its pitch-dark moony eyes puckered as we stared at it. A little blue butterfly landed and lingered at its extruded anus. A raven flew over and looked down, reading the menu.

I was with my bird friend Mark Cocker. We went off for a few hours of mostly birdless birdwatching and got back to the clearing at half past four in the afternoon. We sat in a wooden hide for two hours, quiet all the while, looking out. Ranko Milanovic, a warden in Tara, had escorted us. He had sent a briefing note in advance:

> We are staying in the hide in absolute silence without snacks, hot drinks, plastic bottles, smoking, mobile phones, rustling clothes, toilet. Do not use any kind of perfumes.

I had bought some chocolate biscuits that morning which I had chosen because they were called *Plazma* and made by a company called *Bambi*. They had to stay in my bag.

What followed was a cinema screening of slow-motion close-ups that felt like views fetched back from over a horizon: daisies shutting as the sun moved from them, moths and mayflies levitating in pools of dusty light, blackbirds present but not, as it were, acting blackbird, and the forever quiet of trees. It was the world carrying on as itself; the truth stopped down.

At five-forty the first gaps appeared in the thick weave of bird song.

At six, a bear came. I had the feeling that it had not long been awake. Its entrance was superb – it walked with a lumpen grace out of the trees and paused in the clearing. Its timing – spot on – was totally its own. I felt that. It carried its own clock with it. The animal seemed massive and immensely solid. And old. Its sway was old, its coat, the dabbing of its paws, its grandfatherliness, its sniff upwind and down. It made me want to say out loud that it was real and that I respected it. Its sway looked tremendously genuine: absolute bear, unperformed. Everything around it became part of its walk. The planet streamed away from it on all sides. In Arctic North America, the Inuktitut word for a bear is *pihuqahtaq* – meaning *the one who walks*: that seemed absolutely the case here in Serbia. It walked as if it was passing the ball of the Earth beneath its feet. Its eyes were very small and its claws were yellow and long. Both seemed not quite right for it, and made it look as if it was still at work on itself. Life wasn't perfect. There was effort. The brighter light of the clearing made it screw its eyes smaller still. Its legs were darker brown than the rest of its fur. They looked like over-trousers, and made me think of folk dancing. You could sense its sleep in its coat. You knew it slept in that same fur. Its nose was wet. As it came nearer, I could hear its rasping breath and see insects being blown from its face by its exhalations. Tiny flies and bees scattered.

It walked across the clearing and out of sight – an exit that wasn't really an exit because it hadn't really entered; it was simply on the go. At six-fifteen it came back and took a dried-up cob from the popcorn stall. It had to raise its front legs to reach its treat. It looked then like a bear wearing a bear-suit, and I felt sorry to have seen that. The dead cow it ignored, apart from turning its swaying nose towards its smell as it passed. It left the clearing again. At six-twenty-five it appeared once more on a path that came into the clearing, but stopped before entering and left the path and just walked off through the trees. It looked then immensely ancient and magnificent, like something before words or thought or even seeing, some thing far, far away, some thing still wild from before anything of us.

Of course, I re-made the bear as it came into my head: I cannot really report on what I saw, but only on what I made of what I saw. Everything is italicised by our looking. The wild dries quickly like dew in the sun. I thought the bear like the spring all across those woods – new-come, not long awake, Persephone in drag. But perhaps I should just write as Ranko wrote in his logbook: date . . . time . . . place . . . bear. Yet for a moment, a fleeting moment, as it turned off the path and went through the trees, its absolute presence felt visible to me: a bear perceived or, rather, *received*, yet unmediated by thought, and at that moment, the ever-so present nothings of those other clearings that

I had waited in, were incarnated or embodied or furred – 'The heavy bear,' as Delmore Schwartz had it in a poem, 'who goes with me.'*

It didn't know that. It didn't know it was being watched. And because it didn't give off a sense of being seen we were able to see it – or believe we might – without, as it were, seeing it. We had what T. J. Clark calls in his book, *The Sight of Death*, about looking repeatedly at some paintings by Poussin 'the physical, literal, *dumb* act of receiving the array on the retina'. We caught the bear off-guard and caught ourselves the same. It came like the best stone – stony. And, of the earth – earthy. It came pure bear. And it went.

We were back in the bear hide at seven the next morning. *Villa Medo* said a little sign above the door. An orange-tip butterfly flew past, briefly turning the clearing into a glade.

As before, after one hundred minutes, a bear came. At nine-forty: a small cub, one year old. Its fur had been mussed up; maybe it wasn't long awake – some of its bed of old beech leaves were stuck to it. It made a little cackling noise as it took a corn cob from the dispenser. It was shaggy and had longer fur than the older animal we had seen. It looked like it had been hugged by a bear.

Before we left, I collected two golden leaves that the cub had shaken from itself to the floor of the clearing. I have them still.

Cederberg
33°S

Claire has a friend called Mark Johnston; they met when they went to high school together in Cape Town when rocks (and maps) brought

---

* He was a heavy bear. It was Delmore Schwartz who used 'Time is the fire in which we burn' as a refrain in his poem of grief and mourning for the deaths of friends and the passing of all things. The poem has an ironic title, 'Calmly We Walk Through This April Day'. He died himself after suffering a heart attack when putting out the garbage, from his room at the Chelsea Hotel in New York City in 1966. He was fifty-two, depressed and an alcoholic.

them close. Previously both sets of their parents had taken them to a place called the 'Scratch Patch'. There, in an industrial shed on the outskirts of Simon's Town on the Cape Peninsula, children can rummage through screes of stone and pick out and collect a variety of tumble-polished gems that have been stirred into a mineral aggregate. You pay according to the size of bag you fill. It still operates, listing southern African stones and crystals among its captive offerings, including agates, tiger's eye, rose quartz, amethyst and jasper. Both Claire and Mark got keen on rock-climbing. Growing up beneath Table Mountain makes climbers and rock-hoppers of many in Cape Town. Claire's father Christopher was an avid mountaineer in his youth and still (in his eighth decade) scrambles (at speed) up and down the mountain at least once a week. He roped his daughter and her friend into many of their early climbs.

Mark remains a climber. His flat – under Table Mountain – has boxes of stones he has collected from various peaks in South Africa and other high places. He continues to love rock. As a lifelong student of geomorphology and tectonics, he understands Gary Snyder's New-Age-Stone-Age remark (quoting the Zen masters, Dōgen and Furong) that 'mountains are constantly walking'. Recently he was able to add the subduction thrill of a New Zealand earthquake to his curriculum vitae. As the years have gone round, though, he has found himself feeling less and less comfortable with his collection. There are now fewer boxes at his home. On current climbs and hill trails he often carries a rock in his rucksack that he intends to return to the spot he took it from. This might seem an action too precious for stones, but Mark's rock repatriations have more to do with a return upon himself in his relations with rock. His thieving – when he thought of it as that – made him feel like he had been trespassing, and he has discovered that he wants the rocks to be in their place more than in his, and that any chipped-off flake of the world's surface is best known as part of a mountain and not as a possession or the prize of someone who has stood on it. Taken back to their home, the rocks have their value restored, for there they lie, like Seamus Heaney's river gravels, as *gems for the undeluded*.

In the Cederberg, north of Cape Town, there is clearly no shortage of rocks. Mark has led Claire and me on walks and scrambles into landscapes that are totally mineral, skeletal places, all bone and no flesh. There is stone enough to spare. Indeed, Mark often plays an old mountaineering jape and, when our backs have been turned, has loaded one or other of our rucksacks with secret rocks to weigh down our climb. And we retaliate too – I have managed to get a good kilo of Kogelberg sandstone into his pack. It is not the transport off the mountain, lump by lump, that troubles Mark, but the species of our intrusion and what we have made of it – the capture as a prize relic or its fashioning into some stony medal. Such a discovery might be applied to all our dealings (or getting) with nature and any possessive re-working (or spending) of its material matter. Mark's correction of his younger habits, his self-stripping of hard-won rewards, seems an exemplary way to go. Nature is best known when in its home, even if there it is out of sight.

On our most recent hiking days in the Cederberg, we stayed for one night at the foot of a high cresting ridge of wounded-looking reddish-grey rock. Fire had done that, not a thief. The mountain had burned the previous summer. It was July, midwinter in the Cape (for me, late of England, the middle of a *converse-season*), and frosty up high. We left any greenery behind us in the farmed valley floor around the town called Ceres. There we had travelled between two roadside signs that had pointed towards the getting and spending of various harvests: *This Valley for Jesus Christ*, one devout farmer had planted in the middle of their fruitful estate, and *Smousery Verbode*, the local council instructed on signs at the outskirts of several settlements, *Peddling or Hawking Forbidden*.

The farm where we stayed (one of the last up a narrowing valley) grew peaches for drying and the track to the barns was laid with a gravel of peach stones, hundreds of thousands of them. Pressed into a pavement in the dusty path, they looked like the products of an obsessive modeller, countless full moons or blinking cyclopean eyes, one after another, each picked up, fashioned, and put down. My head torch lit them up as Mark and I walked out in the mountain dark to collect some kindling for a fire to heat our evening.

The sky was clear and shipping in cold air that made our breath flare in front of us. Mark knows the stars as well as the stones, and we fell into conversation with the night. Big rocks were flying high: the marvellous bright purr of the Milky Way, bushy with stars, curdled with them, every wink of the sky having its own, and Orion, upside down for me, and the Southern Cross. And then, when Mark pointed in its direction, I saw, for the first time, the Coalsack, a black muzz forcing a gap above us on one side of the star surge. It's a familiar southern-hemisphere dark sky sight, but I had never noticed it before on any other African night. There it was – or wasn't. It looked like nothing; like a moth hole in the flecked wool of the night. Stars crowded at its rim, but it seemed an empty space.* But closer up, through binoculars, its prickling velvet depth manifested a deeper dark, and then it seemed as if a patch of fine dust had been sprinkled over coarser grains or a pollen cloud was blowing over a distant seedbed. It gave a view – blurry and out of focus – of a space that appeared to have been pushed behind or beyond but which was, in fact, more simply or plainly, obscured by it. For the Coalsack is dust, a nebula of thick interstellar dust that occludes our view of the celestial topography beyond. It comes like motes or floaters in our galaxy's eye. It might be the heavens breathing out cold air. It has got *between*, and yet everything in the night sky is made more beautiful for its smudge and for its putting out of the light. One day the Coalsack will ignite with the glow of many burning young stars, but for now its dust isn't to be had as anything other than a haze, and it makes a kind of agglomeration of nothing that, aggregated in its patch, becomes a blurred truth which sharpens everything around it, making the whole night-field seem like a kind of blueprint. Looking at it, and its

* Various southern peoples have recognised the Coalsack as a (big) bird in the night sky: it forms the head of an emu in several Australian Aboriginal cultures and a (not unrelated) tinamou in Inca astronomy.

black-out, you can see the dark; looking at what it obscures, you learn what light might mean.

Tarquinia
42°N

For D. H. Lawrence, in western Italy in 1927, going into dark spaces in pursuit of a clearer sense of a better life meant stepping behind a guide with a set of keys and an acetylene lamp. At Tarquinia, on a 'necropolis hill' growing with 'rock-rose' and 'asphodels', he followed the man and his light down 'a dark little hole underground: a dark little hole, after the sun of the upper world':

> in the dimness, as we get used to the light, we see flights of birds flying through the haze, rising from the sea with the draught of life still in their wings. And we take heart and look closer. The little room was frescoed all round with sea and sky, with birds flying and fishes leaping, and fragmentary little men hunting, fishing, rowing in boats . . .
>
> There is nothing impressive or grand. But through the paleness of time and the damage of men one still sees the quick ripple of life here, the eternity of the naïve moment, which the Etruscans knew.

Lawrence spent more time in Italy than anywhere else after he left England, pretty much for good, in 1919. He had been there for several stays before then and, by the time he quit his native land, Italy had already given him as near to a home as he ever had in his adult life. In 1912, on his first travels abroad, he and Frieda Weekley – a married woman and mother of three – ran away together across the Alps from Germany, through the Austrian Tyrol, into northern Italy. Then, although Frieda took a once-off lover in a hayloft while Lawrence botanised montane flora (the sex life of flowers detaining him while his chosen partner went to bed with a student friend), and although it rained and Frieda sulked on the Italian side of the mountains, the country still lay before them like Keats' *warm south*. It promised a new spring for their lives.

A plan to visit the remains of old pre-Roman Etruria and write about the two-and-a-half-thousand-year-old Etruscan tombs came to Lawrence in the spring of 1926. He was living then with Frieda at the Villa Mirenda, in Scandicci, outside Florence. The spring that year started wet. The countryside was 'very Tuscan – but green, green, over-green, to set your teeth on edge'. But the *pugging* weather dried, and soon Lawrence could read and write outside once more. That year his own story got in the way of history and, instead of visiting the long dead Etruscans, he went back to Britain on what was to be his last trip. He travelled to Scotland for the first time (he never was anywhere further north) and saw Skye and liked it: 'It restores the old Adam in one.'

There is still something of an Odyssey up there, in among the islands and the silent lochs: like the twilight morning of the world, the herons fishing undisturbed by the water, and the sea running far in, for miles, between the wet, trickling hills, where the cottages are low and almost invisible, built into the earth. It is still out of the world, and like the very beginning of Europe: though, of course, in August there are many tourists and motor cars.

Accessing the *morning of the world* was important to Lawrence. It was his formulation for spring (the *world-morning* as seen in a new opened flower) and it was, in his mind, the time in our species' life when we knew better how to live. After Scotland, Old Adam walked on and went south to spend days close to some of his earliest haunts. Though the Lincolnshire coast was grey, he identified the East Midlands as his part of the world, his home-scar, and he surprised himself in discovering how connected he still felt to his old places. Topped up by what he saw in England, when he was back in Italy, in the autumn of 1926, he began busily drafting *Lady Chatterley's Lover*.

Frieda described him at work – doing home from abroad:

195

He would sit, almost motionless except for his swift writing. He would be so still that the lizards would run over him and the birds hop close around him.

Lawrence worked on his novel into the winter. As it came into being it left him 'in a quandary'. He had written what he needed to write but – with the experience already as the author of difficult books – suspected it would be unpublishable. With such thoughts, in the early Italian spring of 1927, a trip to see the Etruscan sites came into view once more. His book about it, *Sketches of Etruscan Places*, appeared only after his death (and has much to say about the posthumous), but it was written at the time of Lawrence's last great shout for life.

Lawrence persuaded an American friend, Earl Brewster, to travel with him, and they were away for just a fortnight in late March 1927. There were other Etruscan remains to look at and museums of unearthed findings, but Lawrence was most interested in the tombs that you could climb down to, which were built into the earth like houses underground, with rooms hollowed out of rock, and stone beds, and chairs. In these homely sepulchres, carved effigies of the dead were erected as if lying at a dinner propped up on their elbows, healthy-looking and often smiling. It is light where they are. The tomb walls are painted, as if outdoors, with outside scenes. But death isn't denied – there are also wall paintings showing the standing but shrouded dead bidding farewell to their loved ones. And the Etruscans also constructed grave goods to assist in the afterlife travels of their dead, including little ships of death, made of bronze, that are both memento mori and model means of conveyance, ferry boats to remind us of the passages of life. In the tombs they were placed next to the stone beds. They gave Lawrence the motif for his late long poem, 'The Ship of Death', that sets sail, looking beyond any crossing, to the darkness ahead. Yet mostly what the Etruscans wanted underground, and what Lawrence responded to above all, are painted scenes of coming rather than going, of brightness, of life, of living, of colour, of good things like birds and music, fowling and fishing, olives and wine, leopards and bulls, sex and flowers.

From the walls of Tarquinia, the tombs can be seen opposite on a green hill:

> that hill has a soul, it has a meaning . . . that is the hill where the dead lie buried and quick, as seeds, in their painted houses underground . . . they are just like houses . . . It is a home . . . the room seems inhabited still by Etruscans of the sixth century before Christ . . . all is colour, and we do not seem to be underground at all.

These tombs were coffins as well as pretend houses, and Lawrence sees dust where bodies once were, and armour 'sunk' on it, and ear-rings lying on a stone bed 'where the ears were dust', and 'bracelets in the dust that once was arms'. Yet among such stilled life he feels life still. This is most obvious in the paintings on the tomb walls:

> Gradually, the underworld of the Etruscans becomes more real than the above day of the afternoon. One begins to live with the painted dancers and feasters and mourners, and to look eagerly for them . . .
> . . . the dancers dance on, the birds run, at the foot of a little tree a rabbit crouches in a bunch, bunched with life . . .

The tombs and their wall paintings, representing what Lawrence called the 'natural flowering of life', speak to him about how the lives of all of us once might have run and possibly could again if only we would attend. Even underground, the Etruscans made life good, and Lawrence tries to fetch this goodness back to the 'above day' at the surface. He calls one tomb (painted with leopards) a 'charming, cosy little room', and we remember that Lawrence was a keen home-maker wherever he lived, that he was good at sewing and cooking, that he liked decorating and fixing up rooms ('I can't recall that he ever broke a plate or a glass,' said Frieda), that he carried a portable kitchen with him on his travels.

One can almost hear them still, calling, shouting, piping, singing, driving in the mixed flocks of sheep and goats, they go so silently, and leading the slow, white, ghost-like oxen with the yokes still on their necks . . .

It is different now . . . We have lost the art of living, and in the most important science of all, the science of daily life, the science of behaviour, we are complete ignoramuses . . .

Lawrence found in Etruscan happiness a way of life that he had long been arguing for. He had just created Mellors in *Lady Chatterley's Lover* at the time he stepped down into these underground scenes of tangled good times. It seems that his wider enthusiasm for the pre- and (as he saw it) anti-Roman lifestyle of the Etruscans has little basis in what we know now. He ignored the historians he read. He got annoyed with a fellow visitor to the tombs, a young German, who had a different interpretation of what they saw. But the truth is only a fraction of what Lawrence wanted.

'A quiet flow of touch' – the *feeling* of the Etruscans – seemed palpable to Lawrence, and it joined them to his project. They were good at living. They had, or seemed to have, 'the old cosmic consciousness': they knew the seasons and lived in the knowledge of death, but they had domesticated that nexus of connections and brought it intimately and locally into down-home versions of their living spaces cast underground. They wanted their dead to be dead, as they had lived.

'Bunched with life', Lawrence wrote of a frescoed rabbit, and all the Etruscan tomb paintings are figured by him as if they themselves were alive and present, as if moving, as if still going, flowing, forwards. 'An act of pure attention, if you are capable of it,' Lawrence writes in his book, 'will bring its own answer.' All we need to do is to pay attention to what we attend to – no rhetoric, please – and then run the film of our own seeing:

Wreaths hang from the ivy-border above, a boy is bringing a wine-jug, the music goes on, and under the beds a cat is on the prowl, while an alert cock watches him. The silly partridge, however, turns his back, stepping innocently along . . .

. . . The Etruscans are still there, upon the wall . . .

. . . the people and the creatures are all really in touch. It is one of the rarest qualities, in life as in art . . . Here, in this faded Etruscan painting, there is a quiet flow of touch that unites the man and woman on the couch, the timid boy behind, the dog that lifts his nose, even the very garlands that hang on the wall.

The way the Etruscans painted, indicated to Lawrence not only their house-style, but also the *touching* truth of how they lived.

The subtlety of Etruscan painting, as of Chinese and Hindu, lies in the wonderful suggestive *edge* of the figures. It is not outlined. It is not what we call 'drawing'. It is the flowing contour where the body suddenly leaves off, upon the atmosphere. The Etruscan artist seems to have seen living things surging from their own centre to their own surface. And the curving and contour of the silhouette-edge suggests the whole movement of the modelling within . . .

It must have been a wonderful world, that old world where everything appeared alive and shining in the dusk of contact with all things, not merely as an isolated individual thing played upon by daylight: where each thing had a clear outline, visually, but in its very clarity it was related emotionally or vitally to strange other things, one thing springing from another, things mentally contradictory fusing together emotionally . . .

For the sun can warm the world, like a yellow hen sitting on her eggs. Or the sun can lick up the life of the world with a hot tongue . . .

One thing springing from another. A wonderful slow surge – Lawrence describes the carving of a wagon moving along a road on a Volterran burial urn as having this quality. *Surge* is an important word for him – it is an evocation of movement that also asserts a connection or a joining, it means the buzz of life, it means Keats' 'green altar' (in his 'Ode on a Grecian Urn'), it means, to me, greenery.

* * *

No other imaginative writer I know, apart from Gerard Manley Hopkins (also a sometimes sickly, botanist-poet), was as florally determined as D. H. Lawrence. He knew flowers all his life, he knew what time of year it was by flowers, he knew where he was by them; he even, I think, knew *who* he was. They were clock, calendar, thermometer, barometer and compass. He noticed them wherever he went and he wrote about them all the time. Frieda described how he was when outside:

> All those that ever went for a walk with him remember what an experience it was. It seemed all he saw out of doors he saw for the first time, and he noticed everything, every first flower in the spring, every colour, every smell.

Lawrence was also, as the critic M. M. Mahood points out, in her great book on botanically minded literary writers, unique in having studied botany at university. He made Ursula in *The Rainbow* do the same, and thereby roped microscopes and nuclei into his novel. He knew how flowers grew. He knew some botanical science. But he also liked the way flowers worked on us – how they made him feel and think – and he wanted to write about that. As an adolescent, he had picked and mounted specimens of the flowers he found around his home in Nottinghamshire. Soon the same were to be pressed into his fiction, his essays and his poems. At times the flowers fight back, and Lawrence allows that, recognises that they cannot take excessive metaphorical exploitation or symbolic hijacking. It is as if their reality tells him when he has stretched a point and that the best thing to do is correct his vision by concentrating on his attention to what is actually growing. That can say a lot – as much as any flower can take – and it is brilliantly and beautifully done in poem after poem. In Lawrence's letters flowers are even less pranked up.

'The insight is uncanny,' D. J. Enright wrote of Lawrence's goat poems; 'a sort of magic, like Adam among the animals.' (In an essay about his childhood, Lawrence described himself as a 'different *animal*' from the middle-class boys at Nottingham High School.) It is the same if not more so for his flowers. He knew the real things and he knew their seasons. The sequence of their growing mattered to him. His letters – regardless of their addressees – record, like phenologically minded field notes, vegetable succession through the year and around the world. The word ecosystem didn't exist then (it was first used in 1935), but Lawrence was forever describing them in these communications, not just one noticeable bloom, but tangled habitats or ecologies. The same web of life is also implicit in Mellors' radical flower-arranging in *Lady Chatterley's Lover*.

The first poem Lawrence wrote was 'Campions'. The first poem in his *Collected Poems* is 'The Wild Common', and begins: 'The quick sparks on the gorse-bushes are leaping / Little jets of sunlight texture imitating flame.' 'Bavarian Gentians' is among his *Last Poems*:

> Reach me a gentian, give me a torch!
> let me guide myself, with the blue, forked torch of this flower
>   down the darker and darker stairs, where blue is darkened
>   on blueness
> even where Persephone goes, just now, from the frosted
>   September
> to the sightless realm where darkness is awake upon the
>   dark . . .

Between his first books of poems and his last there were hundreds of flowers and one long spring. They thin out, to those dark gentians (an autumn flower), only in the final collection of his life. Before then, almost all of Lawrence's poems are flower-driven, even those without specific floral content. The title of his collection *Pansies* was intended as a reference to the French word *pensées* – it was a bunch of pansies, as he said, 'a handful of thoughts' – but we get the idea, and understand how flowers underwrote everything for him. The *wild common* was, as he acknowledged in the foreword to his *Collected Poems* in 1928, a destination he searched for all of his life: 'The wild common, the gorse, the virgin youth are here and now, the same: the same me, the same one experience.'

Seeds were important too. In Cornwall in November 1915, with *The Rainbow* suppressed and on the point of leaving England and trying to go to America, he wrote in a letter: 'My life is ended here. I must go as a seed that falls into new ground.' Later in his letters he often describes his health as 'seedy'. He was ill for years, and denied it to himself and hid the worst of it from his correspondents. I think he used the word to smuggle into his descriptions of himself a sense of possible growth, a renewal or a wakening from dormancy, from wintry darkness into spring. The season meant more to Lawrence than any other time of the year. Spring meant coming back to life and getting better. It meant making life too. It was also the children he never had.

At the same time, between February and April 1927, as Lawrence was working on the second version of *Lady Chatterley's Lover* and travelling to the Etruscan tombs, he wrote an essay in four parts that is now known as 'Flowery Tuscany'. 'Each country,' it begins,

> has its own flowers, that shine out specially there. The Mediterranean has narcissus and anemone, myrtle and asphodel and grape hyacinth. These are the flowers that speak and are understood, in the sun around the Middle Sea.

Human cultivation there, the 'gentle, sensitive sculpture of all the landscape', has not driven away 'Pan or his children', Lawrence says: 'Man feeling his way sensitively to the fruitfulness of the earth, has moulded the earth to his necessity without violating it.' There are wild flowers in a human landscape and domesticated plants too, all sharing a habitat.

> Spring starts in February, with the winter aconite. Some icy day, when the wind is down from the snow of the mountains, early in February, you will notice on a bit of fallow land, under the olive trees, tight, pale-gold little balls, clenched tight as nuts, and resting on round ruffs of green near the ground. It is the winter aconite suddenly come.

This arrival, this *sudden* appearance, is always important to Lawrence. He looked for any such 'surge' – the kick of spring. It was more often to be found and felt in the 'lands of the sun' south of the Alps. North of the Alps, where he came from, were 'forever' 'lands of greyness'.

Although mute and fixed, although rooted in the earth, not therefore able to passage like Lawrence himself, or migrate like a nightingale, the spring flowers' busy growth is described as vividly mobile.* These are crocuses:

> You cannot believe that the flowers are really still. They are open with such delight, and their pistil-thrust is so red-orange, and they are so many, all reaching out wide and marvellous, that it suggests a perfect ecstasy of radiant, thronging movement, lit-up violet and orange, and surging in some invisible rhythm of concerted, delightful movement. You cannot believe they do not move, and make some sort of crystalline sound of delight. If you sit still and watch, you begin to move with them, like moving with the stars, and you can feel the sound of their radiance. All the little cells of the flowers must be leaping with flowery life and utterance.

In Tuscany, this happens before March. By late April, greenery is all:

> now the pear tree is a lovely thick softness of new and glossy green, vivid with a tender fullness of apple-green leaves, gleaming among all the other greens of the landscape, the half-high wheat, emerald, and the grey olive, half-invisible, the browning green of the dark cypress, the black of the evergreen oak, the rolling, heavy green puffs of the stone pines, the flimsy green of small peach and almond trees, the sturdy young green of horse chestnut. So many greens,

---

* Lawrence's romantically anti-romantic and assertively sexy essay on the nightingale was published – and probably written – at the same time as his Tuscany flower essay; he wrote outside in the spring and nightingales came close to him – 'they are very inquisitive and come nearer to watch me turn a page.'

all in flakes and shelves and tilted tables and round shoulders and plumes and shaggles and uprisen bushes, of greens and greens, sometimes blindingly brilliant, at evening, when the landscape looks as if it were on fire from inside, with greenness and gold.

Regarding these flowers, and their being *fucked into being*, Lawrence says much more in his Mediterranean essay about the sun than about the earth. About earth, he is generally quite quiet. I suspect it was a more northern item for him. It suggests origins, and perhaps the coal-miner's son saw the soil like that. The earth of his first home that he visited once again in 1926 kick-started – an upwelling or an un-mining – *Lady Chatterley's Lover*. In Italy, though, Lawrence never writes of his own flowers, of a garden or anything he has grown – he had no earth of his own. The sun was much more obviously present. He knew the 'cold, dark reality where bulbs live'; he knew that green surges come out of black earth; he knew that in order for Persephone to come up she must have gone down. He knew all of this, but he wanted to talk more about the other side of the story. The sun was magic. At the time Lawrence was writing, the age and the likely lifetime of the sun were topics of scientific concern, but he was having none of it. A calculated end date for our day-star was not of interest; rather, his thinking swung him around in the opposite direction. Southern brightness, sun dazzle, was evidence of the unending rondure and cycling of life. It was a cheering lesson. We don't know 'whether the sun ever came into exist-ence, and we have not the slightest possible ground for conjecturing that the sun will ever pass out of existence', he says:

> Hence, strictly, there is no tragedy. The universe contains no tragedy, and man is only tragical because he is afraid of death. For my part, if the sun always shines, and always will shine, in spite of millions of clouds of words, then death, somehow, does not have many terrors. In the sunshine, even death is sunny. And there is no end to the sunshine.
>
> That is why the rapid change of the Tuscan spring is utterly free, for me, of any sense of tragedy. 'Where are the snows of

yesteryear?' Why, precisely where they ought to be. Where are the little yellow aconites of weeks ago? I neither know nor care. They were sunny, and the sun shines, and sunniness means change, and petals passing and coming. The winter aconite sunnily came, and sunnily went. What more? The sun always shines. It is our fault if we don't think so.

Imagine Lawrence on climate change! If only we had that . . . you wouldn't wish it on him but he would be superb on it.

Lawrence saw two more springs in southern Europe, and died at the beginning – on 2 March 1930 – of a third. The last part of 'Flowery Tuscany' switches its focus from flowers to some human sunflowers that leaned, like him, towards the sun and the south. Several of his travel pieces about Italy include descriptions of encounters with various – usually German – *Wandervögel*, sun-seeking migrants, footing it from further north, pilgrims, 'wandering for wandering's sake'. He meets some of these young men on the Ponte Vecchio in Florence; he had met another in an Etruscan tomb; one, with a different agenda, had earlier managed to pinch Frieda (or she him) for a few minutes, even as Lawrence and Frieda were effecting their own southern runaway. Lawrence is half alarmed by these rucksacked northern youths and half impressed. They are real 'barbarians', he says, 'turning to the sun again, in the great adventure of seeking themselves'. He tries to make something of the Teutonic mind behind these back-to-nature tramps but, coming at the end of pages of ecstatic observation of the Tuscan spring, his argument seems rather forced or hot-housed. After all, in their own way, the flowers of Tuscany move towards the sun every spring as they climb out of the winter dark; and in his own way Lawrence did the same.

'Comes over one an absolute necessity to move.' Lawrence (as here leaving Sicily for Sardinia) arrives everywhere on the go. And moving in this way was his work, his answer to the growth of plants – their 'surge' and their 'utterance'. Lawrence used these words repeatedly of flowers; he also used them to describe the sort of poetry he wrote. Flowers might be poems and poems might be flowers. In 1919 he wrote

205

an introduction to the American edition of his *New Poems* called 'Poetry of the Present'. It is very floral (not flowery or florid). And his language for the continuing *becoming* of flowers jumps the species barrier:

> free verse is, or should be, direct utterance from the instant, whole man. It is the soul and the mind and the body surging at once, nothing left out.

It is striking, if not strange, that the things Lawrence most took stock of were rooted to their spot, yet as an adult he was hardly ever in one place for more than one season. He loved, and lived by, the turn and the turn about, but he usually went somewhere else before it happened again where he was. Was any other writer so restless? Surely no one was also repeatedly out of sorts with wherever they fetched up. For Lawrence, there were a first few days when settled life in the new place looked promising; but soon enough it was time, once more, to get out and get on. Being perennially disappointed by wherever he had arrived meant that Lawrence forever needed launch pads and new places. And although, increasingly as he got older, he knew that there never could be a viable destination – a right place at a right time – he never stopped trying to go.

England, having made him, was his first and deepest problem place and the most necessary to be left, but nowhere was spared. In 1922, having been in Italy for five months, he wrote that it was 'a hateful country'. When he had arrived for that particular stay in Sicily in September 1921, he had described it as 'home' and written: 'Still, like this place best.' A few weeks later he was thinking of moving. Prospects were always promising. Taos in New Mexico sounded enticing from Taormina. For a while, during the same winter of 1921–22, Ceylon was going to be the answer – 'palms and elephants and monkeys and peacocks' – and he took the boat from Naples in February 1922. But, up close, it was awful. He knew it within a week or so: 'The East is not for me.' Then he thought he should go back to England, where life really – surely – mattered and could be explained. But America might do. Actually, next was Australia: 'Heaven knows why.' So it went on. And so on he went.

206

He knew he was hard to please and he was funny about it, even though there was frustration and sadness in his permanent and quixotic errancy. Australia had 'marvellous air, marvellous sun and sky' but, and he says it himself, 'but – But – BUT – Well it's always an anti-climax of buts.' But, there was always also somewhere else. The Pacific, perhaps?

I'm determined to *try* the South Sea Isles. Don't expect to catch on there either. But I love trying things and discovering how I hate them.

Five days later, he wrote another letter, on a ship between Perth and Sydney:

I feel that once I have rolled out of Europe I'll go on rolling. I like it so much. But F. still hankers after 'a little 'ome of 'er own'. I, no.

Australia he liked for the ocean and the fact that no one came to call. But the food was dear and the people he did see had no life. And the Pacific? 'We were a day at Rarotonga and two days at Tahiti: very pretty to look at, but I didn't want to stay, not one bit.' And again: 'reptile nausea [b]ut lovely flowers'. 'Travel', he wrote in the same letter, 'seems to me a splendid lesson in disillusion – chiefly that.' A month later in mid-September (this is all in 1922) they were in Taos, New Mexico:

America is more or less as I expected: shove or be shoved. But still it has a bigness, a sense of space, and a certain sense of rough freedom, which I like. I dread the pettyfogging narrowness of England. Still, I think to come on [back] in the spring. It is still hot, sunny here, like summer.

The United States was spacious but the weather was out of joint. At least in England there are seasons. Two days later he wrote to E. M. Forster:

I feel a great stranger, but have got used to that feeling, and prefer it to feeling 'homely'. After all, one is a stranger, nowhere so hopelessly as at home.

Horner
51°N

Every spring, for forty years and more, the oak woods at Horner, on the north slope of Exmoor in west Somerset, have been a place I have needed to be in. Much of what I think of as the best of spring can be found there. Redstarts, pied flycatchers and wood warblers arrive from Africa in April to breed in these woods. After three or four months, they return to winter, south of the Sahara. Those that survive will then fly north to Horner for the next spring.

My need to see these birds in the oak trees at Horner has grown as I have got older.

There is no re-setting of the clock for any of us, no go-backs are possible or re-starts permitted: we are all older every spring; I am greyer, deafer, slower, more generally autumnal; but to witness the work of time through the oaks and the redstarts at Horner allows me to feel the quickening of the world and its coming to life year after year. And seeing the migrants begin again in that place, and their repeat performances over many years, I find myself feeling – even for a passing moment beneath a singing bird in a green tree – that I too might be commonly sourced, or made at the same time from the same matter. If that is the case, I am then within touching distance, as it were, of life that, unlike mine, might never stop. This is a fantastic thought, of course, but this, I think, is what the spring does: so might we put our ends behind us rather than ahead; so might those clocks and re-starts be oaks and redstarts.

The rills that become streams that become rivers that are the Horner and East Waters have cut deep, muttering valleys away from the heave of Exmoor down towards the Bristol Channel. The moorland heather and grasses on the tops are rarely other than rusty or dun, but in places water has softened the shrug of the hill with greening veins and weedy deltas that seep and run. When all around seems dead, these creases in the earth shine with a soldered silvery dazzle. Spring begins in such places, these springs, and it flows with the water.

The two streams rise on the open moor but soon, falling from the hills, their narrow rocky beds are canopied with trees, mostly oaks. The trees rise up the steep sides of the valleys. On the flanks of the moor, the woods climb to a tree-line and stop below Dunkery Beacon. Lower down, towards the edge of the uplands, the woods climb right over the tops of the valleys and cape the hills between. Green comes out of the brown and grey.

Almost as long as I have been walking the springtime woods at Horner I have been reading Coleridge. Several of his best poems and the 'glistening chaos' (Richard Holmes' description) of his notebooks make very good company there. They might be read as uniquely imaginative guidebooks to the place and its meanings. Much of Coleridge's greatest poetry was made out of the West Country. It got deeply into him and into his writing. He grew or green-housed his 'Kubla Khan' in a wooded combe just five kilometres west of Horner. He knew the trees hereabouts. A map from his time marks them growing along the same rivers as they do today. In his introduction to the 'fragment' he tells us that the poem occurred or appeared to him in the summer of 1797 in a trance or dream when he was sickly in a 'lonely farm-house between Porlock and Linton'. Among the postcards the poem sends of 'romantic chasms' and 'caverns measureless', Coleridge submits descriptions of more familiar, even local, places – a 'green hill' and a river 'meandering with a mazy motion'.

He also coined the word *greenery*. Its first recorded use in the *OED* is in the poem. The word comes at a point where the poem wants to rhyme *tree* with *green*. It is also required to open out, as its blurry and reverberating last syllable does, and to activate – to action green – and multiply, to grow and to leaf. In his *Biographia Literaria*, Coleridge wrote of language's capacity to animate: he knew words to be 'no passive tools' but 'organised instruments, reacting on the power which inspirits them'. Greenery is one such word, a *minting*. As verdancy roots with virility, so greenery grows with energy. It does this both suggestively and literally – an anagram of it gives us *re-energy*.*

'Kubla Khan' wasn't published until 1816, but it was first made at the time when Coleridge and Wordsworth were in Somerset writing the poems that became the *Lyrical Ballads* of 1798. That collaboration has romantic lime trees in it and quasi-poetical nightingales, but it also challenged those well-established poetical tropes and, putting new subjects into new verse, re-started English poetry. It is a springtime book. William Hazlitt, at that time a young stalker of the lyrical balladeers (he walked from Shropshire to see them in Somerset), talked of their book having 'something of the effect that arises from the turning up of the fresh soil, or the first welcome breath of Spring'.

It is still good to read after a day in the greenery.

Not long after I discovered that that was Coleridge's word, and a word that was leafed into the language among the shaggy oaks of the west, I came upon a mention that Wordsworth was colour-blind. He saw, it was said, sand as the same colour as grass. Greenery was likely lost on him. I am not sure why – the sense I have of Wordsworth's sombreness and autumnal sobriety, perhaps, or of the poets' later disagreements after they left the west behind – but that discovery made the green in my mind, conjured there by Coleridge, greener still.

At the same time, after a day walking the woods at Horner, in the company of some new installed spring birds, it was good also to discover that Coleridge referred to his notes as *fly-catchers*. These notes – there are books and books of them – frequently began life in the field and on the spot. The moment of each entry's making can often be evidenced. He writes 'now' repeatedly. *Natura*, he said (though not in a note), *is that which is about to be born, that which is always becoming*. That is what he noticed and what he wanted to record. As a younger poet especially, he seems to have found whatever was passing particularly pressing – most important was to get down the fleet and the fleeting. He wrote about clouds, streams, the wind, the moon, about linnets and wagtails, and

---

* I owe this lexical discovery to Tanmay Dixit, wizard of words, and now super-smart student, with Claire, of cuckoo-finches in Zambia.

starlings and rooks. He wrote about the *jiffling* of leaves. He wrote about people seen or met on the road. He wrote about a chamber-pot of his own urine. He took brilliant and touching snapshots in words of his children's early years and reported their own observations and first adventures into understanding. He also looked within himself, and wrote, like a naturalist, about what moved through his mind and what grew there.

Coleridge's note-taking began in earnest in 1797–98 when he was living in Somerset with his family and near William and Dorothy Wordsworth. He was outside a lot and walked great distances. At that time he consciously tried to take notes, he said, 'with the object and imagery immediately before my sense'. Among his *fly-catchers* are some notes on a flycatcher. Entries in the notebooks record what Coleridge was reading as well as what he was seeing. Having read Gilbert White's *Natural History of Selborne*, he quarried some facts from the 'sweet delightful book':

The Fly-catcher, mutest Bird, save only when maternal anxiety extort an inward plaintive note

This must be the mostly quiet spotted flycatcher, not a Horner pied, but there are spotteds in the Somerset woods too. I am sure Dorothy Wordsworth (I think her likely to have been the most observant and best birder of the gang in Somerset) would have known them in the Quantocks.*

In January 1964 Elizabeth Bishop wrote a letter to Anne Stevenson, the poet and critic, who was working on a book about Bishop's

---

* Coleridge was a fly-catching young man, living in motion, as flycatchers will (and swallows and many other migrants), making do with what he could get on the wing; by comparison, Gilbert White called himself a 'stationary man' and was interested in the world as it came to him. His is truly *found* prose. And perhaps his understanding of his fixity – his stationary life – in Selborne contributed to his lingering belief, contrary to much evidence he himself accumulated, that the swallows, which he so obviously loved, actually never left his parish but remained there – fixed – hidden in the winter in the mud of a pond or in the thatch of a roof.

poetry. Stevenson was interested in Bishop's possible connections with surrealism (including painters like Paul Klee and Max Ernst); Bishop replied that she didn't regard surrealism as an influence and pointed, instead, to her stronger feelings for Charles Darwin's writing. Her enthusiasm for the naturalist's way of seeing, and his dreamy openness that grew paradoxically from his intense concentration, reads as a fine description of how she regarded her own poetry-making and its ties to its world. Think of her 'Sandpiper' on the Atlantic shore:

> The world is a mist. And then the world is
> minute and vast and clear.

Bishop's words on Darwin, generous as to how the universe of facts (both minute and vast) can be taken in by a subjective and wandering eye, as much as by a cool and objective lens, might also stand as some big-hearted instruction for best-practice nature-noting. Close attention and accuracy are important, but so too must be the right to roam imaginatively, *giddily off into the unknown*:

> reading Darwin, one admires the beautiful and solid case being built up out of his endless heroic observations, almost unconscious or automatic – and then comes a sudden relaxation, a forgetful phrase, and one feels the strangeness of his undertaking, sees the lonely young man, his eyes fixed on facts and minute details, sinking or sliding giddily off into the unknown. What one seems to want in art, in experiencing it, is the same thing that is necessary for its creation, a self-forgetful, perfectly useless concentration.

It is Darwin's uncertainty, his blurry thinking, rather than his clarity of perception, that Bishop extols – his looking so hard that he loses himself and cannot quite *see to see*. 'Sandpiper' has a shudder or shake about its looking (as well as about its subject); so do 'The Fish' and 'The Armadillo'. The poems *range* like D. H. Lawrence's animal and flower poems, and as (some of) Gerard Manley Hopkins' poems, and many of Coleridge's nature notes.* The close attention involved enables a vivid capture of the observed life, but also gives us the animal or plant as it has occurred specifically (no matter if blurrily) to the particular observer. When this works best there is no sense of the poet possessing or in any way owning the subject. The animal *takes* the observer and operates on them, not the other way around. *What you look hard at,* Hopkins wrote in his journal, *seems to look hard at you.* Despite the inward re-making of the fish or the sandpiper, the wild animal is released without scarring back to its own realm.

Gerard Manley Hopkins' journal notes are as good as Coleridge's. He too makes a nature note out of urine (the pattern frozen piss makes on a urinal in winter). He too wrote of starlings in flight. He sent letters to the journal *Nature* about sky colours after volcanic eruptions. Clouds, and how to capture them correctly, occupied him almost as much as they did Coleridge and only a little less than John Ruskin (whose madness was part-triggered by excessive cloud-watching). His looking is recorded as a physical action, as if his seeing is feeling. Like Coleridge's *greenery*, this active and engaged physicality can also be felt in his coinages, *inscape* and *instress*, that describe the irreducible essence of a living thing (including rocks, rivers, clouds, as well as kingfishers and bluebells etc.) and its rub against the world. For Hopkins, to walk outdoors and look about was to experience a kind of palpable incarnation. He was marked himself by the marks of what he saw: as things grew (changed, moved), so did he. On 12 December 1872, when still a student priest, he went 'on the fells with Mr Lucas' and recorded his day in his journal:

Ground sheeted with taut tattered streaks of crisp gritty snow . . .
I saw the inscape though freshly, as if my eye were still growing.

On another occasion, 17 May 1874, picking bluebells, he 'fell in blue handed with the gamekeeper, which is a humbling thing to do'. He

---

* See also Thomas De Quincey above, on Wordsworth's *relaxing attention* in 'There Was a Boy'.

hadn't been able to stop himself seeking to touch. Or even to taste. He had picked bluebells during another spring, in May 1871, and was then *caught* by them, not by a nature-policeman. It is their flavour and sound or voice that he was most taken by:

> if you draw yr. fingers through them they are lodged and struggle / with a shock of wet heads; the long stalks rub and click and flatten to a fan on one another like yr. fingers themselves would when you passed the palms hard across one another, making a brittle rub and jostle like the noise of a hurdle strained by leaning against; then there is the faint honey smell and in the mouth the sweet gum when you bite them. But this is easy, it is the eye they baffle.*

19 April. In the spring, the leaves come at Horner when they will – leaf-out some years can be weeks later than others. Never have I known the wood to be in the same state on the same day from one year to the next. The greenery in April is slight and tender at first – often trembling. It takes some weeks for an oak to look more green than grey, more leaf than wood, more alive – often – than dead. But it has happened every year I have walked under the trees, and as the new leaf growth spreads and meshes into a green commonwealth, curtailing the sunlight reaching the woodland floor, so caves open of an almost tangibly gaseous light. As though the chlorophyll of the fresh leaves had sponged at the air, the understorey simmers and flares for a month or so – an *arcade* of green rooms is there, an *arcadia*. This is the wood's most buzzing time.

---

* About this notebook entry, the poet Roger (R. F.) Langley wrote in his own journal on 22 April 2003: 'A never-to-be-forgotten passage, to recall you to the quality of life whenever you feel there is not much to it.' The literary critic Humphrey House, who edited both Hopkins and Coleridge, noticed that Hopkins' use of slashes in his journals was similar to Coleridge's. Both capture the hurry of observation and the excited uncertainty at the time of the note-making about the connectedness of the observation or the thought to its surroundings – slashes are marks of mobile punctuation as physical as a breath or a glance. As a young man, Hopkins, House noted, may well have seen some of Coleridge's original notebooks.

On the lower hills at Horner the woods cover everything, cloaking the dome of one so roundly that I see a marvellous breast every time I look at it. Many individual oaks have bosomy crowns when in leaf. And there is erotic softness – a wet electricity – within the wood too.

My walk, the same walk through Horner Woods that I have taken for forty springs, begins at Webber's Post. I start on the moor's edge, in open country up above the trees, and walk downhill. If, on a first visit, I hear a redstart singing, before the wood has closed around the unfenced road, the year can be made fully whole and wholly good in minutes.

Redstarts arrive in the Horner woods in the first two weeks of April. Males, like many migrants, commonly make landfall a little ahead of females. Singing often at the tops of trees, they delineate their territory and describe their desires. Some will know the woods from previous years, and once again have sought out, or been caught by, the place they want to be detained in. They will have sung there before, perhaps from the same perches and to defend the same territory. Some territories will be vacant because last year's singers are dead. Other singers this year will have hatched nine months before from an egg and been reared in a hole in a tree in these woods. They will never have previously opened their beaks to sing, until something in the sunlight meets something in their bodies, and their life and time condenses into short sprightly rounds of three- or four-second-long tunes.

At Webber's Post, before the trees thicken and the road steepens, there are three hundred metres of heath with bracken and gorse and scattered birches. Here, today, were siskins and redpolls, bouncing overhead, seemingly too slight to be held down to any place, and also two crossbills, heavier travellers and more committed. At the edge of the wood, where the trees shielded the wind, warbler music began: blackcaps were making juice and willow warblers and chiffchaffs were singing together. The chiffchaffs' name-calling song sounds like a soft bolero drawn from a cool engine in the earth. The sweet descants of the willow warblers' songs are greener.

I walked further into the shelter of the woods. It got warmer. The oaks around me were still mostly bare or hung with catkins, like new lambs' tails, tasselled and limp, wan and yellowish and smothered with dusty pollen. On the naked fingers of the crown of one oak, grey mostly with tattered mittens of hoary lichen and just a few shakes of new greenery, there was a male redstart. My first on its home ground this year. I heard it before I saw it, and listened to it for ten minutes before I tried to find it. Its little singing answered so much – I let my head fill with its song, a tune I hadn't heard for ten months: eight phrases one minute, six the next, six the next, then five and then eight, and so on. The music was slight, but it felt alive and it glistened in the air. I listened, and then sang it back, *sotto voce*, to the singer, trying to describe it to myself. It is refreshing, a watery rinsing or the first glance of sunshine after rain; it sounds coy, like an apology, or like the warm-up to a bigger number that never comes. Today I heard the simplicity or modesty of the musical line and its chaffinch-like approach and retreat. *Plainsong*, I said out loud to the trees.

In 1797, Coleridge was kept from the last days of the Quantock spring when Sara, his wife, accidentally poured a skillet of boiling milk on his foot. Immobilized for a week or more, he couldn't walk the hills and combes. The Wordsworths kept at it and took with them their visiting (shared) friend Charles Lamb. In Nether Stowey, Coleridge sat in a leafy arbour that Tom Poole (his inspiring, radical neighbour) had grown in his garden (which adjoined the Coleridges') and thought about what he was missing. His thoughts became 'This Lime-Tree Bower My Prison', which shifts from being a panoramic projection of the sights his walking friends were seeing to a close-up of the delights of the garden where the poet was caged. It is a screening in a green cinema. Coleridge couches it all in friendly conversational terms but in fact it's a monologue, as much about loneliness as about conviviality. It ends as daylight leaves the scene and as 'the last rook / Beat its straight path along the dusky air / Homeward'.* Coleridge

---

*'Light thickens, and the crow makes wing to th' rooky wood' is Shakespeare's best ornithological moment, I think. Macbeth says it. Surely Coleridge was at least half-remembering that here.

has noticed and now recalls how rooks overhead in flight can be heard 'creeking'; and this gives him his last line, which both justifies his one-sided talk and re-describes (a field observation) the leathery sound of the rook's wings, while encapsulating the wider, unitary urge of the whole poem: 'No sound is dissonant which tells of Life.'

26 April. Horner. A gift of a day. So much this morning had come from Africa to these woods – how extraordinary it seems to put this springtime ordinariness like that. Fifteen willow warblers, three chiff-chaffs, three blackcaps, a garden warbler (my first of the year), ten redstarts, thirteen pied flycatchers (my first, again), one wood warbler (my first), five cuckoos, a tree pipit, several swallows and house martins overhead, and a singing whitethroat in a hedge on the road out. Not one of them was here one month ago; most of them, then, were still south of the Sahara.

One male redstart was singing on the crown of an oak. Through my binoculars I could see the bird's warm breath – its African insides – and I watched little puffs of cloud leave its open beak and disappear into the cool morning air. As it sang, the flickering fire of its plumage radiated heat: brick-tile and burnt sienna on its breast, wood ash and soot around its head, flannel grey on its back, a lit lamp bright at its forehead and, as ever, the stoking of its tail, fanning all. I leaned, as always, towards it.

Twenty paces on, another male redstart arrived in the lower branches of a tall oak as I was watching a male pied flycatcher in the same tree. The birds passed one another and as they did I heard, from higher up in the crown, a male wood warbler giving one round of its silvery tremulous song. My three in one tree.

Coleridge's 'Frost at Midnight', made in his time at Nether Stowey along with 'This Lime-Tree Bower' and 'Kubla Khan', is a winter poem, but it speaks for me to those trembling springtime birds. On the night in question, Coleridge has stayed up late, his wife is asleep, his infant son is cradled beside him. He watches the guttering fire in the hearth:

the thin blue flame
Lies on my low-burnt fire, and quivers not;
Only that film, which fluttered on the grate,
Still flutters there, the sole unquiet thing.
Methinks, its motion in this hush of nature
Gives it dim sympathies with me who live,
Making it a companionable form . . .

The trembling *film* – the heat blur raised by the flame not the flame itself (which *quivers not*) – is (as Adam Nicolson says in his book *The Making of Poetry*) half a thing and half a happening. It is also time present. The burning of the fire, its self-consumption, is its life. And we, Coleridge suggests, can (must inevitably) take part in the carbon cycle, its consuming heat and its burn in time, companionably, as do the coals.

Allow me this: we are all due the everlasting bonfire, we come from it and are headed towards it – *time, for sure, is the fire in which we burn.* We are where we are because of our burning of that which was once green. A lump of coal is the fossil residue of photosynthesis, a condensation of ancient Palaeozoic sunlight. A burning log represents a more recent capture and expenditure of the fuel of the sun. Likewise we are all made of transformed sunlight (call it star-dust if you like). Redstarts are too.

Isn't the vital force of the filmy blur, rising from the coal (or wood – youthful coal), that Coleridge notices, also like the redstart's trembling tail (it quivers, that is true), which is half the bird and half what it does? And, being that, why can't the redstart's tremble become, like the low flutter that seems to show the breathing of the fire, a *companionable form?*

The red *starts* and we might run with it.

The same day, in one combe at Horner, there were six willow warblers singing at once. I sprawled on a sofa of dead bracken to listen. Although each male sang a song nearly identical to its rivals, the effect was not a cacophonous log-jam. When crunching their numbers, Claire and her scientist colleagues call meaningless data *noise*. It is a kind of backwash to truth, the tonally generic sea out of which floats meaning but which is itself distracting to that meaning. The warblers' singing said to me that if we knew how to listen adequately there would be no such thing as this noise.

As they moved through the oaks and birches the birds' songs came and went, drawing and redrawing their spaces across the green-lyre of the wood. I couldn't see any of them but could feel their movements by listening. Although it was a rivalrous squabble – singing is a means of fighting without bloodshed – the riot of competing song didn't sound like that. *No sound is dissonant that tells of life.* Neither was it meaningless in its accumulation. They all had the same news and they sang it the same way; it was polyphony, but each bird sang out of itself, from its own centre. Each song was felt therefore as specific; each sounded a beginning, as if the song had started with its singer alone.

Further along the path, at the top edge of the wood adjoining the moor, I had a ten-minute view of a male pied flycatcher. I sat with it in its place. In that time it gave just one round of song. It moved beneath an oak, hopping from dead branches on the ground to the trunk of the tree, with its wings slightly lowered below its body. The white blaze in its forehead shone bright. For a minute it perched quiet and still. Then it flew to a hole in the oak where a branch had snapped away. It was pointing it out. A female appeared in the little clearing and hopped from branch to branch nearer the male. The male must have seen her – or known she was watching him – long before me. He flew closer to the hole and then to the female. She flew away.

I saw another female pied flycatcher on the walk back. It washed in a rocky stream and then flew up to a young tree. It dried itself by rubbing its stretched neck on a twig. The action was very human: seeing the stretch, I felt the colour rising in me, catching myself catching a woman at her bath.

Perhaps that will not do. Birds are themselves. We shouldn't appropriate. The living world beyond us, as Wordsworth said in a poem (from after he left Somerset), is neither for getting nor spending. In

1802, Coleridge wrote (after he had left Somerset too) a letter to his friend, the poet William Sotheby:

> never to see or describe any interesting appearance in nature without connecting it by dim analogies with the moral world proves faintness of Impression. Nature has her proper interest; & he will know what it is, who believes & feels, that every Thing has a Life of it's own, & that we are all *one Life*.

One of the truths that Coleridge knew from being a good observer (and note-taker) of the outside world was how at our peril we move from *outseeing* – our sense of the world we witness – to *inseeing* – what we do with our witnessing. The move is a defining activity of our species, of course, and we are all guilty of not being natural in our dealings with nature. We can't be.*

They are all beasts of burden, Henry David Thoreau said somewhere of animals, all *made to carry some portion of our thoughts*. All the pied flycatchers, redstarts and wood warblers that live can manage very well without me (or Coleridge). Without them, though, I would be in trouble.

27 April. On my way between Bristol and Exmoor I often stop in the Quantock hills. An oak wood there called Rectory Wood once served a

---

* Coleridge described himself as an awkward bird – at different times he was a 'library cormorant' who devoured every book, a caged starling who could not finish anything or escape his own song, and an ostrich who abandoned its eggs in inappropriate places. As an original observer of avian flight – he wrote about flying linnets and starlings as if they made the passage of time through the world visible and even articulate – he put his own dilemmas regarding his over-thinking in avian terms:

> I wished to force myself out of metaphysical trains of thought, which, when I wished to write a poem, beat up game of far other kind. Instead of a covey of poetic partridges with whirring wings of music, or wild ducks shaping their rapid flights in forms always regular (a still better image of verse), up came a metaphysical bustard, urging its slow, heavy, laborious, earth-skimming flight over dreary and level wastes . . .

How not, then, to be a bustard?

tannery at Nether Stowey.* Like Horner, the wood is nestled into a combe on the rising hillside above the village. The trees are protected now. This is a pied-flycatcher wood. There are dozens of nest boxes fixed to the trunks. I cannot resist them. I have spent hours in spring – days overall – sitting on the ground, among dark cushions of bilberry and whortle-berry bushes, watching birds come to the holes. Sometimes I lift a lid of a box and peep inside. Today I saw three male and three female pied flycatchers. The females were going in and out of boxes, prospecting. It was still early days for them. There were blue tits incubating in two other boxes. I also saw a willow warbler, with a moustache of dry grass it had gathered in its beak, heading for its nest hole in a beech-hedge bank.

In the wood the most obvious growing business of the year was in the new leaves on the trees that grew along the top of this bank. One low limb of almost every tree had come alive with *beechen green*. The new-hatched leaves hung from black horizontal branches like levitating flights of just-emerged butterflies, drying and filling their wings. In the surrounding shade, dimmed further by their very brightness, they seemed to float. And they throbbed as if some lightning was passing through them. *Electrict fluid*, lightning was called in Coleridge's day (he pasted a newspaper cutting into his notebook about a storm in August 1804), and that was this. All else, around and behind the wet glister of the brilliant green, looked cave-muddy and cave-old. Hanging apparently *before* everything, the new green added an optical plane to the wood, changing the spectrum but also the space. It stopped my eyes, like lightning will, like a new form in the place, an object of it but not yet incorporated, like a child of the space.

Some myths suggest the golden bough was a magic apple tree, some that it was mistletoe on a winter branch; if you were seeking it, one of these beech branches would do, a spring-leafed branch in a black wood. The leaves were soft and wafery and moist and cool. And edible. I picked one and chewed its communion cud; it tasted of sweet chalky grass.

---

* Tom Poole, Coleridge's friend, was the tanner in the village at the end of the eighteenth century. Oak bark makes a dye and a seasoning for leather. The word 'tanning' comes from old words (in Medieval Latin, French and Cornish) for oak or its bark.

28 April. I had volunteered a day out with spring birds as a prize in an auction to help a friend raise some money for a good cause. I was won by someone I'll call Nigel, a retired bank-manager. I suggested Horner but Nagshead, a wood in the Forest of Dean, was nearer to where he lived. Here are further acres of the western temperate rain-forest, with oaks and beeches too.

I was slow getting going but eventually untangled a pied flycatcher from the green shadows – a male buzzing a great tit that was investigating a nest box. Then, in a sun-splashed glade, with green tongues of wood garlic and bluebells smoking, I showed Nigel a male redstart. His first. I was enamoured, as ever; Nigel didn't seem too bothered. Next I dug out for him, high up near the roof of a beech cavern, a wood warbler event: two singing males in the same tree and a third, probably a female, watching. In a little stir of wind the new foliage shifted with the tremble of the displaying birds' wings miming the shuffle of the leaves. To be in the tree was to be made from it. *A brother of the leaves* he seems, wrote Wordsworth, of the *green linnet*, a greenfinch (was he really colour-blind?). It was the same for the wood warblers. The birds had breasts that were bright white but all else of them – their head, back, wings and tail – was a green that looked dusted with pollen or flor. I could see feathery filaments of sharp lemon yellow, sulphurously bright, suffused within the warblers' cooler base plumage. The two males sang – against one another – and their singing, I heard, once more, as a fine silver wire or molten shimmer, pulled from within, first coiled then unsprung and ductile, a cascade from such miniature toys that it shook their entirety. They seemed possessed, and I was infected and started to blush, as if implicated in the affair. I turned to Nigel – my wife, as it were, in the wood – who hadn't seen any of these birds before. He looked back at me, apparently unmoved. I tried to compose my face and turned again. It was like marshalling myself back into a room after a secret tryst; I burned with it even as I tried to stamp out the fire.

29 April. Back to Horner. Cold, with birds shivering this morning with the chill, not with lust. The pied flycatchers were quiet and slow in the trees, their faces like ponies – dark eyes and a white blaze in

their black brows. I watched marsh tits taking green caterpillars from oak leaves for food for their young. I heard ten redstarts.

30 April. Horner again, until ten in a sparkling morning. I counted six wood warblers, each a glass of lime cordial – simply beautiful, beautifully simple. There were married redstarts – she into a hole on the end of a snapped-off oak branch, he following with a grub in his beak. Two of the ten pied flycatchers were fighting males, dirtying their dinner suits in wet leaf mould at the side of the road. I also saw four tree pipits parachuting into the gorse at the wood edge and two marsh tits nearby. These last, and possibly several of the others, I surely saw yesterday as well. To see the same individuals over and again through a season, all of them in their places, *occupied* – this idea grew in my mind.

The name of the path I take is Boy's Path. A sign has appeared.

2 May. Horner. A fine rain was being blown sideways on a west-southwest wind. The wood carded cloud until it festooned the tree tops. The oaks bowed their heads as if cowed by the weather. For an hour I felt like a sorry moth. The wet air of the cloud forest clogged my hair and misted my lenses. A male pied flycatcher knocked raindrops from its song-post twig. The water fell like tin tears along the twiggy stave. But even in the rain, on the great hillside lawn of tall oaks there were paired redstarts and paired pied flycatchers and a singing wood warbler. All their sounds seemed softened, aptly so, in the submarine rainlight. Every bird I watched shook their feathers and shivered off a jewelled caddis sheath of themselves. A pair of pied flycatchers chased a female redstart; she chased them back. They were quiet, but their dancing movements lent a music of colour and contrast so that, as they flew, the wood lit up and sparkled with the rain that they interrupted, as if the water falling around them was being worked in a woodland forge. *Spangle*, I wrote in my book, and watched the word slide from my page.

By the end of the autumn, half a year hence, all the green pigment in all the oaks of Horner will have been destroyed. The greenest day in the woods is sometime in the first week of May. More shades of green are then to be seen than ever and all the greens are greener than before.

Verde que ti quiero verde, I announce to the goodness, every year, in my skeleton Spanish, Federico García Lorca's *green-how-I-love-you-green* – but what do I know?

Green turns out to be incidental to the oaks. It is the least required colour for the tree and visible to us because it is not wanted. In photosynthesis, chlorophyll absorbs all the colours of sunlight except green. The plant uses the rest of the light's energy while the green is reflected. It is, in this way, unprocessed and secondary, extrinsic or excess. Green is lost light and the greenery only appears energetic. The first colours visible in oak leaves before they fully green up, that reminder of the autumn and the intimation of their end in their earliest days, reveal the leaves' other pigments: yellow, red, brown and orange, the carotenoids and anthocyanins. These accessory pigments remain in the leaves but are masked when chlorophyll is dominatingly present, when plant cells are producing it through the spring and hiding the leaves in green. Green is a front, a blur; the life is behind.

Should green stand, then, not for *go* but for *gone*? Is mould as apt an incarnation of the colour as a lettuce-green oak leaf? *All flesh is grass*, meaning it soon dies. Is green more truly then rot and better thought as a kind of calenture, or green madness, or gangrene (which doesn't mean green) or constant verdigris (which does)?* Is green closer to death than life – is it all outbreath, or tomorrow's coal? Is greenness in fact, as Philip Larkin said in his beautifully miserable poem 'The Trees', 'a kind of grief'?

The green dies and the woods turn brown. And the season departs – with its dying leaves – at the same speed roughly as that it arrived with. Senescence travels south in the fall, moving about sixty kilometres a day away from the north. Someone might walk back to Africa with the autumn as I have tried to walk north with the spring.

---

* Paris Green, an artificial nineteenth-century pigment, was cheap to produce and much used but toxic because it contained arsenic. When Napoleon died on Saint Helena in 1821, some believed the British had poisoned him by wallpapering his room in the colour. Van Gogh was keen on another fake green, Emerald Green (it is especially visible as the background colour to his 'Self Portrait Dedicated to Paul Gauguin' of 1888), and it may have poisoned him too.

6 May. A nest box audit in the tannery wood on the Quantocks:

Empty: 6
Old nests (last year's): 9
New nests, shaped grass cup in a corner, lined with old oak leaves, no eggs yet – pied flycatcher, I think: 6
Nest, lined with moss and feathers, with blue tit eggs: 1
Nest, with incubating blue tit: 1

On this day – 6 May – in 1798 Dorothy Wordsworth was in the Quantocks, three kilometres from Rectory Wood. With her brother and Coleridge she walked from Alfoxden (where she and William were living) towards Nether Stowey (and the Coleridge cottage). Her journal from this time doesn't record a great deal, but after this walk she thought to note that the walkers 'heard the nightingale; saw a glow worm'. Coleridge wrote up this shared observation in his poem 'The Nightingale'. It was first published in the *Lyrical Ballads*, where he dates it to April of that year. Since he includes the glow-worm in his poem too, it is safe to assume that its details came from that walk. Coleridge steals a march; Dorothy's date is more likely to be accurate. The poem is a have-my-cake-and-eat-it poem – Coleridge corrects the sentimental over-poetical appropriation of the bird, though not before he gives a good replica of that.* The poem makes further imports from Coleridge's

---

* On cake and having it, see Coleridge's loving and brilliant capture of his young son Derwent's dismay over time passed being unrecoverable, in a note from 1803:

Derwent (Nov 6. Tea time) came in, & all the *Cake* was eat up, & he was by no means willing to accept dry Toast & butter as a Substitute 'Don't eat all the Cake!' – Well, we will not tomorrow! – O but don't eat the Cake! You have eat the Cake O but don't eat up all the Cake! – His Passion had completely confounded his Sense of Time & its consequences – He saw that it is done; & yet he passionately entreated us not to do it – & not for the time to come / but for the Present & the Past. 'O but you have! O but don't now!'

Arriving in the company of other birders at the site of a rare bird to discover that they have seen it but it has now flown away can trigger similar upheavals, as Derwent's, in me to this day.

life and includes a version of the moment, marvellously recorded in his notebooks, when his crying infant son Hartley was calmed by moonshine. Whatever its biography, the poem is regarded evidential enough to be considered the first published record of a nightingale in Somerset.

22 May. Bumblebees in the bilberries in the tannery wood. Otherwise the oaken hillside had a deep-forest quiet. There was a further silence too: that of the sitting birds, the purposeful silence of incubation – the egging on.

I sat to watch – without seeing – the sitters at their tasks. It was like lying under a night sky. The quietness of all the eggs in the nests in the woods came mutely within my earshot, as planets and stars can sometimes seem to transmit the sparking prickle of space between them. I heard the silence. The curve of each nest bowl would be a cast of the incubating bird's breast. And the future's songs and colours and flights were all curved into their eggs, all dark there, as if waiting but asleep.

I settled into the quiet time. The soft rustle of the wood. One fly passed, and then another bee. A holly blue butterfly visited a holly bush growing at the base of an oak. It was paler than the sky beyond the canopy of oaks – the green leaves dilute anything blue below them.

Nests in these woods are all about secrets and hiding and stillness. Spring is bird song and leaf burst but is also here stopped in its very going, in shade and quiet: nests are like ballast, keeping life down, and eggs, too, spring paradoxes – seeds, germs in the earth-dark, hard-shelled pebbles, solid-cased yet shifting within, growing and changing, wanting to crack.

An hour later, I stood up and walked through the wood, lifting the lids on the nest boxes:

Empty: 12
Old nests: 2
Pied flycatcher: 5 (two females sitting and three other clutches of 6, 7, and 7, holly-blue unmarked eggs), dry grass nests with dead oak leaves. Each egg like a little corner of buried sky.

Blue tit: 3, mossy nests with off-white, brown-spotted eggs
Great tit: 1, mossy nest with sheep's wool with off-white, brown-flecked eggs

9 June. Tannery wood. My uncle died this morning in Taunton hospital. There were wood warblers where I hadn't heard them before in the oaks: four singing males. One nest box on an oak trunk was being visited by parent pied flycatchers, coming every thirty seconds or so with caterpillars and grubs. A wood warbler sang in the same tree, sending down a silvery rain over all. I looked quickly in the box: seven or eight flycatcher chicks, leaf-mould brown, lay on top of one another, like a nest of fat stubby snakes.

Pied flycatcher numbers are down in Britain. Their insect prey is hatching earlier than it did and the birds are arriving too late to get it. This is what *phenological mismatch* means – their timing is out and consequently they find themselves out of time. Wood warblers must also come from the far side of the Sahara to breed in the Quantocks, but are not suffering in the same way. Their breeding season is now less synchronised with peak caterpillar abundance than it was in the 1980s, but the birds seem able to mitigate this mismatch by exploiting other foodstuffs. Breeding success has remained fairly even. Yet since the mid-1990s the UK wood warbler population has more than halved. Land-use changes on the birds' wintering grounds in Ghana and Burkina Faso in West Africa seem to be doing for them. Trees are being cleared in farmed areas and forests degraded into patchy woodland. Wood warbler happiness requires particular woods in the birds' winter as well as for them to breed in, and nowadays there are not woods enough.

14 June. Horner. At Webber's Post my car rocked in the wind streaming off Dunkery. The hilltop melted into the mist and departed as *cloudage*. I had no coat and hid for an hour at my steering wheel. A song thrush came down with a snail in its beak and used the road as its anvil. Along the verge, each slipper-flower of the purple foxgloves was glassed in rain. A green aphid walked the long back of a black slug.

I made it to the path. The light turned frowzy. In one birch there were six willow warblers – adults and their fledged young – calling to one another and shaking the rain from their backs. The young might never have been wet before. A male redstart hunted for caterpillars on a slope of bracken; it found one like something it remembered. As it flew it caught a splash of watery sun. The drizzle had moved on and the morning came to itself. The wet jewelled a thousand spider webs. I tried *spangle* again in my notebook.

The wood was songless. I found a male pied flycatcher feeding two fledged young. The adult had a ring on its leg. Someone had held it in their hands somewhere. I've never met another person on all my days on Boy's Path. A vomit-yellow fungus that I had seen bleeding grimly from some oak trunks had solidified into a mad carpentry of shelves and brackets. Now I could identify it as chicken of the woods.

A male pied flycatcher flew down to the path ahead of me. A female redstart landed ten steps further on. Her tail trembled as if she was sweeping with it, like Hestia at her hearth, sweeping ashes. A blackcap sang for twenty seconds – the only singer all day. The silence of everyone else and the fruit in its music put the end of the season into the wood. I could hear the autumn in the last of the spring.

Nagyszelmenc & Kisszelmenc
49°N

Look up Nagyszelmenc on Google Earth. Flip between the map and the satellite photograph. It's a village in the far east of Slovakia that sits right on the border with Ukraine. Its name is Hungarian (in Slovak it is called Vel'ké Slemence). It is, or was, a Hungarian village. Ninety-five per cent of the people who live there are Hungarians. They speak Hungarian. Look at the border marked on the map. A road at Nagyszelmenc runs up to a line. This road, in Slovakia, meets a road in Ukraine. It is the same road, but the border has severed it. There is a village in Ukraine too. It begins at the line, as Nagyszelmenc ends. Or begins: the border makes a kind of mirror. In Ukraine the village is Kisszelmenc (Mali Selmentsi in Ukrainian). It is, or was, a Hungarian village. Etc. *Nagy* means big in Hungarian, *kis* means small. The villages were once one.

Szel means wind. There is plenty of that. It is flat hereabouts. It is also near the middle of Europe. Uzhhorod, the nearest neighbouring town in Ukraine, once Ungvár in Hungarian, is the European pole of continentality – the place in Europe most distant from the sea. I saw redstarts there one May. They rouged the fruit trees in the gardens of the town without any signs of effort, suggesting that all routes in and out were open to them. As the redstart flies, Uzhhorod is 670 kilometres from the Baltic, the Adriatic and the Black Sea.

Hungary once had a navy. I have a framed map on the wall of my flat in Bristol. It cost a couple of pounds from a flea market in Budapest. It is a map of Hungary showing the country and its borders as they were on 4 April 1939. It must have been printed not long after. That was the *Springtime for Hitler* year. The map is labelled *Csonka-Magyarország*, which means Legless or Truncated or Maimed Hungary. It's an opinionated drawing with topographical attitude.

Hungary spent the first half of the twentieth century shrinking. Having been on the losing side in the First World War, the country was forced to give up territory at its edges (which had included access to a sea coast on the Adriatic). It became smaller. The borders on my map are printed in a bleeding iron-red and show a wrongly caged or confined and punished Hungary – at least, that is what the cartographers must have thought. Nor did the apparent injustice stop there. Because – again – the country was on the losing (fascist) side in the Second World War, not only did it fail to regain the use of its old legs, and recover lands lost in the Treaty of Trianon of 1920, but after 1945 it also shrank further still. My map shows the northern border of Hungary running through much of present-day Slovakia and extending north-east deep into the Carpathian Mountains of today's Ukraine. When the Soviet Union defeated occupying Nazi Germany in Hungary, it stayed on to command the country. Hungary lost all those acres (to neighbouring Eastern bloc states) and today it is as small as it has ever been. Cruelly (perhaps understandably, albeit wrongly) it continues to be politically over-exercised by its edges and remains poisonously troubled by the question of occupation. The present government laments the *csonka Magyarország*, is hostile to the notion of migration (the first Hungarians, like all of us, were a migrant people themselves, of course), and has put fences up to stop the would-be passage of people from elsewhere. Redstarts can get through from Chad or Ethiopia or other places to the south, but human migrant traffic, anyone who might have accompanied the redstarts across the Sahara, is barred.

Nagyszelmenc is marked on my old map. It was then apparently securely nested within Hungarian territory. Nowadays the village must live more like a vagrant bird that has fetched up in the wrong place, lost in a kind of internal exile, spatchcocked across a border, and with its people apparently homeless even in their own living rooms.

In the spring of 1997, I walked east for the last few metres to the wire fence from the last house in Nagyszelmenc – we had called in on Janos, the elderly man who lived there. I was travelling with Ken Smith, poet and friend, and his friend Miklós Zelei, a Hungarian writer. Ken was thinking of a poem in this place that might work on the radio. I was recording the wind in the wire. After a few steps, we got to the border. It was a simple affair. The fences (there were two – one in Slovakia and one, a metre east, in Ukraine) ran over the rough asphalt of the road, from the fields to the south and on across the fields to the north. The through-way where we stood had become a dead-end, a double dead-end: a cul de sac meeting head-on a cul de sac. There was nothing more. The same green grew on either side of the border. Lucerne, I think. Janos' smallholding looked identical to a house and plot we could see on the other side. As I put my hands on the fence and looked through the oblongs of wire, a golden oriole slipped from a willow just a few metres ahead of us, up the road in Ukraine, and flew towards us, bouncing and mustard-bright. It cleared the wire and continued into Slovakia for a hundred metres until it found a willow to dive into. As I watched it go, a trio of swallows came over us and flew in the opposite direction from Slovakia to Ukraine.

It took us a day and a half to make the birds' ten-second journey. We had to drive dozens of kilometres north to be herded at a vehicle choke point and negotiate a jam of officialdom – papers, passports, customs, policemen – and then, once in Ukraine, to drive back south to Kisszelmenc. The journey was long enough and slow enough in the car for us travellers to listen twenty times over to the same cassette, *The Boatman's Call* by Nick Cave and the Bad Seeds. Before we had even got to the queue at the border, Ken began to sing along to one bluesy dirge or another. For the wired-up springtime place we were trying to get to there were several appropriately cracked pastorals set in various dark arcadias. Ken was particularly taken with a song about the spring fall of cherry blossom called 'People Ain't No Good'.

In Kisszelmenc, having talked to Janos' neighbour (who was also a relative), we walked with her to the wire and hailed Janos in one country from another, using the language of neither. As we did, the swallows of both villages were criss-crossing the skies over the fences, and fire-bellied toads bleeped and pulsed in the ditches on either side of the border. One swallow came low and flew between the top strands of the wires. It was like seeing a bird come through an open window.

Birds can fly and need no papers. So what? I first went to Communist Hungary in the 1980s because I was interested in spending time in a place that had a story that seemed far from finished. It was a country still on the move, as my own country seemed not to be. I was smitten. Since then I have gone back many times for the same reason to many places along the east–west European borders. Much has changed since 1986 – including a new unmooring of my own home – but not everything. The wretched recent human history of these places, and what I think of as their long dying, continues, paradoxically, to make them lively.

For me also, the birds in these awkward and wounded borderlands mark the time too. Once in Hungary in the far east of the present country, on a late winter visit I hoped would be an early spring trip, I stopped on a road beyond the Hortobágy having seen half a dozen cranes flying low over the *puszta*. They had lowered their legs and were

231

looking to land after a journey. They counted as spring new-come birds to my mind, although some do now winter in today's milder Hungary. As I was reaching for my binoculars and clambering out of my car, a young woman appeared from behind a scrawny line of bare trees. She was walking towards me. There was some dirty snow on the ground and ice in the air. The woman, who was actually more of a teenage girl, was wearing old army-issue combat boots and a pink bikini. I had inadvertently pulled over at a pit-stop of some kind. Using my best Hungarian to extricate myself from a deal, and too nervous to check on the cranes, I got back into the car. I drove on towards the town of Gyula and the Romanian border and, for the next ten kilometres, my passing seeming to encourage more women, all as crane-legged as the first, to come, as if sprouting or *springing*, to the roadside, all of them dressed for nothing at all.

We returned from Kisszelmenc to Slovakia. After the same slow border chaos in reverse, our car-load felt as though we had got out of gaol and we stopped on the edge of a village to celebrate with honey and wine. It was hot. With a goose wing that he kept for the purpose, a bee-keeping wine-maker brushed his bees from their combs so that he could pour the honey into a jar for us. It settled there like an extravagant golden mud. Other bees were busy flying from the nearby flowering limes and acacias. Their hum thickened the air. Some interrupted their journeys to drink from an iron barrel brim-full of rainwater. I saw the thirsty workers walk head-first over and down the metal lip of the barrel to reach the dark skin of water. You could see them pushing their faces into it and the water surface stretching around their mouths.

Our own drinking took us underground. We followed our host into the cellar he had dug into a low hill. He tapped a barrel, siphoning his best white wine with a glass retort. We drank some straight from the flask and had more of the cool yellow plasma poured for us into metal drinking cups. The wine tasted perfect – like the air had around the bees, of lime flower and green sun and chalky earth. We took another cup. We weren't far underground, but the cave kept us preserved in a level condition. Until we stepped back out into the sunlight we were all sober and making sense. Before, about ten seconds later, I collapsed and fell asleep on the ground, I looked back happily down the hole, our late abandoned home.

The same afternoon for a second time we came out of the dark again and into the day, with a similar effect. Back in Nagyszelmenc, Ken and I went to call on Janos in the last house before the border. I recorded our talk. We sat around a table covered with an oil cloth in the dark room that was almost the whole of his home. An old calendar hung over the sink. It was fifteen years out of date. The Russians had taken Janos from Nagyszelmenc in 1944 when they overran eastern Hungary, as it was then. He was twenty. Many Hungarians were rounded up, as human war booty, and held in a camp nearby at Szolyva (now in western Ukraine). They were told they were being sent further east for some *malenkij robot* or a little labouring work. Janos didn't make it back from Siberia, to what remained of his home, for years. Thousands never got out alive.

Ken took notes and later wrote about this in a poem called 'Wire through the Heart'. Janos served us chaser after chaser of *pálinka*, a special 'kosher' bottle, to toast our arrival and his survival. Eventually we had to leave. Once again, as we stepped from the souterrain, the daylight and the sun-warmed spring air took their prisoners. Outside Janos' house, I made it to the road but Ken toppled into the toad-ditch. I turned in time to see it, hearing him say:

– I've done it.

And then, a moment later, as he fell forwards:

– *Yo no soy marinero.*

We were a long way from the sea but he went down into the water nonetheless, getting soaked to his waist and tagged with green weed. He clambered out dripping, and we made it, still crapulous, to the wire. We greeted it like an old friend and held on tight.

From Kisszelmenc came the sound of music. We had got to the border at the same moment a trio of gypsy musicians, a woman and two men, left the yard of a farmhouse, one hundred metres up the village street on the Ukrainian side. They turned on the road and walked towards us. They were all singing. The woman led the voices; one man played a small guitar and the other a cimbalom. They sang and played as they walked.

The cimbalom sounds like a piano as it sinks to the bottom of a lake. Stretched strings, mounted like a horizontal harp, are hit with soft dulcimer-style hammers held in the player's hands. It makes music of great, often hurrying, fluidity. Its sounds are watery and somewhat calcified or coralline. The guitarist was busy too. Although the song they were singing had a walking beat the music ran as it went, as if the tune was hurrying away from the singers then returning to them, finding a common stride and a step, and then moving off again. It moved like a dog on a walk, off the leash, away and back and back and away.

I knew the song from my time in Budapest. It was called 'Luma Maj' or 'The Gypsies are Coming'. They were. Until we arrived at the wire, the three had had no audience as far as we could see; yet they were singing. And even with us listening they appeared not to need us to do so. The three musicians, walking and singing – it was for them, not us. They were taking outside the inside of themselves: they didn't have much, but they did have that.

> Avile le roma, *luma maj,*
> The gypsies have come
> Avile le mangaven, *luma maj,*
> To propose to your daughter.
> Szode mangesz pe tyi sej? *luma maj,*
> How much will you ask for your daughter?
> Tranda lire taj dopas.
> Thirty lires and a half.
> Akhardeman te khelav, *luma maj,*
> I was asked to go to dance,
> Taj me phendem, csi khelav, *luma maj,*
> I said I was not going,
> Ingerdeman te khelav, *luma maj,*
> I was taken to dance,
> Taj me phendem, csi khelav, *luma maj.*
> I said I could not.

The woman's smoky voice made a blackened blues of the story. It sounded like a strong crying. Life is hard, that is a given; everything else must be lived in this knowledge.

The guitar, which was a tambura, I think, jangled like a dirty ukulele. The guitarist sang just behind the woman's words, as a kind of echo to her voice, putting a drag or delay on it so it went out into the air around them all and lingered there. The cimbalom player departed on a quickstep run, dragging the feet of the tune and then skipping on – that dog, again, always running somewhere – and he sang, as well, or rather made a percussive drumming sound, a rolling bass hum-cluck, from somewhere in his throat. It added a beat, like their footsteps, to the project: a *lifted-up over-singing*. They walked towards us at the border, singing of their walking towards us, a description of the condition of their lives, a song about moving being given on the road. Everything was hard. Everything was coming. Everything was moving. It had always been that way and it always would.

At the wire, the song ended and they stopped. We said hello and put our hands as best we could through the Slovakian fence towards them beyond the Ukrainian fence. They said hello back. Miklós had a daughter, Bori; he promised to send her when he could. We laughed. We couldn't shake hands as we couldn't reach across, and only at the height of a swallow flight was the wire open enough, and that was above our heads. The singers asked for nothing. We smiled and waved again at the air between us and they started another song.

They sang in a Romani language. I had known a version in Hungarian. It was a prayer about homelessness (all their songs are about homelessness) and was, again, addressed to themselves.

> We have no lives any more,
> Even the wind blows us,
> Even the wind blows us, Gypsies!
> Get up, Gypsies,
> Get up, and let's go . . .

JUNE

Cavenham
52°N

1 June. An evening on the Suffolk heath, with Claire, for stone curlews and, perhaps, nightjars. United States Air Force transporter planes circled and banked low above our heads every minute of the first hour. They lumbered around, nuzzling at the thick air, like dor beetles or cockchafers, not really wanting to be aloft but frightened to come down. There was one stone curlew, locked on the turf, incubating eggs or brooding chicks. It looked like a lizard in a sandpit. The old dust of chalk and sand, and threadbare turf, and rabbit fur, and grasshoppers and cinnabar moth caterpillars, and prickling gorse and sapless heather: all is rolled into this bird, and then some old goat conjoined to give it eyes. The shock of its making steers the rest of its life. It looks damned. A *petrified* curlew, Thomas Browne once called it, after an accident in translation – that name suits too.

The planes kept coming, now like old cart-horses running the ring at a knackers' market, surely too slow and too heavy. The last one circled and then the light turned loose and made as if to undress the clouds. Another stone curlew, invisible, started up with warped curlew calls, a kind of yowling. Then, the day all but gone, a third flew from one side of the heath to the other, all gawky and hexed, with a still wilder and more urgent cry. I lost it in the smoky twilight.

Claire heard a nightjar, one brief broadcast purr, another distillate of the place. Though I had turned up my aid, I missed it, and all I got was the reverb of the stone curlews' cries and a last shudder from the earthquake of flying hooves. For a while the evening seemed spoiled

– it and I had failed one another – until rescue came with a soothing sliver of moon, which boated through the clouds above the birch wood at the edge of the heath, a *sky-canoe*.

The wood at Cavenham holds a roost of jackdaws and rooks. I was surprised there were so many black birds so early in the season. What had happened to their appointed springtime homes? Were they bystanders to breeding or had they already bred and were now winter-minded? Long after night had fallen and the moon had paddled higher, stragglers continued to arrive, with both their wings and voices creaking. In the restless dormitory the racket eventually dimmed but it never stopped; deep into the dark they were still talking in their sleep.

Lerwick
60°N

5 June. Shetland: I crossed the path of the little boy of the house where I was staying who was coming up the steps from his garden. He was talking to what I took to be a toy mobile phone that he had held to his cheek. As he passed me, he stopped talking, lowered his hand and opened his palm, and showed me the hen's egg he held there, speckled brown, new fetched from a straw nest in the little coop to the side of the garden. Its warmth had warmed the boy's cheek, and he was talking to it before his mother scrambled it with others and we shared it for our breakfast.

The same day on Fair Isle I watched a fulmar trying to land on its breeding ledge, its feet lowered and paddling for purchase in the chimney of wind at the top of a geo, a cleft in a cliff. It took twenty-five attempts: a man, home from the pub, patting over and over for his keys. On our way to Shetland, the previous day, the cloud had sunk near Sumburgh and we had mimicked the fulmar when our plane had to *go around*, as the pilot said, and try again.

For six days on Fair Isle there was no tree taller than my ear. And every bird that wanted a tree was shown to me. The spring migrants had no place to hide. The island is unhedged, its one plantation has five stunted conifers and they are dead. The wind comes from all quarters. At night the great black flood of it polished the stars. In the daylight, I saw a frog orchid so blown about that its flower couldn't leave the shelter of the soil. I heard a marsh warbler sing from a dead Christmas tree, a chatter-box, plaiting its mimicking tunes with the voices of those birds it had lived among before it blew, by mistake, onto the island: blue tits and robins from Sweden (where it might have hatched and, another year, bred), scrub-robins and weavers from Zambia (where it might have wintered). At Shirva, Stewart Thomson, in his tenth decade, sat outside his house on a blue pew spinning brown wool from the island's fleeces. In his garden roses there was a western subalpine warbler, less than a year old, just in off the sea and 2,000 kilometres off course. One in the roses – how many more on the seabed?

Swaffham Prior
52°N

7 June. Four blackbird eggs have become three chicks and one egg. It was pipping. I held it to my ear and heard the quietest labour, the clicks of the chick's egg tooth working at a way out of its egg. It is the bird's first song.

Vence
44°N

At the end of the 1920s, as D. H. Lawrence got sicker with tuberculosis he was able to move less and less. This was especially cruel for a life that up until the last was always shifting. He liked it like that. The damned and the dead were stopped and he didn't want to join them. He was always looking for life, and dreams of getting up and going on crowded at him until his end.

Rimbaud was the same. He is not a poet who often makes you cry but his last letter, by one of the greatest of all leg-stretchers in art and in life, is wretched to read. Early in 1891, in Ethiopia, where he worked as a trader (in coffee, elephant tusks and guns – he had long abandoned poetry), his right knee became inflamed and then septic. Within a few weeks, the man said by Verlaine to have *soles of wind* couldn't walk. Knowing there was no help for him where he was, he designed a litter and had himself carried out of Africa, north from Harar and up the Red Sea coast. It was an emergency passage for a stranded migrant. Travelling was agony, but he survived the journey and landed at Marseilles, where his right leg had to be amputated. With just one leg, he made it to his family farm in north-east France where his mother was. Then, intent on heading south again, he returned to Marseilles. But he was at death's door, not in a departure lounge. Bone cancer had been diagnosed.

His sister, Isabelle, who had accompanied him, sat at his bedside and recorded his delirious visions:

– 'We are in Harar, we are always leaving for Aden, and we have to look for camels, to organise the caravan; he is walking very easily with his new articulated leg . . .'

That was his madness talking. In reality:

– 'He's as thin as a skeleton and has the colour of a corpse! And all his poor paralysed, mutilated, dead limbs around him!'

There was no return to travel or to health for Rimbaud. He got worse. Two weeks later, on 9 November 1891, he attempted to book a passage with the director of a steamship company at Marseilles. His sister took down his request. Rimbaud begins with an ivory inventory, as if he were still trading from Africa; then, acknowledging that he cannot move, he makes it clear – even in his terminal confusion – that he is still desperate to go:

Send me therefore the prices of the services from Aphinar to Suez. I am completely paralysed: I wish therefore to be on board in good time. Tell me at what time I need to be carried on board . . .

239

He died the next day at ten o'clock in the morning. He was thirty-seven.

It would be possible to put together an anthology of the desired last-minute departures that marked the exits of a number of spring-seeking writers. There have been some wretched endings.

Chekhov, who released a herd of deer to run through the last thoughts of a dying man in his story 'Ward 6', is himself supposed to have asked, as he died: 'Has the sailor gone?'

'Now comes good sailing,' are said to have been Thoreau's last words, to which he added 'moose' and 'Indian'.

Thoreau was forty-four when he died. So was Chekhov; so was D. H. Lawrence.

Chekhov wrote of seasonal blossom – the exhalation of the spring – together with his clouded lungs in a spring letter of 8 March 1901 from Yalta:

> Our almond and apricot trees blossomed long ago, it is gloriously warm and all would be fine and merry were it not for the cough which has been troubling me for ten days now.

His last letter from Badenweiler on 28 June 1904 includes queries about boat timetables, like Rimbaud; he fancied a trip from Trieste to Odessa: 'It would be an absolutely ideal trip for me, if the boat is a good one and not an old tub.' He died four days later (and his body was returned to Russia in an old oyster barrel).

An entry in her journal by Katherine Mansfield, a few days before she stopped writing, three months before she died of tuberculosis, aged thirty-four, in January 1923, mentions Chekhov's last letters – 'Illness has swallowed him' – and goes on to assert why she wants to recover her own wellbeing: 'to live a full, adult, living, breathing life in close contact with what I love – the earth and the wonders thereof – the sea – the sun'.

'A child of the sun,' she said she wanted to be. Her last entry, written eight days later, on 18 October 1922, records a view from the fall. She's making, it appears, the beginning of a story (her journals often depart into settings and scenes for fictions), but it is also a description of where she was that autumn day, far from the sun:

In the autumn garden leaves falling. Little footfalls, like gentle whispering. They fly, spin, swirl, shake.

Running upstairs on 9 January 1923 (at Gurdjieff's 'Institute for the Development of Man' near Paris, where she was a patient/student) she suffered a pulmonary haemorrhage and died half an hour later.

Lawrence died thinking of his next move, at the beginning of spring. Boats were part of his getaway plans. He always had plans and was never really a writer in *residence*. He wrote his last letters (without knowing them to be that) from his last but one bed (he was moved once more on 1 March 1930 and died the next day).

The sanatorium where he lodged was called Ad Astra – 'To the Stars'. Virgil used the phrase in the *Aeneid*. It was in Vence, near Nice, in the south of France. In the same hill town, little more than a decade later, Henri Matisse designed and decorated (stained glass, murals, furnishings) the Chapelle du Rosaire – and was so ill and infirm that he had to work from a wheelchair and use a brush mounted on a stick tied to his arm. At Ad Astra, Lawrence was a patient (though not that) for less than a month. Confined to bed, he wanted above all to get downstairs to where the world carried on.

Space travel had previously been on his mind along with his perpetual restlessness. Like a bird trying to escape the winter, he had headed south with Frieda from Germany in September 1929 to France and the sea: 'I feel that *nothing* will ever again take me north of Lyon,' he wrote in a letter on 27 September. 'I dread and hate the north, it is full of death and the most grisly disappointment.' Their new home was called the Villa Beau Soleil. And for a time the sun shone enough for the new arrived migrant to detect a living engine even further south:

From here, one feels Africa. It is queer – but the direct vibration seems to be from Africa. Next winter, we'll go.

They didn't; he was dead. But until the last he wouldn't stay still and was intent on getting better. At the Beau Soleil he was often in bed. He could manage 'little walks', but wrote: 'I keep mostly indoors. It's a bit too sharp for me.' A doctor from England was found, though the patient was loath to trouble him. Lawrence spent the winter working on new books (the posthumously published *Apocalypse*) and overseeing existing publications – the flood tide still ran high around *Lady Chatterley's Lover*, which had appeared (or half-appeared in privately printed and pirate editions) in 1928; he wrote his *A Propos* of the novel, and he sorted his Italian essays ('The Nightingale', 'Flowery Tuscany' and 'Fireworks'), and there were new stories ('The Escaped Cock'), and pamphlets (*Pornography and Obscenity*), and poems ('Pansies' and 'Nettles').

He looked at the sea from his bed and watched the moon over the Mediterranean. Friends visited and hangers-on gathered. Lawrence and Frieda acquired a marmalade cat, sometimes called Mickie Mussolini, and two goldfish (the cat caught one); Frieda played records on her gramophone, which Lawrence hated (earlier he had broken over her head her much loved Bessie Smith disc, 'Empty Bed Blues'), but they also baked bread together; he asked for a blue jacket from Italy ('I love the colour so much'), and for a Christmas pudding and 'half a pound of tea' from England, along with '2 large meridian undervests' and '2 knickers' for Frieda. The narcissus began to flower in December.

All the while, however, he was dogged by his 'tiresome' health, though he was adamant (until the very end) that it wasn't his lungs, and he repeatedly made light of it, describing himself as no worse than 'so-so' just six weeks before he died. 'Somehow I am not ill,' he wrote, 'but my bronchials and asthma *get me down*.' He took to spitting into old envelopes that, when filled, he kept in his jacket pockets. In 1925 doctors in Mexico City had diagnosed Lawrence's tuberculosis, but he only ever used the word tubercular once in relation to himself after that, and that was less than three weeks before he died. Similarly, only in a roundabout way did he own up to the awfulness for him of having to stay still and the meaning of such confinement. Once, he declared that he was improving, but in the same (struggling) breath admitted that he wasn't: 'I'm really rather better again – only I never want to walk or move about.'

That was an inadvertent declaration of how bad things were, but still he didn't stop – he hoped that demonstrating a hunger to be on the road again could start him off on it once more. After all, the season demanded it. In October 1929 he had written a poem about a migrant butterfly pausing on his (static) shoe before committing itself to flight south over the Mediterranean. On 6 January 1930 he wrote to Maria and Aldous Huxley: 'Already the year is changing round . . . It might pick me up again, who knows?' In fact, by this time he could barely move under his own steam and had on occasions, as his health got worse, to be literally picked up by others and carried. He didn't mention that to the Huxleys or his other correspondents. He told Mabel Luhan that he planned on going again to Taos in New Mexico: 'Here's to the Spring, and a little new hope.' The whole of 'old moribund Europe' was now giving him grief, not just the north: 'I shall just die if I linger on like this in Europe any more.' On 8 January 1930 he wrote: 'I wouldn't mind a long sea trip.'

In late August or early September of the year before, Lawrence had begun drafting his poem 'The Ship of Death', inspired by his eschatological travels underground to the Etruscan tombs and their grave goods. In his notebook this poem followed a first version of another stunning death-haunted poem, 'Bavarian Gentians'. In an Alpine village that August, a bowl of cut autumn gentians had added the only décor to Lawrence's room in an otherwise spartan inn that smelled 'terrifically of cows'. 'The Ship of Death' was revised and finished in October 1929. Two months later, Lawrence was talking of taking a boat from Marseilles to San Francisco.

He liked boats, he said, but to be able to walk again would have been better than sailing. When he had arrived at Ad Astra he had written: 'I'm going to practise walking again.' That is a sad remark from someone who had once been a great walker. Frieda had admired his legs, and David Ellis (one of the heroic team of recent Lawrence biographers and editors) points out that many male characters in Lawrence are noted for theirs: 'Quick, alive, vital, the leg is a metonym for animal vigour and sexual prowess.'

243

By the middle of January 1930 there had to be sanatorium talk alongside the runaway talk. He was still promising Mabel that he'd make it to New Mexico: 'We can begin a new life,' he wrote; 'by the end of March, surely, I shall be well enough again'; meanwhile, 'I watch the sea and the white foam.' But there was to be no ship to San Francisco. He accepted, at last, some medical advice: 'Dr Morland assured me I should get better so much more quickly in a sanatorium, and be able to *walk* again – and that is what I want, I want my legs back again.'

In Lawrence's mind, the moon might have been a helpful agent in this. He craved lunar magic and lunar movement. Writing in *A Propos of Lady Chatterley's Lover* of our 'pettifogging *apartness*', he asked:

> How are we to get back Apollo, and Attis, Demeter, Persephone, and the halls of Dis? How even see the star Hesperus, or Betelgeuse? We've got to get them back, for they are the world our soul, our greater consciousness lives in. The world of reason and science, the moon a dead lump of earth, the sun so much gas with spots: this is the dry and sterile little world the abstracted mind inhabits . . .

He was wrong about the science, but let us forgive the sick man. In three poems he wrote in his last year, he expressed his needs better – his imaginative hope that the moon might move us, as it draws its tides, and not be a dead lump, and let us not be the same.

Another spring he might not make (and didn't, in fact), but surely he could aspire to live beneath another full moon. He asks for it in the last poem in *More Pansies*. It is called 'Prayer'.

> O let my ankles be bathed in moonlight, that I may go
> sure and moon-shod, cool and bright-footed
> towards my goal.

In 'Invocation to the Moon' in *Last Poems*, he asks for a 'last great gift':

who will give me back my lost limbs
and my lost white fearless breast
and set me again on moon-remembering feet
a healed, whole man, O Moon!

And in 'Shadows' in *Last Poems*, at a time of a dark moon, when it is 'in shadow' though nonetheless operative still, he talks of a half-life rescued for him in the moon's half-withered light, of being broken down to come back, not in the world's morning of spring but in some seasonless but personal place, 'on a new morning, a new man'. The poems, like much of Lawrence's late writing, are made of words that have come the *whole way*, of words that have *been there*:

and still, among it all, snatches of lovely oblivion, and snatches
of renewal
odd, wintry flowers upon the withered stem, yet new, strange
flowers
such as my life has not brought forth before, new blossoms of
me –

Is it too far-fetched to think of Lawrence *blooming* with his tuberculosis – to think of the blood-spotted flowering of a tubercular root system occurring to him, even as he coughed into his envelopes; to ask if there might yet be a strange dark and bloodied spring within him? Walter Benjamin, in his essay on tubercular Kafka, has a brilliant insight on the animal within the writer of 'Metamorphosis', 'Josefine, the Songstress or: The Mouse People', 'A Report to an Academy' and 'The Burrow':

because the most forgotten land is one's own body, one can understand why Kafka called the cough that erupted from within him 'the animal'. It was the most advanced outpost of the great herd.

Even in his last months Lawrence was never entirely moonstruck. Almost all of his declarations of intent are acknowledgements that life is unlikely to go the way he would have it. He watched himself closely and owned up to his fantasies almost as much as he entertained them. Much of his greatness as a writer lies in this self-knowledge. In 1927 he had written in a book review:

> We travel, perhaps, with a secret and absurd hope of setting foot on the Hesperides, or running our boat up a little creek and landing in the Garden of Eden. The hope is always defeated. There is no Garden of Eden, and the Hesperides never were.

When Lawrence arrived at Ad Astra he weighed less than forty-five kilograms – as near to weightless as he had ever been in his life. To begin with, as so often for him in new surroundings, the place was promising – it was more like a hotel than a sanatorium. 'The mimosa is all out in clouds . . . and the almond blossom very lovely.' Upstairs, in a building up in the hills behind Nice, he felt 'aloft': 'I feel better, I feel I've escaped something' – 'Here one is in the sky again, and on top of things.' But he was already too *light*. Trying to plan what was next, he managed to read a life of Columbus and when reviewing a book by Eric Gill he wrote an article that re-phrased his preoccupations:

> Only in the country, among peasants, where the old ritual of the seasons lives on in its beauty, is there still some living, instinctive 'faith' in the God of Life.

But by this stage of his sickness he could only report on what he'd read: he hadn't been allowed to walk out to see the almond blossom – he couldn't walk – and had had to make do with others' news of it. He didn't put on any weight; and soon, as ever, the new place no longer suited: 'shan't stay long', he wrote on 21 February of his room, unwittingly also of his life. A week later, he was carried to a new bed, but he lived only one more day.

The spring that year came without him in it.

Aarhus
56°N

All flowers and every animal might be good to think with. Every life form might be relevant. Some, maybe, more than others. Picture a reindeer. Following the spring north, you might follow the herds that have done the same and are still trying to move with the season. In the springtime of Europe, around 15,000 years ago, at the warming end of the last ice age, reindeer were an expression of the changing climate, they travelled with it, and they took people with them. To this day, they remain seasonally affected animals still living, and struggling to live, as such.

Felix Riede knows about the old reindeer. He is an archaeologist at the university in Aarhus in Denmark. He works mostly on past planetary disasters (volcanoes, earthquakes, meteor strikes) and their impact on early human life in Europe, but he is also interested in the very first people who walked into what is now Denmark after the end of the last ice age. These people – Felix thinks there were about twenty of them – were in pursuit of reindeer that were retreating north, following the ice, wanting to cling to its hard shoulder or hug its cold shadow. As the climate warmed, and a version of spring came from the south, the reindeer had gone on ahead – backwards, as it were, in search of the best of winter, older weather, and away from the new temperate conditions in Europe to the south, which bred insects that pestered the grazing animals and allowed the growth of lush vegetation that they couldn't eat.

There aren't any reindeer in Denmark now. They had to move further north as the post-glacial ten-thousand-year-long European spring took hold. Felix and I spoke in his modern office on a late-spring Danish day. It was blowy and cool but green all about. Swallows flew low to the ground in the academic precincts.

The people who followed the reindeer were Hamburgians – named for a site near the present-day German city that they occupied. As the first post-glacial Danes, they are known from just a handful of places in southern Denmark: Jels Oversø and Slotseng in Southern Jutland

and at Krogsbølle (where Felix excavated) and Sølbjerg on the island of Lolland.

They were in those places because of reindeer. These sites are on or near relatively high ground: good for observing prey. The people hunted with spears or arrows with flint tips, but as yet it is not known how they followed the herds.

– Their activities could be thought of, in human terms, Felix said, as a proto-colonisation around the harvesting of natural resources, or, in ecological terms, as part of natural succession, whereby our predatory mammal species moved northwards with plants and other animals occupying (or re-occupying) lands that had been frozen over and life-less for thousands of years.

Those two families were an expression of the spring of the continent. The Hamburgians themselves might put it another way: reindeer were what they wanted – they lived by them. The people who walked into Denmark were a group from a larger population who had survived the end of the last ice age in the Franco-Iberian refugium in south-west France and the north-east corner of Spain. As the grip of the ice less-ened, some of these people moved north into France, towards the Rhineland, and up along other large river corridors, into the north European plain (made up of today's countries around the southern portions of the North Sea and the Baltic Sea, from Britain to Poland, and areas of those seas not then under salt-water). Reindeer were the only large animal present in this area. There were wolves somewhere, but there is, Felix said, surprisingly little evidence of them keeping up with the new herds.

– Reindeer are very good at escaping in space.

People therefore had the chance to play wolf – just a few of them.

– Very few.

The received thinking is that the Hamburgians occupied southern Scandinavia around 14,700 years ago and stayed. Felix isn't so sure, and suggests that there were actually two short 'colonisation pulses', one around 14,700 to 14,600 years ago and a second around 14,300 to 14,200 years ago. There is enough difference in the artefacts at the Hamburgian sites known in Denmark to suggest these two discrete times.

248

– These are the archaeological signatures of a few people making forays into the edges of the known world. No one had been there for many thousands of years, and these people had no knowledge of where the resources were. They had to learn as they travelled. The landscape type might have been familiar, but the deglaciated specifics of the terrain – including where the reindeer were – weren't. It was also immature, ecologically speaking: a barren and sharp place.

'Altogether elsewhere', wrote W. H. Auden in 1940 in the last stanza of 'The Fall of Rome',

> Vast
>
> Herds of reindeer move across
> Miles and miles of golden moss,
> Silently and very fast.

I see a silent movie filmed from a light plane crossing the tundra. These dream-powered images are put into play by Auden to describe the opposite of the human. They evoke life on the flip-side of the world, far from civilisation and its discontents as catalogued in the rest of his poem. The reindeer are like an intermission in a news bulletin, a screening for when times otherwise are tough.

Now we know there were a handful of people down there on the golden moss in that *altogether elsewhere* during the morning of the European world. Talking to Felix, listening to him, I saw at once how young everything is in the north where the ice was: where the swallows come, where the reindeer walked, where Felix lives and works, where we were speaking, and where I come from too and have been departing from and returning to for so much of my life. Migration from the south into these places is an event of the world's morning, or from the spring-time of a world era. Migration evolved here in a shifting time – climate change prompted the adaptation that is migration; it is young, still new, and it happened (and is happening) in the Earth's own expression of a springtime. Spring itself, as we know it in our northern places, is still young: we've only had 15,000 springs – everything that we think of as spring has evolved in that time. Spring *in* the north has evolved in the spring *of* the north. The annual defrost is a mirror of the epoch's thaw. We are all here, still waking up in our interglacial, warm between icy sheets. The world truth – spring as an opening up of life – that thrills us, is itself a *becoming* of the world. The buzz of earth *is* the buzz of the Earth.

– These people came out of a cultural tradition that they shared with others who decided not to go north. Those who stayed south diversified their economies. They had deer, not reindeer, to live by. But some had decided to follow the reindeer. They were the animals they knew. That decision-making is something to think about. How did they do it? As the herds moved north, so the people followed. Who can say whether these people were therefore pioneers or traditionalists? What we see as an obligation to step in with ecological succession in a dynamic landscape were actually human decisions taken by these people that we might recognise as familiar. Politics comes into this as well. Perhaps influential people pulled families with them on the journeys they had decided to make. Were there charismatic leaders who broke from some traditions in order to pursue others? Did they all fall out over reindeer?

To catch reindeer on Greenland, the first people there modified the terrain at migration bottlenecks, building cairns and flying flags or pennants to steer and direct the animals. There is no evidence of the Hamburgians doing that. Nor did they become herders like the Sámi. That sort of animal management or open-range husbandry only developed in the Middle Ages. There is even debate as to whether people can actually follow reindeer herds, because the animals move so constantly and across such distances. Reindeer can run at seventy kilometres per hour; a herd easily travels more than thirty kilometres a day; in a year they move as much as 2,400 km; they are also expert swimmers.*

---

* From Montastruc in France came a brilliantly seen and precisely made three-dimensional carving in mammoth ivory of a male reindeer swimming after a female. Dated to 13,000 radiocarbon years ago (about 15,000 calendar years), it is the oldest sculpture in the entire collection of the British Museum.

It is certain, nonetheless, that the humans who walked into what is now Denmark 14,000 to 15,000 years ago were people of the reindeer. The two species were tied together. One mammal made a culture for two. All parts of the reindeer were put to use, and the animals also had immense significance beyond their function to the reindeer-hunters. These people had been cave-painting people. Animals meant a lot to them: they thought with them as well as eating them. In the cave at La Madeleine, near Lascaux in France, an engraved drawing of a young male reindeer was found – it was made on the foot bone of a reindeer. In the quasi-steppe where the Hamburgians went in today's Denmark there was no wood for timber. Reindeer bones became a building material. Being the tallest thing around, ribs and other bones from the animals became the trees of the bare lands. Tools were made from bones too, clothes from fur, and everything that could be was eaten. Moss and lichens the reindeer had eaten were made edible to humans by the animals' digesting gut chemistry. The guts themselves gave the reindeer-people string. Reindeer stomachs and bladders became containers. So overlapped and intertwined were the two sets of lives that we might say the people *were* reindeer in another form.

Reindeer are not difficult to catch so long as you know where they are, and so long as you can keep up with them. Their seasonal migratory behaviour is 90 per cent predictable. That doesn't sound like bad odds for a hunter, until you realise that that means a totally reindeer-dependent people will have a bad year one year in ten.

– A very tough year. There is a lot of evidence of hunter-gatherer groups coming into severe trouble when specialising in reindeer. The animals have a really volatile boom-and-bust demography, and it is hard for hunters to keep pace. But that doesn't mean they didn't try. With the Hamburgians, we might be dealing with attempts to follow reindeer into new territories that ultimately failed.

The precariousness of the Hamburgian enterprise and its likely failure has, paradoxically, allowed individual people to become visible across the dark spaces of intervening time. Had they succeeded, the accumulating evidence of their occupation might have covered their first traces and destroyed the record of those who first walked that way.

Because it appears that the families of hunters failed we can raise them into a second life.

Reindeer were killed with flint-tipped javelins or spears. Most of the evidence of the reindeer people is their flint weaponry. It is possible to track one maker across many flints. No two tool-makers handled and worked a flint in exactly the same manner. They all left their signature.

– We can actually recognise the same shapes – the cutting marks on flint weapons – at a series of sites, and deduce that it was actually the same person who was making these flints and working in different places. Through their material traces, we can see, and move with, an individual.

One maker, 14,000 years ago, leaves their mark. Their *handedness* can be seen, their particularities still legible in what they did, their blows are recorded and the lean of their fist.

Felix showed me pictures.

– The tools tell us more too. They are amazingly well designed. You would be impressed. There is a high frequency of combination tools. They are neat solutions to a problem of a vagrant people who needed to travel light. They made multi-tools: both ends of a flint were modified – it is like having a screwdriver at one end and a wrench at the other.

The reindeer came, like birds, without any bags; the Hamburgians had Swiss Army knives and made bags out of the reindeer.

– It was all about movement with the reindeer. But it was hard. They didn't have travois, or skis or sleds. There were no dogs in northern Europe. There were massive constraints on how much you could take. It was hard too for elderly people and small children. Female fertility was probably reduced by the walking life. Everything had to be done on two feet. Two feet only.

It didn't work. The old story is that it did: that people arrived in Denmark and stayed. Felix thinks that doesn't fit the evidence. There is a great difference between these Hamburgians and those people who followed. And those who followed were living and working in a new boreal landscape that had trees, not reindeer. There was also a short cold phase, a throwback icy snap that might have sealed up the

Hamburgian world, before a more substantial warming began, ushering in the rest, as we know it, of life.

– These groups were so small. The landscape was raw and extremely challenging. Colonisation proceeds by trial and error. The landscape seemed familiar but key features were different. Landscape-learning takes time. And the people couldn't handle it.

– And there were only twenty of them?

– Perhaps I am joking a little. But not much. Each of the few sites we know is small. There is no evidence of any substantial structures or of any long-term occupation. The people clustered in two parts of the country. There was no fanning out, no general presence elsewhere. The material culture that we see in the flint projectile points is near identical. I think there were very few people and they were only here for a few years, one generation perhaps, and the bid for a new home failed. Three hundred years later others tried again.

I left Felix and hurried to the airport to fly north to look for some living example of the reindeer we'd been talking about. As I walked into the terminal a hail-storm began. It had been brewing for an hour in a pile-up of clouds. I watched the end of it from inside the departure lounge. On the wet concrete apron at the base of a big window I could see the body of a swallow. A *papirosa*. It must have collided with a pane of glass. If it wasn't a wet cigarette it was a dead moth. I've never seen a swallow casualty like that before, but sometimes they must fly wrong. The little fluster of its dark body and *roundy* head was briefly shrouded in dabs of greyish hail. The sun came out and I watched until the ice melted from it.

Troms
70°N

Five hours after I left Denmark, I was on Kvaløya – Whale Island – in northern Norway. There was a bull reindeer walking along a rush-hour road towards the bridge to the neighbouring island on which the city of Tromsø lies. Vehicle traffic was quite heavy. The animal, like a good pedestrian, moved onto the pavement and walked there with an air of entitlement. I wound my window down as we passed to better take in such a holy cow. Its hooves clicked on the tarmac like tap shoes. A vinegary whiff came off it, as if it had just run a good distance. Its fur, pale charcoal grey, seemed to be being shed in clumps from various patches on its body. And its mood – head-down, hips-lurching, dance-marathon veteran – lent it ramshackle character: it looked like a king of infinite space, an animal going where it wanted, but also deluded, waylaid by its own imagined or misread magnetism, and a prisoner in its own potently disabled body. Its biggest problem was the trophy of itself that it had to carry on its head. The velvet that stretched over its growing antlers was the same colour as its face and its body, but this branching helmet of bone seemed to be crushing the animal beneath it, like kingly armour put on a boy prince – a heavy and venerable crown slipping over his soft pink teenage ears.

Reindeer are part of urban life in the Tromsø area. The cars and trucks slowed but didn't stop. Everyone had places to get to. Nick Tyler, translocated Englishman, reindeer scholar and car-driver, told me the animal's antlers were not only heavy but also living – and that that day they would grow a centimetre, and it would be the same every day at this time of year. The reindeer was budding. And building. If it ever stopped walking, we might focus on a branch or more of its headgear, fingering up towards the midsummer sun. And today it would reach higher than yesterday. You imagine such a tree would need roots to grow and to anchor it in the animal's head. Then you wonder where those roots must reach.

This story, or variants of it, is often told: the hunter Actaeon, when punished by the huntress-goddess Artemis (Diana in Roman myth) for gawping at her nakedness, felt himself becoming a deer, first going 'on all fours' (in Lavinia Greenlaw's poetic re-telling), and then being clobbered about the head as a bony tree began to sprout from the top of his skull. A few moments later all his thinking – a view down the long pale corridor of his life – was truncated as he was torn apart by his own hounds.

As it walked, the reindeer on the road chewed the cud and topped it up by nibbling at tulips in people's front gardens. For May, June and July male reindeer are solitary beasts. Nick filled me in on the cycles. In the winter the herds mix. In the autumn rut the males fight.

– And? I asked.

– A guy like that, fully grown, five or six years old, is building up strength and condition for the rut, for mating. He looks a bit shaggy but he's moulted already and he's fattening on rich spring greens, and growing his antlers.

The antlers are like our fingers: bone in their middle, cartilage at their tips, blood vessels pumping life around. Their velvet is skin. Come October, and the rut and mating, a massive rise in testosterone will kill the antlers, turning living bone into dead bone. Turning it from something soft, that could be injured, into a hard, insensitive, fighting weapon. Normally a body rejects and sloughs off dead material, but the male reindeer needs its antlers. One of the qualities of multi-purpose testosterone is that it blocks this process. It inhibits the activity of osteoclasts – specialised cells at the base of the antlers – that would otherwise nibble away at the dead material of the antlers causing them to fall off. Hence, though dead, the antlers remain attached. After the rut, testosterone levels subside and the osteoclasts get to work and the antlers are cast.

On one tine, the reindeer had hooked a young bracken frond. A bright green wreath hung on the budding green horn. The greenery can't be that important to them. Reindeer are red/green colour-blind and, Nick said, though they do often pick the freshest stuff to eat, we don't know how they do that except that we can say that their choice is not based on colour. The world the reindeer live in is beyond green, north of it. Still, though, the bracken gave the crowned beast a wayward Dionysian look.

At one point, late in his play and deep into his rut of toxic madness, King Lear comes on stage 'dressed with weeds' or 'fantastically dressed with wild flowers' according to different stage directions. He has got himself pranked up into a green suit – appropriately, as he is becoming a green man and is on his way into the earth. At the end of his life he thinks of flowers, as well as trying, in his lucid moments, to make some corrections to the awful man that he was. He hands out flowers (a role more often taken by women – Perdita, Ophelia *et alia* – in Shakespeare) but it is too late. Having made the time run out of joint, he is now so far out of step – so seasonally disaffected – that he cannot get back. First he tries to give flowers to Gloucester, who is blind and cannot see them. Then, when he realises that Gloucester is Gloucester, Lear takes off his own floral crown, since his kingliness has now been discovered as meaningless, and speaks some of his late-flowering bleak truths: 'When we are born we cry that we are come / To this great stage of fools.' Moments later, his wrath and madness rise up again. Six times he says 'kill' as – so one set of stage directions says – 'he throws down his flowers and stamps on them'.

The reindeer on the pavement on Kvaløya was semi-domesticated. It belonged to the Sámi herder who owned all the reindeer on the island. All owned reindeer are supposed by law in Norway to have their ears marked – nicked with distinctive cuts – indicating to whom they belong. There is only one herder on Kvaløya, so he doesn't cut his animals, though the authorities say he must. Elsewhere in Norway an uncut reindeer is considered wild and therefore deemed – in the logic of the anthropocene – the property of the state.

Sámi herders are pastoralists. They don't own land but have long established grazing rights: rights of usufruct. Reindeer are in principle allowed to graze anywhere they can reach, including people's tulip beds; it is the job of farmers not herders to put up fences in order to keep reindeer off their land. Conflicts arise in Norway comparable to those anywhere in the world where pastoralists meet settlers. The new-come temporary swallows I saw zipping along above the reindeer in Kvaløya might overhear similar arguments in the Arctic to those they heard between farmers and nomads in Chad when they themselves were in transit through the Sahel.

Some people are fed up with the reindeer. They say there are too many and they are eating too much. That might better describe the complainants. Some reindeer are given a certain amount of supplementary fodder in winter but this is because, in part, their ability to roam and graze (and be grazed) and move in search of natural forage has been much reduced over the last century by man-made barriers of one kind or another. Their wild food supplies are also otherwise compromised. Changing land use patterns have contributed to the advance of shrubs and woody plants. Warmer temperatures, thanks to anthropogenic climate change, alter the wild pastures reindeer have grazed and browsed for thousands of years; evergreen lingonberry or cowberry is more abundant than it was and is not palatable to reindeer. What pushed them north at the end of the last ice age is affecting them once again today. And movement is not necessarily the answer for the animals that it once was. Even when they can roam they seem more reluctant to do so than they did before. Though reindeer are colour-blind (in a similar way to Wordsworth and many other humans) they can see ultraviolet light (like no human). Electricity cables appear to reindeer to 'crackle and spit fire', Nick said; the animals can see, around the wires, disorienting coronas of fizzing discharge.

Because reindeer live in a world of extremely variable light (all-day night for some of the year, no night at all at other times), they have evolved a unique mechanism to optimise their vision in addition to their UV awareness. In winter the physical structure of their eyes changes in order to improve their vision during the dark season. They have eyes like cats' eyes. The *tapetum lucidum* is a mirrored layer behind the retina, which reflects light back to photoreceptors and improves vision in poor light. It is what makes the eyes of many animals shine in the dark (ours don't, which is why flash photos show 'red eye'). In reindeer the *tapetum lucidum* changes: it is golden-coloured in summer, reflecting light straight back through the retina; in winter, it shifts to a deep blue colour, which scatters light around inside the eye, rather than reflecting it straight back. This greatly increases the animal's visual sensitivity in the low light of winter. The trade-off that arises – the boosted sensitivity comes at the cost of reduced acuity (scatter reduces spatial resolution) – evidently does not matter. Though reindeer see less sharply in the dark months of the year, their motion perception remains intact. They might not be able to detect the expression on a wolf's face but they will still see the predator's prowl.

The next day in Tromsø, there was smoked reindeer salami for lunch, cut with a knife that Sámi reindeer-slaughterers use. I tried dried reindeer heart too. I preferred the salami. I asked everyone in northern Norway about her or his favourite reindeer cuts. Heart was used to frighten the tourists, someone said. We sat in Nick's study, beneath his treasured oars from his rowing days at Cambridge University. He showed me a recent purchase: a vintage tobacco urn marked with his College crest for his pipe shag.

We were waiting for Karen Anette Anti, a Sámi reindeer-herder. She arrived – didn't want any lunch – and at our request she sang or yoiked her dead father. He had been a reindeer-herder too. It was a sad Arctic song, cold but deep – half lullaby, half lament. It began in its middle somehow and ended abruptly. Sounding as if it had no obvious start or finish, it seemed perfect for a song that would be made under one long sky, the dark of winter or the light of summer.

Karen Anette talked about the shapes of reindeer antlers. No two reindeer look the same. Three Sámi words are sufficient to identify any particular animal in a herd. Notches cut in the reindeer's ears are the owner's mark. But they are not really needed. Or they haven't been. A rich vocabulary of sex and stage of life and face and body conformation and coat colour and antlers (in season) identifies each animal.

Even before she gathered herself for her yoik, Karen Anette was troubling to listen to. Much is in jeopardy for her people and their animals. The Old Earth as she saw it (and called it) is running out of time, or rather, she corrected herself:

– It is being run out of its time.

– The government listens a little but not much, she went on. It listens more to the mining corporations. I feel closer to the American Indians than I do to the Norwegian people – and we know what happened to the Indians when their relationship with their animals was broken.

There are eight seasons, Karen Anette said, eight seasons in a reindeer year, which is also the Sámi year since the animal and the people are one. 'These are the days that Reindeer love,' wrote Emily Dickinson in a poem – and the Sámi year begins when the reindeer calves are born.

Spring-winter: *gidádálvve*, in March and April.
Spring: *gidá*, in April and May.
Spring-summer: *gidágiesse*, in May and June.
Summer: *giesse*, in June and July.
Autumn-summer: *tjaktjagiesse*, in August.
Autumn: *tjaktja*, in September and October.
Autumn-winter: *tjaktjadálvve*, in November and December.
Winter: *dálvve*, in December, January, February and March.

– I have been born to this life – we haven't done anything else in my family, just reindeer. I like my caffè latte, but I like my reindeer more. They haven't changed, but now the modern world is coming nearer. We use motorbikes and snowmobiles and helicopters and it makes our life easier as herders, but other people are also coming into the pastures and the mountains and making life harder for the reindeer and for us. The reindeer's nature is to go away and it still can just about do that, but soon maybe not. Modern life cannot be matched with the reindeer. Each season, you have to migrate with the animals, and when they cannot move then reindeer-herding cannot work. We cannot manipulate the reindeer's nature. The reindeer decide for us. Modern society wants to plan, but we cannot plan anything other than what nature does – it decides.

– You can *yoik* a reindeer. My *yoik* is my father's – it just comes, I get it from him. He's been dead for five years. But you can *yoik* a place too, even a motorbike.

I flew back from Norway to London. Beneath the North Sea the sands of the Kentish Knock were obvious. They made a kind of brown bloom or sandy inflorescence that clouded some sea within the sea, as if a shoal of sand was swimming and growing there. It was like the

Coalsack in the southern night sky – an obscuring presence – but it was in the sea.

As we stacked and banked over south London, I looked down again and could see the scar tissue of my first secondary school: location for the two least happy years of my life. There was the doctor in the san on day one who pulled open my underpants, as he might his desk drawer, cupped his palm beneath my retreating baby balls – such a strange nest to look down into – and asked for a cough; there was a teacher who liked to cut boys' hair when they were naked in the changing rooms after games; and there were the games themselves: from the plane I could see the cricket pitches where once I was winded by a ball to the chest and once by a ball to the balls. But I could also see the trees at the edge of the grounds and the outfield that ran to them where I often took comfort and hid as one sort of long-stop or another. And there was the great hall too – site of my dancing for *The Rite of Spring*.

Before the reindeer, I had seen in the National Museum in Copenhagen the 2,000-year-old Gundestrup cauldron. Found in a bog in Himmerland in Jutland in 1891, it is made of silver (with lesser quantities of lead, tin solder, gold and glass) and it is big (70 centimetres in diameter and 45 centimetres tall, and weighing 9 kilograms). Nothing bigger in the silver-work haul of the Iron Age has ever been found anywhere. The museum describes it as the most image-rich object in Danish prehistory. The *repoussé* design (scenes hammered from the reverse side of a piece of metal into low relief) is of a series of curved rectangular plates depicting religious or sacred moments. Mostly these are gods at work; and they are probably deities that were foreign to the religions of the people who lost or hid the cauldron in the Jutland peat where it was stowed for 2,000 years.

There are many theories about the cauldron's origin, and about its function and significance. Perhaps it was commissioned by Celts from Thracian silversmiths (working in present-day Romania or Bulgaria) and brought north by a tribe of people retreating from the Romans. The cauldron might have been a precious object carried by a refugee. It might have been a gift. It might equally have been war booty. Whatever the truth of its beginnings or the truth of its meaning, it represents, in any case, an amalgam, a fusion of European cultures – a stew or *suppe, gulyás,* or potage, or bouillabaisse; a melting pot for *portable soup.*

One of the inner plates of the cauldron especially merits the attention of reindeer-watchers or followers of Actaeon (or King Lear or Orpheus or the spring itself). The scene shows a human-looking figure wearing a vest and long-johns and sitting among other animals – a deer, three lions, a wolf, two antelope-types, with a second human riding a dolphin. The man – it's a man-type – has antlers sprouting from his head almost identical to those of the deer at his side. He is horned but he doesn't look burdened by his headgear, and he sits in a serene pose like a yogi in a lotus position. He might be meditating or chanting or singing. The wolf and the stag appear to be paying attention as they might have done to a singing Orpheus. He looks out at us with a face that seems to be also looking within himself. I've seen St Francis painted like that among his birds.

Cernunnos was the Celtic horned god associated with pretty much everything of his time: animals and fertility and life and the underworld. Perhaps it is he on the cauldron. In his right hand he holds up a torc. In his left, he holds a snake, grasping it just behind its head (although the head looks more ram-like than serpentine). The torc could be a tambourine; the snake looks like a microphone, with a cable curling across a stage. Here is Nick Cave, our Orphic rock 'n' roller, giving us what he has got ('People Ain't No Good' – Ken Smith's favourite, or the double album of *Abattoir Blues/The Lyre of Orpheus*), and supported by his band, the Bad Seeds – the wolf who leans in on backing vocals, the deer that *yoiks, clippity-clop*; while, down at the front of the stage, in the charmed and wowed audience, there's someone, as always, riding on a dolphin.

Porthmear & Tallinn & Riga
50°N & 60°N & 57°N

One recent year, in February early in the spring, I called on my friend Jane Darke who lives in a house on the beach at Porthcothan in north Cornwall. Jane is a writer and film-maker; I wanted her to sing for me. She wasn't sure that she would. First we walked out southwards on the coastal path. Jane lives off *tideluck*. From the beach, she collects driftwood *wreck* for her stove. Washed-up coal from long-sunk collier ships and other coal-powered steamers heats the rest of her house. Shelves and surfaces in every room jostle and crowd with what Jane (accompanied by her late husband Nick) has found on the strand: Lego figurines from a container lost overboard, sea-beans that have floated from South America, defunct cigarette-lighters from sailors' bars in dockyard cities, lobster-pot tags from New England, stray fishing buoys, drowned little auks . . . there seems to be no end to what the sea might bring ashore.

A storm had passed through that morning and brought behind it soft weather. Jane was hoping for coal. D. H. Lawrence stayed in Porthcothan in 1916 and, in the early spring there, sensed 'incoming' and 'uncreated days' blowing ashore. As we walked, I decided we could taste the spring on the mild air as though the salt tang had been taken from it. Violets were out, flickering soft and dabby flames at the foot of a hedge. Skylarks went up and sang and stayed there.

Thanks to Jane, at Porthcothan I also met her friend the naturalist Richard Pearce. He has spent many days of every year for more than half a century counting the limpets on the shore in north Cornwall. After the 1967 *Torrey Canyon* disaster oiled this coastline (the rock-struck sinking ship spilling crude), he began marking quadrats on rocks and counting and mapping the limpets. In the first years after 1967, the oil and the equally toxic detergent used to clear it killed almost everything on the intertidal beach at Porthmear, but more recently, though gouts of oil from various sinkings and spills still materialise on the shore, the limpets on the beach have returned in numbers.

Towards Porthmear, Jane turned for her home: she had not long had a new knee. I walked on to the beach. Thanks to Richard I had had the biological concept of a home-scar explained to me – the mark made on the surface of the rock by the limpet's grip and the corresponding shape cut into the mollusc's shell, the limpet marking the rock and the rock marking the limpet. I addressed myself there, at the deep rocky cove, to the one million home-scars Richard had been keeping his eyes on.

A black redstart flew across the beach and shook its tail at the sea – a tiny violet warmth against a vegetable-green ocean. There were several new-paired herring gulls in the fields at the cliff edge. They looked like couples at the early stages of a party, standing nervously close to one another, moving together as if tied at the ankles, speaking inadvertently at the same time, trying to break their own ice. A wren called a single alarm *tick* from a hedge of flowering gorse – sunshine itself – and that one note, released into the day, seemed to call out the time. A raven overhead gave a *cronk* as I walked on, and I felt something like a pendulum swing between the small bird and the big. The thorns along the hedge were budding with fists of tight green leaves. The air continued soft. *Here comes everything.*

I turned back to Jane's house on the shore. We drank coffee, cheering for the new spring and her new knee, and then, leaning against her cooker in her kitchen, she sang:

> O! Where is St George,
> O! Where is he O,
> He is out in his long boat on the salt sea O.
> Up flies the kite, down falls the lark O.
> Aunt Ursula Birdhood she had an old ewe,
> And she died in her own park O.

It's a song from May Day at Padstow. A greening song for a sea place made (evolved or grown probably over hundreds of years) to be sung at the heart of the spring. It is sung still every May Day. On that morning, still weeks away from where we were, the fishing port streets are decked in greenery and an obby oss dances and swives to the tune that goes around and about the town over and over through the day.

Padstow is only seven kilometres up the coast from Jane's kitchen, but she isn't from there and she didn't think the song was hers to sing.

– It's theirs, she said.

Just a couple of years after the Baltic nations escaped from the rusting cage of the Soviet Union, I spent some midsummer days in Estonia and Latvia. One night in a clearing in a dark forest outside Riga, I listened to village choirs from all across Latvia singing on behalf of the light when it began to dim at the solstitial crux of the year. At midnight on an earlier night the same week, I leapt over a bonfire on the Baltic shore near Tallinn with various friendly Estonian pop singers. In our jumps we were to straddle the middle of the year. After the leaping the remainder of the night was somewhat subdued. There was the slight wash of the slight sea, a wan light continuous in the dusky sky, drizzle spitting into the fire, soft bubbling resin from the burning pine and apple tree logs, and human introspection, brought on by a sauna and vodka, then endorsed by the singers' maudlin tunes. One of their songs was about a nightingale (they are thrush nightingales here) that stops singing at midnight on midsummer's night.

That night we seemed to have lived the ebbing of the year. But the next day, still in the swim of solstitial light, it came back to life in the form of a strange bird. In an old orchard just behind the bonfire beach I saw a wryneck. Among my imaginary friends in my imaginary aviary – though none of them speak to me – wrynecks are neighbours of woodcock and nightjars. They are all complicatedly brown birds, all interested in hiding, and they all behave for part of their lives as something other than a bird. All also have unorthodox relations with movement. They all must fly, all are migrants, but much of their lives is spent sitting still or making themselves inconspicuous.

The wryneck used to be a British breeding bird, but never has been in my lifetime. This absence, or the bird's historical exit, makes it feel old-fashioned, even folkloric. It looks like that too. The wryneck is a cryptic woodpecker. It nests in holes in old trees. It eats ants. The bird looks like bark or like a wood ants' nest. The way an ants' nest seethes is congruent with the way a wryneck moves. They ripple and flex, and are named for their habit of twisting their bodies in snaking writhes to distract or jinx a predator; the effect is hypnotic. They hiss as well.

Once, at Lake Naivasha in Kenya, I saw a wryneck in its wintering wood, and was struck by the bird hiding among the pale grey-brown acacias (where a leopard also concealed itself), just as it had hidden in the previous spring in some pale grey-brown trees, perhaps in an old orchard somewhere in old eastern Europe. How strange it seemed, an antique, spending its life flying up and down the world in order to hide away twice from everything.

Three times out in the open I have seen migrant wrynecks that ended up in spring or autumn Britain missing the cover of trees: my first was caught in a net in an old quarry at Portland Bill and, in the hand of the ringer, it twisted and writhed and raised on its crown a crest of feathers the colour of wood ash; my second was flushed by my bike from a verge as I left my work as a junior nature conservationist in Cambridge, shaking me from my indoor bird concerns (the preservation of threatened species on Madagascar) and restoring me to passing life, and its migrant energy; my third was on a drystone wall on treeless Foula in western Shetland (the same day, I saw the even more deranged stone curlew), part of the widespread scattershot of spring that takes some of its avian traffic every year and throws it to the wind.

In the Estonian orchard the wryneck was piping its spring song from an old apple tree. In an entry for the willow in his tree alphabet chapters of *The White Goddess*, Robert Graves says the wryneck is the moon goddess' 'prime orgiastic bird'. We can get lost (intoxicated, bemused) by those words (as in much, if not all, of *The White Goddess*): Orpheus is in Graves' pages and Persephone, as well as the moon, all entangled with the twisting bird, but the wryneck bewitches beyond or outwith its association. As it is, it is wilder than any human construing.

It was the same for me at Riga and the midsummer song festival. The raw is so often better than the cooked. The journey better than the arrival. Nothing I saw or heard performed from the stage – choir after choir of mostly young women singing mostly of spring – matched the moments when I stood behind the arena in the shadowy pines, where the waiting singers put on crowns of twisted oak leaves, adjusted their dresses, cleared their throats, and lined up to sing as they walked towards the clearing and the light.

To be backstage was to be in a forest. There were wood ants' nests there as well – brown barrows on the bare soil below the evergreens. There were close-growing pines, with bark the colour of dried blood, there were dark firs at the edges of the pines, and there were oaks at the edges of the firs, lighting with their deciduous greens the paths through the trees. It was a flat place. And I think it had been a killing place for the Jews of the city in the Second World War and perhaps for others both before and since.

Singing festivals in the Baltic countries were stages of opposition in the struggle against Soviet power in the 1980s. As folk music in Communist Hungary was cultivated by the state as a kind of peasant pop, so village choirs in Latvia had been permitted and marshalled by governments loyal to Moscow. But the commissars in the client countries misread the national anthems they thought they heard in the grinding dance music for drunken village weddings and the songs of teenage flowering made for long midsummer days of field work. Peasant expressiveness wasn't as politically correct as they wished. The cabbage-heads with their earth-feet wouldn't dance and sing as instructed by any central committee. Today the same tunes might even be endorsing the desperate dive to the right in these countries, still hobbled by their devastating experiences in the twentieth century. I had an inkling of this even in the early 1990s in the arena in the forest at Riga. It was already too clannish. That is another reason why I preferred those spring rites, and those Persephone-replicants, when they were warming up, in the murk of the night forest; then the songs were truly theirs.

Being under the dark pines made a darkroom, and I stood against a trunk as files of young women walked past, *developing*, en route, singing already of the sun goddess and the moon god, her lover. A dozen or so came as one, each in a white or off-white dress, each silky and slubbed so that they silvered, even in the half-dark, as bright as wood warblers will. Each was crowned with green: most wore oak twigs in leaf, plaited and woven, every one different, each made by its wearer to fit; some head-dresses made green horns; some had flowers studded through their hair. You couldn't not see young saplings in leaf or a meadow dotted with wild gems. Deeper in the forest, the waiting women looked like mushrooms in a dark shed. Deeper still, I could hear thrush nightingales singing behind all the human voices.

It had rained that day and it was raining now. The women wore low shoes. The mud of the forest floor spattered almost everyone's legs. As they took the steps to the stage their earth-feet were there for all to see.

It rained more through the short dark, and when I came to a bus-stop the next morning in Riga, there were a dozen sodden crowns in the gutter – green wreaths now. It felt as though autumn had arrived overnight. 'After the leaves have fallen', wrote Wallace Stevens, 'we return / To a plain sense of things. It is as if / We had come to an end of the imagination . . .'

Lynford
52°N

28 June. I went back to the Brecks to retrace my steps where, a year before, I had accidentally flushed a nightjar off its eggs. That day in June I had been alone. Alone, but not lonely. I heard redstarts and then saw them at the fence below the warning flag on the border of the Stanford Training Area army grounds. Seeing them, even flying into a forbidden zone, meant all was well with the world: there are more than one kind of fluttering red flag. A male flew through the wire, towards the live-firing range, and landed in a hawthorn, spreading its tail to slow its flight and show its name. I saw a soldier too, in camouflage kit in the distance, and I remembered a photo-graph I had seen (Helen Macdonald, friend and student of war and bird studies, had sent it to me) of John Buxton, biographer of the redstart, in army uniform. His book on the bird (as I have said, the best bird book I know) is an account of seeing, then studying, breeding redstarts when he was a prisoner of war in a German camp in Bavaria, where the birds were free to come and go through the camp's perimeter fence, and where Buxton and other inmates became their captive audience, the caged men liberated, at least in their questioning minds, by witnessing around them the free passage of the migrant birds.

At Lynford, my day made because of the red-tails, I turned for home as the afternoon sun lengthened every shadow, but then I heard, towards the limits of my hearing (in the shadow of my ear), a woodlark, and it held me on the heath. I couldn't see the singer – they sing mostly in flight and often high up – and I caught only a mist of notes in two brief showers of song. All was tentative, as it is with woodlarks, tentative but lambent. Of the bird songs I know I think their music is my favourite.

My slight hesitation in calling it my best could also describe the quality of what the woodlark says. I first heard them sing at Beaulieu Road in the New Forest in the spring of 1975, and have since listened to perhaps one hundred. Early on, as I have said, I heard the birds' singing as similar to the pre-echo of music, that kind of mouse-speak you could hear sometimes if you dropped your head to a record player and listened to the grooves at the start of a song. The woodlark's cool and whispered tentativeness made for a sound like that, like a cast of a song rather than a song itself. Later, I heard the bird (on a vinyl record) as sung by a Hungarian opera singer, and that made me cry; now their song sounds to me like a kind of bird blues: a country blues such as Skip James sang, like 'I'm So Glad', a sad song dressed up with happy intentions that no one really believes. And the woodlark's music sounds sad too, sad yet sustaining, a faltering but realistic transcription of a love life, sweet phrases with lonely gaps between them.*

Woodlark springs are as long as I would like mine to be. They are early migrants to parts of their European range, and they can start singing up the new season even before the calendar end of a year. They can sound as frosted as a winter heath or as dry as a felled acre of woodland in July. They sing late in the day and early in the morning. They sing at night. They are pan-European birds occurring from Morocco to Finland: birds in the north and east migrate to the south

---

* In describing how Josefine, the mouse-singer, sounded, Franz Kafka accidentally gave a marvellous description of a woodlark's song: 'Something of our poor, brief childhood is in it, something of lost happiness which can never be found again, but also something of active present-day life, of its small gaieties, unaccountable and yet real and unquenchable.' (Michael Hofmann's translation.)

and west in the winter; all remain in Europe. My friend Adam Nicolson, for whom I am an occasional ornithological adviser, sent me a message one October from where he was walking in Crete, asking whether there was such a thing as a 'nightingale-lark'. He was right. Woodlark song starts cautiously, with separate long notes, before accelerating and tumbling over itself. It says life, which we are rightly cautious about, can yet be good, but it also says how little of life there is for everything. Skylarks are habitually – magnificently – profligate in their singing, woodlarks never. Every woodlark I have heard has told me how few woodlarks I have left to hear.

The singing bird at Lynford was invisible somewhere in the sky and I imagined it turning, up there, as I have seen them do, circling high, and making its unemphatic broadcast. It was hard to hear, but then much of my hearing these last few years has been pushed back to the edge of my senses: thinned in what it can detect, and compromised by the raised noise of my inner ear's static output – its panning for sound – trying to get back an echo off the quietening world. I often hear the frequency but not the notes, the noise but not the data. But for a moment or two I had had that woodlark come inside and talk to me.

I walked towards the singing bird through green croziers of bracken rising from a cleared plot of cut forestry. I strained my eyes looking up above my head, and held my hand cupped behind my one so-so ear hoping to trap more song. An onlooker might have assumed I was having a religious moment. I was, in a way. Then, from beneath my faraway feet, up sprang some short flailing sticks of grey and brown bark that, three metres or so from my arrested stride, became a bird. I had trodden on a nightjar. Being triggered like that into the air, it took flight in bits and pieces, and only assembled itself after a few sprawling and chaotic flaps. Then it clattered into shape and became a bandaged balsa-wood model: a great moth's head with the wings of a dark dragonfly. Hugger-mugger it hurried away at the height of the bracken tops.

I had chased it from the earth, and it wanted to get back there as soon as it could. The day was still bright and the nightjar hated it. Its name said so. Its flight said so. I watched it slice into the interior of a shrubby line of trees to find some shade or dark. But it really wanted to return to where I was, for in falling on the bird's tail or back my foot had been prevented from crushing its eggs. And there they were now, below me, a clutch of three, still frighteningly close to my boot.

The nightjar makes no nest. The incubating, then brooding, bird pushes with its belly a slight depression into the ground – here it was loamy and littered with bark chippings – and that is that. The eggs are miraculous. Such is the genius of their crypsis that my camera couldn't bring the three at my feet into focus. They were extraordinarily like the complexion of the ground they lay on, all grey streaked with brown, and randomly dropped in an arbitrary scrape, surprisingly small and somewhat elongate, rather reptilian, and looking like a triptych of long-exposed pictures of a not-quite-full moon taken through rain or mist, everything being a little fuzzy, with whites sullied, and seas showing.

Pained by my accidental blunder, I didn't stay long, and soon moved off hoping that the adult found a quick way back to its charges. The eggs were warm but not very. Before I left, I knelt down briefly and put the back of my hand against them, as I have felt my children's temples, and as my parents felt mine. They were still alive, I'm sure, when I walked away.

I need a nightjar every year. My desk in Bristol is under the flamboyant wings of a pennant-winged nightjar that was cut from a roadkilled bird in South Africa by Claire's late friend Kirsten Louw. I never met Kirsten. Claire showed me living examples of the birds in Zambia on our first African date. I have pinned Kirsten's to the wall, so that the two fifty-centimetre-long pale brown streamers of an extended primary feather put inverted commas around everything I write.

Our nightjars – 'our' – come to Britain as end-of-spring birds, and are one of the last migrants to arrive. By the time they find their heath or plantation of evergreen saplings, the juice and juvescence of the year has mostly dried. That suits their browns. All the night-working birds have related but different arrangements: woodcocks are made of wet mud and worms, tawny owls stick to the trees and are sleepy bags of leaves, a nightjar is a mixture of dry heath and dusty moth incarnated as a bird.

They come from the south. They need moth-soft warmth every night of their lives. And they go back south. In Africa every conceivable substrate has a nightjar of its own to match; they dress in all the dirts. European nightjars spend their winters alongside local species from Sudan to the Cape. They all fly like something somewhere between a magic carpet and a lasso. Most of them sing like dust humming. Day is anathema to them all.

It is that churring I need to hear to make me know that the season in England has done most of what it must. (The soporific purrs of turtle doves – the mildest bird song I know, warmer still than a nightjar's cooking – would say the same and have done so for me, but they are now hardly heard in Britain.) I am consoled with a churr. It has all the *burry* selvedge of spring in it: the purr and buzz, its good tremble, its sway.

When I went back to the bracken at Lynford, one year after the nightjar eggs, with my birdwatching friend and Claire's ornithological colleague, Gabriel Jamie, the first nightjar began churring at ten to ten at night. It was dusk for sure, but with enough light left of the day for us to be able to see the birds that then appeared in the first half-hour of our watch. I have never been to a séance, but perhaps this was one. One hundred metres from where I had flushed the breeding bird the previous year was a hot spot for this year's nightjars. Four birds came to and from this place, in the bracken, as if wound to it on invisible wires. Some arrived, others got up from the ground. We saw males, with their white wing and tail spots, and females, without. All of them flew with a strange stiff-winged deliberateness. Sometimes a clap came from one – a softish woody slap as it raised its wings high above its back. Sometimes a bird dropped down in a crumple, as if collapsing the toy glider of itself, to fall out of sight, hidden by the bracken. Two others kept up their churring further off. Those drawn to their spot made *kewit* calls too, more intimate and domestic sounds, and then two nearby males clapped their wings and made me think of flamenco. The sombre ground and the shadowy sky seemed to be put into a dance or a

271

conversation by the birds, they had so much of both in their voices and their looks and their actions. Being themselves, they made the darkness visible and its silence audible: the earth's purr and the nap of the sky.

As the night thickened, all distances became those between the singing nightjars and the soft whewing judder of their flights. They got harder to see, and my impoverished night sight chopped at the birds with a kind of visual stutter, making their jerky flight look jerkier still. For a time, nothing else told except for the strobe of dark birds, until the sky above grew comparably marvellous. It got brighter as the night went on and raised a light-studded blue-black roof over the sooty shadows and earthy churring. Distances then became astronomical. First Mars arrived, all big and cooking with a reddish simmer, hot to see; then, in the west, Venus flickered low, but electric. More stars surged between the planets, as if coming to life. There was a show of sorts going on, a lovely mummery in the night. It felt like the sky was watching the sleepy Earth. And then a stunning full moon of impossible size and total theatre broke out from behind the pines at the edge of the heath. Doing so it appeared to explain everything beneath it as if it had conjured the lot. More astonishing, truly charming, the flying nightjars appeared to feel the effervescing moon as much as we did. Two flew from the dark edges of the sky into the widening silvery tide of moonlight, sailing it with taut wings and stiff tails, with white discs juggled between the moon and the birds, and then, for a moment, they passed right over the moon's face, looking like first one thought and then another crossing its brow, and showing the mind of the night.

Látrabjarg
65°N

Nightless June with Claire on the seabird cliffs, north-west Iceland in astounding, terrific daylight.

An arctic fox, sandy and sinuous, hunting for guillemot eggs, worked the auk ledges like a feather duster hurried along a mantelpiece.

Short-legged, fluffy, running fast on the narrowest of ways high above the sea, it beat me by ten metres to be the westernmost land mammal in Europe.

Nothing else I saw in twenty hours of walking the peninsula – the seabird-storeyed cliffs on its south side, and the sloping lower hills and boulder beaches on its north – was as *in-between* as the fox running along that cliff ledge. It was an anomaly of the middle ground, a rarity of near-human scale, in a world otherwise elementally at large, a world where the Arctic might rhyme with the Sahara, where what wasn't very close to hand looked very far away, what wasn't sun-cooked felt ice-cold, what wasn't rock was sea, what wasn't black was white, and where there was either life in teeming abundance or apparently nothing at all.

In such a world we struggle to measure up. The long day – a day that lasts weeks from May into June and on towards July – rules every-thing. There is no night to speak of. 'We are', as Tomas Tranströmer said in his poem 'Below Freezing' (translated by Robert Bly), from the other end of the hyperborean year, 'at a party that doesn't love us'. Like well-behaved children (as if with partying parents downstairs), Claire and I put ourselves to bed in our hostel bunks in a pine-panelled room with a bible on the table between us. But I got grumpy. Since the sun wouldn't set how could I? We were inside, but daylight came, relentless with an oiled glare, through a thin curtain at a small window. It made me wince. Outside, nothing else of the sleeping kind seemed to have its eyes shut. Everything indoors seemed improperly – unnecessarily – roofed. This was cabin fever. We gave up, got dressed and went out, and within minutes were repaired, or, rather restored, to the melee, to what and where we had been when we had been out before – hung over with a mixture of Arctic sunstroke and benign jet-lag: *day dreamers*.

As we were failing to fall asleep in our bunks, I remembered a similar feeling in my childhood when slow-departing spring dusks, all silvery and calm, used to steal through the gauzy curtains of the bedroom I shared with my sister. It told me then, aged seven, that the day was not yet done. The same twilight, one evening in May, after Jenny and I had been put to bed, gave our parents the time to erect a swing in our back garden. Their plan was that it would appear magically the following morning, Jenny's birthday – as if it had sprouted from the lawn – except that the same light that let them work kept me from sleeping, and I heard their labours and got up to sneak a view of them through the curtains. It's the only time I have seen my mother with a spade in her hands.

Eventually, even under Icelandic midsummer light, you have to sleep, but by then – another twelve hours away – the night and the idea of the dark had slipped far from my mind and a new clock began to tick within. All the time-keeping apparatus I had previously accepted seemed questionable. My body counted photons not hours, and I was adding rather than spending, while the sun, the supplier, urged all under it to keep up.

At Látrabjarg, a vast day hung over everything. We walked ten kilometres following the cliff edge – a dell then a ness, a ness then a dell – up and down and out and in, but always west and always in the most *general* of light. The sea that began 330 metres below us, to our left, stretched far away, a great slow slop. Wind came, gentle but cold: there was ice off there, somewhere. Once or twice a gust of auk jabber and tenement guff crept up over the lip of the cliff: a noisy reek that smelled and sounded old. Otherwise, there was empty air everywhere; it streamed ashore, apparently making landfall for the first time since its creation.

Near and far there was black and white, tiny and epic. A male long-tailed duck swam alone across a cliff-top tarn – black over white. Close to us, careless of us, male snow buntings – black over white – made song flights from rock outcrops just back from the cliff edge: the flutter of a lacy handkerchief and a little metalworked song of beaten tin. Their song was all I could hear. The sound of sea at the base of the cliffs stayed there. When I looked down through my binoculars I knew the noise though I couldn't hear it. In the winter, when the wind hammers furiously out of the south-west, the sea can be heard hitting these cliffs from twenty-two kilometres away on the far, north side of the peninsula. Inland-facing windows get frosted with salt spray that has crossed from Látrabjarg. Our landlord told us that. They are his windows – the same windows that let the summer light in on us.

On the next western peninsula to the south of us, more than eighty kilometres across the great bight of a vast sea bay (when a distant sea-eagle flew towards us, it appeared as slight as a floater drifting in my eye), was the colossal glacier-capped volcano, Snæfellsjökull. An ice pyramid crouching over a sometime oven, it had bred all the clouds in the sky so far today. These lingered where they had been gathered, mantling the summit like the opened wings of a snowy owl.

The scene was too big for the world itself, as if beyond its scale, and the view exhausting. I lay down – doggo, doggone – on the cliff top. Far below – nauseously far – the cliffs there were 440 metres high – ten thousand auks and fulmars and kittiwakes and a few glaucous gulls dotted the sea like mica sparkles on a dark rock. Closer in – no less disconcerting – came a carousel of a thousand guillemots, flying in front of their ledges, each only centimetres from another but never touching. I tried to see a way into the flock, where it might have begun, the point where one bird might join the swirl, but the wheel, a continuous *side*, had no entrance or exit. The helix of turning birds brought on a kind of meditative fever: here was something like perpetual motion in an endless day. The sun caught the blow or rain of the auks' chalky shit – their mutes – as they wheeled, and enamelled it brilliant white as it slipped to the sea.

I looked beyond. Greenland was 330 kilometres further west. Between Iceland, which was green grass where I was on the cliff top, and Greenland, which I knew in my mind as ice, whaleback islands came and went. The day to the west was so bright and so prevalent that the water turned silvery black all the way to the skyline. Under such sunlight the sea seemed stunned. It spread so wide it appeared beyond time, it was so lit it appeared everlasting. But then, as I scanned, I saw its surface being torn – tiny slits in its massive crêpe carpet – by whales breaking through from below: the fin-peaks of killer whales and the long barrows of humpbacks.

Their breathing made them do this. In order to stay under water they need to break its surface. They were kilometres apart and appeared only every five minutes or so and without a discernible rhythm, but the movement of the animals and the sequence they made across this great plain put a clock of sorts into the sea. Even from three or four kilometres away, through my binoculars, I could detect the world before me being given a pulse, with the whales marking time. Their going over, the way they bowled forwards into the sea, turned them into a sort of counter, with the animals' fins and backs appearing as movements on a great watch, and the roundness of their swim asserting – part under the surface and part above – that planetary time was being kept. As one humpback came and went, I said, out loud, *an atomic clock*.

A fluster on the cliffs woke me up. A raven was stealing a fulmar's cream egg from an unguarded nest and flew inland with it wedged in its beak. Ten minutes later a glaucous gull stole another from another nest and did the same. There followed more blacks and whites. The ledges near the cliff top had Brünnich's guillemots breeding on them. Black above, white below, with a silver-white line drawn, like a gentle ripple on the sea, from their beaks through their black cheeks. Those with cliff duties bent to the eggs cradled at their feet and nuzzled them. Others were diving for food offshore and twisting back with great torque up to the surface. They re-appeared as if launched from below. Beads of baffled seawater rolled from their backs. A kilometre further out, killer whales came, as before, through the sea's skin. Their white flanks and black backs struck a rhyme for the guillemots, the birds' pied curves chiming with the whales'. How similar they seemed – how conjured from that place – and yet how difficult it is to measure the adjoining worlds of these sea creatures, to construe the spaces in a guillemot's life and a whale's: paltry centimetres of ledge together with unending ocean, seconds with the sun on your back and years beneath the waves.

High shifts of milky thin cloud came in from the direction of Greenland and plumed to mare's tails. They showed the shape of the wind's drift and marked time over my head. Not the whales' time but not so different from it either, and somehow, in all that stretched light, of the same ilk. I could see the weathered past above me – the way things were – written into the sky even as I studied the present moment. There was still a line of cloud where it had first condensed and formed, but some of its high ice had been shifted in the wind, as if combed or brushed. Thus, older clouds and newer clouds were there at once: one had made the other and the journey in between – the working of the cloud – was visible as well. In this way I could see the passing of an hour or more of this long day described by that which was passing; in this way at once I could see *now* and *then*.

I shivered and stood up to walk some more. The air was chilling. I left the cliffs and went, for half the night that wasn't, to the north side of the peninsula along its softer shore. Still the day would not go. The sun hung around. After eleven, in the notional evening, the day star sank no lower in the sky and it moved across rather than below the horizon. And in my dazzled head it printed everything bright. Three kilometres away, I could see a swirl of fulmars above an iron-red breeding cliff, a drifting chimney of lit dust. Each bird – a hundred or more – made a white dash, a filament in the light. As they wheeled and circled, their shit fell from them and caught the light, just as it had from the guillemots earlier, falling like sleet sparkles.

At midnight, the valleys that ran north to the sea channel at Patreksfjörður were bright with buttercups and electrified with the non-stop *muzz* of drumming snipe. They laboured up the sky in a rocking-horse canter with a whickering call, and then reached a toppling over/tipping point where their exertion gave way to abandon, and they launched themselves back towards the ground into comet-streak head-long plunges. There is Icarus in these falls and land-rhymes for the seabirds' mutes and the whales' blows. Falling through the sky – as if dashed down from above or burned by the sun – the snipe spread their tail feathers to play the air, fantastically, like a bull-roarer or a wind-harp, and produced an itchy, stammering sound, as if some fur in the air was being stroked. I walked under a dozen drummers. It was like being able to hear mosquitoes from a kilometre away.

ticka ticka ticka

ticka ticka   *ticka ticka*

wuwuwuwuwuwuw

ticka ticka ticka ticka

wuwuwuwuwuwuwuwu

At one o'clock in the morning I came alongside an estuary and woke a sleeping red-necked phalarope – a bird I'd last seen at the other end of the Atlantic in Cape Town sewage works. It was the only sleeping thing I saw in days in Iceland. Phalaropes are waders that voluntarily swim. It was floating on the soft rise of the tide like a drifting paper boat. You don't often see birds waking up like this. Nor feel yourself waking them. I had got somehow into its head. It looked like a little toy to me, but as it came around and woke, it returned itself to its world and began to spin away, swimming its own clock, circling on the still water, picking at insects that had settled on the calm.

At two o'clock I flushed an eider from her nest. As she left, she shat (more shit and good shit) and spattered her down. I felt around for her clutch of four spinach-green eggs, and put my hand into the nest's springy grey muff. It was hot in there. It seemed a kind of world felt – a soft fence against everything.

There was more softness, too. In this hard place the long spring is kept alive in this softness. Up the fell from the eider nest were small pale-green orchids no more than three centimetres high (northern green, I think, *Platanthera hyperborea*). There was also a wheatear, a bird that had made it out of Africa for a few weeks, feeding three new-fledged chicks. They chirruped the same grown-up calls – like the sound of knapping stones – as their father, although they were still dressed in down that was like dandelion clocks. A whimbrel – another African; I've seen them at the Cape Town shore – sang like a nervous curlew. And I walked between stereophonic golden plovers – one rising from the hillside to call to my left, another rising and calling to my right – *pews* in both my good ear and my bad. From the corrugated roof of an old whaling station on the fjord, a snipe was singing its up-sky song – *ticka ticka ticka ticka*. As its beak opened so its tail rose, the opening of the one raised the other; the tail was instrumental to its song as much as the beak that gave it sounds. It couldn't be helped; the urge was felt and expressed there. The snipe stopped singing and its tail settled. Then it started again, and its tail followed.

At three – but the time meant nothing – I went at Örlygshöfn around the outside of a museum that had gathered one local man's collection of old trucks and boats and aeroplanes. It looked no different from a junkyard. There were rusting Russian planes and rusting American ones. There was a Bedford fire engine from Britain that had been customised for Icelandic use by sticking labels with Icelandic words over the switches and buttons for the ladders and hoses. I peered at the dashboard – the long extinguished spread of bulbs in little glass cases – and it looked like a midsummer memory of the stars in a night sky.

On one side of the museum there were a series of monuments to lost ships mounted on rough boulders, steel plates etched with engravings of trawlers and the names of drowned sailors. All the evidence pointed to the short life of machines and the even shorter life of their men.

In December 1947, the *Dhoon* trawler, out of Fleetwood, hit the rocks at the foot of the high cliffs at Látrabjarg. Men from the farms, who were also whalers and fishermen and eider-keepers, went to help the *Dhoon*. On 13 December farmers from Hvallátur (named for its whales) and neighbouring farms (including the father and grandfather of our landlord) descended the cliffs, 260 metres down to an outcrop called Flaugarnef, sixty metres above the sea. A party of four was lowered to the beach at low water and they walked 500 metres to the wreck of the *Dhoon*. The skipper, the mate and a deckhand had already been lost to the sea – Fred Kirby, Harry Ellison and Fred Wolfenden. A line was shot and twelve survivors were helped ashore. Not all could be hoisted to safety up the cliffs before the tide returned, and an overnight shelter was set up on an icy ledge for seven crewmen. They were brought up the following day and taken inland.

On 4 February 1968, a message was received from the radio of the Hull trawler *Ross Cleveland*, from Ísafjarðardjúp, 100 kilometres further north around the coast from Látrabjarg: 'We are going over.' There was a pause of a few seconds. 'We are going over. I am going. Give my love and the crew's love to our wives and families.'

Next to the engraved texts that described these wreckings there was a redundant steam trawler called *Mummi*. Next door but one, a pair of redwings carried food to their nest in the opened head of the ruined cockpit of a stranded United States Navy plane. The mummy bird had craneflies in her beak; the daddy sang from his perch above the sockets of the eyes of the plane: *dee dee dee-day* and then a swirl of chewed notes. It was three-thirty in the morning. The redwing flew to a satellite dish on the wall of the museum and broadcast again.

Pandrup
57°N

I stood with my foot on the bottom rung of a ladder as Anders climbed twenty steps, four metres up, to the roof of the barn. There he leaned out, with his ruler in his hand, towards a wooden cross beam, to measure a nest made of mud.

I had come, towards the end of a spring, around midsummer, to rural northern Jutland in Denmark to watch swallows and a swallow-watcher-in-chief.

There were no cows on the first farm where we stopped, but there were birds still. The barn was empty of farm life, but a sweet smell of shit and of silage lingered in the air – the leftovers of grass. We manoeuvred the ladder. The barn's corrugated metal walls and concrete floor threw harsh echoes. The breeding swallows – barn swallows – we had come to see – and disturbed – were making *chiddit chiddit chiddit* calls as they flew off their nests. Other birds answered as they came into the barn through the open entrance and turned tight corners around the shadowed interior. Their sounds and the stony reverb could have put us in a cave.

I love Anders Pape Møller, though he would wince to hear me say it. He laughed, quietly, when I asked him if he was the king of the swallows. Local people do call him the bird king, he said. Though the remark was meaningless to him, I am sure he is. He is also bright, smart, mordant, kind, funny, and Danish. He grew up not far from where he leaned his ladder and has been studying swallows in northern Jutland every spring since 1970. He has surely forgotten more about them than all of the rest of us will ever know.

280

Beyond his professional achievements and generous nature I have personal reasons to warm to him. He encouraged Claire when she was a young student of evolutionary biology to spend time in his laboratory in Paris. And, years later, without apparently a moment's pause, he agreed to let me accompany him to watch his work on the radiation-raddled swallows of Chernobyl. Every year still, he travels to Ukraine to monitor the birds' body-burdens, the weight of their curse. Since 2011, he has added Fukushima to his annual migrations, where he studies the fall-out of another power station disaster – a nuclear harvest and an irradiated environment. There are sick swallows in Japan too. But Anders is interested in everything the birds can tell us of themselves and, more widely still, how life goes in general. His attention to swallow-*going*, in both senses of the word (how life progresses and how it departs; how it starts and how it ends), is what took me to Jutland.

Very few barn swallows breeding in Europe build nests in places that are not man-made. The species has been our intimate for thousands of years. Swallows come to Europe to live next door or even within our homes. They occur where we do. It follows that they also die where we die. Skeletons of swallows 8,000 years old have been found in flint mines dug in chalk. On a day off from our tour of the barns, Anders and I found them breeding in a Second World War concrete bunker looking across the sea towards Norway. The swallows posted themselves through the gun slits with an aerodynamic suppleness that made us smile. The species' literal proximity to us through our shared history has made us feel close. Their choosing to nest around us we regard as a blessing. Their stopping down amongst us in the midst of their coming and going speaks of hospitality. They have liked us; we have liked them. Their expert mud-worked homes might even have inspired our species to emulate them and attempt to build the same.

They also like the flies that have long been associated with the way we have lived on the land. And flies, as much as swallows, were our concern in Jutland.

In his shirt pocket Anders had a little notebook. At the foot of the ladder, before we began speaking again, he wrote down the dimensions of the nest he had measured. From another nest we could hear nestlings begging. An attending adult gave an alarm call to shush them.

– That's because we're here, but the call isn't very loud because it has a beakful of insects. You can hear their food.

Anders had ringed forty-four swallows in this barn this spring. But there weren't many insects around. We put a mist net across a window opening in the side of the barn and retreated further into the shadows. The adult birds were still building the nest he had measured – there were no eggs yet – although the next nest along the beam already had chicks in it. Nowadays the birds like to be as high as possible. Nests that are low down are more vulnerable to predators. In 1970, when Anders started work in this barn, he could reach all the nests from the ground except one. Nearly fifty years later, he couldn't reach any without a ladder, and some were twelve metres up.

Cats on farms reduce the swallows' reproductive success. The birds' chicks aren't necessarily eaten, but where there are cats swallows breed later, have fewer chicks, and fewer second clutches. In this way, the cats suppress reproductive activity, making the swallows take fewer risks.

– Some farms have fifteen cats.

– And?

– Yes, I've been counting them, as well as the swallows, since 1970. The swallows here are not very happy, you can hear that.

Anders knew what they were saying. I've listened to them for almost as many years as he has (he's a little older than me), but I hear just *swallow*. And I make something for me of their music: that familiar chittering that I want to call lovely, its soft stoniness, which sounds looped and joined, and warm. Anders will have none of this – although, in his own way, he too has designs on the birds. That loveliness is an alarm call.

– I didn't start on swallows although they were the birds of my childhood landscape. I began ringing birds in winter, it was sparrows and yellowhammers. But so many swallows came in the spring. They were easy to find and easy to catch. And at least some of them came back the next year. The farmers opened their barns in the spring and the birds came in.

Some of the swallows in the barn flew in through the wide-open space of its doorway. They arrived at full pelt. Others entered through a narrow crack along the apex of its roof. To do so they had to momentarily fold their wings and angle their flying bodies, as cavers must contort themselves to get around obstructing rocks on their journeys underground. Watching these various arrivals took me back, as every swallow flight into and out of a building flickers in my mind, to my first bird memory, now more than fifty years old, of watching a swallow fly from the brightness of outside to the blackness of indoors, from the sky above my first childhood house through an open door into the dark of a shed: a bird making the same journey as we do, all the time, from without to within, from away to home, from flight to nest, and back again.

Attractiveness in swallows (to each other – Anders' concern) is determined by a number of characteristics. The most important is the length of the tail feathers. Males with longer feathers are more attractive to females. Anders and colleagues have shown this by looking at variations in tail length in the natural populations of the bird and by experimentally manipulating it, cutting some birds' feathers and gluing extensions on others. Birds with symmetrical tail feathers also do better at attracting mates than those with feathers of variable length.

Throat colour also has an effect: males with darker chestnut throat patches are more attractive to females. And the intensity of the ultra-violet reflectance of the birds' upper parts – the colour we see as slaty-blue – also relates to mating success.

Song is important too for attracting partners and even more important in competition with other males. One particular note at the end of the male's song is a 'tremolo note'. It sounds to me like an electrical shorting or fizz. It is longer in males with high levels of testosterone. 'You can actually hear', Anders said, 'the testosterone in the structure of the song.' The bird sings its physiological status. Above us, a young male swallow obliged – we could hear the long tail to its tune.

– He hasn't a female yet but is trying to get one. If we can hear the testosterone then surely all the swallows can too.

Anders has ringed more than 6,000 swallows in his life, mostly in these barns in Jutland. While we waited, having set his nets, he pointed out a bird that flew into the barn.

– That one, I know, always sits on that beam, it always comes through the window at the same height, it always turns at the same spot under the roof, and I've only ever caught it once.

– If you weren't here, I'd be hiding more, waiting for the net to catch some birds. It is better when I am out of the way. They most definitely recognise me and see me as an interfering type. I used to ride a bike from barn to barn and already, when I was still about 500 metres from a colony, the first alarm calls would start up. They knew this bicycle was somehow associated with further activities. Now I hide in my car.

– They are clever. One man I know, near here, didn't like them because they were putting their shit on his car, so he installed a light-trigger mechanism to close his garage. The swallows learned to cut the beam and open the door. Another man also didn't want their shit in his garage so he closed the door. Within a few days the birds had scratched a small tunnel under it.

The net in the barn caught three birds. They were regulars. Anders unpicked them from the mesh. They looked small in his hand, a bit messy, and oddly dopey, furled like a moth in its daytime sleep.

Anders went back up his ladder.

– Please don't stand this time too close to it. I've fallen here a few times. When it happens I try to fall not at the same time as the ladder, but sometimes that isn't possible.

We could hear a bird calling – *dee dee dee dee* – from high up in the barn.

– A young male trying to attract a female's attention, but he won't be successful.

I don't know how he knew that, but I believed him right away. Was it because it said my name? Being in the company of scientists – it's the same being married to one – makes me even more of an eejit than I am at other times.

I asked what the farm was called. Anders wasn't sure.

– I know it as Edward, which is the first name of its previous owner, the father-in-law of the current farmer.

They aren't the same sort of farmers here any more. Edward had sixty dairy cows until 2016, but all had been sold. Farmers could make a profit only when assisted by agricultural subsidies. Milking the cows didn't pay. When the subsidies went the herd had to follow.

Fewer cows meant fewer insects, and swallow numbers have fallen. The insects, especially flies, which swallows like to eat, often spend their youths in cattle dung, and there are many more flies where there are cows. A pair of swallows and their young consume approximately one million flies a year (so Angela Turner, biographer of the species, queen of the swallows, calculated once, Anders said, on the back of a napkin). In the barn we weren't bothered by a single fly. Though the birds are still breeding where the animals once lived, they must travel further to feed. Formerly, the swallows in Jutland (especially in a cold and wet summer) could feed indoors on flies busy around cattle; now, no more.

People like to believe the swallows – 'their birds' – come back, and the thought of the returning migrant underwrites much of our emotional response to those birds that come and go. But only 30 to 40 per cent of all adult swallows return the next year, and after just a few years, as Anders said, 'There's none of those old guys left.' Of course, there are younger ones instead, and there will be yet younger ones too (young birds that survive their first winter away return but often disperse; 11 per cent of chicks come back to the neighbourhood where they were raised, males more often than females). We hope for more swallows and more springs. But knowing can be cruel, and I could see the facts mark Anders' face as the truth passed across it, even though he has long known it and must have explained it – a necessary disillusionment on behalf of the verifiable non-human world – many times before.

In Chernobyl, a permanent crisis gets renewed every year: swallows arrive into its empty (maybe anti-) spring and sicken, they attempt to breed, very few return, the toxic sink draws more birds in, and they too sicken. Mutations harrow the population. There are many breakages of DNA sequences. Abnormalities in swallows are more common in the Exclusion Zone than anywhere else Anders knows. The birds' tails can be short and asymmetric; their beaks, feet, toes and plumage wrong.

On the farms of Jutland it is not so bad, but neither is it wholly good. When swallows breed they do well (more than 95 per cent hatch and fledge out of a first clutch of, commonly, five eggs), but overall numbers are down. At the end of our first day in the barns, Anders drove us through his study area. First he checked a nest he had spotted in a bus shelter on the grassy verge of a village street: a sweet image of a benign occupation and inter-specific place-making – the co-existence of passaging people and passaging birds; except, although the nest was still fresh, there were no eggs in it. Then we picked up speed and the story darkened. Swallows all across western Europe face compounded woes: farming has industrialised the old green world and climate dysfunction is wrecking the seasons. The birds' flies have either disappeared, because livestock has gone indoors or vanished, or they are now appearing at different (usually earlier) times, because they have changed their diary and clock to keep up with warming weather. Insect phenology is shifting. Spring in temperate latitudes is getting earlier. The birds must shift too. Swallows, among many migrant species, now have to be back relatively early from their winter quarters. If not, they are late and risk being out of time, like vagrants in their own places, estranged in their own lives, doomed to miss the bus. And soon, thereafter, presumably, dead.

It was a grey day, heavy with clouds. Rain had lurked in the air for hours. As we travelled the straight roads across the boggy fields, the black peat beneath everything threw, from below, an extra darkening of the place. The spring felt done.

Anders has been travelling back and forth here for fifty years, for roughly forty-two swallow generations, and in that time he's tried to know every bird that has lived here. I told him how much I liked (and at times have lived by) Gilbert White's annual swallow diary from eighteenth-century Selborne.

Anders had read the entries, of course. As he drove he looked ahead, but called out each swallow place that we passed.

– This year there were seventeen pairs in this barn, with one more in a neighbouring building. There were fifteen pairs last year, thirteen the year before; I've checked here since 1971 and this year's count is the highest yet – they'll have space problems soon. They still have cows there . . .

– This next farm, here, only ever had one nest, in 1972 . . .

– Here there are two farms, no swallows . . .

– In this house the man opens his garage and a pair comes . . .

– That is the old shop and that the old school; both are shut and no swallows . . .

– There's a nest half outdoors around the back of this house . . .

– There are fewer and fewer farms and even fewer cows.

– Here's another small farm; there were eight pairs, now none. Pasture has been replaced by potatoes or rye or wheat. No flies.

– It is still thought bad luck to knock down a swallows' nest, though people do it. This small farm has had up to eight pairs. The tradition was that in spring you had to open your windows and doors to the birds. Preventing them from entering could have severe consequences: cows will stop producing milk or the farm might burn down. Things might end badly if you don't show some care for the birds. They are strong medicine and can change people's attitudes. If you are looking for a wife in Jutland, and have a woman in mind who isn't showing any interest, you must catch a swallow, dry and powder its heart, and tip it into the beer of the object of your attention.

We were quiet for a minute.

– Luckily, I didn't need that myself.

We slowed to watch family parties of cranes walking the fields. When Anders' father knew this area, around Store Vildmose, the peat was seven metres higher than it is today, but there were no cranes then. Two horses stood in fields on opposite sides of the road; they looked at one another in the way they do – that stare that seems old wherever it happens. Their tails twitched in time, and the skimming stones of half a dozen house martins crossed from one horse to the other, as they dipped close to take the insects drawn to the animals' warm blood.

– In this barn there were twenty-two pairs, then a barn owl moved in and ate them all. It moved on but the swallows didn't return . . .

– This is a pig farm with new buildings, everything is indoors and sterile, you have to put on a space suit – it's like Chernobyl – no swallows, of course . . .

– There are five pairs here in a tractor barn, but there were twenty-five before. As the farms change, and the cows go, the swallow population goes down. That is the general pattern . . .

– This farmer has stopped farming; there were sixty-nine pairs here once; he's a truck-driver now, and this year, here, nothing . . .

– Next farm, here, in the early 1980s there were up to sixty pairs; today eight.

– Now I am looking for swallows at Christmas.

This is possible in Europe today. Some swallows have started wintering in Portugal and Spain. They aren't bothering to go any further south. Anders would like to know where they come from and whether they do better or worse than traditional migrants. That would be one way of quantifying the cost of long-distance migration. That's how he sees it. I warm to the thought of winter swallows. That is stupid, I know, and I don't want the time to be so out of joint – migration is meaningful because of its going and its coming, its clearing of the breakfast things and its setting of the table for dinner, its exhalation and its inhalation; but the keeping-back urge is still strong, the dream of running ahead of time and outwitting death, the fantasy of spring everlasting . . .

Science regards migration as a derived character or an adapted behaviour in the evolutionary lives of species. Swallows have much to say about this. As well as the annual European–African barn swallow exchange, there are migratory and related subspecies in Asia and in the Americas, flying from the northern hemisphere to the south, and then back again. Meanwhile, in the Nile Valley there is a unique resident population of barn swallows that doesn't migrate. Might they be the ancestral birds from which all others have come? Genetic molecular analysis could answer that, Anders says. He's also waiting to hear from Argentina and Uruguay where a barn swallow population has emerged, presumably genetically isolated, that breeds in those southern countries and then flies north in its winter season in a counter-direction to the species' movements throughout the rest of the world.

– Many times these birds have changed my mind.

We stopped on our way home from the swallows to watch three cranes in a field. They looked like grey bundles of wet washing. Anders talked of the 'human dream' in the idea that cranes pair for life. 'There's very little data,' he said.

I had arrived in Jutland on 23 June. It was Sankt Hans Aften for the Danes, St John's Eve, the birthday of John the Baptist; people would be singing in Riga and others would be jumping bonfires along the Baltic shore. This day was the time, Anders thought, when 'witches are sent to a mountain in Iceland'. Towards dusk we were standing in a clearing in a public park in Pandrup, a suburban dell rimmed with young oaks and cherry trees, with bungalows not far beyond. It was raining. A bonfire of fir branches and a dismembered wooden pallet was proving tricky to ignite. Children ran around with their faces raised to the rain; they were laughing, as they got soaked. A ring of their parents and other townspeople had been pushed back by the drizzling wet to shelter under a corral of temporary gazebos and picnic tents that circled the fire.

We were trying to sing. A page of lyrics had been handed around, though most of the singers knew at least some of the words. It was a midsummer verse, written in 1885, with a text by Holger Drachmann and 'melodi' by P. E. Lange-Müller. Where I stood, the tune was sluggish and the singing somewhat desultory. Anders joined in, just a half-beat behind, and was, I thought, intentionally coming to the song but wanting to keep a certain sceptical distance from its moment. But as I looked around and listened, it was clear that everyone else was also behind the tune.

Public singing anywhere can sound like coerced embarrassment, but here the entire event, even mid-performance in the civic garden, registered as *late*. It was as if the singers stood for us all, as a species as well as the individuals present, as if everyone had been found, or had found themselves, out of time. Perhaps that is what midsummer means. And more than that, the *delay* seemed in keeping with the wider drift or slippage of the present day, and that made the untimeliness feel oddly timely. It captured the awkwardness of signing up to a seasonal mood-song that signifies less to us than before, and in an era when the seasons themselves don't seem to stick any longer. As it dragged its way around the ring of singers, the song asked (inadvertently or not) what it would mean to be in time. And whether being out of time, although more tunelessly sad, might be a truthful reflection of what has happened to our centrally heated world.

Paraffin was added to the fire and it took and roared for a bit as the song petered out. The burning branches hissed, with sap seething and resin blistering in the cuts. Despite the rain, chiffchaffs and chaffinches sang from the surrounding trees and swallows hawked the dell for the insects raised by the bonfire's damp smoke.

After the singing there were speeches. I asked Anders if a woman talking was reciting a poem. He said she was listing the donors to the children's playground in the town.

We walked back to where Anders was staying. And there, thanks to birds, life began again.

When on swallow duty, Anders lodges in the home of his old friends William and Agnes. William is William Carøe Aarestrup: a chimney sweep and lifelong bird-ringer, pigeon-fancier and aviculturist – an all-in total bird-man. Noah, or better still St Francis, might play William in a film of his life.

On the way to his house we walked down streets of modern bunga-lows. Pandrup has grown and colonised various grassy fields where William used to ring. In trapping cages, baited only with water, he once caught 1,000 linnets in a day where the houses now stand. Anders knew William then. They met in 1966. William had started ringing in 1960 and since then has processed 160,000 birds (I was born a little after William starled ringing in 1961 and have lived 21,000 or so days – he's ringed an average of eight birds every day of my life). Many were caught in his small back garden. He lives in a (older) bungalow too.

To this day, his house and garden are full of birds; I heard them as we turned into his street and their noise was continuous throughout the time I was visiting: a diverse flock including wild birds, tamed birds, caged birds, rescued and sick birds, lifelong pets and temporary holdings, an ancient red-lored Amazon parrot and a waxwing waiting for a winter release. There were many silent birds as well: dead birds skinned, feathers and skulls, cups for champion pigeons, and the details on paper of thousands of free-flyers that had passed through William's hands.

In the house's dining room were eight top hats, ascending the wall, mounted like ceramic flying ducks used to be. William's father was a chimney sweep as was his grandfather. His brother was as well and his two sons still are. He was eighty-five when we met and still working: before the singing in the park he had ringed a brood of six swallows that he had found on a sweeping job. He mimed taking the young out of their nest to me and I could see the soot-inlaid lines on the palms of his hands.

His first recovery came only two months after he had started ringing in 1960. An icterine warbler he had caught in Pandrup was found on its southbound migration in northern Italy. He was amazed. As he told me this, he drew a line across his forehead with his finger, a line I took to mean both the passage of the bird and the opening of his mind.

Everything about birds remains interesting to William. More than that – everything about them, as seen through his fast-moving, cornflower-blue (and forever young) eyes, was *good*. Surrounded by birds in his house and garden, hundreds of the living present, thousands of records of the elsewhere and now dead, William suggests – without so gushing a thought ever being said – that he could love every individual bird in the world there is, or has been, or could be. Before I had met William, I'd asked Anders if he knew of Dr Dolittle, and the story, in one of the books by Hugh Lofting, about swallows massing together to pull a becalmed ship up the West African coast. He had laughed, of course, and shaken his head; but here now was the doctor at home in Pandrup with as much swallow (or any other avian) back-up, surely, as anyone could ever need.

In a semi-circle of wire cages that radiated from the back wall of the house (I thought of the sweep's stiff-spoked brush I had seen in a lean-to) was the hurry and flutter and whistling din of many small birds. I saw the rescued waxwing, and bullfinches, a female blackcap, a scarlet rosefinch, a nuthatch (extraordinarily), goldfinches, siskins, redpolls, at least one twite and, my favourite (of course, yes!), a redstart. It was a female. William had reared it from a chick when he saved it from a rain-dashed nest. It flew about the lower half of the cage it shared with half a dozen waxwings and a medley of finches. Its tail trembled and the shivering red proved it was still a redstart. William had had a male too, but it died not long after the birds had paired and the female laid an egg. I had never seen one in a cage before.

All the birds were busy and, because William was looking after them, all his captives appeared content. Almost all of them were never going to go anywhere else, but William made their stopping easy. He spoke sweetly to them in a sort of whistled collusive whisper. His eyes moved over his flock as fast as the little birds travelled their cages. And he poked green lettuce leaves through the wire with his thick fingers with his sooty nails.

More than a half-century of William's ringing had yielded a fabulous harvest. His records imply an abundance that is hard to imagine now. Where are those bungalow linnets today? But it is also difficult to conceive of every one of these birds passing through his hands. What kind of knowledge exchange or species of intimacy does that imply? He has held them all: 15,000 greenfinches, including 4,352 in twenty-one days in his garden in April 1970, with 789 on 1 April alone; 2,515 siskins from his garden in twenty-one days in February one year; 20,000 starlings, 4,000 out of his garden.

Of the 25,000 swallows William had ringed by the time we met, 15,000 were trapped at roosts. He caught hundreds in a single net. He would carry home bags of the birds and hang them overnight on hooks in his ringing room. Some swallows, like the midsummer's brood he had caught the day we met, he got out of chimneys when cleaning. He would always take rings with him when working. Before he was an official qualified ringer his curiosity prompted him to devise his own rings. He showed me a rectangle of bent wire that, sixty years previously, he had threaded with home-made rings and kept ready in his sweep's bag.

Where will they go, then – will they be heard from again? Always there are these questions as the ring is fitted. Contemplating this, anyone might draw a line across their brow. One starling William ringed in his garden in 1960 was found dead in Helpston, John Clare's home village in Northamptonshire.* One of William's ringed swallows went to the Congo (his only African swallow recovery). A sandwich tern flew into overhead wires in South Africa. One of three woodcocks he ringed was shot in Russia. A turtle dove was shot in Ukraine. Subsumed places, long overgrown borders, lost geopolitical configurations – they all spring from William's albums of ringing data. He has letters from the USSR, the once-divided Germany, the former captive states of the Eastern bloc, apartheid-era South Africa, letters from dictatorships with secret policemen and from people's republics, letters from places with electric fences, letters swapping grid references and details on deaths. The nonsense of our gated and wired world is exposed in such exchanges of information: a nine-year-old hawfinch first ringed in East Germany that William 'controlled' (another ringer's bird re-captured); the starling that made it from William's garden in Jutland to Archangel in Russia.

– *Starlingrad*, we joked, looking at his cages, talking of freedom.

At dinner we toasted all birds and drank elderflower champagne from hedgerow flowers fizzed in a bucket by Agnes just days before. Then we ate Pandrup pork with new potatoes from the garden and spinach followed by a bowl of small tart strawberries, also home-grown and dribbled with fresh honey donated by a neighbouring bee-keeper. The talk was of honey-bee losses, the value of nettles as vegetables, and the best way to toast edible hay. Then the *porse snaps* came out – akvavit

---

* Clare knew starlings year-round there, breeding birds, as well as the autumnal comradely influx and springtime exodus of migrant visitors, and he wrote of 'the starnel crowds that dim the muddy light'.

steeped with bog-myrtle for forty days. Tradition demands you hold the eyes of your fellow drinkers as you drink. I said some faltering words about the end of spring.

Anders talked about some of the other William-like men he knew. There was the wryneck obsessive who spent his springs looking for the birds' nests in Denmark, and then sprinkling cayenne pepper around the base of any breeding tree in order to discourage pine martens from stealing the birds' eggs or chicks. Then there was Jan, the raptor obsessive, who had lent Anders his folder of goshawk feathers – a book of one thousand different greys. He had monitored up to fifty nests every year for decades, accumulating data for the equivalent of 1,400 nest-years. He was a forester and spent most springs climbing slippery tree trunks in rubber boots. The nests (some massive and weighing 500 kilograms) are on average eighteen metres above the forest floor. I thought of William's extending brushes, Anders up his swallow ladder, Jan climbing goshawk trees. Jan once told Anders when out climbing together: 'I'm not a religious person, but I say a prayer.' On the same trip, up a tall tree, Anders lost his footing and thought he was going to die. Jan also had collected 36,000 feathers of the prey species of sparrowhawks. 'Enough material for ten PhDs,' thought Anders. 'But, fuck you, Jan said, when some academics approached him for his golden eagle data.' Why? I asked. Anders did one of his smiles. (Later in my stay we tried to return the great grey encyclopaedia; there was no reply when we knocked at Jan's door: he was out, almost certainly up a tree.)

It was getting late, and I asked about singing and about the sea, where I was headed next. Anders started on a song for the end of the day: 'Solen er så rød mor . . .' – 'The sun is so red, mother . . .' It is lonely at sea at night and the gulls and the terns have no place to go . . . no place to call home. Anders' mother had sung it to him as a lullaby. William's mother did the same. Anders had last sung the song when his own children were small, fifteen years before. He is louder in Danish than he is in English, but not much.

William, listening to Anders sing, spilled his tea. Agnes laughed at her husband, her face creasing, and the whole of her upper body shaking with mirth. William had spilled his wine just minutes before as well;

he was tired after his day's sweeping, ringing and singing. I had misunderstood – he had ringed sixty swallows that day, not just one brood of six.

– We Jutlanders always smile, Agnes said, and we laugh at adversity.

Anders saw me out; it was after midnight and there was still rain in the air, but the sky throbbed with a greenish glow.

– Tomorrow we'll eat less, he promised. But you could come for a herring breakfast.

I stopped on my way back to my bed to listen for corncrakes in an old peat bog. One wet grassy field was crowded with dandelions. There were still some buttery golden flowers, but most had gone over to grey seedy clocks that looked, that night, like William's brushes. *Chimney-sweeps*, the clocks were called in England once, and it has been suggested that Shakespeare knew this and made part of the elegy-dirge in *Cymbeline* from his botanical knowledge. In the low-thrown ashy light of midnight, the dandelions looked like a universe of suns and moons scattered deeply through a big sky: *golden lads and girls all must, as chimney-sweepers, come to dust.*

Around the Baltic, swallow dances were once performed by people – usually young women. The steps the dancers took mimicked the flights of the birds. The dances were to bid farewell to the birds when they flew south to warmer lands. A Danish observer recorded what he witnessed one time in nineteenth-century Lithuania:

> I saw this dance one summer evening in a little birch grove. Couple behind couple take up positions in two sets facing each other, they swing around, bend down and pass through quick as a flash so that really in a way it reminds one of the swallows' twisting and rapid flight.

In August each year, Anders goes back to finish with the swallows in Denmark, checking on the birds' breeding success. He swims then, sometimes, in the cold bight of the Jammerbugt. This run of rough sea off north-west Jutland is named for its deathly fury; it is a bay of lamentation and wretchedness, dangerous for sailors and fishermen. But on certain windy days, when braving the waves, Anders has watched swallows over his head flying south across the sea, coming from Norway and heading for Africa.

Troms
70°N

One day I'll see my last redstart – perhaps I already have. Perhaps it was the one that I followed across the bog on the hill behind Gabi Wagner's house at Balsnes near Tromsø in northern Norway at midnight on a midsummer's day.

Claire and I had gone out for a walk. Another walk – because it is light all the time at that time in Troms County and there seems no reason not to be up and out in it as long as it lasts. And it lasts long. It lasts so long that lasting is not what it does. It plainly *is*. The light is. Elsewhere, days might be where we live, but for three months of the Arctic summer there are no days, or rather there is just one long day, and everything lives in its light.

My legs were tired at three in the morning when we came back down the hill but otherwise I was wide awake. So was the male redstart that sang from a fir tree in a rocky outcrop halfway across the wet bog. It did its work right away and made my day. But this day was abundant – it stretched and everything in it stretched with it. And in all that light, I pictured the bird as my last redstart. Not because I felt death coming, but because I felt life going on. There was no reason for the redstart to stop what it was doing. It could go on. It went on.

The sun wasn't there at that minute, clouds were thickening, but there was as much brightness at midnight as there was or would be at midday. In that light – under it but also within it, since you feel it streaming into you and pouring through you – time slides away. There is no night, no day, no difference between them; everything is displayed in a long, *lasting* now. In that light, there and then, the redstart sang and shook its tail – simply shaking and simply being.

I knew the bog would freeze; I knew the sun would go behind the mountains; I knew the redstart would leave; I knew most of its babies would die. All that – all the world-weariness that is everywhere alongside our own botched, debris-strewn and put-up lives – I knew. But here everything was numinously on hold – on hold and yet moving.

Florizel is in love with Perdita in Shakespeare's *The Winter's Tale*. He watches her dancing. It is beautiful to see and it makes him speak beautifully to her:

> when you do dance, I wish you
> A wave o'th' sea, that you might ever do
> Nothing but that – move still, still so,
> And own no other function.

Move still – there was that in the redstart on that long day: a be-all and end-all.

Still so.

To still be in the world's morning in June you must move north, to where the European spring ends. In England today, no matter how early I might walk in Horner Woods, the pied flycatchers will be finished. The trees will be quiet; there is no more song. Some of the birds will already be done with the place and slipping south and away. Better then, if you can, to seek the start once more, to begin again, pass go, find spring eternal, and enjoy the all-day breakfast.

It was cold for June, even for an Arctic June. I was wearing five layers, plus a hat and gloves, in order to drink my coffee sitting on the hammock between the birches at the back of Gabi's house. A male pied flycatcher was resident in the little stand of trees. It sang on and on. The cold didn't seem to bother it. Yet its summer life must be colder than its winter life – the summer life when its partner must hatch naked chicks in frosty air and the pair find caterpillars for their begging mouths. There were swallows flying too, near Gabi's barn, and willow warblers singing. All must be colder when breeding than when wintering. Sometimes it must be too cold. There was snow in late June just before I pitched up. And still the southerners come.

I had tried to arrive with these birds, or at least not long after. Perhaps some were still touching down, even at midsummer. After a squall dashed along the fjord, we came upon one bright field which seemed to have collected a fall from the south: a pair of whinchats were on the fence, three pale wheatears worked the cow-cropped turf, two cuckoos swung their tails on a telephone wire, a male ring ouzel jumped through the long grass where the field climbed a hill, and a pair of redstarts flew out from some straggly birches. Perhaps they were all already at home, and just happened to coincide as we passed, but to me they seemed a welcoming committee.

We drove to the sea to the north-west of Tromsø. Swallows flew along the rocky beach. Arctic terns flew between them.

Because it doesn't get dark here for about one hundred days – the so-called 100 Growing Days – there seems to be very little death. There being no night means there is no sense of the dark as an end-stop to life; there is no switch-off, no snuffing out. Yet there is something in the highest tide that speaks of its turning; something in a zenith registers a nadir, knowing that what is now the nearest will become the furthest, knowing that light contains its opposite. That feeling is here. The light has been thrown up over the top of the world as far as it can be. It caps the time at the middle of the year; but on its far-flung travels we sense the other end of its life too; so much light these days must mean, at the other end of the year, so much dark.

Arctic terns might tutor us in this understanding, though the birds themselves avoid its truth. In Norway, they were moving up and down every fjord. The last I had seen were in the depths of the northern winter in midsummer South Africa. They go further south than that too, into austral midsummer light at the edge of Antarctica. Arctic terns probably see more daylight in their lives than any other species of bird – they fly from the lit north to the lit south, from one midsummer brightness to another. Sea swallows, terns have been called and, in their flights from south to north and back again, the Arctic tern and the barn swallow are as one. No bird could better fly the long Arctic/Antarctic day than the tern. I've never seen one look weary at either end of the world. Their calls are brittle like glass. They appear to be made from bright skies: they are strip-lights steering a bird, or batons of the sun, engineered by it, and always rising towards it in their *lightness*. And after lighting the lit Arctic, they will turn about and, cleaving to the light, will leave with it and fly to the bottom of the planet, south to where the lit Antarctic can nurture them, until the tilted world is ready to receive them in the north again, always shunning night, always wanting light.

I got to know Gabi Wagner because she put me up when I had to come to Tromsø in the middle of the winter to make a radio programme about ice with the geographer Hayden Lorimer. Hayden was an old friend of Gabi from when she lived, where he does, in Aberdeen. Gabi is a chronobiologist. She works on time and life, or, more specifically, on seasonality and animal clocks and calendars. When Gabi subsequently welcomed me on two further trips in midsummer (one on my own, one with Claire), she was living with her then partner David Hazlerigg, who is also a chronobiologist in Tromsø. Gabi works mostly on ptarmigan and David mostly on salmon. Both were warmly welcoming in the Arctic summer as in the winter, and so were their three children, Valerie, Tom and Lilou.

In the day that was the night of the European Union referendum in Britain, David took Claire and me out canoeing on the fjord to fish for cod. We headed off as the polls were closing and landed again as the first results were being called after midnight. It was night in Britain but light throughout in Tromsø – a new day in one place, more of the same in the other. As the results began to stack up, the continuing light, where we were, made me think (feel, really) that since the day hadn't closed or the light decayed, the debate ought to be still alive with the vote still to be won. The depressing outcome – something caught that I hadn't thought was being fished for – looked unbelievable in the continuing light. Someone was trying to stop what was manifestly still going on: we were still in the morning from before, still joined to an earlier day. How then were we to be torn from that, without a deadly night being put between us?

299

In our canoes we were low to the sea, pushed just slightly into its skin. We had short rods with spinners and one hundred metres of line. Claire made the first catch. As the cod came up into the air it had a surprised face. David took the line and the fish in his canoe. He hit the fish on its head with the handle of an axe. The fish's face turned from surprise to shock. It got hit again. The shock froze.

Afterwards it all seemed meaningful. I had cast my vote by post but never got a bite on the water. We drifted on the tide towards where our fjord joined another that ran west to the open sea. The second take was harder to secure. Claire hooked another cod in the gills, but it was too small. The tide pulled at us more and more. We spun like a compass needle seeking iron. The meeting of currents birthed whirlpools that drew down the surface of the water into apprentice maelstroms. Sea froth creamed around these scoops. Our canoes bucked. Big ships heading for Tromsø loomed over us and scared me. We had to paddle hard. At least, I thought we should; David and Claire wanted more fish. The vestiges of brighter earlier hours came and opened cracks of soft wet gold in the clouds. The light picked out the whites of the gulls resting on the fjord surface; from the level of sea they looked very big. An adult white-tailed eagle flew down the fjord over our boats, heavy with itself: a bone club for a beak and a ripple of heft and effort passing through its body to its deep-fingered wing-tips. I thought of the Dam Busters. We landed and carried our rods and our meagre catch ashore. A woodcock came roding between the red barns and the birch wood. The light was opening again and the clouds thinning still further, but by then we really needed bed. *Adieu.*

I fell asleep still feeling the bob of the canoe on the fjord; an hour later when I woke, my right arm was trailing from the bed, as if drawn through the water at the side of my boat. I could hear a redstart some way up the hill behind the house.

On Gabi's bog, moss-covered mounds, some with soft hearts, and some with stone, make miniature *mogotes*, or inselbergs, each a micro-biome. I liked them for leaning on, feeling like Gulliver in Lilliput, squinting at a model village: there were tiny moss trees hung with single water droplets like Venetian lanterns, moss lawns of rust, plant seeds like boulders, lichen rugs, cushions of green, little stick tents, goblin markets, dripping-seeping places like swamps drawn on a treasure chart. There were a dozen mounds across the bog; I tried to reach them all. Each was different but similar and each was also like a 3-D map of the whole northern world, the domed top of the planet, light flooding over all, wetness underwriting everything, the give of a great mire, a swaddled place, almost everywhere moving beyond green.

When I was leaning on one of these *mogotes*, I saw a male redstart land on another. I could have worshipped that bird. Then, on the next *mogote* beyond that one, another male popped up, all shimmer and quiver. Their territories must have met in the bog somewhere between them. The islanded kings flew at one another and tangled for a moment, falling towards the sphagnum like burning coals, before righting themselves and hurrying back to their kingdoms. I couldn't resist stepping nearer the birds, wanting this heat that was theirs.

I talked to Gabi many times when we were her guests. The light was our continuing subject, and how she and her family and all the animals she knows live with it: this light, and the way that seasonality – so marked here – plays across her life and her work. We talked at one in the afternoon and at one in the morning, we talked as we cooked meals, we talked as she walked her dogs, and we talked when she showed us her Svalbard ptarmigans and the other animal residents of the research enclosures at the university in Tromsø.

Early in her career Gabi studied at a research station of the Max Planck Institute in Germany, working on sparrows and their day–night rhythms, asking what light signals do to their brains and how their brains continue to use the information signalled by the light. She kept her study birds in the same underground bunkers where much work was done on bird migration (*Zugunruhe* studies – on seasonal restlessness and directional intentionality), and also where Rütger Wever and Jürgen Aschoff carried out many, now famous, human sleep experiments from the 1960s to the 1980s. In these trials, volunteers were kept underground for three months in low light levels. Some people loved it, some disintegrated. It's like that too in the Arctic north through the winter: all sorts of souls are kept in the dark, waiting for the light.

– Everything in an organism must be timed to function properly, Gabi said.

– But these timing processes have to be separated – they have to happen at different times. Asking how that is achieved got me going as a scientist.

– The first question you always ask is, does an organism's timing come from within or from without? Does it have a biological clock within it or does the organism follow the external world? To answer this question I would put my subject animal into a constant environment where light or dark do not occur as they usually do. If a rhythm persists under these conditions, which might be constant light or constant darkness, then we know the organism isn't just following the external world but is following a rhythm from within. Its clock is endogenous.

– Biological clocks are not exact. The sun's light–dark rhythm is twenty-four hours, but the endogenous rhythm that comes from within organisms never exactly matches that. Biological clocks are like old grandfather clocks that have to be re-set every day, and if they are not, they get out of time and become desynchronised.

– There is a further interesting complication here. In the Arctic, the daily light–dark signal is not available for parts of the year. For months it is dark all the time and for months it is light. Yet organisms that live here need this signal as much as any other animal anywhere. The signals help separate processes in time. A reindeer cannot rut and moult at the same time. To be ready to do either of these, they have to be able to anticipate the change in season. You cannot start growing winter fur only when the temperature falls. You cannot grow antlers for a rut that starts that very day. But if you have no signal to tell you that the days are getting shorter or longer, how can you do these things at the right time? Much of the life of an organism has to be anticipated by it. Clocks and calendars help with this.

Back-timing in order to be, as we used to say at the BBC, *out on time* (finished without *crashing the pips* or bumping into another show) – the only radio-production skill I ever seemed to have – is crucial in nature. The talk of clocks and calendars suggests something external to the animals that use them. But the terms are ours only: the animal has no such baggage, no watch other than one within which is wound by world time, in a collaboration made with (in David Abram's phrase) the 'animate rondure' of the Earth.*

– Anticipation is everything, Gabi said. Long-distance migrant birds have an apparently extraordinary task. Redstarts or pied flycatchers need to arrive here in Tromsø on their breeding grounds at the right time – a certain time. But the day length, that would tell them what time of year it is, is wrong where they are and cannot be a signal to them. It's fascinating therefore to study how they organise that – how without an appropriate environmental signal they synchronise their circannual cycle. Moult, reproduction, preparing for migration – it all has to be anticipated and added to the birds' forward-planning diary in order for it to be triggered at the right time. And, amazingly, they get it right every year.

We went to see the study animals at Gabi's university. A musk-ox came up to its fence to say hello. It was wearing its go-every-where-regardless-of-heatwave-or-blizzard coat, which made it look like a mad thing out on a walk. It snorted great gusts of green rumen into our faces. Musk-ox wool, Gabi said, is called *qiviut* in Inuktitut (the same word means the downy feathers of birds) and is fantastically warm. A neighbour of hers shot some in Greenland in the 1970s and sent the wool to NASA to line astronauts' space suits.

The reindeer in their pen were not so friendly. There were eiders on a pond and seals in an indoor pool. Gabi's Svalbard ptarmigans were in hutches outside. They looked like swatches of material

---

* Likewise maps – a *word* we need to describe some quality animals *have*. David Abram – 'Cranes and Butterflies would have little use for a separated *re-presentation* of the Earth's surface, for they have never torn themselves our of the encompassing *presence* of the wide Earth'.

undergoing camouflage experiments. The winner would be the best replica of a grey-brown rock spalted with creeping vegetation and a spreading bleed of rusty lichen. All the birds had won first prize. Each ptarmigan was patterned in the same way, but so busy and multi-layered was their cryptic plumage that my bamboozled eyes saw them all as different.

– This last winter was rubbish. It was very long. I have colleagues who were sitting miserably on two metres of snow where their study birds should have been breeding. Everything changes year by year in this way. Nothing is predictable. In the face of this, evolution has latched on to the one available constant, which on average keeps you on the right track, and that is day length or photoperiod. It seems enough for many organisms to get their timing information for their whole year from just a few days. It seems – and we see it in the north especially – that they don't need this information every day. Here there is midsummer madness – so much light – and life runs free beyond clocks and calendars for a while. Organisms can afford to do this. A few days on either side of such times (when there is separate day and night) seems time enough for photoperiod signals to be put in place and clocks to be corrected. This can be done by comparing a few days to the days before – are they longer or shorter, are we running into winter or are we running into summer? A re-set or a correction is then made. The circadian – free-running, endogenous – cycle gets entrained or synchronised by the light–dark cycle. And the year-round circannual cycle takes it from there: moult, migration, mating – all might now be scheduled.

Gabi told us about a ptarmigan trip she had made. There's a highly successful German bird-breeder who has hatched and reared many unlikely species at his egg plant in the middle of Germany. His successes include puffins, guillemots, red-necked phalaropes and saddle-billed storks. He has also managed to breed Scottish ptarmigans. Gabi was interested in how he had done that. He, in turn, was keen to know about her Svalbard birds.

– In reindeer studies, as in ptarmigan, the current dogma is that, as Arctic animals, they have very strong circannual rhythms but very weak circadian or day–night clocks, since there are long periods of each year where the difference between day and night is not clear. In other words, they have a good sense of the time of the year but no idea about the time of day. These beliefs come from activity measurements – reindeer activity is regulated by their rumen. They need to chew the cud and they do this at any time and show very little day–night rhythm when doing it. That is true, but their circannual clock still needs to be entrained and it can only do this in response to a photoperiod – a day – or a series of photoperiods. They need to know when to march, when to moult, when to fatten, when to rut, when to breed. They can only do such longer-term calendar-setting if they know what time of day they can expect the next sunset or sunrise. In the Arctic they only have a few weeks in the year when there is any visible sunset or sunrise. Their clock therefore needs to be susceptible to that brief signal. I don't buy the weak-clock thinking. We might not see the reindeer taking all this on board as their activities are very arrhythmic (that is what constant light or constant dark has done to them), but I would be surprised if we don't see evidence of rhythmic activity in their brains and elsewhere in their bodies.

Gabi talked, Claire asked questions; I put my face to the wire and tried to get the reindeer to share a thought. New work had been done in Tromsø on their highly adapted noses. They are crucial in allowing the animals to survive super-cold winters. A reindeer's nose releases as little heat and conserves as much water vapour as possible. Because it has a very large internal surface area, incoming air is warmed up extremely quickly. If the temperature of the outside air, as inhaled by the reindeer, is minus forty degrees Celsius, by the time the air reaches their lungs it is plus thirty-eight. Their convoluted nasal geometry can change the temperature by seventy or eighty degrees in less than a second. Oryx living in hot and dry desert environments have equivalent sophisticated nasal structures that do the same as the reindeer, but in reverse. Engineers of heat exchange systems for houses are very interested in all these noses.

There were swallows above the reindeer pen in Tromsø, keen on the flies that followed the animals; I pictured the same birds flying above oryx in Chad; the same birds taking flies those grazers had disturbed, the same birds breathing the same shared air. One roundy head must do for the swallow in both Chad and Norway.

– As a chronobiologist, I am obsessed by anticipation. I like all this forward thinking myself. There is a wonderful anticipation around the sun returning in the new year when you realise the twilight we have is getting longer and longer and brighter and brighter day-by-day, and then there is enormous excitement on the day that the sun finally pops up over the horizon and you see your first shadow for months. Spring starts, in this way, before the sun returns and long before the season itself properly begins. The sensation of the darkness retreating begins in mid-January. There is still a lot of winter ahead, but the feeling is already one of growth and of going into a light season. It is incredibly invigorating. For everyone, I think. From there on, hope just rises. And I love then the speed or the drama of seasonal change – the way the hills get green from their bottom to their top in a few weeks, the way the snow retreats upwards.

– People from elsewhere ask how we deal with the darkness here. Actually we have more light in a year than almost anywhere else, in terms of hours of daylight. This is especially the case if you count the civil twilight – the time when it is light although the sun is below the horizon – which is also important to organisms. Thanks to the all-day light of May, June and July, the total energy of the sun arriving here is much higher than anywhere at the Equator. This is the basis of all the great migrations to where we are – that is why everything that can afford it comes here. There's incredible growth, incredible biomass production, and that doesn't stop for those months. It is not very hot, but the light makes it worth flying from Cape Town.

In the night-time hours at Balsnes the wind often dropped. Then the sky overhead was chalky, ether-tinted, pink.

On the bog there were cuckoos. One made a *cuckoo* and then it, or another, came out with a weird mashed-up swallowed laugh: *wah wah wub wah*. Cuckoos are sometimes called gowks. I think that is what the bird on the bog was saying. Gowk comes from the Old Norse *gaukr*. The Norwegian for a cuckoo is *gjøk*. When the bird spluttered those

306

notes it made the hillside sound ancient. Birds can do that: some are time-travellers; some are trapped as birds of the old money, pre-decimal, or pre-digital birds. The cuckoo is one of those. The bird on the bog flew further off and carried on, as of old. Cuckooing its clock. I counted for half an hour: twenty-three *cuckoos* in a row, a pause and then thirty-one, then three, then thirty, then thirty-four, then five, then twelve, and then thirty-eight. Then it stopped.

A cuckoo is a calendar. People in Russia will count the birds' calls to look into their future. Tolstoy's extraordinary story about a horse, 'Strider', begins strait-laced and zoologically segregated, with people over here and other animals over there; but then it crosses into its horses' consciousness and profound horsey talk. It ends with Strider meeting the knacker and then – as seen from his dead horse flesh – being eaten by a wolf and her cubs. At the point where the story begins to shift into the heads of its non-human animals, Nester, groom to the horses, listens to a cuckoo and counts its calls to ascertain how many years he has to live. Tolstoy doesn't say what he hears.

We went out for another walk from Gabi's house. We were out until three in the morning. By the time we got back we were all sleepy, but the light tugged at us. Melatonin was our topic.

It is very old: plants have it (it was discovered in some in 1995) as well as animals. We need darkness in the evening and brightness in the morning to re-set our body clock. In the winter in the Arctic it is difficult to get enough light and in the summer it is difficult to get enough darkness. To sleep well in the light nights it is recommended that you maintain a regular bedtime. Don't go haywire. No *mayhem*. Curtains – heavy ones – help, but you also shouldn't have any sort of digital screen in your bedroom. Delay in accessing darkness gives you jet-lag and that feeling that your body has been robbed of time. Melatonin release is triggered by darkness. We can't go to sleep without it. Light stops melatonin production. If you open the fridge for a midnight feast, the light from it causes your melatonin levels to crash. It takes hours to revert. The same thing happens if you look at your phone at night to check a referendum result.

*   *   *

Towards the end of one stay in Norway I walked alone for ten hours up and down a mountain north-east of Tromsø. Of all the walks and all the stake-outs I have attempted into the season, I think this one said the most of its time and place, or rather, its times and its places.

I began at sea-level alongside a fast black-water river where it jostled coldly into a fjord. The birch trees there were tall and their leaves were losing their fresh green shimmer and their downy lanugo, turning darker and glossier. In wetter places where the peat had thickened, an under-storey of bracken grew stiff with juice, electric-green and rampant. All around, there were chiffchaffs and willow warblers, redpolls and redwings. The scene was domestic – the birds were singing but well established, paired and working on family matters, some nest-building, some already carrying food to their young. There were sheep in the woods too: belled ewes with chunky lambs at their side moving leisurely beneath the birches, the dull cloche of their bells timed to their grazing nods.

I began to climb. The leaves got younger with every step I took. Little disturbances of the air under the open canopy of the trees made breezes so local that one leaf only on a birch tree shivered. I flushed a woodcock from the leaf mould; it went off with the crack of a dead branch, something brown and mobile built from something brown and static. There was no green in it whatsoever.

Higher, now, and cooler and grey-brown prevailed – the leaves were shrinking back into the trees. There were willow catkins and birch buds – soft things furred to keep them warm. A willow warbler was singing in a tree that was surrounded by snow – there and then the winter seemed collapsed into the summer, with my spring season squeezed out of existence. The trees got smaller and thinned. I stopped at the last one. There was another willow warbler in it. Singing to take its mind off things, it seemed, like a pioneer whistling at a campfire, nervous of wolves.

The ground got wetter as the woods fell below. My leaky boot tasted the mire and, as I felt the swill of peaty water at my toes, a great snipe unfolded itself, a mix of fluster and aplomb, from a wet patch of brown bog grass. It made a ripping sound as it lifted off as if it was being torn from the earth. In my binoculars it looked like half a pillow fight. Its dead-grass camouflage was so good it gave the bird an ecstatic air as it jinked away through the dwarf trees.

I left the bird's footprints in the peat, and after a few steps of my own was walking through snow. In a patch of it, there was a dead tangle of a woody plant that had called in a wintry caravan of redpolls – streaky brown finches with one rationed dot of red on each of their pilgrim foreheads. At the bottom of the mountain there were paired and breeding redpolls; here the same species seemed weeks away from that. They gleaned; and I shivered to watch. In a two-hour climb I had walked the time back to winter. Among the finches, a bulky one with a pale rump was my first ever Arctic redpoll. It twisted and puffed after the seeds it wanted, looking like a dirty snowball trapped in a cage of dead twigs.

Five minutes higher and colder, with still more snow on the ground and now sleet in the air, and there was a wheatear and then another – a pair, two hero migrants from Africa – here on a snowfield, looking as sorted as ever. I glanced up from watching them, marvelling at their survival, to see a bumblebee steering its unlikely furry helicopter out across the snow.

I reached a col and passed a half-frozen lake – a frosted eye looking sightlessly up into the grey sky. But even there, there was life. A grey heron trying to fly through the sleet, as hopelessly and as heroically as the bee, lowered its legs and landed at a run onto the little island in the middle of the cataract of ice, only to provoke a mob attack by the common gulls that were sitting on eggs there, trying to incubate their genes in a slow-melting deep-freeze.

The sleet pitted the snow. Where the snow ended there was dead ground – all brown. The plateau, where I was, ran away on all sides. There were higher mountains to the north, and the sea – lit like a sword – glinted far away to the south-west. The light all about was grey but bright. The air was cold but the sun spoke in the brightness. As I spun around, taking in the top of the world, a long-tailed skua appeared over my head, sharp-winged and skate-tailed, painted in shades of strong brown, and looking like a mountain crucifix, a sort of wind-sculpted iron assemblage, half pitchfork, half lightning-rod. The bird called once, like a tough black-headed gull. They breed up here on the high ground.

Years of my birdwatching life rose before me as I watched that skua. One May when my now big children were little, we had a few days on Coll in the Inner Hebrides. We saw corncrakes and basking sharks and the children found oystercatcher nests and collected dead gannets and tiny pink cowries – like babies' toes – on the beach. And I watched – as they were busy – a long-tailed skua moving north off shore. A year later, also in May, at the ancient Greek ruins at Chersonesus in Crimea, meeting veteran Tatars to talk about their enforced emigration in the Stalin years, I watched three long-tailed skuas leave the Black Sea behind them and head north – fast and buoyant – over the ruins and on inland. There are known annual passages of the skua across the sealess bulk of Europe between the Black Sea and the Baltic as well as up the Atlantic edge of the continent. Any of these migratory skuas might have been heading for the fell where I stood in Norway. Here I was, looking up at the other end of the birds' story. Yet it wasn't an end: I could tell that even as I built it as such in my mind, for there are none in nature; the bird told that too, and that was the best thing then to know in the world.

I was beginning to descend – not yet re-tracing my steps but leaving the col and dropping down from its plateau into the head of a broad valley. A few still bare trees had their existence on the banks of a river. None were taller than me. I ate my sandwich crouched between a willow and a birch. On the far side of the river a reindeer calf was being steered by its mother through scrubby vegetation. It was sedge-brown; its mother was grey, a dirtier snow than an Arctic redpoll. I wondered if anything remembered green here. The trees, perhaps? They were not dead. They would know green again. The summer solstice had passed but their spring was yet to come. But it would, wouldn't it?

A willow warbler began to sing at the edge of the little scrubby assemblage. There was green in that too. And then, near me, a male bluethroat started up. A rocky stream of cold-frothed song. Its red spot

310

lifted in its blue enamelled throat as it sang. It was like an Arctic flower, a crocus or a gentian: the flame in its throat held a heat within the shelter of itself, warmer than all of the ice in all of the north. The trees where it sang were leafless still, but it had elected to be there. These birds had come from Africa – to here, where snow covered one-third of the earth, the air was iced and it was raining painfully – but soon they would make a nest and fill it with eggs.

I turned back to begin my walk down; three snipe chipped and whickered overhead. As I stepped away, the bluethroat and a redwing were still singing. It felt wrong to leave such song and such singers. Ten hours later I woke up in bed and thought immediately of the birds singing and how they would be still be at it.

I belayed down the mountain on the songs of willow warblers – one gently roping me to the next and it passing me on. One of them had an aberrant voice. It seemed to be echoing itself as it sang. At first, I wondered if it might be an Arctic warbler, but I think it was an unschooled willow that perhaps had never heard its father sing or had heard, as an impressionable youngster, only the song of a neighbouring bird bumping off the rocks. I sat and listened and realised that, in the place where I had stopped, I could lie down for the first time that day. There was a dry rock for me. It fitted and seemed *quite soft*. I had already walked fifteen kilometres. A spring bubbled at the edge of the rock: slivers of peat and grains of mica tumbled in the crystal bucket of the little pool, pushed about by the renewing flow from below; one young birch leaf had fallen there and swirled greenly over and over in the milling water. Close by I heard a redwing – not only its four familiar thrushy notes but also the more gnarly chew of the sub-music behind, that which says something of the bird's personality beneath its perform-ance. A song, like my favourite woodlark's, that should sound like love that comes out as an elegy. A willow warbler – the wrong-singer, I think – came silently into a birch sapling growing between my bed and the spring. It said nothing now, but it was alive.

If I wasn't betrothed to the redstarts, the bluethroats might have me. There are suggestive similarities. Redstart intensities in the bluethroat are found in its breast and tail and song. Between these it is a drab-brown and off-white robin-shaped bird. Bluethroats are in the same genus – *Luscinia* – as nightingales (they were previously thought robins – *Erithacus*). Their tails, which have rufous panels towards the base, flick and flirt a little, though not as habitually as redstarts'. Their throats (males in breeding plumage especially) are a metallic enamelled blue (cobalt, the books say), a rare colour in birds and made even more striking – they do *strike* – by a red spot or patch in the middle of a bright blue sea (another race of bluethroats has white spots instead of red). This makes their throats look like open gapes. They sing and it seems that their throat is opening as well as their beaks. The blue and red feathering rustles and wavers as they sing, as if made from a sharper, more metallic material than their other feathers, and as if it was a song source as much as their syrinx.

Bluethroat song is better – I must tell the truth – than the redstart's: it often begins in a similar way, with a modest call-like *hooet* but, rather than tinkling on as the redstart's, the bluethroat recruits any surrounding or remembered singers and reproduces a chorus of voices. Up to fifty species are mimicked – a diary of where the bird has been and what it has heard. It's a sweet riot, less madly furious than a marsh warbler's snared cacophony of far-fetched song, more sober and chilled. They sing through the day and through the Arctic night. Unlikely – un-musical – source material is added to their playlists: the sounds of snipe and willow grouse and long-tailed skuas have been noted, and also crickets and frogs and train klaxons. I hear it as an anthology of the spring.

On a walk with Claire, to the east of Tromsø where Norway and Sweden and Finland meet, we saw in a wet birch copse three bluethroats, two females and a male. One of the females was washing in a peaty pool at the mossed roots of a tree – a jewelled Diana. All the colours were there: green beneath her and on the leaves, the blue of the sky and her little throat patch, the silvery ash of the birch branches, black crusts of lichen and yellow of fungi, and the red of her red tail. Water droplets ran from her as she shivered and they polished everything. She flew a metre or so and, on landing, flicked her tail and, in the dappled light on the Arctic woodland floor, it seemed like a breath made visible.

As we pitched our tent in the same bright night, Claire talked to me about light and bluethroats. Understand light, she said, as a source of information. Most animals use it as such (all but a few cave-dwellers). A bird's colour, as we see it, might be constructed in three ways: by its feathers' intrinsic colour, by the light that is available to bounce off them, and by our sensory system – that of the receiver sensing the light. Different animals perceive the same spectrum differently. We see light on a fairly narrow portion of the electromagnetic spectrum, whereas many animals, including birds and fish and ants, can also sense ultraviolet light (and the polarisation of light – as we saw dragonflies doing in the desert in Chad when they misidentified our car bonnet as a pool of water).

The bluethroats were living with their UV vision around our tent. The species breeds mostly at high latitudes, and they display before dawn or in the relatively low light of a midsummer night when short-wavelength light predominates. Their throat plumage is highly reflective of UV. To their eyes their blues look even brighter than they do to us. In 1996 and 1997, Arild Johnsen and other Scandinavian researchers experimentally manipulated the throat colours of wild bluethroats in Øvre Heimdalen in Norway (at 61° north), painting some with sun-block cream mixed with preen oil. UV-blocked males had lower mating success, lost more paternity, and gained less extra-pair paternity. Their blue is their life; the bluer the better.

At our campsite glade, a breeding pair of the same birds came close, foraging before flying off deeper into the little wood. I offered them some crumbs of my oatcake, but they were busy with mosquitoes. The mosquitoes were feeding on me. Perhaps my blood fed a bluethroat. The birds were brilliantly present in that little clearing. We are very here, they said, very *living*. They worked their tails as a redstart would, with a slow pump. The male turned its red-spotted blue throat towards me. It was dazzling even without UV vision. Its red was not a single patch but a short chain of red spots, like a necklace, and its bright throat shone like a dish or a receiver of some sort, able to focus a whole world onto its tiny plate of hot metal. It sang and, as it sang, the bright feathers broke apart on its throat and each variously caught the light. I watched it, the light working on the bird and the bird working the light, and I was taken by it, so taken that I wanted never to stop looking.

Claire is half French. Sometimes she tutors me in her mother's tongue as well as about biology. We lay side by side in our sleeping bags, talking and looking out of our tent.

Émail, she said, is the French for enamel – and so I put here as an attachment what we saw and what I wish I might forward to all: the bluethroat's blue throat . . .

At midnight, above the midsummer midnight bluethroats came a midsummer midnight swallow. It flew silently over our tent. It was the last bird I saw before we slept and it was the first bird visible when we woke into the same light of the next day. It had been elsewhere, surely, when we were dreaming, but it was there again up above our heads. It had made it here just as I had. My journey from Good Hope to the North Cape was done and my spring come.

JULY

Swaffham Prior
52°N

1 July. A stalled day, muggy, all traction spent; the year here begins now to coast for a month or more. A meantime. *Now it is autumn*, D. H. Lawrence begins 'The Ship of Death'.

By day: in the garden, I deadheaded roses, picked up the June-drop hard-pebble apples, and thought of threading a daisy chain. The trees wheezed with fledgling birds. One blackcap was making a last stand among the tombstones in the churchyard: the sometime fruit juice of its song thickening to jam. On the pavement near our front door was a flattened toad, pressed dry and leathery, like the sole of a shoe; nearby were the eelskin skids of a dozen squashed slugs. All life was slow-hurrying to death, at slug speed, like a toad walk, or a falling star. A dragonfly caught a mosquito and ate it perched on a bramble. In its windowed wings was the glistening memory of its life that began underwater. The dry stick of the present-day thing was like a fossil. All other insects looked made out of dust. I itched at hoverflies and burnet moths. For an hour around midday I lay on my back in the garden under an exhausted sky, smudged and old, with a wood pigeon's drone close by and with asthma higher up in the short-lived shift of a cloud, some milky tendrils condensing from the air, and then, fast but vague, the bloom thinning back to nothing.

There was carnage on a drive to and from the Devil's Dyke. In the gutter below the rookery at Burwell there were four dead *branchers* – fledgling rooks – that had been hit by cars. They had crumpled in the dirt, like broken umbrellas, only a few metres from their nest trees after perhaps nothing more than a maiden flight. On the main road was a crashed barn owl, perfection brought down: a brown-and-white stew of stubbed-out cigarette and dropped ice-cream cornet. On a hard shoulder, back towards home, a family tragedy: three blackbird corpses, an adult male and two short-tailed brown fledglings, like shoes kicked off to the side of a hallway.

The back of my hand is marked with melanin rosettes like lichen scabs on a stone. I noticed the dark brands today, when holding the steering wheel and avoiding the bodies, and then again when writing down the death toll as I sat in the car outside our house. I am caramelised for my own autumn drive with these spots of time. The French call them *fleurs de cimetières*. There are more this year than last. I count them.

By night: three or four elephant hawkmoths were dazed by the street light in front of our house; they looked besotted as they crawled on the road, like Turkish slippers on the asphalt, a brocade of soft pink, mild green, dusty apricot. I winced as a car passed. *So quick bright things come to confusion.*

I cannot remember when I first registered it, but I have long known that *Tim*, my first name, is held within *time*. I live within it. I often notice this: how my name is meshed with time, woven into it, or nested or budding there. *My time* therefore is underlined by the fact that my name – hence all of me – is contained in it. *My time is Tim.*

Long ago, I also discovered that my monosyllabic surname does some of time's work. It wants to become a preposition. Put at the front of a word, it will mostly undo it, turn it back, or reset its meaning.

If time *is* the fire in which we burn, as Delmore Schwartz said it was, then Tim might be his own kindling or fire stick. On keypads and screens whenever I type *Tim* I am offered *Time*. On my own laptop, which has learned to predict what is most likely to be required, *tim* flowers into *Tim Dee* even if I want *time*.

An anagram of the six letters of my name is Edit Me.

2 July. Swaffham Prior: bike ride with thrip mascara. A roadside sign: *Meat Bingo and Horse Carrots*.

Utne
60°N

For five July days I sat on the shore of Hardangerfjord in western Norway. I had gone north to celebrate a birthday but with half a hope for a bit more spring. It was mostly grey. And though the fjord is salty and a tide of sorts ran to and fro past the beach chair I'd dragged onto the verandah of our wooden cabin, the season was already winding down. Sitting there, served peanuts and wine by my growing sons (it was nearly Lucian's twenty-third birthday), I watched slack water and heard the quiet lisp of the turning year as it began to make its exit.

Plums and cherries were for sale in little makeshift stalls alongside the road at the edge of the fjord. When we were there, the plums were being picked from the orchards that grew up the steep slopes for a hundred metres or so, between the salt water and a band of morose-looking firs. 'Plommer' or 'Moreller', the handwritten signs said, or 'Frukt & Gront', *fruit and greens*. We were just north of 60°, the fabled threshold of harsh and stark latitudes, but here a deciduous season had been enabled between sea-level and mountain top, with soft flesh coaxed from a narrow farmable contour. We bought punnets of fat plums, admiring the glaucous bloom on the deep purple fruit, their pruines-cence, that summery frost that is like the marvellous scurf on a baby's head. The bloom is waxy and stops moisture leaving the fruit and prevents water getting into it. But when I left a plate of the plums out in the soft rain – it was always more or less raining – the lovely pallor dissolved and ran from the fruit and never returned.

Birdwatching was slow. There wasn't much to spot. I glimpsed the sorrel-red tail of a skulking redstart and a female pied flycatcher flew from one birch to another, like a shaving of bark. Both birds – silent now and subdued – seemed hardly there. Almost everything gave off this all-passion-spent summer quiet; the whole place might have fallen asleep.

I sat and watched time pass. The slow flow of the fjord. A squall crossing it, keeping pace with a car ferry. One dozen porpoises that arrived on an imperceptible tide, their short fins tearing the dishcloth surface, before they dived deeper to leave neat circles of stunned water, calm and rimmed like the lily pads on the pond at the shore. Our more energetic holiday-making neighbours going out in a rowing boat to spin for cod but catching nothing. And when the mizzling cloud parted, on the far side of the water, beyond the fishing couple, the ferry, the porpoises and the rain, the sight of the long plunge of a high waterfall over a cliff edge and the stop it put to everything.

A stop, because I could see the water coming apart as it fell. When the gradient steepened and the mountain top became the mountain side, the rushing stream left its rocky bank and bed as a joined and continuous flow, but then, in the stretch of a moment, unhindered by anything but gravity, it lost its watery substance – all that was solid was melting into air – and for 300 metres what was on show was time itself made visible.

I meditated on the fall through my binoculars, drinking it down. Tumbling liquid was passing into countless bulbs or teardrops of light. It was all-moving but all marbled and dreamily slow. Time scattered in its flow. There were stoles and shawls of it; the braiding stream became various nets or fretmarks of mist that slid over themselves, some shifts moving faster than others, some slower. Veils of grey vapour broke away horizontally from the vertical cascade, denying any gravitational draw-down, and slowing even further as they fell, their smoking dissolve drifting out from the cliff. It poured on or kept doing whatever it was doing, and in all the hours that I watched, the fall never looked the same from one moment to the next.

In the winter the falls freeze here. I surprised myself thinking of the relief that such a fixing would bring. I knew then that the year was done for me.

I put aside my binoculars for a day and went up to the melting face of a glacier. It was tremendously dirty and tremendously sad, the most apparently redundant – laid-off – of all the heavy industry I have seen on the Earth. That was the climate crisis talking to us all, but it was also July speaking directly to me, announcing itself as the end of a line and a stop on time.

* * *

318

Back in my chair at the fjord, a few birds tugged me away from the falls. Fledglings were on the wing. Parties of young blue tits and great tits came by. Families of common gulls worked the shore, the adults yapping at one another like cartoon doglets; their youngsters, sandy brown with kohl-rimmed eyes, wheedling behind, reluctant to commit to any grown-up world. Four white wagtails walked the water, crossing the pond, lily-pad by lily-pad, hurrying after flies; I could hear the slight scratch of their feet.

Swallows flew low at the water's edge close to our cabin. They were leaving. You could hear that in their quiet. They said nothing; their wings made the slightest creaks. There was a gathered silence around them, yet they carried in their intense purposefulness (she makes the *casual perfect*, said Robert Lowell of Elizabeth Bishop; a swallow does the same) a ghost of their once-sounding selves. All their twitter was stopped but still latent – this past spring's noise, next spring's noise – in the heavy silence of the afternoon. Because we know their sounds – I knew it this year and have done for fifty previous years – we hear its absence all the more in July's soft pedal. That particular nothing I have always thought to be a sound of autumn.

A family party of willow warblers came around the lily pond; they were fast-moving and feeding hastily but travelled in a cloud of quiet, with just their beaks snipping every now and then. Singing was now in their heads only. They had heard enough of one another, and for now there was nothing further to say.

A spotted flycatcher woke me with the snap of its beak as it took a fly, just a metre from my chair. I've heard their beaks more often in my life than their song, which is thin and slight and often lost in the leaf shuffle and green linctus of late-spring trees. They are dusty-grey and mousey birds. In the summers of my teenage years (when summer still existed for me) a pair nested in the broken wall of the back garden of my home in Bristol; and as I lay in bed late into the day, I used to hear them, through my open window, snapping when all else was quiet. In May, I had heard one sing at Horner Woods on Exmoor, or rather I saw its beak move and convinced myself that some slight song was added to the sound-stream of the wood in full utterance.

Otherwise it was only snaps: the Hardanger bird, and one in the churchyard opposite my house in the Fens in June, and the same sound from a wintering migrant the previous December in the bone-dry Cederberg in South Africa, as it made flycatching sallies from some burnt trees along a river edge. The species returns to breed where it was bred and it shows fidelity also to its wintering places, rhyming the swing-swoops of its flights in Africa with the same in England or Norway, one perch on one continent conjuring a second on another. That tiny snap sound, at the quiet limits of my hearing, at the quiet limits of the world's ear, had also moved from southern Africa to Scandinavia; its curtailed and midget percussion, like one soft click of the fingers, makes the planet beyond it feel – sound and seem – vast to me, and the bird's journey, from one snap to another, equally bewildering. Vast and bewildering, yes, but also minutely real as well: local, actual, and total.

Somewhere between the top of Europe and the bottom of Africa, a spotted flycatcher snaps after a fly every daytime minute. Think of those snaps as heat (as any sound wave ages and moves away from its source it becomes heat), warming the world between the bird's summer and its winter homes, its spring and its autumn flies. Think of its *catch*. A snap, as I have written the word. A *take*. And another, now.

The Way Down

Shake
17°N & 70°N

In the desert in Chad in February, I had spent two weeks sleeping on sand. After the quick end of the day, some couscous, our bird notes and the prayers of our driver and cook, we unrolled camping mattresses and lay on our backs under the night sky. The stars prickled over us. Hours later I woke before the last ones were put out. Often I found my right arm trailing from me, and my sleeping hand buried in the sand. Every morning, my right side felt as if it had slept differently from my left. As if the night had ridden me. My arm shook, in shakes and spasm, clawing awake, scattering fistfuls of desert. I thought perhaps that the ripples of sand beneath our thin bed had pressed upwards into me. I thought perhaps that an earlier failure, the asymmetrical hearing loss that has baffled my right ear, was making me sleep too much on one side. Then I stood up for my first steps of the day and foundered with a limp. All that right of me was out of sorts and I felt *beside myself*.

There were often camels near our camps. I watched the bony origami of their sitting down and standing up and I saw, once, a young boy, their herder, sleeping on the neck of one, a hump for his pillow. Feeling disabled in the desert, I had started looking about for examples of how others unthinkingly managed what I had discovered I could not. We had seen migrant birds flying on north; there was the boy sleeping on a sleeping camel; and there was me not doing anything like either. The world grows away from the sick like this, as they must grow into themselves; I didn't want this to happen to me, but it did.

321

Between my new shakes, I had seen two birds that I had hoped to see in the desert – migrant redstarts and resident blackstarts. Before our time in Chad I had never seen redstarts on their wintering grounds in the Sahel or as they began their northward spring flights across the Sahara. The blackstart is a desert-adapted specialist and was entirely new to me.

The redstart's tail, the colour of brick-tiles, slides and fuzzes – we know that, I've said it often enough, and we know of its defining intrinsic glow. The blackstart's tail shivers like roof slates in a heat haze. We saw both birds in the desert, and I renewed my love for the one I already knew and fell almost equally for the novelty. On waking one morning, I heard a blackstart singing on the other side of the sandstone cul-de-sac where we had camped. It made the stony song of a little thrush that spends its days on rock. I stood up, shaking, and watched it trembling and singing.

I returned to England. I thought my own tremors would pass. They didn't. I sought doctors. And I began to accommodate myself to my new blurred self. Or tried to. We were not in step. Trying to meet my new movements – the tremor, the limp, an imbalance – I brought the thought of moving myself to the front of my head; I felt it come, a new muscled self-consciousness, as I never had had to do before. Still I shook.

Hospitals shifted me from radiology to neurology: from animals with backbones to animals with minds. Ease, meanwhile, kind ease, left me. I felt abandoned by myself: all the unthought going-forward went, the turn and turn about, any sweet ataraxy of gesture and stride. Even as it singled itself out, my body, that right side, my leading edge, had never been less me. My living hand: out there, it was, not here at home.

Within thirty seconds of our handshake the neurologist knew what he was looking at. I walked a line. I held my arms out in front of me. I picked up beads with my left hand and then with my right. I tapped my fingers against my thumb as fast as I could. And I wrote out a poem, of a kind. Dr Sarangmat asked for it: one line five times over in his notebook.

Mary had a little lamb
Mary had a little lamb

Mary had a little lamb
Mary had a little lamb
Mary had a little lamb

I did my best. The day before my appointment I had returned to Britain from northern Norway. I'd seen, as I have said, redstarts there. They tremble in the Arctic at the edge of snowfields as they do in the desert.

On my last day in Norway, still spring-seeking but now short of time – the season's and mine – I went on a nature trail with the daughters of my Tromsø chronobiologist friends. We were looking for nests. Valerie was twelve then and Lilou nine. Valerie was an excellent observer, full of questions and curious about what we saw. Lilou was keen too, especially when it came to holding baby birds, which she did with confident tenderness. I'd seen her hold the family chickens like that.

Valerie asked how some birds mimic other singers and why.

– I want to be a scientist, she said.

She knew pied flycatchers and their songs, and bramblings too. She learned within minutes how to identify tree pipit song and willow warblers and redpolls. She told me that she had watched the beaks of oystercatcher chicks gradually turning red as the young birds grew up on the fjord shore in front of their house. She hoped we would find a cuckoo chick.

– What's the point of flies?

That was Lilou; she knew the words to many scenes in *Monty Python and the Holy Grail* and we laughed about the African and European swallow joke in the film and its taxonomical niceties. She offered to bite my legs off as well.

We were walking on what the girls called Long Mountain. We peeped in on nest boxes: five had chick-guarding adult female pied flycatchers; two had great tits that snaked and hissed at our fingers. At the sea-level start of our walk, the flycatcher chicks were ready to fledge. At the top, they were blind and naked babies still. We talked about time running backwards uphill. Lilou found a downy redwing in the wet grass of a birch wood and cuddled it for a minute.

I told them that the redstart was my favourite bird. They were curious to hear about my children. They were grown-ups now, I said, but when he was about six, Dominic painted a redstart for my birthday and Lucian, about seven, wrote me a redstart limerick. Ever since, I have kept the picture on my mantelpiece in Bristol and the poem in my mind, and I recited it to the girls in the wood. Lucian wrote it like this:

> there once was a man called tim
> who carred his bonoclars with him
> his favrote bird i'm sure you have herd
> was the RedstarT it was a Pashonot thing

A minute later, I found a redstart's nest in a hollow tree and I reached in to bring out a chick to show, but the young bird was ready to fly, and my clumsy grip couldn't stop it escaping the cage of my fingers and it flew up into the birch beyond me. As it landed, its baby tail rose and fell behind it. A redstart.

Two days later I got a name for my condition. After *Mary had a little lamb*, Dr Sarangmat looked directly at me and told me I had Parkinson's disease. His eyes watered slightly as he spoke. The line from the nursery rhyme, a spring song of a kind, that I had known since my childhood but had never written down, was announcing my end and how things will go for me. Micrographia is a Parkinsonian trait. My notebook entries had been getting smaller. I had guessed what the exercise was looking to prove and I tried to keep each line the size of the last. But my data were there to see for Dr Sarangmat.

Everywhere that Mary went the lamb was sure to go. Every so often the world is bound to shake, as Elizabeth Bishop's sandpiper knew. I was the dancer of my dance and we would be partnered forever more.

I cycled home from the hospital to my flat in Bristol. A van was parked on my road. An old blue Transit. Hand-painted on its side in white lettering was: *Simply Shake Simply Be*. I smiled to see it. Maybe it toured the West Country festivals with an offering of some sort: something to drink or a way to get in touch with yourself.

The same evening I told my children of my diagnosis. Both were themselves in their responses – lovably so. I put on a brave face and telephoned Claire to tell her my news. She was in Tanzania in the thick of a field-work season with her honeyguides. The connection was good: I could hear the African night fizz and seethe behind her as she paused after I spoke. When there are difficult things to say she has a stammer that sometimes judders in her mouth. In all the talk of all of our life together – our talk, when she is herself and I am me – she never falters, but when I told her of the meaning of my shakes, a stammer came into her reply. I could hear her crying in Tanzania, and she shook with her words. Her sympathy set me off. We trembled together.

Wake
52°N

I had thought my redstart shake and Claire's redstart stammer would be the place to end a book about the spring – birds and people not stopped by their impediments but set going – but another year turned us around again.

It was midwinter once more, the shortest day, the year's midnight, the beginning of spring, the merry-go-round, the light coming back – whatever we call it, whatever it means . . .

Claire and I were together in the Fens. We woke on the solstice morning. A message had arrived overnight from Steve, the brother of my close friend Greg Poole. Greg had had a heart attack, Steve said, and was not expected to recover. He was in hospital in Bristol. Steve was arriving from his home in Japan.

Greg never regained consciousness, and died on 28 December 2018. Where is he now?

I knew him since we were school-age birdwatchers in Bristol. He kept a soft Bristol accent throughout his life. He was very funny and had a wild laugh all his own. For a time we tried to play saxophone duets, him on alto and me on tenor. He was good and stayed the course, and I wasn't and didn't. He was also a true naturalist. After studying biology at university, he became a painter and print-maker and quickly established himself as one of the most original wildlife artists of our time. He was bold and constantly evolving as an artist. The more he saw – and he was forever seeing more – the more he sought to draw. There were never only birds in his pictures. Nothing looked like an illustration in a field guide, but everything looked like what it was – what it was and how he saw it. He felt the world (ecologically and emotionally) as un-edged and continuous and joined, and he put that in his art. He sat directly on the ground to make his work in the field, his paper put on the surface of the Earth (he carried a kind of mat in his cavernous rucksack for wet days; sometimes he climbed into his rucksack for further protection, sometimes he slept there). Such an earthing was important to him, but from there he painted how everything living was in motion and connected. It is wretched to think of him as stopped. The cover of this book was made by him, although he didn't know that his picture would get me going and see me home. I am grateful to Greg's partner Susan, and to Steve, for letting that be the case.

Greg's pictures hang above the three hearths that were or are fireplaces in the three living rooms where I have written these words: in Bristol I have some oystercatchers piping on a wave-washed rock; in Swaffham Prior in the Fens, a saltmarsh scene from the Norfolk coast with wading birds and fishing boats; and in Scarborough, south of Cape Town, two Prince Ruspoli's turacos in southern Ethiopia flying above two women walking and carrying backpack burdens – swaddled babies, perhaps, or bundles of firewood.

On that midwinter morning in the Fens, Steve's message had said that Greg's heart attack had happened four days before. That same day Claire had discovered that she was pregnant.

Things dying and things new-born, and the meeting of both – they weren't my words when I was a schoolboy actor in *The Winter's Tale*, but they came that morning directly into our bedroom. There they were: two arrivals that became part of our lives at the moment we met them; firsts of their year, death sentences and new lines, throwing time out ahead and behind us, re-framing our existence; and moving on us with love, too, love and grief, flowering at the moment of their discovery and immediately felt or *taken* – as daffodils take the winds of March – for a coming and a going, into and out of this world, for something of its spring and for something of its fall.

I spoke at Greg's funeral. The tremor in my right hand was bad, and I had to hold my page against my chest to stop the paper flapping. At the end of the service, I had to press a black button at the side of the lectern, to send the poor man on his way alone, down and underground first, and then into the oven.

Cycling to Greg's wake from the crematorium in north Bristol, I heard a mistle thrush singing its midwinter song on Coldharbour Road. As sharply as ever, it made its point.

And where is he now? All of my spring journeys seem to have been in search of a fit enough answer to that question. Where does all the time go? And how does life run? What havens, what harbours, might we call on as we journey? How can we love what has gone? And how might the lost return? Who and what goes on ahead and who and what will follow?

Most of my recent field days out with Greg had centred on not seeing things. My last time had been the previous May when we went to listen for nightingales at Highnam Wood in Gloucestershire. When we were teenage birdwatchers, there were nightingales nearer to Bristol at Inglestone Common – we'd seen and heard them together forty years before. They aren't so easy there any longer, and Highnam is now the most reliable local site I know for the birds. Because dogging had become popular in the car-park at the wood, it has been closed, so we stopped further up the main road and walked back to the entrance. Greg drove his camper van: he had made a wooden holster which he had fixed to his dashboard to hold his satnav machine. His having the contemporary technological kit, but customising the rig to live with it, as if in the Iron or Stone Age, said something to me about his character, and we'd joked and talked about that as we began to walk towards the thick green heart of the wood. He had been keen to show me his close-focus mini binoculars too, which he used for watching – and then drawing – butterflies.

After nine in the evening, as the light went and other birds began to fall silent, three or four nightingales started up in a hazel coppice.

We stopped talking as the birds' music began to plumb the night. Two males were close to one another and battled in a flyting performance, each listening to the other and answering back, seeming to up their game in each renewed round of their song. We saw nothing of them, but all the old nightingale sounds were there, all the sounds and all their messages. Every nightingale I hear summons the songs of all the nightingales I have ever heard. Maybe Keats loaned me that thought (he says the same in his 'Ode'). Each song I hear as a performance of a performance – their singing comes out of the dark as some oracular utterance, like the half-heard, half-remembered phrases of some ancient culture, and I feel it shepherding the listener, taking us back, as Lawrence said in his 'Piano' poem, *down the vista of years*. I whispered something about this in the woods at Highnam. Greg was more switched on by the jazz specifics of the singer. His friend Kim Atkinson *paints* bird song, and he spoke a little about how that might be done.

The singing continued and we fell quiet once again. I sat on the ground at the edge of a hazel brake and recorded the song of one bird on my phone. Greg walked a little further on and also crouched to the ride and listened. I wear a hearing aid in my right ear and Greg had both ears wired (an infection, perhaps developed after scuba diving, had flannelled his audio command a decade before), but the singing was loud and it went in as deep as any deep song could, *cante jondo*. It was coloured black in my mind. I've listened back to my recording many times. Just about audible is the sound of Greg bending himself to the grass.

The previous spring we had both cupped our hands behind our failing ears on a similar warm late May evening, when we had gone out to listen for nightjars at Black Down on the Mendips, south of Bristol – again, it was a re-walking of old routes we had taken, both together and alone over the years. The birds were harder to locate than the nightingales were to be, and they were trickier to hear. For two hours we stood in the dark at the edge of a fir plantation on the heath, hoping to receive the nightjars into our disabled heads. There was one, finally. Our aids were hard-pushed to pick up the reeling and the churring of the distant singer. Its dust-speak came and went like the grey sand of the heath blowing on the wind. We got it eventually, but it was only ever at the edge of our hearing.

Earlier in the same year, before the nightjar, two springs before the nightingales, three springs before I am writing, Greg had shown me his favourite butterfly spots in the Mendips at Burrington Combe and Rowberrow and Dolebury Warrens. I knew the place for birds – it was once a grasshopper warbler site, and spring redstarts are still possible there. As a teenager, I lost my bird notebook at Dolebury on the terrace-tumble of the limestone hillside, but then, with great good luck, had it returned to me. Months after it fell from my pocket, a couple out walking their dog found it fallen between some rocks. They fetched it back into the light, saw my address written inside, and posted it to me (they had read my notes, they said, and had known from them that I would be missing my lists). It was too early for warblers or for butterflies when Greg and I clambered up the pale rock to the Iron Age hill fort at the top of Dolebury, but he talked of forthcoming dingy and grizzled skippers, and of the kidney vetch and the life-cycle of small blue butterflies – their caterpillars dormant in the flower-heads of the vetches at our feet where the whole bony hillside was waiting out the winter.

A conical hill south of Bristol towards Bath has a small wood on its peak. The hill is called Kelston Roundhill, the trees Kelston Clump. The trees give the green hill a noticeable green cap in the spring. Greg liked the place, and in 2019, in the early springtime after his death, before the leaves came to the beeches, his family put some of his ashes there. Susan wrote to me later in the spring of how well the pocket-sized meadow was doing that Greg had encouraged behind their house in Bristol. She said:

Greg would have loved this springtime. Trefoil, thyme, clover – all flowering. I am less sad for my own loss than for Greg's loss of this season.

You can see the beeches at Kelston and the green domed hill they crown from many parts of Bristol. I've known the prospect for fifty years but I have never been. I will go next spring and see how it grows.

My grandfather (my father's father – he died not long after I was born) used the same trees for his own purposes. He worked as a clerk in the Fry's chocolate factory at Keynsham between Bristol and Bath. He could see the hilltop from his desk, and my father says his father felt that, when he looked up and saw the trees, they did him *good*. My dad always called, and calls, the clump *my father's trees*. I have never known them as anything else, until now.

I saw them today as I cycled through the city.

Before I walk to the trees in next year's first greenery, I hope to meet our son. He should come, in his own time, in August, at the Cape of Good Hope, in the spring.

20 May 2019
Bristol, Swaffham Prior, Cape Town

13 November 1780

Tortoise goes underground: over him is thrown a coat of moss. The border being very light & mellow, the tortoise has thrown the mould entirely over his shell, leaving only a small breathing hole near his head. Timothy lies in the border under the fruit-wall, in an aspect where he will enjoy the warmth of the sun, & where no wet can annoy him: a hen-coop over his back protects him from dogs, etc.

Gilbert White

BIBLIOGRAPHY & NOTES

Introductory material and 'The Way Up'

And now in age is from George Herbert's 'The Flower' (1633), in *The Complete Poetry*, edited by John Drury (Penguin, London, 2015).

Gilbert White's journal entries on Timothy the tortoise are in *The Journals*, edited by Francesca Greenoak (Century, London, 3 vols, 1986–9). See also *Gilbert White's Year: Passages from 'The Garden Kalendar' and 'The Naturalist's Journal'*, selected by John Commander (Oxford University Press, Oxford, 1982); Sylvia Townsend Warner, *The Portrait of a Tortoise* (Chatto & Windus, London, 1946).

Albert Camus, 'Summer in Algiers' (1954), in *Selected Essays and Notebooks*, edited and translated by Philip Thody (Penguin, London, 1979).

Elizabeth Bishop, 'The Sandpiper', in *Poems* (Chatto & Windus, London, 2011). Bishop's words on her poem are quoted in Colm Tóibín, *On Elizabeth Bishop* (Princeton University Press, Princeton and Woodstock, 2015). See also Mark Ford, 'Elizabeth Bishop's Aviary', *London Review of Books*, 29 November 2007.

W. S. Merwin, 'Shore Birds', in *Selected Poems* (Bloodaxe, Hexham, 2007).

On surfing the green wave see Ellen O. Aikens, Mathew J. Kauffman, Jerod A. Merkle, Samantha P. H. Dwinnell, Gary L. Fralick and Kevin L. Monteith, 'The greenscape shapes surfing of resource waves in a large migratory herbivore', *Ecology Letters* 20: 741–50 (2014); Brett R. Jesmer, Jerod A. Merkle, Jacob R. Goheen, Ellen O. Aikens, Jeffrey L. Beck, Alyson B. Courtemanch, Mark A. Hurley, Douglas E. McWhirter, Hollie M. Miyasaki, Kevin L. Monteith and Matthew J. Kauffman, 'Is ungulate migration culturally transmitted? Evidence of social learning from translocated animals', *Science* 361: 1023–5 (2018).

On the speed of spring see maps of the ten degrees Celsius isotherm in Ian Newton, *Bird Migration* (Collins, London, 2010). See also Robin Robertson's poem 'Primavera', in John Burnside and Maurice Riordan (eds), *Wild Reckoning* (Calouste Gulbenkian Foundation, London, 2004).

James Pearce-Higgins, 'Birds and climate change', *British Birds* 110: 388–404 (2017).

Robert Herrick, 'Corinna's Going a Maying', in *Poet to Poet: Selected Poems*, edited by Stephen Romer (Faber, London, 2010).

John Stow on May Day is quoted in Christopher Logue (ed.), *London in Verse* (Penguin, Harmondsworth, 1984).

Now each holt is from Lavinia Greenlaw, *A Double Sorrow: Troilus and Criseyde* (Faber, London, 2015).

Theodore Roethke, 'The Far Field', in *Collected Poems* (Doubleday Anchor, New York, 1990).

Rainer Maria Rilke's line *O Earth on holiday* is from 'Spring', in *Orpheus: A Version of Rilke's 'Die Sonette an Orpheus'*, translated by Don Paterson (Faber, London, 2006).

Robert Lowell, 'Brunetto Latini', in *Collected Poems*, edited by Frank Bidart and David Gewanter (Faber, London, 2008). The poem was first published in Lowell's collection *Near the Ocean* (1967). His version of Horace, 'Spring', is in the same book. Lowell is the greenest of poets: the word *green* must outnumber any other colour by ten to one in his poems.

George Orwell, 'Some thoughts on the common toad', first published in *Tribune*, 12 April 1946, reprinted in *Narrative Essays* (Harvill Secker, London, 2009).

world's morning is from D. H. Lawrence's letter no. 1,958 from Sicily. Lawrence's letters throughout are quoted from *The Letters of D. H. Lawrence*, edited by James T. Boulton and others (8 vols, Cambridge University Press, Cambridge, 1970–2001).

John Keats, 'Ode to a Nightingale', in *John Keats*, edited by Elizabeth Cook (Oxford University Press, Oxford, 1990).

simple flowers and *flowers growing over* are from letters from Joseph Severn to William Haslam, including one written the day before Keats' death, 22 February 1821; see *Life and Letters of Joseph Severn*, edited by William Sharp (Sampson Low, Marston, London, 1892). Severn said violets were Keats' favourites and that they grew in the graveyard in Rome.

Spitting out blood is from Robert Lowell, 'Picture in the Literary Life, a Scrapbook', in *Collected Poems*, op. cit.

Henry David Thoreau, *The Journal of Henry David Thoreau, 1837–1861*, edited by Damion Searls (New York Review Books, New York, 2009).

José Ortega y Gasset is quoted in W. H. Auden, *A Certain World: A Commonplace Book* (Faber, London, 1971).

Look deep into nature: Albert Einstein's remark is widely quoted – most recently I found it on the label of a sporty woollen T-shirt.

transport of cordiality is from Emily Dickinson's poem which begins 'Several of nature's people', in *The Poems of Emily Dickinson*, edited by Ralph W. Franklin (Belknap Press, Cambridge, Massachusetts, 1998). Dickinson's handwriting was described by Thomas Wentworth Higginson as being like *fossil-bird tracks*.

Nadine Gordimer, *The Conservationist* (Penguin, Harmondsworth, 1983).

W. S. Merwin, 'Threshold', in *Selected Poems*, op. cit.

Shakespeare quotations throughout are from *Complete Works: The RSC Shakespeare*, edited by Jonathan Bate and Eric Rasmussen (Palgrave Macmillan, Basingstoke, 2008).

giant memory of one known longitude is from Robert Lowell, 'For Elizabeth Bishop 2: Castine, Maine', in *Collected Poems*, op. cit. The poem was first published in Lowell's collection *History* (1973).

the buzz of earth is from an untitled poem dated 8 February 1937 in Osip Mandelshtam, *Selected Poems*, translated by James Greene (Penguin, London, 1991). The poem was published posthumously. Mandelstam died aged forty-seven on 27 December 1938 in a transit camp near Vladivostok.

John Buxton, *The Redstart* (Collins, London, 1950).

time is the fire is from Delmore Schwartz, 'Calmly We Walk through This April's Day', in *Selected Poems (1938–1958): Summer Knowledge* (New Directions, New York, 1967).

John Clare, 'The Firetail's Nest', in Simon Armitage and Tim Dee (eds), *The Poetry of Birds* (Penguin, London, 2009).

Birds return is from Robert Lowell, 'Spring', in *Collected Poems*, op. cit. The poem, a version of Horace's *Odes* I.4, was first published in Lowell's collection *Imitations* (1960).

Thick flies is from Robert Burns, 'Song in Autumn', in *Selected Poems and Songs*, edited by Robert P. Irvine (Oxford University Press, Oxford, 2014).

December & January

slant is a word in Emily Dickinson's poem no. 1,263, which begins 'Tell all the truth but tell it slant – / Success in circuit lies', in *The Poems of Emily Dickinson*, op. cit.

Patrick McGuinness, 'Blue Guide, 1, Gare du Nord', in Christopher Ricks (ed.) *Joining Music with Reason* (Waywiser Press, Chipping Norton, 2010).

February

Aimé Césaire, *Return to My Native Land*, translated by John Berger and Anna Bostock (Penguin, Harmondsworth, 1969). Translation slightly amended.

Louis MacNeice, 'All Over Again', in *Collected Poems*, edited by Peter McDonald (Faber, London, 2006).

Rainer Maria Rilke's line *The word is old* is adapted from 'Cycles', in *Orpheus*, op. cit.

The birds of Chad are described and illustrated in Nik Borrow and Ron Demey, *Birds of Western Africa* (Christopher Helm, London, 2001). For present-day life histories of European migrants in the Sahel and south Sahara see Leo Zwarts, Rob G. Bijlsma, Jan van der Kamp and Eddy Wymenga, *Living on the Edge: Wetlands and Birds in a Changing Sahel* (KNNV, Zeist, 2010).

tawny grammar is a phrase coined out of Spanish by Henry David Thoreau in his essay 'Walking': see *The Portable Thoreau*, edited by

Jeffrey S. Cramer (Penguin, New York, 2012); Gary Snyder wrote an essay with this title which has put Thoreau's phrase into the modern world.

Antoine de Saint-Exupéry's orange trees and captive gazelles are in *Wind, Sand and Stars*, translated by William Rees (Penguin, London, 2000). First published in 1939 as *Terre des hommes*.

Tomas Tranströmer, 'Upright', in *The Half-Finished Heaven: the best Poems of Tomas Tranströmer*, translated by Robert Bly (Graywolf, St Paul, Minnesota, 2001).

Charles Darwin, 'An account of the fine dust which often falls on vessels in the Atlantic ocean', *Quarterly Journal of the Geological Society of London* 2: 26–30 (1846). Darwin wrote: 'The little packet of dust collected by myself would not have filled a quarter of a tea-spoon, yet it contains seventeen forms.'

Amato T. Evan, Cyrille Flamant, Marco Gaetani and Françoise Guichard, 'The past, present and future of African dust', *Nature* 531, 493–5 (2016).

D. H. Lawrence, 'The Gazelle Calf ', in *The Complete Poems of D. H. Lawrence*, edited by Vivian de Sola Pinto and Warren F. Roberts (Penguin, London, 1994). All Lawrence's poetry quoted is from this edition.

Dorothy Wordsworth, *The Grasmere and Alfoxden Journals*, edited by Pamela Woof (Oxford University Press, Oxford, 2008).

Samuel Taylor Coleridge, notebook entry, 18 June 1801; all Coleridge's notes quoted here are from *The Notebooks of Samuel Taylor Coleridge* (the Bollingen Series L edition), edited by Kathleen Coburn and others (5 vols, Routledge, London, 1957–2002). The single-volume *Coleridge's Notebooks: A Selection*, edited by Seamus Perry (Oxford University Press, Oxford, 2002), is portable and well annotated.

When I was a boy is from Peter Reading, C (Secker & Warburg, London, 1984). *Again the Homeric dream* is from Peter Reading, *Faunal* (Bloodaxe, Hexham, 2002).

Michael Longley, 'The Bed of Leaves', in *The Ghost Orchid* (Cape, London, 1995).

The rock paintings of the Ennedi massif are described and illustrated in Roberta Simonis, Adrian Ravenna and Pier Paolo Rossi, *Ennedi: pierres historiées*, translated by Jean-Loïc Le Quellec (Edizioni all'Insegna del Giglio in Firenze, Sesto Fiorentino, 2017).

Little trotty wagtail is in *John Clare*, edited by Eric Robinson and David Powell (Oxford University Press, Oxford, 1984).

Ronald Johnson, *The Book of the Green Man* (Longmans, Green, London, 1967). Re-published by Uniformbooks (Axminster, 2015), this is a remarkable and too little-known collection of poetry and highly recommended.

What I do is me: for that I came is from Gerard Manley Hopkins, 'As Kingfishers Catch Fire', in *The Major Works*, edited by Catherine Phillips (Oxford University Press, Oxford, 2009).

If I am pressed to say is quoted and discussed in Sarah Bakewell, *How to Live, or a Life of Montaigne in One Question and Twenty Attempts at an Answer* (Chatto & Windus, London, 2010).

March

Edward Thomas, 'Thaw', in *Collected Poems* (Faber, London, 2004).

Barrie E. Juniper and David J. Mabberley, *The Story of the Apple* (Timber Press, Portland, Oregon, 2006).

The Roman story of the golden bough (Aeneas instructed to carry the ever-growing branch as a token for admission to the underworld and an audience with Proserpina) was told most famously in Virgil's *Aeneid*, but also appeared in several other versions in the ancient Mediterranean world. Among the translations of Virgil's passage are C. H. Sisson's in *Collected Translations* (Carcanet, Manchester, 1996) and Seamus Heaney's in *Aeneid, Book VI* (Faber, London, 2016). See also J. M. W. Turner's golden-shimmer painting *Lake Avernus – The Fates and the Golden Bough* in the Tate collection. 'Avernus' means birdless – this imagined entrance to the underworld was a toxic lake which poisoned anything flying over. Lake Avernus is north of Naples. South of Rome, in 2010, an ancient stone-walled enclosure was found that perhaps fenced and protected a huge cypress or oak tree; here, it was speculated, grew the tree that grew the golden bough.

Eudora Welty, 'Music from Spain', in *Stories, Essays and Memoir*, edited by Richard Ford and Michael Kreyling (Library of America, New York, 1998).

Samuel Taylor Coleridge, 'Aria Spontanea', in *Selected Poems*, edited by Richard Holmes (HarperCollins, London, 1996). All Coleridge poems quoted are from this edition. Richard pointed me in the direction of this poem.

On bog bodies see P. V. Glob, *The Bog People: Iron-Age Man Preserved*, translated by Rupert Bruce-Mitford (Paladin, London, 1971), first published in Danish in 1965; Julia Blackburn, *Time Song – Searching for Doggerland* (Jonathan Cape, London, 2019); Christian Fischer, *Tollund Man: Gift to the Gods* (History Press, Stroud, 2012); Steven Mithen, *After the Ice: A Global Human History, 20,000–5000 BC* (Harvard University Press, Cambridge, Massachusetts, 2006); Karin Sanders, *Bodies in the Bog and the Archaeological Imagination* (University of Chicago Press, Chicago and London, 2012); Pauline Asingh, *Grauballe Man: Portrait of a Bog Body* (Moesgård Museum, Aarhus / Gyldendal, Copenhagen, 2009); and several Seamus Heaney poems, mostly in his collections *Wintering Out* (Faber, London, 1972) and *North* (Faber, London, 1975).

On the birds of Ethiopia see John Ash and John Atkins, *Birds of Ethiopia and Eritrea: An Atlas of Distribution* (Christopher Helm, London, 2009); Nigel Redman, John Fanshawe and Terry Stevenson, *Birds of the Horn of Africa: Ethiopia, Eritrea, Djibouti, Somalia, Socotra* (Christopher Helm, London, 2011); and Claire Spottiswoode, Merid Nega Gabremichael and Julian Francis, *Where to Watch Birds in Ethiopia* (Christopher Helm, London, 2010).

R. E. Moreau, *The Palaearctic–African Bird Migration Systems* (Academic Press, London, 1972). Reg Moreau died in May 1970 before his book was published. He wrote at the end of his preface: 'For reasons of health I should be surprised if I set eyes on reviews of this book. How delighted I should be if someone somewhere thought it "no bum swan-song".'

Eschew luggage is from Peter Reading, 'Apophthegmatic', in *Untitled* (Bloodaxe, Hexham, 2001).

Marcus Tullius Cicero's remark, of the philosopher Bias of Priene, one of the Seven Sages, is in *Paradoxa Stoicorum* I.8.

Teevo cheevo cheevio chee is Gerard Manley Hopkins' transcription of a woodlark's song, in his unfinished poem 'The Woodlark', in *The Major Works*, op. cit.

I have seen Africa is from Coleridge's notebook entry for 19 April 1804. See also Alethea Hayter, *A Voyage in Vain: Coleridge's Journey to Malta in 1804* (Robin Clark, London, 1993); Richard Holmes, *Coleridge: Early Visions* (Hodder & Stoughton, London, 1989); Richard Holmes *Coleridge: Darker Reflections* (HarperCollins, London, 1998).

no there there is from Gertrude Stein, *Everybody's Autobiography* (Random House, New York, 1937).

On the avifauna of Gibraltar see Clive Finlayson, *Birds of the Strait of Gibraltar* (T. & A. D. Poyser, Calton, 1992). Gilbert White wrote of Gibraltar and of migration in *The Natural History of Selborne* (Penguin, Harmondsworth, 1977), first published in 1789. He was never there but his brother was: see Paul Foster, 'The Gibraltar collections: Gilbert White (1720–1793) and John White (1727–1780), and the naturalist and author Giovanni Antonio Scopoli (1723–1788)', *Archives of Natural History* 34: 30–46 (2007).

Ana T. Marques, Carlos D. Santos, Frank Hanssen, Antonio-Román Muñoz, Alejandro Onrubia, Martin Wikelski, Francisco Moreira, Jorge Manuel Palmeirim and João P. Silva, 'Wind turbines cause functional habitat loss for migratory soaring birds', *Journal of Animal Ecology* doi.org/10.1111/1365-2656.12961 (2019).

April

roundy head is quoted in Tom Paulin, *Crusoe's Secret: The Aesthetics of Dissent* (Faber, London, 2005).

Steven Feld, *Sound and Sentiment: Birds, Weeping, Poetics, and Song in Kaluli Expression* (University of Pennsylvania Press, Philadelphia, 1982).

Seamus Heaney, 'The Blackbird of Glanmore', in *District and Circle* (Faber, London, 2006).

Adam Zagajewski, 'Houston, 6 p.m.', in *Mysticism for Beginners*, translated by Clare Cavanagh (Farrar, Straus & Giroux, New York, 1998).

Bertolt Brecht, 'When in My White Room at the Charité', in *Poems 1913–1956*, translated by John Willett and Ralph Manheim (3 vols, Eyre Methuen, London, 1976).

the navel is from Seamus Heaney, 'Mossbawn, Omphalos', in *Finders Keepers: Selected Prose 1971–2001* (Faber, London, 2002).

Seamus Heaney, 'A Herbal', in *Human Chain* (Faber, London, 2010).

Charles Darwin, *On the Origin of Species*, edited by Gillian Beer (Oxford University Press, Oxford, 2008).

Marjorie C. Sorensen, Graham D. Fairhurst, Susanne Jenni-Eiermann, Jason Newton, Elizabeth Yohannes and Claire N. Spottiswoode, 'Seasonal rainfall at long term migratory staging sites is associated with altered carry-over effects in a palaearctic–African migratory bird', *BMC Ecology* 16: 41 (2016). See also Marjorie C. Sorensen, 'Singing in Africa: no evidence for a long supposed function of winter song in a migratory songbird', *Behavioral Ecology* 25: 909–15 (2014).

On willow warblers in Sweden and much else migratory see Ian Newton, *Bird Migration*, op. cit. This book and also Ian Newton's *The Migration Ecology of Birds* (Academic Press, London, Burlington, Massachusetts, and San Diego, California, 2008) are highly recommended.

Seamus Heaney, 'The Gravel Walks', in *The Spirit Level* (Faber, London, 1996).

walking on air is from Dennis O'Driscoll, *Stepping Stones: Interviews with Seamus Heaney* (Faber, London, 2009).

Seamus Heaney, 'The Underground', in *Station Island* (Faber, London, 1984).

Seamus Heaney, 'What Passed at Colonus', *New York Review of Books*, 7 October 2004.

Seamus Heaney, 'Digging', in *Death of a Naturalist* (Faber, London, 1966).

Seamus Heaney, 'In Time', in *New Selected Poems 1988–2013* (Faber, London, 2015).

Leonard Blomefield (formerly Jenyns), *A Naturalist's Calendar Kept at Swaffham Bulbeck, Cambridgeshire* (Cambridge University Press, Cambridge, 1903).

Vaslav Nijinsky is quoted in Jerry Mason (ed.), *The Family of Children* (Jonathan Cape, London, 1977).

On *The Winter's Tale* see Wilbur Sanders, *The Winter's Tale: Critical Introduction to Shakespeare* (Harvester Wheatsheaf, Hassocks, 1987); Jonathan Bate, *Shakespeare and Ovid* (Clarendon Press, Oxford, 2001); Patricia Storace, 'The "darkness and radiance" of the tale', *New York Review of Books*, 12 May 2016.

Richard Mabey, *Flora Britannica* (Sinclair-Stevenson, London, 1996).

D. H. Lawrence, *Sea and Sardinia*, edited by Mara Kalnins (Penguin, London, 1999).

Mary Taylor Simeti, *On Persephone's Island: A Sicilian Journal* (Vintage, New York, 1995).

Matthew Arnold, 'Empedocles on Etna', in *Selected Poems and Prose*, edited by Miriam Allott (Everyman, London, 1993).

Ian Hamilton, *A Gift Imprisoned: The Poetic Life of Matthew Arnold* (Bloomsbury, London, 1998).

John Milton, *Paradise Lost*, in *The Major Works*, edited by Stephen Orgel and Jonathan Goldberg (Oxford University Press, Oxford, 2003).

Ovid, *Metamorphoses*, translated by Arthur Golding and edited by Madeleine Forey (Penguin, London, 2002). This translation was first published in 1567.

D. H. Lawrence, *Lady Chatterley's Lover*, edited by Michael Squires (Penguin, London, 1994).

Robert Frost, 'A Servant to Servants', in *Collected Poems, Prose and Plays*, edited by Richard Poirier and Mark Richardson (Library of America, New York, 1995).

Ere your spring be gone … you grow old … those who cannot use the present is from Ben Jonson, *The Alchemist*, in *The Alchemist and Other Plays*, edited by Gordon Campbell (Oxford University Press, Oxford, 2008).

the brief span of life is from Robert Lowell, 'Spring', in *Collected Poems*, op. cit.

J. W. Goethe, *Italian Journey 1786–88*, translated by W. H. Auden and Elizabeth Mayer (Penguin, Harmondsworth, 1970).

Ted Hughes, 'The Rape of Proserpina', in *Tales from Ovid* (Faber, London, 1997).

Heinrich Gätke, *Heligoland as an Ornithological Observatory: The Result of Fifty Years' Experience*, translated by Rudolph Rosenstock (David Douglas, Edinburgh, 1895).

William Eagle Clarke, *Studies in Bird Migration*, (2 vols, Gurney & Jackson, London, 1912).

R. M. Lockley, *I Know an Island* (Harrap, London, 1938).

Otto Herman's list is quoted in Michael Walters, *A Concise History of Ornithology: The Lives and Works of Its Founding Figures* (Christopher Helm, London, 2003).

Carlo Rovelli, *Seven Brief Lessons on Physics*, translated by Simon Carnell and Erica Segre (Penguin, London, 2016). First published in Italian in 2014.

Stefan Garthe, Verena Peschko, Ulrike Kubetzki and Anna-Marie Corman, 'Seabirds as samplers of the marine environment: a case study of northern gannets', *Ocean Science* 13: 337–47 (2017).

Sebastian Conradt, 'Der Basstölpel – Seevogel des Jahres 2016: Der Fluch des billigen Plastiks', *Seevögel* 37(2): 4–13 (2016).

Coleridge's 1798 North Sea crossing is recorded in his notebook and in a more worked-up form in *Biographia Literaria*, (2 vols, J. M. Dent, London, 1956).

May

William Empson, 'Fairy Flight in *A Midsummer Night's Dream*', in *Essays on Shakespeare*, edited by David B. Pirie (Cambridge University Press, Cambridge, 1986). First published in 1979.

John Clare, 'The Fern Owl's Nest', in *John Clare*, op. cit.

Alfred Newton, *A Dictionary of Birds* (Adam & Charles Black, London, 1896).

Elizabeth Bletsoe, 'Birds of the Sherborne Missal', in *Landscape from a Dream* (Shearsman, Bristol, 2008).

For woodcock facts see William Yarrell, *A History of British Birds*, 4th edition, revised by Alfred Newton and Howard Saunders (John Van Voorst, London, 1871–74); J. H. Gurney, *Early Annals of Ornithology* (H. F. & G. Witherby, London, 1921); Stanley Cramp (ed.), *Handbook of the Birds of Europe, the Middle East, and North Africa: The Birds of the Western Palaearctic, vol. 3 – Waders to Gulls* (Oxford University Press, Oxford, 1983); Kenneth Richmond, *Birds in Britain* (Odhams Press, London, 1962); William Wordsworth, *The Prelude* (1805), edited by Ernest de Selincourt and revised by Stephen Gill (Oxford University Press, Oxford, 1978); Leo Tolstoy, *Anna Karenina*, translated by Rosamund Bartlett (Oxford University Press, Oxford, 2016); W. B. Alexander, 'The woodcock in the British Isles', *Ibis*, 87: 512–50 (1945); David Lack, *The Birds of Cambridgeshire* (Cambridgeshire Bird Club, Cambridge, 1934); Gilbert White, *The Natural History of Selborne*, op. cit.

On green see Michel Pastoureau, *Green: The History of a Color*, translated by Jody Gladding (Princeton University Press, Princeton, 2014); Simon Schama, 'Blue as can be', *New Yorker*, 3 September 2018.

that greeny flower is from William Carlos Williams, 'Asphodel, That Greeny Flower', in *Collected Poems, vol. 2: 1939–1962*, edited by Christopher MacGowan (New Directions, New York, 1991).

how many colors is quoted in Sam Stephenson, *Gene Smith's Sink: A Wide-Angle View* (Farrar, Straus & Giroux, New York, 2017).

Gertrude Stein, 'Celery', in *Tender Buttons* (Claire Marie, New York, 1914).

Rainer Maria Rilke, *Letters to a Young Poet*, translated by Charlie Louth (Penguin, London, 2014).

Thomas De Quincey, *Recollections of the Lakes and the Lake Poets*, edited by David Wright (Penguin, Harmondsworth, 1971).

Don DeLillo, *The Body Artist* (Scribner, New York, 2002).

pihuqahtaq is from Frédéric Laugrand and Jarich Oosten, *Hunters, Predators and Prey: Inuit Perceptions of Animals* (Berghahn, New York, 2015).

The heavy bear and *Time is the fire* are from Delmore Schwartz, 'The Heavy Bear Who Goes with Me' and 'Calmly We Walk through This April Day' respectively, in *Selected Poems (1938–1958)*, op. cit.

T. J. Clark, *The Sight of Death: An Experiment in Art Writing* (Yale University Press, New Haven, Connecticut, and London, 2006).

mountains are constantly walking is from Gary Snyder, *Practice of the Wild* (Farrar, Straus & Giroux, New York, 1990).

D. H. Lawrence, 'Sketches from Etruscan Places', in *D. H. Lawrence and Italy*, edited by Simonetta de Filippis, Paul Eggert and Mara Kalnins (Penguin, London, 2008).

He would sit, almost motionless is quoted in John Worthen, *D. H. Lawrence: The Life of an Outsider* (Penguin, London, 2006). In addition to this one-volume life, the three-volume *Cambridge Biography of D. H. Lawrence* by David Ellis, John Worthen and Mark Kinkead-Weekes (Cambridge University Press, Cambridge, 2014) is highly recommended; David Ellis, *Death and the Author: How D. H. Lawrence Died, and Was Remembered* (Oxford University Press, Oxford, 2008) is also excellent.

I can't recall that he ever broke a plate or a glass is quoted in *D. H. Lawrence: A Critical Anthology*, edited by Harry Coombes (Penguin, Harmondsworth, 1973).

John Keats, 'Ode on a Grecian Urn', in *John Keats*, op. cit.

All those that ever went for a walk with him is quoted in *D. H. Lawrence: A Critical Anthology*, op. cit.

M. M. Mahood, *The Poet as Botanist* (Cambridge University Press, Cambridge, 2015).

D. J. Enright is quoted in *D. H. Lawrence: A Critical Anthology*, op. cit.

different animal – in an essay about his childhood class Lawrence described himself as a 'different animal' from the middle-class boys at Nottingham High School – see Mark Crees, 'Another animal', *Times Literary Supplement*, 18 March 2005.

glistening chaos is from Richard Holmes, *Coleridge* (Oxford University Press, Oxford, 1990).

no passive tools is from Samuel Taylor Coleridge, *Biographia Literaria*, op. cit.

William Hazlitt is quoted in the introduction to Nicholas Roe (ed.) *English Romantic Writers and the West Country* (Palgrave Macmillan, Basingstoke, 2010).

On Wordsworth's colour-blindness see Geoffrey Madan, *Notebooks: A Selection*, edited by J. A. Gere and John Sparrow (Oxford University Press, Oxford, 1984).

On Coleridge's notes as *fly-catchers* see Walter Jackson Bate, *Coleridge* (Weidenfeld & Nicolson, London, 1969).

Natura is that which is about to be born is from Samuel Taylor Coleridge, *Aids to Reflection* (George Bell, London, 1884). Adam Nicolson lent me this observation.

see to see is from Emily Dickinson, 'I Heard a Fly Buzz – When I Died', in *The Poems of Emily Dickinson*, op. cit.

Elizabeth Bishop, *One Art: Letters*, edited by Robert Giroux (Farrar, Straus & Giroux, New York, 1995); on Bishop's Darwin letter see Zachariah Pickard, 'Natural history and epiphany: Elizabeth Bishop's Darwin letter', *Twentieth-Century Literature* 50(3): 268–82 (2004).

What you look hard at is from Gerard Manley Hopkins' journal; quotations are from Gerard Manley Hopkins, *Collected Works, vol. 3: Diaries, Journals and Notebooks*, edited by Lesley Higgins (Oxford University Press, Oxford, 2015) or *The Note-Books and Papers of Gerard Manley Hopkins*, edited by Humphry House (Oxford University Press, London, 1937).

R. F. Langley, *Journals* (Shearsman, Bristol, 2006).

Humphry House, *Coleridge: The Clark Lectures 1951–52* (Rupert Hart-Davis, London, 1953).

Gilbert White as a *stationary man* is mentioned in Don Gifford, *The Farther Shore: A Natural History of Perception 1798–1985* (Faber, London, 1990).

Samuel Taylor Coleridge: Selected Letters, edited by H. J. Jackson (Oxford University Press, Oxford, 1988).

beasts of burden is from Henry David Thoreau, *Walden*, in *The Portable Thoreau*, op. cit.

Verde que ti quiero verde is from Federico García Lorca, 'Romance Sonambulo', in *Selected Poems*, edited by Christopher Maurer (Penguin, London, 2001).

Philip Larkin, 'The Trees', in *Collected Poems*, edited by Anthony Thwaite (Faber, London, 2003).

Dorothy Wordsworth, *The Grasmere and Alfoxden Journals*, op. cit.

On recent population trends in pied flycatchers and wood warblers see 'Seeing the wood warblers for the trees', *British Birds* 110: 302–3 (2017).

cloudage is Coleridge's coinage in a notebook entry for 2 November 1803.

Ken Smith wrote about several journeys that we took together to the old and persisting borderlands of Hungary, Slovakia, Romania and Ukraine: see especially his *Wire through the Heart* (Ister, Budapest, 2000) and some poems in *Shed: Poems 1980–2001* (Bloodaxe, Hexham, 2002).

June

petrified curlew: see R. Rainbird Clarke, *In Breckland Wilds* (W. Heffer, Cambridge, 1937).

We are in Harar is from Arthur Rimbaud, *Selected Poems and Letters*, translated by Jeremy Harding and John Sturrock (Penguin, London, 2004); see also Graham Robb, *Rimbaud* (Picador, London, 2000).

Has the sailor gone? is quoted in V. S. Pritchett, *Chekhov: A Biography* (Penguin, London, 1990); see also Anton Chekhov, *A Life in Letters*, edited by Rosamund Bartlett and translated by Rosamund Bartlett and Anthony Phillips (Penguin, London, 2004).

Now comes good sailing: see David Markson, *The Last Novel* (Shoemaker & Hoard, Emeryville, California, 2007).

Illness has swallowed him is from *The Journal of Katherine Mansfield*, edited by John Middleton Murry (Albatross, Hamburg, 1933).

Quick, alive, vital is from David Ellis, *D. H. Lawrence: Dying Game 1922–1930* (Cambridge University Press, Cambridge, 1997).

D. H. Lawrence, 'A Propos of *Lady Chatterley's Lover*', in *A Selection from 'Phoenix'*, edited by A. A. H. Inglis (Penguin, Harmondsworth, 1979). First published 1930.

Walter Benjamin, 'Franz Kafka: on the Tenth Anniversary of His Death', in *Illuminations*, translated by Harry Zohn and edited by Hannah Arendt (Schocken, New York, 2007).

Felix Riede's webpages at Aarhus University list his many papers and book contributions; see especially 'Success and Failure during the Lateglacial Pioneer Human Re-colonisation of Southern Scandinavia', in Felix Riede and Miikka Tallavaara (eds), *Lateglacial and Postglacial Pioneers in Northern Europe* (Archaeopress, Oxford, 2014); and 'The Resettlement of Northern Europe', in Vicki Cummings, Peter Jordan and Marek Zvelebil (eds), *Oxford Handbook of the Archaeology and Anthropology of Hunter-Gatherers* (Oxford University Press, Oxford, 2014).

W. H. Auden, 'The Fall of Rome', in *Collected Poems*, edited by Edward Mendelson (Faber, London, 2007). See also Jill Cook, *The Swimming Reindeer* (British Museum Press, London, 2010); Jill Cook, *Ice Age Art: Arrival of the Modern Mind* (British Museum Press, London, 2013).

Nick (Nicholas) Tyler's webpages at the Arctic University of Norway list his many papers and other reindeer publications; see especially David G. Hazlerigg and Nicholas Tyler, 'Activity patterns in mammals: circadian dominance challenged', *PLoS Biology* 17(7): e3000360 (2019); and Nicholas Tyler, Karl-Arne Stokkan, Chris Hogg, Christian Nellemann and Arnt Inge Vistnes, 'Cryptic impact: visual detection of corona light and avoidance of power lines by reindeer', *Wildlife Society Bulletin* 40: 50–58 (2016).

Lavinia Greenlaw, 'Actaeon', *London Review of Books*, 25 August 2011.

Karl-Arne Stokkan, Lars Folkow, Juliet Dukes, Magella Neveu, Chris Hogg, Sandra Siefken, Steven C. Dakin and Glen Jeffrey, 'Shifting mirrors: adaptive changes in retinal reflections to winter darkness in Arctic reindeer', *Proceedings of the Royal Society of London B* 280: 20132451 (2013).

These are the days that Reindeer love is from *The Poems of Emily Dickinson*, op. cit.

The Gundestrup cauldron is described and pictured in Poul Otto Nielsen, *Danish Prehistory* (Nationalmuseet, Copenhagen, 2016).

Robert Graves, *The White Goddess: A Historical Grammar of Poetic Myth* (Faber, London, 1961).

Wallace Stevens, 'The Plain Sense of Things', in *Collected Poems* (Faber, London, 2006).

Franz Kafka, 'Josefine, the Songstress or: The Mouse people', in *Metamorphosis and Other Stories*, translated by Michael Hofmann (Penguin, London, 2008).

Tomas Tranströmer, 'Below Freezing', in *The Half-Finished Heaven: the Best Poems of Tomas Tranströmer*, op. cit.

Anders Pape Møller has published more on the barn swallow than probably all other swallow scientists put together. His *Sexual Selection and the Barn Swallow* (Oxford University Press, Oxford) appeared in 1994, and since then he has continued to publish on the bird as a result of his studies in Jutland and in Chernobyl. Many papers can be accessed online. See for example 'The effect of dairy farming on barn swallow *Hirundo rustica* abundance, distribution and production', Journal of Applied Ecology 38: 378–89 (2001); A. P. Møller, A. Barbosa, J. J. Cuervo, F. de Lope, S. Merino and N. Saino, 'Sexual selection and tail streamers in the barn swallow', *Proceedings of the Royal Society of London B* 265(1394): 409–14 (1998). I wrote on Anders at Chernobyl in *Four Fields* (Jonathan Cape, London, 2013). See also Angela Turner, *The Barn Swallow* (T. & A. D. Poyser, London, 2006).

the starnel crowds is from 'Autumn Evening', in *John Clare*, op. cit.

I saw this dance one summer evening is quoted in Nigel Allenby Jaffé, *Folk Dance of Europe* (Folk Dance Enterprises, Kirby Malham, 1990).

Gabi (Gabriela) Wagner's chronobiology papers (and David Hazlerigg's) are listed on the website of the Arctic University of Norway.

David Abram, 'Creaturely Migrations on a Breathing Planet', *Emergence* 1, available at emergencemagacine.org.

Elisa Magnanelli, Øivind Wilhelmsen, Mario Acquarone, Lars P. Folkow and Signe Kjelstrup, 'The nasal geometry of the reindeer gives energy-efficient respiration', *Journal of Non-Equilibrium Thermodynamics* 42: 59–78 (2017).

Leo Tolstoy, 'Strider', in *'Master and Man' and Other Stories*, translated by Ronald Wilks and Paul Foote (Penguin, London, 2005).

Arild Johnsen, Staffan Andersson, Jonas Örnborg and Jan T. Lifjeld, 'Ultraviolet plumage ornamentation affects social mate choice and sperm competition in bluethroats: a field experiment', *Proceedings of the Royal Society of London B* 265(1403): 1313–18 (1998).

July

So quick bright things come to confusion is said by Lysander in *A Midsummer Night's Dream*.

casual perfect is from Robert Lowell, 'For Elizabeth Bishop', in *Collected Poems*, op. cit.

ACKNOWLEDGEMENTS

More than fifty years of season-watching have gone into this book, and my biggest thanks must be for the spring itself as I have known it in every one of those years in Europe and, more occasionally and more recently, in Africa. More and more, I think it a kind of *world-luck* to live in parts of the planet that are seasonally driven: every time the spring comes around it seems like a boon. That we leave our own springtime behind as we grow up and get old, and that we are now, as a species, screwing over the life-making timekeeping of the Earth, means it isn't all holiday smiles, but I still love the coming of the green, and feel I must thank the sun and our off-kilter planet for what they have given and for what they still give.

Three places accommodated me in the writing of this book during all my journeys. In the last house but one, before the southern tip of the Cape Peninsula in South Africa, I both started and finished. When I started (in a Cape summer) there were barn swallows from Europe outside our house; when I finished (in a Cape winter) there was a sleepy wild tortoise in our garden. Claire will not allow me to call it Timothy (there are more than one anyway), but I am lucky to have had such a place and such animal company, as well as the counterseasons to live in and to live against.

In the sleepy tortoise time in the Cape midwinter, we have used the old nests of Karoo prinias from our garden to kindle our wood stove into life in the fireplace below Greg Poole's Ethiopian picture. In the springs in our cottage in Swaffham Prior in the Cambridgeshire fens, I have collected, as Gilbert White said his poor parishioners did, would-be nest twigs dropped by rooks or jackdaws, either in our garden or down the chimney into our fireplace. I made a bonfire once and cooked

351

sausages on the embers of the sticks. The jackdaws in our village tell the time as well as the church clock. The recent English springs I have known occurred there more than anywhere else.

My fireplace in my flat in Bristol is blocked, and the room there is crowded with several thousand books and two dozen stuffed birds and too many pebbles and shells and fulgurites and sea-washed glass and driftwood wreaths and dropped feathers and birds' bleached skulls and all the other wreck or crapola that I pick up, and cannot stop adding to my baggage. The whole flat is, in effect, the continuation of the nature table I started keeping when I was a boy. Some call it my bat cave. Yet without that stuff and those books there would be nothing to read here.

There again, this book has more people in it than any other I have written. It is made of others' presences and words as much as my own. Everyone who appears in its pages has been kind to me, giving me their time, their art, their understanding. Some knew when we spoke that they were being recruited; others might be surprised – all were beyond generous. Deep thanks to Mark Cocker (and to Mary Muir), David Hazlerigg, Gabi Wagner (and children Tom, Lilou and Valerie), Anders Pape Møller, William Carøe Aarestrup (and Agnes), Felix Riede, Ole Nielsen, Julia Blackburn, Nick Tyler, Karen Anette Anti, Patrick McGuinness, Barrie Juniper (and Jonathan Davidson), Keith Bensusan (and Ian, Steve and Yvonne), Jesus of El Cabrito, Pier Paolo Rossi (and Hugo, Issa and Johnny, drivers and desert cooks), Rian (and Lorna) Labuschagne (and Gus and Margie Mills), Anna Giordano, Mark Johnston, Tessa Hadley, the late Peter Reading, Michael Longley, the late Ken Smith (and Judi Benson) and Miklós Zelei, the late Greg Poole (and Steve Poole and Susan Morgan), Robin Robertson, Luci Gorell Barnes, Ferenc Márkus, József Kárpáti (and Judit Fehér), Márta in Budapest and Louise Henson, Tom Nichols, Adam Zagajewski, Gabriel Jamie, Richard Pearce, Jane Darke, Ranko Milanovic in the Serbian bear hide, Gyula in the Romanian bear hide and my friendly Egyptian taxi-driver in Bristol. I thank also all the authors of the ornithological books and the scientific research that have given my flights of fancy some truthful underpinning.

In addition to those mentioned or quoted above, many friends and other acquaintances have, over many years, shown me what the spring means to them. Their book of the season wouldn't be this one, but this one couldn't have been written without my knowing them and their take on the times. Especial thanks are due to some long- and still-standing heroes, all one way or another companion botanisers on both asphalt and wild-stone pavements: Hugh Brody, Susannah Clapp, Paul Farley, Jeremy Harding and Beth Holgate, Alexandra Harris, Fraser and Sally Harrison, Richard Holmes, Kathleen Jamie, Richard Mabey and Polly Munro, Adam Nicolson and Sarah Raven, and Christopher Ricks and Judith Aronson.

I have stolen less from the following friends and others but thank them as much: Richard Alwyn, Sandra Anderson, John Andrews, Simon Armitage, Ken Arnold, Paul Bailey, Jeff Barrett, Barbara Bender and John Torrance, Ronan Bennett, the late John Berger, Simon Blackwell, Julie and Tim Blake, Sean Borodale, Sue Brookes, Jon Buck, Will Burns, John Burnside, Antonia Byatt and Sam Collyns, Nancy Campbell, Lesley Chamberlain, Nigel Collar, Adrian and Gracie Cooper, Holly Corfield Carr, Callan Cohen, Rob Cowen, Susie Cunningham, Nick and Jan Davies, Vanessa Daws, Mike Dibb, Paul Dodgson, Steve Ely, Sinead English, John Fanshawe, Joe Farrell, Steven Feld, Rose Ferraby, Peter Fiennes, Will Fiennes, Gavin Francis, Lavinia Greenlaw, Jay Griffiths, Sam Guglani, Eric Hadley, the late Ian Hamilton, Tom Hammick, Robert Hanks, James Hanlon, Diva Harris, the late Christopher Hitchens, Michael Hofmann, Matthew Hollis, Jonathan Holloway, Matt Howard, Martin Jenkins, Suzy Joinson, Vicky Jones, Paul Keegan, Andy Kershaw, Zaffar Kunial, Angela Leighton, James Lasdun, Alastair Laurence, Peter Lawrence, Richard Long, Hayden Lorimer, Jay and Guy Louw, the late Derek Lucas, Gerard McBurney, Simon McBurney, Michael McCarthy, Helen Macdonald, Robert Macfarance, Jamie McKendrick, Bill McKibben, Pippa Marland, Glyn Maxwell, Steve Mentz, Catherine Merridale, Dominic Mitchell, Mary Morris and Arvon, Andrew Motion, Rachel Murray, Daljit Nagra, Mary Nichols and the late Geoff Nichols, Redmond O'Hanlon, Alice Oswald, Ben Parker, Chris and Helen Parker, Ian Parker, Don Paterson,

David Perry, Dexter Petley, Nik Pollard, the late Roy Porter, Bethan Roberts, David Rothenberg, Chris Routledge, Fiona Sampson, Sukhdev Sandhu, Neil Sentance, Jos Smith, Zoe Smith, Cécile and Christopher Spottiswoode, Greta Stoddart, Lydia Syson, Jack Thacker, Rose Thorogood, Hanna Tuulikki, the late Derek Walcott, Mike Walker, Marina Warner, Eliot Weinberger, Catherine Westcott, Brett Westwood, Francis Wilson, Jon Woolcott, Jenny York, Zinovy Zinik.

Mr Koupparis and Mr Timoney and their NHS teams at Southmead Hospital saved my life halfway through this book; Dr Sarangmat at Southmead and Dr Worth at Addenbrooke's are making it possible to still feel alive. Alastair and Kev at PD Warrior, Bristol and my fellow movers and shakers there are excellent provocateurs.

Some parts of this book occurred to me on BBC time – when I was working as a radio producer. I would like to thank Richard Bannerman, Brian Barfield, Elizabeth Burke, Kate Chaney, James Cook, Jeremy Howe, Clare McGinn, the late Sam Organ, Tony Phillips, James Runcie, and Gwyneth Williams. Friends at the BBC made my last years working there more than friendly: thanks to Sarah Addezio, Tim Allen, Mair Bosworth, Mike Burgess, Alison Crawford, Sarah Goodman, Sally Heaven, Caitlin Hobbs, Iain Hunter, Mary Ward Lowery, Siobhan Maguire, and Ali Serle; and also, from earlier times, to Christopher Cook, Sarah Jane Hall, Fiona Maclean, Julian May, Sue Roberts, Beaty Rubens and Jules Wilkinson.

Some preliminary sketches for this book appeared in other places: my thanks to the websites The Clearing and Caught by the River, the book *Arboreal* (edited by Adrian Cooper, Little Toller, 2016), the *TLS* and the *LRB*, Andrew MacNeillie and the magazine *Archipelago* and Craig Raine and *Areté*.

I am generously homed at United Agents, with great thanks to Anna Webber and Seren Adams; and at Jonathan Cape, with thanks to Daisy Watt, Graham Coster, Bea Hemming, and above all to Dan Franklin.

My family get the worst of me and are very kind about it. John and Kate Dee, my parents – forever young – have now been making this book possible for nearly sixty years. My sister Jenny Dee is a true kindred spirit. My parents gave me their car and my sister sold me hers (for 50 pence). As is my wont, I killed both vehicles, soon enough, but before they died they got me properly on the road. For that and much more, my thanks and my love. Once again I thank Stephanie Parker, the mother of my big boys, for making life far easier than it might have been for decades. Those big boys, Dominic and Lucian, are two-thirds of my dedicatees. My new boy, Adam, is my third. Children are our greenery, our spring, and these three coming into the world and growing here have been the very best thing.

Claire Spottiswoode is on almost every page of this book; she was with me for more than half of it, and she informs every page even where she isn't mentioned. I met her when she had come, like a swallow, from the south. She's taken me back with her now, giving a spring to a man in fall. Everything is because of her.